William D.
PAWLEY

William D.
PAWLEY

THE EXTRAORDINARY LIFE OF THE ADVENTURER, ENTREPRENEUR, AND DIPLOMAT WHO COFOUNDED THE FLYING TIGERS

Anthony R. Carrozza

Potomac Books
Washington, D.C.

"Epitaph on an Army of Mercenaries" from Last Poems by A. E. Housman. Copyright 1965 by Henry Holt and Company, New York. Reprinted by permission of Henry Holt and Company, LLC.

Library of Congress Cataloging-in-Publication Data
Carrozza, Anthony R., 1942–
William D. Pawley : the extraordinary life of the adventurer, entrepreneur, and diplomat who cofounded the Flying Tigers / Anthony R. Carrozza.—1st ed.
p. cm.
Includes bibliographical references and index.
ISBN 978-1-59797-714-2 (hardcover : alk. paper)
ISBN 978-1-59797-719-7 (electronic edition)

1. Pawley, William D. (William Douglas), 1896–1977. 2. Ambassadors—United States—Biography. 3. Diplomats—United States—Biography. 4. United States—Foreign relations—1945–1989. 5. United States—Foreign relations—Latin America. 6. Latin America—Foreign relations—United States. 7. Flying Tigers (AVG), Inc. I. Title.
E748.P38C37 2012
327.2092—dc23
[B]

                                                        2011042169

Printed in the United States of America on acid-free paper that meets the American National Standards Institute Z39-48 Standard.

Potomac Books
22841 Quicksilver Drive
Dulles, Virginia 20166

First Edition

10 9 8 7 6 5 4 3 2 1

CONTENTS

ACKNOWLEDGMENTS

The life of William Douglas Pawley was an adventure waiting to be written. One of the main sources of research material was in his own words. An autobiography he was working on was never published, but it holds a fount of information and offers insight into his thoughts. I am grateful for two sources of the manuscript. Richard Tryon, who was working diligently on putting the manuscript into a readable form, provided me with one version. The second version is in the archives at the George Marshall Library in Lexington, Virginia.

When I obtained the photograph of the dedication of Rancho Boyeros Airport in Cuba, I could identify only two people in the picture. George G. Fariñas identified everyone in the photo, for which I am deeply indebted. Eugenie Buchan, who is presently working on a doctoral dissertation about airpower and Sino-American relations during the period between the World Wars, not only provided me with a selection of photographs, she also identified the people in the photograph of the CAMCO Loiwing factory opening.

The interlibrary loan system enabled me to tap into a wealth of sources. I was able to receive microfilm reels of the *Miami Herald* and the *Miami Daily News* as far back as the 1920s. Books from practically every library in the country, as well as graduate thesis manuscripts and monographs, were provided through the Steele Memorial Library in Elmira, New York. I wish to thank Owen Frank, Maria Rupp, Rose Woodard, Cola Thayer, and Pat Cuthbert at the Steele for the extra effort each made to fill my many requests.

The presidential libraries—Hoover, Roosevelt, Truman, Eisenhower, Kennedy, and Nixon—provided me with material essential to this book. The James Marshall McHugh Papers at Cornell University were invaluable in presenting an unbiased portrait of the aviation business in China.

PART I
Fledgling Entrepreneur

1

An Adventurous Early Life

Before the end of World War II, the U.S. government reached the conclusion that an effective intelligence-gathering service was vital for the nation's security. The Office of Strategic Services (OSS) served that purpose during the war, but now it was deemed necessary to establish a permanent and well-funded organization. Congress approved the Central Intelligence Agency (CIA) as the entity to gather intelligence, interpret data, and make recommendations of policy to negate effectively foreign countries' subversive activities.

During the postwar years the power granted to the agency began expanding, and its original purpose seemed to have been forgotten. Covert activities against other countries, dossiers compiled on U.S. citizens and foreign nationals, illegal wiretapping, and the reading of private mail became commonplace CIA practices. The boundaries established at its formation began to be pushed beyond mandated congressional and presidential limits.

In 1954, Congress established the Commission on Organization of the Executive Branch of the Government (known as the Hoover Commission), with one of its assigned duties to study the organization and operations of the CIA. Its members were to review methods of agency operations and make recommendations to reduce expenditures, eliminate duplication of services, define the responsibilities of agency officials, and consolidate functions for more effective performance. As the commission began its work, President Dwight D. Eisenhower ordered Director of Central Intelligence Allen W. Dulles to form a separate panel of consultants to review CIA covert activities.

Fearful that the Hoover Commission would uncover embarrassing activities, Eisenhower directed the panel to "undertake a comprehensive study" of the CIA's covert operations and make recommendations to ensure "the field of foreign clandestine operations is adequately covered and that there is no unnecessary duplication of effort or expense." While the Hoover Commission would be submitting its report to Congress, Eisenhower directed the special panel of consultants to send its findings in a classified and "top secret" report directly to him. In his directive dated July 26, 1954, Eisenhower asked the panel to consider the "relative costs of these operations" and to "equate the cost of the over-all efforts to the results achieved."[1]

Lt. Gen. James H. Doolittle, who led the first bombing raid of Tokyo during World War II, headed the panel. Indications suggest that Eisenhower, and not Dulles or Doolittle, appointed the panel's other three members. One of the members was William Birrell Franke, a Wall Street wizard who was serving as assistant secretary of the navy on financial matters and would later be appointed secretary of the navy during the period when planning of the Bay of Pigs operation began. The second member was Morris Hadley, chairman of the board of the Carnegie Corporation, whose law partner, John J. McCloy, would later serve on the Warren Commission investigating the death of John F. Kennedy. In 1967 Hadley's family Rubicon Fund would be revealed as a conduit of CIA funds. The third appointee was William Douglas Pawley, a former ambassador to Peru and Brazil, a personal friend of Eisenhower's, and a self-made millionaire businessman.[2]

The Doolittle Group, as the panel became known, held its first meeting on July 14, 1954, at CIA headquarters, where the CIA director and key members of his staff briefed the group's members on problems they felt needed attention. Subsequent meetings included briefings by the Departments of Defense (DOD) and State, the Federal Bureau of Investigation (FBI), the Bureau of the Budget, the three armed services, and the Atomic Energy Commission (AEC). All paperwork was kept within the immediate office area; all working copies, files, and records were either destroyed or returned to their source; and no archives were developed. On September 30, 1954, the group's sixty-nine-page report was sent to President Eisenhower.[3]

A White House press statement on information contained in the report concluded that the CIA was doing a "creditable job," but there were areas in which "administration and operations can and should be improved."[4] The secret report made several recommendations to raise the competency level of CIA covert operations. The suggestions were aimed at the core of the CIA's function:

Elimination of personnel who can never achieve a sufficiently high degree of competence to meet the CIA standard. This will entail a substantial reduction in present personnel. There is no place in CIA for mediocrity.

Continual improvement of the present excellent training facilities and capabilities in all covert activities to keep step with future requirements.

Imposition of severe penalties upon employees at any and all levels who advertently or inadvertently violate security.

The panel also emphasized the importance of covert operations in a "continuing cold war situation as well as the requirements of possible hot war" and stated that funding of such operations was vital to the security of the United States.[5] As a peripheral member of the intelligence community, William Pawley aided in establishing guidelines for the CIA that would affect U.S. foreign policy over the next four decades.

By the early 1950s, Pawley had become a staunch, conservative Republican who felt the United States was "pandering" to communism and being caught up in the "swing to socialism."[6] His backing of attempts to overthrow Fidel Castro were reminiscent of a James Bond thriller, complete with daring undercover operations aimed at deposing or discrediting the Cuban leader. Pawley's involvement with anti-Castro groups brought him in contact with shadowy figures such as Mafia gangster John Martino, Watergate figures Frank Sturgis and Howard Hunt, and an unidentified anti-Castro youth who tape-recorded Lee Harvey Oswald during an interview when Oswald tried joining a New Orleans anti-Communist group as a hired gun.

In late 1975, a Senate subcommittee headed by Senator Frank Church began investigating the assassination of John F. Kennedy. Two committee members—Pennsylvania Republican Richard Schweiker and Colorado Democrat Gary Hart—made several attempts to reach Pawley by phone to elicit his testimony regarding both the name of the unknown Cuban and Pawley's involvement with underground anti-Castro groups. Pawley kept ducking the senators. When they finally talked to him, he assured them he had nothing to reveal. The Oswald tape recording had been turned over to the FBI but was not given to the Warren Commission. The Senate subcommittee considered subpoenaing Pawley to testify, but before they could, he was dead.[7]

The life story of William Douglas Pawley, an extraordinary, controversial, and daring individual, covers several continents, involves numerous world leaders, and is placed in the center of world events that shaped twentieth-century history. A cross between Indiana Jones and Donald Trump, Pawley was a shrewd and fearless man who never backed down when faced with adversity. He became a millionaire at an early age, lost his fortune, regained it, and continued to accumulate sizable wealth while serving as an influential adviser to every president from Franklin Delano Roosevelt to Richard Nixon.

The Pawley family traces its roots to South Carolina. George Pawley took the following oath on January 22, 1689: "I doe hereby promise to bare faith and true alliegiance to or: soveraighne Lord King James ye second & fidellity to ye Lords Proprietors of Carol - according to ye fundamentall constitutions, dated ye XXIth July, 1669."[8]

George Pawley's grandson, also named George, was a dedicated public servant elected three times to the Assembly. He served on road commissions and was a member of the delegation to settle the boundary between North and South Carolina. In 1746, Royal Governor of South Carolina Province James Glen sent Pawley as his personal agent to deal with the Cherokee Indians. Pawley was later appointed adjutant-general of the provincial militia.[9] The South Carolina summer sea resort of Pawley's Island was believed to have been named after George and his brothers, Anthony and Percival.[10]

George Washington, who kept a diary during his trip through the South, made the following entry on April 28, 1791:

> Mr. Vareen piloted us across the Swash (which at high water is impassable, & at times, by the shifting of the Sands is dangerous) on the long Beach of the Ocean. Five miles from this we got dinner and fed our horses at a Mr. Pawley's, a private house, no public one being on the road; and being met on the road and very kindly invited to dinner by Mr. Flagg to his house, we lodged there, it being about 10 miles from Pawley's and 33 from Vareen's.[11]

The Pawley mentioned in the entry was George Pawley III.

Edward Porcher Pawley, William Pawley's father, was born in 1864. In 1890, he married Mary Irene Wallace who gave him five boys, beginning in 1893 with George Plummer Pawley. William Douglas Pawley, the second child, was born September 7, 1896, in Florence, South Carolina. Edward ran a retail dry goods business in Florence with his partner, S. A. Gregg, Jr.[12] But Edward had dreams of becoming a rich man. He owned two farms where he grew spot cotton, but a friend convinced Edward that the real money to be made was not in "spots" (cash sales) but in "futures." By selling his spots for futures, Edward stood to make ten times the money.

Unfortunately, the cotton market went into a steep decline as Edward began investing heavily in futures. To cover his futures contracts, Edward mortgaged his farms and retail business, but the market kept dropping. Having speculated every penny he owned, Edward finally gave up and filed for bankruptcy. His timing was disastrous. If he had waited two more days, Edward would have reaped the benefits of a boom market that eventually would rise to three times his initial investment.

When the hired help working on Edward's farm learned of the bankruptcy, they hid seventeen mules from the receivers. Spiriting the animals to a nearby town where they were sold by one of the farmhands, Edward used the proceeds to begin a new life. The Spanish-American War had recently ended, so Edward decided to seek business opportunities in Cuba, possibly a job working for the U.S. Army. Leaving his family behind, Edward arrived in Havana sometime in 1898 or 1899.

To make ends meet, Edward met boats docking in Havana, transporting tourists to their hotels and tending to their luggage. He finally got a job with the U.S. Army managing the post exchange in Matanzas. With a steady income, Edward returned to Florence in 1900, packed up his wife and two children, and returned to Cuba. Two more sons were born while the family was in Cuba—Edward in 1900, and Eugene in 1905—and a fifth son, Wallace, was born in New York City in 1908.[13] The U.S. Army transferred Edward to Cienfuegos, where he was placed in charge of the military's food supplies and commissaries.[14]

The United States signed a lease agreement with the Republic of Cuba in February 1903 and a supplementary second agreement in October that same year for the Naval Reservation at Guantánamo. Both agreements provided for the United States to maintain a coaling station, but article 3 of the agreement stated "no person, partnership, or corporation would be permitted to establish a commercial, industrial, or other enterprise within the reservation."[15] However, article 5 allowed importation "for exclusive use and consumption therein" of merchandise free from customs duties. Based on this provision, Edward was granted a license to operate a store "to do business with the officers and enlisted men of the Navy and Marine Corps on duty at that station in the discretion of the commandant."[16]

In 1908, Edward obtained a license to open a branch store on South Toro Cay near the station's wharf, in direct violation of the agreement. The new store provided a needed service because there were no ship's stores at the time.[17] Local merchants complained that Pawley had an unfair advantage over them, not only because of the store's location but also because his goods were duty exempt. Responding to the complaints, the Cuban Ministry of State requested a clarification of article 3 from the U.S. State Department. An investigation showed the U.S. Navy had permitted the commanding officer of the Marines at Guantánamo to allow Pawley to operate his business under "such conditions and restrictions as he may impose," with the understanding that Pawley's license could be canceled at any time.[18]

But the United States was seeking to expand the boundaries of the coaling station, and the Pawley store was a minor sore point with the Cubans. While not admitting the store had been operating in violation of article 3, but that it had been "granted solely for the purpose of providing by the most expedient means" supplies for the needs of men on the base, the navy acquiesced and revoked Pawley's license in August 1910. The order specified that "such revocation to become effective within a reasonable time granted for closing out the business."[19] Without any further mention of the matter by the State Department, Pawley's store closed its doors.[20] Edward opted to leave Cuba and moved his family to Haiti.

Young William attended private schools in Cuba, where he learned fluent Spanish. His entrepreneurial roots began at the age of eleven when he loaded a small rowboat with fruit, candy, and treats that he would sell to American sailors on warships in Havana harbor.[21] At twelve, while his family remained in Cuba, William was sent to a college preparatory school in Stamford, Texas. "I ran away, acutely homesick," Pawley recalled. "I rode a cattle train the 600 miles to New Orleans on nearly empty pockets and emptier stomach. I worked my passage by freighter to Havana."[22]

In 1913, at the age of sixteen and a half, William was given $500 from his father and was sent by him to attend Gordon Military College in Barnesville, Georgia. Along the way he lost the money. When his father refused to send any more, William wrote to five prominent families in Haiti and offered to teach their sons conversational English for $100 apiece when he returned on break.[23]

According to two students at the school, Pawley found another way to supplement his income. Working on the school yearbook committee, Pawley collected $100 from advertising solicitations. H. D. Solomon, the student yearbook editor, claimed that Pawley told him the money was paid to the yearbook printer. A few weeks before graduation, according to Solomon, the printer appeared at the school looking for the money Pawley supposedly had paid him. Solomon paid half of the printing bill out of his own pocket and assumed that the school president paid the balance. Pawley neither repaid Solomon nor was ever held accountable for the missing funds. William dropped out of school in the first semester of the 1915–1916 academic year.[24]

At the age of eighteen, he wrangled a job with Dodd & Restoy, a Cuban export firm in New York, to sell stearic acid and candle paraffin in the remote jungles and backwaters of Venezuela. Traveling by burro, William honed his business skills while perfecting his Spanish to the point where he knew "all the accents and inflections and idioms of every place it's spoken by banker or laborer."[25] After less than a year, he was back in Cuba, but two years later, he returned to Venezuela, selling diving suits to pearl divers on Margarita Island.[26] Diving for pearls was a two-thousand-year-old industry on the island, and it was rumored that Columbus gave a necklace of Margarita pearls to Queen Isabella.[27]

While William was developing his salesmanship skills, his father was establishing an import-export firm in Port au Prince, Haiti. The E. P. Pawley & Co. became such a success that Edward incorporated the business as the West Indies Trading Company. William joined his father in Haiti and continued his on-the-job training as a future businessman.

The trading company grew rapidly and provided Haiti with modern manufactured goods produced in the United States. The company operated one of the largest grocery and dry goods store in the republic and also built a well-equipped garage to service and repair cars that it imported to Haiti. The West Indies Trading Company became sole distributor for the Ford, Hudson, and Essex Motor Car Companies. Pawley's company also had exclusive distribution rights for six other companies: Victor Talking Machine, Singer Sewing Machine, Indian Motorcycle, Goodyear Tire & Rubber, Delco Light, and H. W. Johns-Manville.

The West Indies Trading Company became the first firm in Haiti to stock modern agricultural implements and gasoline tractors, the first to use electric advertising signs and newspaper advertising, and the first to have a soda water fountain. The company became so popular that if anyone needed a particular article, he or she was told, "Ask the West Indies Trading Company." The export side of the business did rather well, also, handling Haitian products such as logwood and lignum vitae, or ironwood (a very hard tropical wood).[28]

When World War I began in Europe, Pawley learned the Haitian government owned three freighters that were laid up for repairs. Knowing that ships were sorely needed in the war, he set out to buy them. A competent chess player, Edward discovered the president of Haiti also loved the game. During frequent visits to the palace, the conversation soon turned to the subject of the three small ships. Pawley purchased all three for $30,000.[29]

The three ships were in such bad shape that they had to be towed to New York to be reconditioned. The voyage was an adventurous undertaking. The crews had to fight off salvage pirates, deal with broken tow cables, and constantly pump out seawater filling the leaky hulls. While the ships were being refitted in New York, it was discovered that the largest had been a private yacht with carved mahogany interior paneling. Pawley sold it for $125,000 and the second ship for $85,000. The third steamed back to Haiti, where it was put into service for the West Indies Trading Co.[30]

In 1918, twenty-two-year-old William returned to the United States, where he became engaged to Louise DeJarnett, but a chance encounter made him change his mind. While visiting his friend Bruce Millner, in Barnesville, Georgia, Pawley happened to look out his hotel room window. On the opposite side of the street, he saw a young girl, neatly dressed in a blue outfit and strolling down the street. Pointing out the pretty young lady to his friend, Pawley said, "That's the woman I'm going to marry."

Arranging an invitation to a party he knew the young lady would be attending, he met Annie-Hahr Dobbs. A dark-haired Southern beauty, Annie-Hahr had been approached by film director D. W. Griffith to appear in *Cardinal Richelieu*. Although Annie-Hahr fell in love with William that evening, impediments prevented their becoming engaged. Pawley did not have a job, and Annie-Hahr was seeing a West Point cadet from her hometown of Marietta, Georgia, at the time. Complicating matters even more, Annie-Hahr's father objected to Pawley as a suitor.

Nevertheless, Pawley was determined to win her hand. Looking into her eyes and trying his best to convey a serious tone, he told Annie-Hahr that he would come back in exactly one year to marry her. Returning home to Marietta, Annie-Hahr spent the year without receiving any word from her ardent suitor. But William Pawley meant to do exactly what he had promised.

One year later to the day, Pawley appeared at Annie-Hahr's home in Marietta. The father, recognizing the young man on his doorstep, immediately grabbed a shotgun to block the way. It was do-or-die time for Pawley, who brushed past the irate father, bounded up the stairs, and entered the bedroom of his love. Annie-Hahr was sitting at her desk, penning a letter to the West Point cadet, the future general Lucius DuBignon Clay, Jr., and accepting his proposal of marriage. Halfway through the letter, she tore it up.[31]

On July 25, 1919, William married Annie-Hahr Dobbs in Marietta.[32] The couple sailed to Haiti, where William and Annie-Hahr joined his parents and brothers.[33] Before their first anniversary they returned to Marietta, where their first child, William Douglas Pawley, Jr., was born. Leaving his wife and infant son behind, Pawley returned to Haiti. While aboard the steamship, he copied out a love poem to his wife, proclaiming his love "is so far greater than you will ever know."[34]

Although his father was prospering in Haiti, Pawley decided to strike out on his own. Returning to Marietta to pick up his wife and child, he set off for Montreal in 1921 to sell gold mine stocks.[35] The venture didn't last long. Broke and without any prospects in sight, he decided to seek his fortune elsewhere. He went with his wife and child to the train station, took out all the money he had in his pocket, and dropped it on the counter. He asked the clerk for two tickets to wherever the money would take them.

Arriving in Wilmington, Delaware, a city he had never visited, he took a job delivering milk. Unfamiliar with the streets on his route, Pawley offered a shoeshine boy half of his first day's wages if the boy would ride along giving directions. When he began earning a sizable commission, the owner of the company told Pawley he would either have to quit or buy the company. He bought the firm and later sold it back to the original owners.[36]

Pawley took care to look successful at all times by maintaining a neat, well-groomed appearance. At night, he placed his pants between the mattress and box springs to press them and hung his jacket above the bathtub so steam from the hot water would get out the wrinkles.[37] Every day he would chuck the flower girl on the corner under the chin, make a pleasing remark, and end up with a free flower for his buttonhole.[38]

His efforts soon paid off when he landed a job as a salesman with the Delaware Tire and Rubber Company. He became president of the firm within a year and owned it a few months later.[39] He next opened an automobile agency in 1924 but went broke again. In 1925, he took a job in Atlanta working for the Nunnally Candy Company. According to a company official, Pawley was hired to set up a

West Indies distribution. After three months, the deal was terminated because it was "not profitable to either the company or the appointee."[40] A 1944 investigative report (run as a background check when he was considered for ambassadorship) by the Department of State noted that Pawley had left the firm because he had become "involved in financial difficulties with that company."[41]

Hearing stories of the real estate boom in Florida, Pawley decided to join a Wilmington banker on a trip and see for himself. The frenzied buying of property in the Miami area had been in full swing for several years, and although he hadn't arrived early enough to get in on the best deals, Pawley was confident he still had time to make some investments. A quick study, Pawley walked into the office of realtor Edward E. "Doc" Dammers and offered $250 as a down payment on a $1,000 lot.

A legend in Florida real estate, Dammers had been selling lots in the Miami area for twenty years. "I sold the late William Jennings Bryan his first lot out in Biscayne Heights," he had proudly claimed. "One corner lot on Flagler Street that I sold for a thousand, sold last season for a million and a quarter."[42] After hearing such tales, Pawley quickly caught the land boom fever. "It was the first piece of real estate I ever bought," Pawley recalled, "but I never got to see the lot." Selling the lot the following day to a guest he had met at the hotel where he was staying, Pawley returned to the real estate agent and bought two more lots, which he also quickly sold.

Away from his wife and lonesome, Pawley tried reassuring Annie-Hahr that he was doing the right thing. "I want to stay down and work as I feel sure I could do something worthwhile with lots less hours," he wrote.[43] "We are making lots of paper *profits* that are just as good as cash," he reported to his wife, but he also confided he was having doubts about himself. "You are so much prettier than anyone I saw, even with their millions, that they will stand up and take notice when you walk out on the sand or pool. But just one thing, the boys are so rich and fine looking, you will be ashamed of your Bill."[44]

Having caught the Florida boom fever, Pawley convinced his Wilmington banker friend to return to Delaware and bring back $25,000. He assured the banker that they would make a killing together. "I'll go to work for Dammers," he told the banker. Through Ed Romfh, a leading Miami banker, Pawley persuaded Dammers to make a deal. "If I sold $100,000 worth of real estate in 30 days," Pawley recalled, "he would pay me a two percent override, plus my 10 percent commission. If I did not sell that much, he would owe me nothing."[45]

The deal became a sure thing when the Wilmington banker returned with $25,000 to be used for down payments on $100,000 of property. With Florida teeming with anxious investors, Pawley had no difficulty making a quick turnover at a substantial profit. The banker returned to Wilmington, but Pawley remained and became partners with another real estate salesman. They purchased twenty acres of land on LeJeune Road, subdivided it into lots, and sold out within seventeen days, realizing $400,000 on their initial $200,000 investment.

Pawley then decided to get into the home construction business. He bought twenty acres near the recently sold property, subdivided it, and began building houses. Even his father-in-law, Herbert Clifton Dobbs, decided to buy property and put it up for resale.[46]

The Williams & Pawley Investment Company teamed up with several other real estate developers to sell lots on an extensive piece of property purchased in Hillsboro Beach. Located east of Pompano, the development was named Boca Del Faro, with lots starting at $5,200.[47] "It was fantastic," Pawley enthusiastically remembered in an interview. "I was making $25,000 to $30,000 a day. Between January and September of 1925, I made $1.2 million." He wrote his wife that he had purchased a new Cadillac and was confident he could "make half million dollars in the next 8 months."[48]

By this time, Pawley had organized a sales force of a hundred men, and on September 7, 1925, he rented the ballroom at the Coral Gables Country Club and invited three hundred guests to celebrate his twenty-ninth birthday. He announced his retirement at the party, but "they begged me to stay until January 1st." His decision turned out to be costly because within four months the boom market bottomed and Pawley lost $800,000.[49]

The next three years were lean for Pawley, who had become a millionaire but lost it by staying too long in the market. Although he spent more and more time away from his family as he tried to get back on his feet, Pawley sired two more children. A son, Clifton Dobbs, was born March 8, 1926, and a daughter, Annie-Hahr, was born November 30, 1927. Strapped for cash, Pawley wired fifty dollars from New York to his wife, advising her to "make it go as far as you can—as we are about busted this time for sure."[50]

In 1928, the Curtiss Flying Service, Inc., provided a "taxi service" for fares wanting short-notice flights between cities. The company also planned to establish flying schools and provide parts and services for airplanes, much as automobile agencies did. "Establishment of the schools, flying stations and service stations should act as a boon to aviation in the United States," Casey Jones, president of the new company, told the press.[51]

Having had enough of real estate speculation, Pawley decided his future was in aviation. Remaining in Florida, he worked as a sales manager for aviation pioneer Glenn Curtiss, and during that time he sold some airfields to the Curtiss-Wright Flying Service, as it was now known. Under Curtiss, Pawley helped set up the airfields and start flying schools. Pawley became a member of the Miami Aero Club, which listed among its members Curtiss and Doyle E. Carlton, the governor of Florida.[52]

During the Florida aviation period of his life, Pawley helped promote air race shows in Miami. He held the number 2 life membership card in the Greater Miami Aviation Association, the organization that started the annual fest that brought fliers from around the world to compete in the speed and performance events. In 1928, together with James E. Yonge, a World War I pilot who was later an attorney for Pan American Airways (Pan Am), Pawley went to Washington to convince the U.S. Army Air Corps to participate in the air races.

"A friend sent his seaplane up to bring us home on Christmas Eve," Pawley recalled. "Over the North Carolina coast an engine failed and we had to make a forced landing." They spent the holiday with a family at a nearby farmhouse. A few weeks later the army fliers showed up—as did Amelia Earhart—and the air races held for the dedication of the Miami Municipal Airport were a success.[53]

The achievements of the Miami air show prompted city officials and aviation enthusiasts to make it an annual event. Starting in 1930, the event, called the All-American Air Races, featured 350 planes competing for trophies in various events.[54] Unfortunately, the third air meet in 1931, promoting the dedication of a new flying field at Opa-Locka, was marred when three men died in a crash. Not entered in the competition, their plane had taken off without authority from the Miami Municipal Airport, hit a high-tension wire near the air show, and crashed in view of thousands of spectators in the grandstand.[55]

Although Pawley was occupied with business matters in Cuba, and later China, he would try to make it back to Miami each year for the air races. He missed the 1933 and 1934 shows, but he was at the January 1935 air show when Capt. Claire Lee Chennault led his "Men on a Flying Trapeze" trio of acrobatic fliers in a spectacular performance. Meeting the army aviator after the show, Pawley began a relationship with Chennault that lasted for years. Stormy and contemptuous, they were often at odds with each other, but together they were to achieve a shining moment in U.S. military aviation history.[56]

In 1929, Curtiss-Wright formed Compañía Nacional Cubana de Aviación Curtiss, a subsidiary to provide air service between Havana and Santiago de Cuba.[57] Eighteen airlines submitted bids to be chosen as the first national airline in Cuba, and after reducing the final selection to three—including Pan American—Curtiss won the contract and began service on November 3, 1929.[58] Pawley was made company president and returned to the Cuba of his childhood.[59]

"We opened the Rancho Boyeros airport at Havana on Dec. 27, 1929," Pawley recalled. "I remember going out on horseback to view the site the first time."[60] The largest aviation facility in Cuba—it covered 165 acres—Rancho Boyeros included an administration building, large hangars, and workshops. President Gerardo Machado y Morales attended the dedication on February 24, 1930. The opening ceremony included an air circus provided by the Cuban Army Flying Corps and the Goodyear dirigible *Defender*, which had flown in from Miami.

During the air show, tragedy struck when the Cuban aviators competed in a balloon-bursting contest. While attempting to dive under a balloon, one of the pilots crashed his plane, killing himself and his passenger. In an unrelated accident, ten passengers on a bus going to the airport were killed in a collision with an electric train.[61] President Machado called off the remainder of the dedication program.[62]

Undeterred, Pawley began operating the air service and even found a way to pick up additional income. "We barnstormed in the country towns," he recalled, "taking people up for a ride for $5 or $2 or whatever they had. In some places we were accused of cleaning out all the ready cash." Casey Jones, president of the Curtiss-Wright Flying Service, was dumbfounded and told him, "Pawley, you got some nerve for a guy who's not even a pilot."[63]

Resourceful and enterprising, Pawley was desperately trying to get back on his feet by traveling to wherever business took him, but it was taking a toll on his personal life. Annie-Hahr and their three children were staying in a rented house in Miami while Pawley divided his time between New York and Havana. Shortage of funds was a constant problem. Returning from the beach one day, Annie-Hahr found the water and phone had been cut off. Pawley had expressed feelings in the past that his wife was "too good for him" and might find other men more desirable, but Annie-Hahr was beginning to feel that she was the one who should be worried.

"I am always conscious of a sort of ridicule from people when I 'turn my back,'" Annie-Hahr wrote to her husband. "I seem to think that they're thinking 'She's a dunce if she believes he's not having a good time.'" Annie-Hahr felt the only reason she wasn't by her husband's side was because of the children. "The women trying so hard to attract you, and the ones who are so attractive, are invariably and without fail, the ones who haven't been thru H—— to have any children," she wrote. "My looks have faded—I can see how much—but I have something to show for it, they still have their 'looks.'"[64] Her intuition told her she was losing her husband.

In what was to foreshadow his future in aviation, Pawley brokered a deal for his company to sell three Curtiss P-6 Hawk warplanes to the Cuban government. Costing more than $20,000 each, the planes featured two fixed mounts for guns, Wasp engines, and Nelson synchronizer gears.[65] But selling military planes was a sideline as Pawley looked to expand the commercial Cuban airline. A proposed link between Havana and Miami was announced on July 30, 1930, with service beginning before the end of the year using Ford Tri-Motor planes.[66]

On September 3, 1930, a hurricane with 160-mile-per-hour winds, slammed into the Dominican Republic. The capital city of Santo Domingo was devastated as the storm passed through heavily populated areas, leveling buildings, killing 5,000 people, and leaving thousands more homeless and without water or medical supplies. The roof of the American legation was blown away, and the insane asylum was destroyed, releasing inmates to run wild in the streets.

Many sought refuge in the four-hundred-year-old cathedral containing the tomb of Christopher Columbus, but others were not as fortunate. A maternity hospital, roofed with sheets of zinc, became a scene of horror when the hurricane ripped the sheets away and turned them into giant scythes that decapitated fifty patients and babies in their path. Bodies began piling up in the city, and lacking the time to bury them, the army was forced to incinerate them.[67] Rafael Trujillo, who had been installed as president of the Dominican Republic a few weeks earlier, took advantage of this expedited disposal process to get rid of the bodies of opponents who had been killed prior to the hurricane. He also issued a governmental decree to seize all Dominicans' funds held in Santo Domingo banks. Ostensibly used for the national emergency, the funds were never reimbursed.[68]

Trujillo petitioned President Herbert Hoover for immediate aid. "We are in need of everything," he begged. With widespread looting and most forms of communication destroyed, Trujillo suspended all constitutional rights and called upon the army to protect the people and property.[69] Maj. Cary I. Crockett, personal aide to Puerto Rican governor Theodore Roosevelt, Jr., was sent to survey the damage and reported, "Doctors, medical supplies, food, tents urgently needed and should be expedited."[70] Emergency relief began arriving from the United States via the Red Cross, and Marine Corps planes flew in needed supplies.[71] Cuban president Machado also asked Pawley to use his airplanes and fly supplies to the beleaguered island.

Acting as copilot, Pawley flew to the island in an amphibian plane. Because too much debris was on the runway, they decided to set the plane down in the bay. Absentmindedly, they forgot to raise the landing wheels, and Pawley hadn't fastened his seat belt. When the plane hit the water, the wheels caught the surf, bringing the nose of the plane down. The impact sent Pawley flying through the windshield, cutting his face wide open and badly damaging his chin. With the hospital out of commission, Pawley walked to his hotel and tended to his wounds using alcohol, sewing thread, tape, and cotton. Eventually his patch job healed, leaving him with only a tiny scar beneath his chin.[72]

Flying out of San Juan, Pawley's planes brought in ether, chlorine, water filters, alcohol, and other medical supplies from Governor Roosevelt.[73] "I took twenty-one doctors over there and stayed ten days," Pawley recalled, "bringing in supplies from Haiti with one airplane and from Puerto Rico with the other one."[74] For his efforts, Pawley received Trujillo's everlasting gratitude, which in later years resulted in lucrative business opportunities.

Returning to the United States, Pawley attended the inauguration ceremonies in Atlanta commemorating Eastern Air Transport Service's scheduled flights between New York and Atlanta. As a guest of Thomas B. Doe, president of the airline, Pawley predicted that Miami would soon be added to the scheduled route. "Mail planes are being supplemented by passenger service," he told a reporter, adding that Florida and Cuba were major contributors to the rise of aviation in the country. His Havana airport and facilities were considered "showplaces in Cuba," and with the Cuban government awarding him the airmail franchise between Havana and Santiago, Pawley was on his way to developing a lucrative business.[75]

For airmail to be collected in Cuba by Pawley's airline and transported to Miami and then to New York, cooperation among competing airlines was a necessity. Pawley had nurtured a friendly relationship with Juan A. Montalvo, Cuba's postmaster general, solidifying Pawley's control over the airmail in Cuba. Pan American provided service for the leg from Havana to Miami, and Eastern Air Transport, whose president was also an officer of Pawley's airline, provided the final flight from Miami to New York. With this three-legged arrangement, a letter mailed in the morning from Santiago on the extreme tip of Cuba was delivered in New York before noon the following day.[76]

The small airline expanded its operation to fourteen airfields with eleven planes flying routes entirely within Cuba that totaled 850 miles. After being acquired by North American Aviation, Inc., the airline was sold to Pan American Airways. At the time of the sale in April 1932, the airline was valued at $1 million, but the transaction was made entirely through stock transactions.[77]

Pawley was now out of a job. He had found the experience of running an airline a worthwhile and enjoyable vocation and decided he would like to stay in the aviation business. During his stay in Cuba, it had been rumored that Pawley had "resorted to measures" in business dealings that were frowned upon, and "eventually he was practically run out." Pawley claimed otherwise, saying he had left Cuba for "political reasons."[78]

2
China

Young, talented, and ambitious, Pawley always found work. H. E. Talbott, chairman of North American Aviation, felt Pawley "had more ability and initiative than any other man" in the company. He offered him the presidency of USL Battery Corporation and the vice presidency of Electric Auto-Lite Company at a salary "more than double" of what Pawley was earning. It was tempting, but Pawley wanted a career in aviation.[1] Leaving his family behind, he sailed on the SS *President Taft* for Shanghai, China, in January 1933.[2]

China! To an American in the 1930s, that distant land evoked fantasies of adventure set against the backdrop of a landscape lush with tropical vegetation and terraced rice paddies. To this land of romantic mystery with strange customs came businessmen and adventurers—all congregating in the bars and hotels made famous by the literature of the day. It was common to see soldiers of fortune, sea merchants, and entrepreneurs gathered together in rattan-decorated watering holes swapping stories of exploits and tales of unusual encounters.

Prior to his departure, Pawley arranged to act as Douglas Aircraft's commission salesman for airplanes in China. But selling aircraft was a sideline; he was made president of the China National Aviation Corporation (CNAC). He was also installed as president of Intercontinent Aviation Corporation, a Sperry Corporation subsidiary.[3]

Originally formed by Clement Melville Keys of North American Aviation, in partnership with Clarence Dillon, Intercontinent aimed to advance American aviation in foreign countries. "Ten percent of aviation is in the air," Keys said, "and ninety percent is on the ground."[4] Through Chinese finance minister Tse-ven (T. V.)

Soong, Intercontinent obtained a franchise for air mail contracts in China, but when North American was dissolved, Sperry Gyroscope Company took over.[5]

When Pawley went to meet Thomas A. Morgan, president of Sperry, Morgan had a strange feeling the two had met before. A former electrician in the U.S. Navy, Morgan couldn't place the face of the man he was interviewing. During the conversation, Pawley talked about his boyhood years in Cuba, which rang a bell for Morgan. They soon discovered that when Morgan served on the USS *Vermont*, the ship had made a stop in Havana and Morgan had bought ice cream from the young Pawley in his rowboat in the bay.[6]

Succeeding Capt. George Conrad Westervelt, USN (Ret.), as president of CNAC, Pawley was to reorganize the airline originally known as China Airways Federal, Inc., which began operations in 1929. Curtiss-Wright had provided financing for China Airways Federal, in conjunction with other companies that Keys owned, to operate the exclusive mail contract between Hankow, Peiping, and Canton.

Keys had invested $700,000 of his own money in CNAC, which was losing $250,000 a year.[7] Uneasy about an American-owned company flying strategic routes within its borders, China had balked at renewing the airline's contract, so China Airways Federal was dissolved. When CNAC was formed, the Chinese held 55 percent of the stock and appointed a majority of the board, while Intercontinent had the remaining 45 percent of the stock.[8] Sharing ownership of an airline was not unusual for China. When it formed the Eurasia Aviation Corporation with Berlin-based Lufthansa, China owned two-thirds of the airline.[9]

The only other commercial airline in China was the Southwestern Aviation Company (SAC), a small company financed entirely with Chinese capital. However, although some SAC planes carried passengers, that was not its main interest It hauled one specific cargo: opium. Transporting opium overland was costly because of taxes imposed by warlords as it passed through their territories. Air freighting the opium from Yunnan with American-trained Chinese pilots eliminated the duties imposed along the way.[10]

During his voyage to China, Pawley pored over books and articles on the life and times of Generalissimo Chiang Kai-shek and his efforts to unite his country. The more he learned of Chiang's nationalistic fervor, the more Pawley realized the importance of his own mission:

I soon realized that I was about to become involved, not merely in another business venture, but in the immensely complex problems of a great nation in turmoil. Whether I liked it or not, my activities in trying to create a modern air transportation network would be inextricably meshed with the struggles of the emerging Nationalist regime of Generalissimo Chiang.[11]

Upon arrival, Pawley called upon the new Chinese finance minister, Dr. H. H. Kung. Able to bridge his country's cultural differences with the West, Kung was a Chinese scholar and direct descendant of Confucius. He had graduated from Oberlin College and later received a master's degree at Yale University. His tie to Chiang Kai-shek was through marriage; Kung's wife, Ai-ling, was the eldest of T. V. Soong's three sisters. Her youngest sister, Mei-ling, married Chiang Kai-shek and was more famously known as Madame Chiang Kai-shek. The third sister, Ching-ling, married Dr. Sun Yat-sen, the first president of the Republic of China, and was herself the co-chairman of the People's Republic of China from 1968 to 1972.

Pawley found Kung to be "affable and informal" and felt at ease with him. Both agreed that CNAC would provide an opportunity to unite China by expanding air routes that would cut travel time between major cities. After the meeting, Kung arranged for Pawley to meet Madame and Chiang Kai-shek. Face-to-face with the head of the Nationalist government, Pawley was impressed by Chiang's "tremendous controlled personal power" and his "courteous reserve, dignity and complete self-control." Madame Chiang and Kung acted as translators while Pawley presented his plan to broaden CNAC routes south to Canton and north to Peking and recommended that Douglas DC-2s be purchased for the expansion. Chiang nodded his approval after hearing Kung supported the plan.[12]

Pawley's tenure as president of CNAC was short lived because Curtiss-Wright had begun negotiations with Juan Trippe of Pan American Airways to sell its share in the airline. The United States had refused reciprocal landing rights with foreign countries, so Trippe, in his efforts to establish a world airline, had to deal directly with foreign governments to secure landing privileges. To accomplish this goal, he formed or purchased subsidiaries in other countries, thus allowing Pan Am to operate terminals. Trippe's plan to circle the globe with his airline ran into difficulties when the Russians and the Japanese refused permission to fly over their territories. He abandoned a polar route for transpacific flight from California to Honolulu to

Manila, then to Hong Kong and Shanghai. CNAC would easily serve as the last leg in China.[13]

Pawley, wanting to modernize the airline by adding new airplanes and expanding routes, left for Shanghai in late January 1933 to negotiate building an aircraft assembly factory with the Chinese Nationalist government as a partner. To further his sideline business, Pawley sold a Douglas plane to T. V. Soong. "I hope by having sold him a ship worth $46,000 for $30,000 that I will be able to sell him 20 more next month," Pawley wrote to his wife.[14] But Pawley was spreading himself thin by dividing his time between running CNAC, selling aircraft, and establishing a factory.

In Pawley's absence, Trippe took up the matter with Tom Morgan of acquiring CNAC, and per the agreement made March 31, 1933, Pan Am received the 45 percent American interest in CNAC in exchange for 3,000 shares ($28 a share) of Pan Am common stock. The deal involved purchasing the entire interests of Intercontinent Aviation and China Airways Federal, which held the 45 percent of the CNAC interests.[15] Although Pan Am accountants put the book value of CNAC at $282,000, the actual value of "obsolete planes, spare parts, and a very small and dwindling cash balance" was only $165,000.[16]

As spring arrived, Pawley still worked for CNAC but now under Juan Trippe. "I don't like to work with Trippe," Pawley wrote his wife. "He is very unfair in most things and with me he seems worse." From his letters, it was apparent that Pawley was unhappy with the new management and looking for another business opportunity. He reached the crucial decision to spend his energy developing a market to sell Curtiss-Wright military aircraft in China.

During the twenties, the Chinese Air Force had a ragtag collection of aircraft left over from World War I, and the proper training of pilots and ground crews was almost nonexistent. Aircraft manufacturing within China consisted solely of a Chinese Navy aircraft plant at Foochow in Fukien Province, which, because of financial limitations, had built only twelve amphibious aircraft between 1918 and 1934.[17] The United States had imposed an embargo on arms shipments to China in May 1919, but after Chiang Kai-shek came to power, the U.S. government lifted some restrictions in April 1929, allowing prospective exporters to apply for licenses through the State Department.[18]

An aviation conference was held in Nanking in April 1931 to discuss improving the Chinese Air Force. Conference members recommended establishing an aircraft industry in China, training pilots, constructing airfields, and developing a modern air force to give China "a much more potent force than either the army or the navy in national defense."[19] Even a national lottery was set up to provide funds for developing the air force. The first was held in the summer of 1933 and netted $750,000.[20]

In December 1934, the Chinese started constructing a new air base—the largest in China—250 miles north of Shanghai in Haichow. The following year, construction began on another in Loyang. Chiang Kai-shek chose Loyang because it had long been considered the luckiest city in China; it had better feng shui, a fortuitous combination of wind and water that the Chinese considered favorable. In addition to hangars and repair shops, the new air base also had facilities for a flight instruction center.[21]

China had reason to develop an effective air force as quickly as possible. Japan, a longtime adversary, was beginning to encroach on Chinese territory. Japanese soldiers staged the Mukden, or Manchurian, Incident in September 1931 as a pretext to invade Manchuria. A three-month undeclared war starting in January 1932, known as the First Shanghai Incident, (more commonly known as the January 28 Incident in China) began with Japanese forces deliberately attacking the city of Shanghai.

Hoping to build an effective air force to solidify his position and prepare for the eventual Japanese intrusion into China, Chiang instructed Finance Minister Soong to seek the Americans' help in setting up pilot training facilities in China. Harvard educated with graduate work at Columbia, the articulate Soong became an important link between China and the United States as China sought financial and military support to fight Japan. Never one to limit his options, Soong also sought help from the French and the Italians.[22]

On March 24, 1932, the U.S. War Department officially noted it was "not interested in sending an aviation training mission to China," but it advised the Department of Commerce to consider "civilian aviation interest."[23] The State Department eventually granted that the trade commissioner could discuss "civilian aviation," but warned it would be "inadvisable" for the United States to be involved in military training.[24] The Department of Commerce, prodded by the American air attaché in Shanghai, Maj. Edward P. Howard (who was trade commissioner), made arrangements for Col. John Hamilton Jouett to head a mission to provide an aviation program and set up flying schools in China using American-built airplanes.[25]

"There is no doubt in my mind," wrote Leighton W. Rogers, head of the U.S. Aeronautics Trade Division, that this would be "of tremendous assistance to American manufacturers selling in the Chinese market."[26] Taking over a "ramshackle hangar and a small, bumpy field," Jouett developed the Central Aviation School into one of the most modern in the world.[27] Based on U.S. Army Air Corps training methods, remarkably he was able to improve the Chinese Air Force so that it was significantly better than it was, but the change was not enough to deter foreign aggression.[28]

Problems plagued the Jouett mission from the start. Although Chiang was eager to upgrade and modernize the Chinese Air Force, internal squabbling presented a hindrance. Disagreements with T. V. Soong resulted in Chiang replacing him as chief of the Aviation Bureau with Chiang's brother-in-law, H. H. Kung. As for the aviation school that Jouett headed, Madame Chiang Kai-shek assumed the duties as an intermediary for her husband, taking charge of "all correspondence regarding the school, its administration and its policies." But Chiang was becoming disillusioned with Jouett because he felt the Americans were more interested in selling American airplanes than in building a formidable and efficient Chinese Air Force.[29]

Accusations also were made against Jouett that he took commissions from aircraft salesmen for recommending planes to China, and some of the accusers were American instructors at the aviation school. Jouett's response—that he "took candy from babies, murdered old women, and a few other things, including the taking of squeeze [bribes]"—did nothing to dispel rumors in a competitive market where American aircraft companies "fought like dogs over a bone."[30] Chiang was also upset with Jouett because Chiang wanted the American pilots to direct combat attacks against the Chinese Communists, but Jouett refused.[31]

Competition and splintered resources ensued when Kung tried unsuccessfully to secure credit from the United States so he could purchase surplus aircraft parts from American companies. During a European tour, Kung stopped in Italy, where he received an offer from dictator Benito Mussolini to build an aircraft factory in China.[32] Anxious to supply China with his aircraft, Mussolini offered his personal guarantee: "If a single Italian plane is not up to specification I will close the factory."[33]

Although the American consul general at Shanghai, Edwin S. Cunningham, had warned Secretary of State Henry Stimson in 1933 that the Italians would gain a foothold in China, his pleas fell on deaf ears. The Italians supplied not only fifty planes but also pilots and ground maintenance crews to the Chinese Air Force.[34] T. V. Soong discovered that although the Japanese disliked the Americans' participation in the Chinese air program, they voiced no protests regarding the Italians.[35] During the three years prior to the Italians' participation in China's air program, China had purchased $2.5 million worth of aircraft and parts from U.S. concerns. Within a few months after the Italians' arrival, they had secured a $2 million order for aircraft, and Italy's foothold was in place.[36]

Not until late 1933 did the United States relax the prohibitions to allow "limitations and exceptions" and began issuing export licenses for military aircraft to China.[37] Northrop Aviation took advantage of the policy change and sold twenty-five airplanes valued at $1,034,550 to the Chinese in October 1934.[38] The following year, the U.S. State Department modified its position, at the request of the Chinese, by limiting American military aircraft sales to the central government.[39] The Chinese minister for foreign affairs, Dr. Alfred Sao-ke Sze, claimed that American arms merchants, "in their greed for profits," bypassed *huchaus* (permits) being issued and asked the State Department to advise exporters to conform.[40] Chiang Kai-shek was concerned that overzealous salesmen would furnish rebel provincial governments with weapons that they could use to unseat him instead of being used against the Japanese invaders.[41]

The U.S. government's concerns about supplying military aid, albeit indirectly, was outweighed by the depressed domestic economy and the worry that American aircraft companies would not survive. From 1925 to 1938, China was the most important customer to American aircraft manufacturers, accounting for more than 13 percent of exports. Protecting that interest seemed to outweigh political considerations, so the government set aside diplomatic considerations and viewed the Japanese-Chinese conflict not as a war but as the "Incident in China."[42] It also felt that it could offset the expense of research and development, which burdened the U.S. Army Air Corps, by passing these costs to the Chinese. Another benefit in supplying American aircraft was that the U.S. government would be in a position to influence Chinese foreign policy by threatening to withhold supplies.[43]

The Far East seemed to be far enough away that a war between the two belligerents wouldn't affect any U.S. concerns adversely and might help its ailing aircraft industry. The U.S. War Department, concerned with increasing the nation's capacity to manufacture combat aircraft in the event of war, came under pressure to allow newer aircraft models to be exported. With an open market, manufacturers expanded production, built new plants, and began setting up mass-production assembly lines. As a result, China was flooded with representatives of American airplane manufacturers looking to land orders at premium prices.[44]

The Chinese way of doing business was also a major concern that had to be confronted. Widespread payment of "squeeze," or bribes, to secure lucrative government contracts had led to upheavals in the Chiang Aviation Commission. In October 1934, a rumor circulated—widely believed to be true—that the chief of the air force, Gen. Hsu Pei King, had received $1 million on several deals. Following an investigation in which accounting records were mysteriously destroyed in a fire, the general and two other high-ranking officers were executed and fourteen others sent to prison. Soong attempted to solve the problem by dealing directly with American aircraft manufacturers, but he quickly became involved in a controversy with Gordon B. Enders, who had offered his services to deal with U.S. companies without receiving a commission.

Enders secured a purchase agreement with United Aircraft Exports for planes, but he then asked for a fee from the company. Realizing that his direct-contact method had failed, Soong demanded that United Aircraft reimburse the Chinese government for the commission fees that had been paid. Soong quickly learned that eliminating graft in aircraft deals had no easy solution.[45]

While other aircraft salesmen scrambled for orders, Pawley had problems getting started. His arrangement with Curtiss was unsettled because he hadn't been given exclusive rights. To acquire the rights, Pawley had to impress Tom Morgan, who would have to recommend Pawley for the commission. Moving into a new office, Pawley was pressed to make a sale. A Curtiss Hawk arrived in China to be used as a demonstrator, but it was held up in customs, frustrating him more. "How I want to make a sale no one knows," he wrote Annie-Hahr. "It's not easy here to get orders but when they come they are good ones." Working long hours, Pawley was trying to get the new office in shape in order to quote prices on planes to all departments that purchased aircraft in China.[46]

Even when customs finally released the Curtiss Hawk and Jimmy Doolittle arrived to pilot the plane, not everything went smoothly. Pawley wrote, "I was sick as a dog and had to come home about 1 a.m. Yesterday at 4 we had to fly the Hawk for some government officials. It rained all day and I got wet to the skin, so today, Monday, I have been in bed with fever 102 & a bad head."

With his wife expecting their fourth child, Pawley was concerned that because of the fierce competition he would have difficulty in getting a purchase order from the Chinese. He had hopes of making a sale, which would earn him $15,000 or $20,000, but his real concern was getting the exclusive agency from Curtiss. "If Tom gives me the agency we should make enough in two years not to worry any more," he confided to Annie-Hahr.[47]

Pawley continued writing to his wife, often sending two or three letters a week. The Chinese had not yet placed any orders for planes, and he was worried about failing:

> I have not cabled you about the Hawks yet because they are hard to sell. France, England, Italy and the U.S. are all working day and night for this order and dear I must have it (for you & Baby).
>
> I can't lose—If I sell them I will leave for home soon—3 weeks or a month more, then come back to build a factory here. It's so nice to feel that I will put it over for Curtiss. (If I fail?) it will hurt but I will not let it make us blue. We will have our children to make us happy.[48]

Grasping the situation, Pawley realized that if he were to garner the lion's share of business in China, he would have to do two things: deal directly with Dr. Kung, who was now the top Chinese official making decisions on aircraft purchases, and build an aircraft assembly plant in China to build and repair planes at a lower cost for the Chinese.

In his report to the naval attaché in Peiping on the American aircraft industry in China, James M. McHugh noted, "From then on the fur began to fly and complications to arise." McHugh added, "[Pawley] plays for big stakes and usually wins. He cannot, in fact, bear to lose—in the vernacular, it 'burns him up' . . . his method is the distinctive and the spectacular—money is no object."[49]

Pawley's main competition was United Aircraft. Its representative, a Mr. Lowe, was offering a plane to the Chinese for $22,000 while Pawley had one similar in design for $23,360. "If I get the order at more than United is asking it will be nothing but salesmanship," Pawley wrote his wife. Starting the day at ten o'clock in the morning with one of the Chinese buyers, Pawley talked for hours but reported, "I would not meet Lowe's price." After having lunch, then tea, followed by dinner, the buyer finally left Pawley's hotel at 10:00 p.m. Pawley wrote his wife that it had taken twelve hours, but "he has promised to try to buy at my price."[50]

One week later, Pawley was jubilant. He had closed the deal and was hoping to return to the United States to be with his wife:

Hahr—the deal is good. I sold 18 Hawks for $400,084.00 and 10 Hawks
more for $222,700.00 and $150,000.00 of spare parts—and I also got the
contracts for the airplane factory. If ever in my life I have had a hard job
it was this one. The English, French, Italians and United Aircraft were all
after the business. Lowe of United almost took it away from me 4 or 5
times—but today I closed it for all the business. I am very happy to wire
the office we got the order.

✗ He asked her not to think hard of him coming to China. "I had to, it was for
the best. I knew it would work out that way—it has, and now we can be together
without worry."[51] His confidence restored, Pawley was determined to make his
China venture a success.

Keeping his promise to return, Pawley was with his wife in Miami when
their fourth child, Irene Wallace Pawley, was born on June 13, 1933. However,
his thoughts were on business, and four days after his daughter was born, he left
to confer with Curtiss-Wright officials in Buffalo, New York.[52] After briefly visiting his family in Miami, he was off to China again. Having completed the sale of
planes to the Chinese, he was now eager to form a company to assemble and repair
the planes.

The only other aircraft assembly plant in China at the time was a small facility that Charles H. Day organized in 1934 at Suichow. The company assembled
planes from parts imported from the United States and repaired damaged aircraft,
and it had even designed and built a two-seater biplane trainer of its own.[53] What
Pawley wanted was an aircraft assembly plant on an even grander scale that would
outdistance the competition.

The Central Aircraft Manufacturing Company, Federal, Inc., U.S.A. (CAMCO)
was incorporated as a China Trade Act company on April 14, 1934, under the contract Pawley had secured on December 8, 1933, with the Military Council of the
national government of the Republic of China.[54] A factory built near Hangchow at
Shien Chiao at a reported cost of $5 million (actually, only $206,892 came from
American interests) for assembling airplanes, repairing and maintaining them, and
training Chinese personnel was later moved to Hankow on property purchased
November 20, 1937, from Standard Oil Company.[55]

Curtiss-Wright and Intercontinent (which Pawley purchased outright from the
Sperry Corporation in 1938) advanced funds for construction, which the Chinese

would repay over a five-year period. The agreement with the Chinese called for the assembly plant to purchase 75 percent of its engines from Curtiss-Wright and 50 percent of its aircraft bodies from Curtiss-Wright or Douglas Aircraft with Intercontinent being the sole purchasing agent for the factory. In addition, the Chinese guaranteed a minimum yearly purchase of $500,000 in aircraft. Although construction of the plant was widely reported in the American press, the Chinese went to great lengths to conceal its existence. The factory was not listed under its correct name in the telephone book, and any mention of it in Chinese newspapers was strictly prohibited.[56]

Not content to rely on one factory, Pawley approached the Canton government to pay for constructing another at Hsiukuan in northern Kwangtung Province. Pawley assigned L. R. Dooley, his former number two man in Shanghai, to broker the deal. But Pawley claimed he caught Dooley paying "squeeze" on several dealings with the Central Trust, the purchasing department of the Chinese central government. After he revealed this information to Dr. Kung, it was agreed that Pawley would transfer Dooley to Canton. Dooley counterclaimed that when the new factory deal was close to being signed, Pawley suddenly appeared and took over the closing. Dooley threatened to sue Pawley for his commission, and although Pawley asserted he only "wanted to avert unfavorable publicity to the American aviation game," he settled by paying Dooley $11,000. Another version had Pawley trying to cut or completely eliminate the amount of "squeeze" being paid to a Gen. Huang Kuang-jui, but the results were the same: Dooley was out, and Pawley closed the deal.[57]

After the Japanese invaded China on July 7, 1937, and Hankow had to be abandoned, the original contract was amended to allow a new factory to be constructed at Kunming, but the location was changed to Loiwing near the Burmese border. "Most of our buildings were flattened but much machinery was saved," Pawley recalled.[58] In addition, contract guarantees were raised to provide for purchases of 66⅔ percent Curtiss-Wright engines and 50 percent Curtiss-Wright airplanes to be bought with a yearly minimum purchase of $1 million. Pawley advanced more than $150,000 out of his own pocket, which the Chinese repaid, to purchase new equipment for the factory.[59]

Part of the original agreement called for CAMCO to procure "at cost" all blueprints from Curtiss-Wright, its subsidiaries, and Douglas Aircraft to be used for manufacturing and assembling aircraft in China, and for Intercontinent to act as purchasing agent (at 5 percent commission) for all materials used in operating the factory. In May 1934, a question was raised as to whether the Chinese order for twenty-two Northrop planes would require CAMCO to buy the blueprints. Pawley had stated that Douglas Aircraft had no subsidiaries, but when the Northrop contract was negotiated, he acted as the representative of Douglas, of which Northrop was a subsidiary. To avoid the $80,000 out-of-pocket cost for the blueprints, Pawley induced Northrop to turn over the prints if China purchased thirty more planes. Shuttling to Nanking to present the offer to Dr. Kung, Pawley received a counteroffer: Kung's order for twenty planes "would not be conditioned upon the securing of the blue prints."

Complicating the matter, Pawley lost the Douglas agency on March 1, 1934, and Northrop's new representative, Edward P. Howard, objected to Pawley's brokering the deal. Howard's offer was to sell thirty bombers to China in return for manufacturing rights. Two months of bickering followed, with Pawley insisting that only he could conduct negotiations while Howard countered that Pawley was trying to regain the Douglas agency. Although Pawley insisted he wasn't receiving a commission from Northrop, his attorney, Dr. George Sellett, revealed that Pawley would receive a 5 percent commission "in order to meet incidental expenses." Pawley also claimed that even though Howard was the "accredited" representative of Northrop, the Chinese refused to deal with him. "In the interest of aviation business," Pawley added, "he [Pawley] was endeavoring to complete the sale through the Intercontinent Company."

In a cable to Douglas Aircraft, Howard wrote that unless the contract was consummated through Pawley, Dr. Kung might refuse the sale. On August 26, 1934, a deal was struck in which Intercontinent would pay $60,000 for the blueprints and the Chinese would purchase twenty-five Northrop planes through Intercontinent. Edwin S. Cunningham, general consul at Shanghai, made the statement that "Pawley has practically monopolized all the aviation agencies in the United States that are in this market." In a conversation with Cunningham on August 29, 1934, Pawley said that upon the recommendation of Dr. Kung, he was attempting to consolidate all American aircraft companies under one firm, "thus preventing bickering, cut throat competition and general washing of our linen before the Chinese." In truth, having established himself as a major player in the Chinese market, Pawley was now hoping to crush the competition.[60]

In March 1934, Annie-Hahr made the trip to China with her infant daughter, Irene. Life in Shanghai was not easy for her, but she made the best of it and tried to adjust to Chinese customs. Although she wanted to be with her husband, she had to settle for those occasional times when he wasn't working. To help his wife, Pawley hired a young Chinese girl to look after baby Irene, but this arrangement resulted in a frightening incident.

While shopping at a local outdoor market, Annie-Hahr suddenly realized Irene and the young Chinese girl were no longer by her side. Frantic and alarmed she searched everywhere but to no avail. Her daughter had disappeared. Worried that the Chinese girl had kidnapped her daughter, Annie-Hahr returned to her hotel to seek help. A few hours later, the Chinese girl strolled into the hotel with Irene in her arms. The girl had what she felt was a reasonable explanation. Irene was such a beautiful baby that she wanted her family to see her, so she had taken her home. Three months later, Annie-Hahr and Irene were on their way back to Miami.[61]

Pawley had made important friends in the Chinese government, including Generalissimo and Madame Chiang Kai-shek and madame's brother-in-law, H. H. Kung, and Pawley intended to use these relationships to establish himself as the main supplier of warplanes to the Chinese. Although he represented Curtiss-Wright and other companies such as Vultee Aircraft, Douglas, Kollsman, and Sperry Instrument, Pawley was met with stiff competition from other salesmen hawking the planes of their respective manufacturers.[62] Pawley relied on the out-dated Curtiss Hawk II biplane as his main product. Marketed to the U.S. Navy as the F11C-2 Goshawk, it doubled as a fighter-bomber. After the navy passed on the plane, Pawley convinced the Chinese to use the design and commission him to build them at his Hangchow factory.[63]

Between March and September 1933, fifty of the Hawk II fighters were de-livered, but by May 1936, the Chinese had managed to lose all but four of them to accidents. Grasping the opportunity to continue supplying the Chinese Air Force, Pawley convinced the Chinese to rely on the newer Curtiss Hawk III fighter, which featured a 750-horsepower engine and retractable landing gear. The first of the new model was delivered on March 19, 1936, and by August another seventy-one planes had been assembled. Few of these planes ever reached combat because the Chinese pilots destroyed most of them in training. Continuing to fill his order book, Pawley delivered thirty Hawk III replacements by June 1938.[64]

Aircraft salesmen tried peddling their latest models by using foreign pilots to conduct demonstration flights that featured aerial acrobatics to show how in-destructible their products were. Pawley hired Frank Hawks to demonstrate the

Curtiss BT-32 Condor, the first twin-engine bomber with retractable landing gear. Madame Chiang Kai-shek feared the young Chinese pilots would forget to lower the landing gear, but Pawley reassured her there was a built-in safety feature to prevent that from happening. When the throttles were retarded, an alarm bell in the cockpit rang if the landing gear had not been lowered.

During the presentation, Hawks flew the plane past the spectators at an altitude of a hundred feet while using only one engine to demonstrate the plane's capabilities. He feathered the other engine by retarding the throttle, setting off the alarm. To silence the irritating noise, Hawks stuffed his handkerchief under the bell. Unfortunately, when Hawks finished the demonstration, he forgot he had disabled the alarm.[65] As one observer of the flight noted, Hawks "absent-mindedly landed the ship on its belly with wheels still up."

The Chinese, always optimistic and offering to help Hawks "save face," concluded that an emergency must have occurred and that the pilot, through his courageous actions, had prevented a disaster in which innocent lives could have been lost. Although the Chinese ignored Hawks's statement that he had been "just dumb and absent-minded," Pawley had to practically give the plane away after observers gave it a reputation of being unsafe and not very reliable.[66] Despite the setback, Pawley continued selling aircraft to the Chinese and made a fortune in the process.

PART II
War in the Far East

3

Pawley and Chennault

In October 1934, Pawley boarded the RMS *Empress of Canada* out of Shanghai bound for New York with stops in Hong Kong, Singapore, and Manila. While at sea he wrote to his wife and expressed concern that he might have to appear before a Senate committee in Washington about the planes he had sold in China. "I know that we have nothing to hide," he wrote, "but still the Chinese Government do [*sic*] not like this idea of the investigation and I do not want to get mixed up with it because it will kill the business in China if Wash. keeps this thing up."[1] There is no record of Pawley's having to testify.

Arriving in New York before Thanksgiving, Pawley finished his business meetings and headed to Miami to be with his family. There, he attended the Miami air show, where he met Capt. Claire Lee Chennault for the first time. A few months later, he was back in New York. All the while, his thoughts were divided between family and his business in China:

> I can't make up my mind about leaving for China. I should go at once and want to very much only because my business needs me. If I could afford to take you all I would not mind. I am tired of being away from you and the children all the time. I am sure that this trip that I am trying to make for only 3 months will be 6 or more, so what to do? I need you with me Hahr—and I am worried when we live as we do.[2]

Family matters would have to wait. Pawley returned to China, this time taking a route to make a stop in London. "Today I found out that I cannot do the business with Canton," he wrote home. "The Consul will not sign the invoice for the shipment."[3]

Business matters were a major concern for Pawley, but his personal life was on the verge of becoming a disaster. Annie-Hahr was weary of being away from her husband, and her discontent led to heated arguments. Pawley tried reassuring her, but he couldn't find the right words to express his feelings. "I get sick every time I think of the way we have been talking to each other, and with little Annie-Hahr around," he wrote from London. "Dear, don't let's do that ever again. *Let's stop raging at each other*. I love you Hahr, and sooner or later it would all end badly for us all, if we don't stop now."[4] Whatever their differences, on September 20, 1935, Annie-Hahr left her children in Miami and traveled to Los Angeles to board the SS *President Hoover* to Shanghai.[5]

Annie-Hahr spent the winter with her husband in Shanghai but sensed her marriage was in trouble. She couldn't place the reason for the feeling, but her intuition told her there might be another woman. It was a lingering thought, but she knew she would do whatever was necessary to keep him. On her return trip to the United States, she headed in the opposite direction. Accompanied by Ethel Rewer, a woman who worked at Pawley's Shanghai office, Annie-Hahr traveled through Singapore, India, Egypt, Italy, and France before arriving in New York in July. It should have been an enjoyable experience for her, but a shipboard incident spoiled the trip.

Planning to disembark at Singapore, travel by train through India, and reboard the ship in Bombay, Annie-Hahr was informed she could not leave the ship unless she had a vaccination. After receiving the shot, she spent two days in Singapore before boarding a train to India. In her compartment she woke up in the middle of the night feeling a burning sensation on her arm. "I saw these big vermilion color patches—raised, rough, solid, and burning as though they were real red-hot coals tied to my arms." With some effort she managed to sleep, but the next morning her arm was still sore and she now had a fever.

Upon her arrival in Agra, India, the heat rising to 118 degrees in the shade made the pain unbearable. At her hotel a Hindu surgeon examined her and said he had never seen anything like it before but felt it must be a reaction from the vaccination. He suggested she leave for Bombay, where she could tolerate the heat because it was moist. A German doctor in Bombay diagnosed the condition as a nervous breakdown brought on by a reaction to the vaccination and aggravated by the intense heat. He recommended two weeks in bed, but she wanted to leave India. While in Bombay, she sent her husband a cable saying she was "being treated for severe nervous breakdown." Pawley never responded to the message, telling her later "it embarrassed him."[6]

Meanwhile, without the support of the State Department, which was beginning to buckle under pressure from Japan to remove its American advisers from China, coupled with the newly arrived Italian mission, Jouett's contract with the Chinese Air Force had been allowed to expire on June 1, 1935.[7] Chiang urged the U.S. military attaché in China to let him invite a U.S. Army Air Corps officer to accept an appointment in the Chinese government as Jouett's replacement.[8] Secretary of State Cordell Hull notified the chargé d'affaires in China that the U.S. government would regard the "lifting" of an officer with "definite displeasure," and it might be construed that we were "inciting the Chinese Government to military prepared-ness" to defend China proper.[9] When Jouett left China, eight of the eleven instruc-tors remained, but by August only one officer and two mechanics were still at the school.[10]

Chiang welcomed the Italian group, but its efforts to establish an air program were limited at best. Regarding both ceremony and swaggering around in blue uni-forms to impress the generalissimo as important, the Italians were ineffective and might have set the Chinese Air Force behind in modern air warfare. The Chinese Air Force boasted having five hundred aircraft by 1937, but only a hundred of these actually were able to fly.

The Italian training school at Loyang enrolled cadets selected from prominent Chinese families regardless of their qualifications, and any student "who survived the training course . . . regardless of his ability" was graduated.[11] Students who washed out at the Jouett facility exerted influence on Chiang Kai-shek through their families and found a place at the Italian school, in effect creating "two op-posing factions" within the Chinese Air Force.[12] The aircraft assembly plant that the Italians established at Nanchang didn't fare much better. The Fiat fighter was a "firetrap in combat," and the Savoia-Marchetti bombers "were of such obsolete vintage that the Chinese could use them only as transport."[13]

To deal with the complexities of securing contracts for airplane sales, Pawley hired Lucius Roy Holbrook, Jr., as a technical adviser for CAMCO. Holbrook, the son of a U.S. Army major general, had accepted a two-year contract as a technical adviser to the Central Trust, the Chinese government's purchasing department. He was an intimate of H. H. Kung's and was employed to study the American market and make recommendations on Chinese aviation. By exerting influence, in 1936 Holbrook steered a contract through Intercontinent for the Chinese to purchase eighty bombers for $11 million in Chinese currency, with $5 million being paid in cash.[14]

As aircraft sales increased, the importance of securing American flight instructors and mechanics to supervise ground crews became critical. As a former associate of the American flying school at Hangchow, Holbrook was instructed to find five American flying officers to replace those whose contracts, like his own, had been terminated.[15] Someone was also needed to conduct an overall study of the Chinese Air Force and report to Madame Chiang Kai-shek, who had replaced her brother-in-law as head of the Chinese Commission of Aeronautical Affairs.

Madame Chiang delicately walked a thin line, incurring disfavor with the State Department for hiring American aviation personnel while pleading for more assistance in obtaining war matériel to fend off the Japanese. She pressed Holbrook to find an aviation expert to evaluate and make recommendations to improve the floundering Chinese Air Force. He wrote to Capt. Claire Lee Chennault, who at age forty-seven was being forced to retire after twenty years in the Army Air Corps. He was found physically unfit to fly because of his low blood pressure, partial deafness, and chronic bronchitis due to chain-smoking three packs of cigarettes a day.[16] While in a Louisiana hospital, Chennault received the letter from Holbrook asking if he would accept a three-month assignment to evaluate the Chinese Air Force at a salary of $1,000 a month.[17]

Chennault began his military career as an infantry lieutenant in 1917. At Fort Travis, Texas, he instructed air cadets in parade drill at nearby Kelly Field. Although he wasn't in the air school, Chennault managed to receive a few flying lessons, and after the war he returned to Kelly Field as a cadet. Graduating in April 1919, he flew a short tour of duty along the Mexican border before being discharged from active service. When the National Defense Act of 1920 called for recruiting pilots, Chennault was back in service as an army flyer. After a stint at Ellington Field, Texas, in 1924, he was made commander of the Nineteenth Pursuit Squadron stationed at Ford Island, the U.S. Army air base at Pearl Harbor.[18]

Promoted to captain in 1929, Chennault was assigned to the Air Corps Tactical School to receive fighter tactics training. Completing the course, in 1931 he was made an instructor at the Tactical School at Maxwell Field, Alabama, where he began formulating methods to use fighter planes to defeat enemy bombers. By the mid-thirties it had become challenging to bring down a bomber with a fighter plane because modern bombers had outpaced the fighters' capabilities. The top American fighter plane, the Boeing P-26, had a top speed of 230 miles per hour and carried two machine guns, while the Boeing B-17 Flying Fortress bomber attained speeds of 250 miles per hour and was defended by machine guns strategically placed to cover any angle of attack from enemy fighter planes.

Military aviation experts, led by Gen. Giulio Douhet of Italy, did not see any future for fighter planes against bombers because they felt the outgunned, slower planes could not stop bombers from reaching their target. Douhet's aerial warfare philosophy was considered textbook doctrine in aviation schools throughout the world. When fighter planes in U.S. Army war games in 1931 failed to intercept any bombers, Maj. Gen. Walter Frank stated, "It is impossible for fighters to intercept bombers."[19] His verdict carried weight, and advocates at the Air Corps Tactical School pushed to have fighter plane tactics eliminated from the curriculum.[20]

Chennault was given an opportunity to demonstrate the fighter plane's abilities when his commander asked him to form a precision flying team at Maxwell Field. With Sgt. John Williamson and Lt. Haywood Hansell (later replaced by Sgt. William McDonald) as his team, Chennault spent hours perfecting their acrobatic air routine, which resulted in spectacular performances featuring death-defying stunts. The team, dubbed "The Men on a Flying Trapeze," performed at air shows throughout the country until their final performance in December 1935 at the Eighth Annual All-American Air Maneuvers in Miami.[21]

Two air race shows were held in Miami in 1935—one in January and the second in December—with Chennault's trio performing at both.[22] Col. Mao Pang-chu, Chinese Air Force, along with several members of the Chinese Commission on Aeronautical Affairs, attended the January show as Pawley's guests.[23] The Chinese had just finished a tour, begun in Russia, to study aviation programs in other countries. At the German air show they were Adolf Hitler's guests, and in Italy they attended a dinner in their honor with Mussolini. Stopping in France and England, the group arrived on January 3 in New York.[24]

Mao was scheduled to tour U.S. air bases and aircraft factories after the Miami show. He also was recruiting instructors for the aviation school in China and inspecting the Curtiss-Wright combat fighter Pawley was trying to sell to the Chinese.[25] To honor the visiting Chinese, Pawley held a reception for three hundred guests on January 9 at the Roney Plaza Hotel. Pawley always entertained in style, and this dinner party was no exception. The event included a "colorful floor show" and dancing to Enoch Light's big band. Among the guests were American military leaders and representatives of various agencies in the Roosevelt administration.[26]

Keeping close company with the Chinese, Pawley joined them as they attended a formal tea reception that the city of Coral Gables held at the Chinese Village, a park featuring Chinese-style houses in a garden setting. Dressed in a dark tropical jacket and white trousers, Pawley resembled more of a diplomat than of a business-man.[27] The Chinese were also Pawley's guests at the All-American Aviation Ball held January 12 at the Biltmore Country Club.[28]

At the Miami air show, the Flying Trapeze team won a trophy for group acro-batic flying with a stunt featuring the two wingmen revolving around Chennault in precision maneuvers while the three planes maintained a unified position in the air.[29] After their performance, Pawley invited the trio to a party he hosted for the Chinese aboard his yacht in Miami harbor. Mao, impressed by their precision flying, offered all of them positions as flight instructors at the Hangchow aviation school.

Williamson and McDonald declined because they hoped to receive U.S. Army Air Corps commissions, but after being passed over, both accepted and left for China in July 1936.[30] They were flight instructors at the Hangchow school for "monthly cash payments of more than that of an American Army major."[31] Joining them were mechanics Sebie Smith and John Holland from Chennault's old army unit, along with pilot Sterling S. Tatum and armorer Rolfe Watson.[32] Chennault didn't want to resign his army commission, but he kept "the other project in mind."[33]

Williamson later became concerned about his Chinese service and asked the State Department's advice on whether to remain in China. He disclosed to the consul general at Shanghai that instructors at the aviation school were expected "to advise and to instruct from the ground" during combat, and he was worried that he might be violating U.S. laws.[34] Instructions from Secretary of State Cordell Hull were sent to advise Williamson and other Americans that their actions "reasonably come within the purview" of laws prohibiting U.S. citizens serving with a combat-ant power against another not at war with the United States.[35]

When Japan formally protested the participation of American aviation instruc-tors in the Chinese Air Force, Hull moved quickly to prevent the Chinese from hiring other Americans. He instructed that all U.S. passports be endorsed with the following statement: "This passport is not valid for travel to or in any foreign state in connection with entrance into service in foreign military or naval forces."[36]

Madame Chiang complained to the State Department that China also employed German and Italian advisers and that China would be at a disadvantage not having American instructors since American planes were 90 percent of China's Air Force. She was also upset that four American instructors, along with the pilot of her private plane, had been persuaded to leave China. Noting replacement parts were needed for their American planes, Madame Chiang wrote, "I hope that the United States will really be neutral in this matter and not place any obstacles in China's way when it is fighting for its very life."[37]

Hull may have been overly concerned about American public opinion, which he claimed was strongly against its citizens' participation in foreign conflicts. He agreed that giving "instruction in China's aviation schools would not be entering the military service of a foreign country," but he was worried about the perception of what "military service" was generally understood to be. Quoting State Department policy of not encouraging American citizens to enlist or take part in foreign military operations, Hull went one step further by stating, "The Department is for the time being not issuing passports valid for travel to China except in unusual circumstances."[38]

The Chinese offer to Chennault was increased from a three-month advisory inspection to a two-year contract at $12,000 per annum. His involvement would include input on any fighter planes the Chinese purchased, responsibility for drafting training manuals and aerial tactics handbooks, and organizing an early warning system of approaching enemy aircraft.[39] To circumvent U.S. neutrality laws, his employer would be the Bank of China, placing Chennault within the inner circle of Chinese power since Madame Chiang's brother, T. V. Soong, was the bank's president.[40]

With no other prospect except retiring to his forty-nine-acre farm in Waterproof, Louisiana, Chennault resigned from the U.S. Army on April 30, 1937, and boarded a train to San Francisco, where he sailed on the SS *President Garfield*. Also sailing from San Francisco that same day, but on the SS *President Coolidge*, were Gen. Douglas MacArthur and his bride of eight days, Jean Marie Faircloth. They were on their way to MacArthur's new post as commander of American forces in the Philippines.[41]

En route to China, Chennault stopped in Japan, where he was met by William McDonald. Sneaking entry into Japan with papers identifying him as an official of a Chinese acrobatic troupe, McDonald traveled with Chennault on a spying mission and gathered information.[42] Reprising the role of Japanese agents who traveled the United States disguised as tourists while photographing military installations, Chennault described their mission:

> We hired an open touring car and, with cameras concealed under our top-coats, set off to see the country through the eyes of experienced airmen gauging potential targets. . . . We filled notebooks full of data on building construction, industrial districts, shipping routes, and areas where industry seemed to be expanding with the suspicious speed of a military enterprise. . . . We toured the flimsy ant heaps of Kyoto, Osaka, and Kobe and sailed down the Inland Sea, noting well the isolated and heavily industrialized islands that housed many of the new war industries.[43]

Stopping at two more Japanese ports, they arrived in Shanghai on May 31, 1937, where Australian journalist W. H. Donald, Chiang Kai-shek's political adviser, met them.[44] Roy Holbrook escorted Chennault to the French Concession in Shanghai, where he met Madame Chiang Kai-shek on June 3, 1937. Chennault was immediately captivated by his Wellesley-educated employer and so charmed by her beauty and power that from then on he referred to her as the Princess.[45]

Reports listed almost six hundred planes in the Chinese Air Force, but after close inspection Chennault determined fewer than a hundred were combat ready. He learned "no plane was ever removed from the official roster for any cause. It could be a total wreck, scrapped for parts or completely obsolete, but it was still carried on the air-force rolls."[46] At the flight school in Hangchow, he conferred with his Flying Trapeze teammates Williamson and McDonald. He also made inspection tours of four airfields, including the Italian flight school at Loyang.[47]

While Chennault was evaluating the Chinese Air Force, Pawley was steadily becoming the main source of military aircraft for the Chinese. While business was succeeding, his personal life showed signs of further weakening. Annie-Hahr moved into a magnificent home on Pine Tree Drive in Miami Beach, where she devoted her life to her children. "I have been working hard around the house—making repairs of all kinds—that required immediate attention," she wrote, but she felt another matter needed his attention. Their son, William Pawley, Jr., had become a handful and her pleas to her husband (whom she nicknamed Cuba) seemed desperate:

> Cuba, you must live with Billy! He needs you. I can manage boys to ten
> years old, but after that they must have a man who is their father or guardian. I am afraid to leave Billy again. I just cannot. He is getting to resent
> our leaving him. We cannot leave him anymore at any cost. . . . He idolizes you and he's been waiting and waiting for you. He needs you to make
> his life for him—and it's in the making now. The next four years are all
> you have, you owe it to him! What he fails to do can't be blamed on me.[48]

Billy had been enrolled at the age of twelve (1932) at the Riverside Military Academy in Gainesville, Georgia, which also had a winter campus in Hollywood, Florida. He was about to graduate and Annie-Hahr wanted his father to give him direction as she was busy tending to her other son and two daughters. Not active in Miami Beach social circles, she preferred remaining home. An accomplished artist, she spent hours supervising her children with arts and craft projects.[49]

Pawley returned to the United States in the spring of 1937, but after a short stay with his family in Florida, he was off again. Instead of returning directly to China, he boarded the RMS *Queen Mary* in New York on May 4, 1937, and sailed to England for the coronation of King George VI. Traveling in style, Pawley had purchased a set of white luggage trimmed in bright brass. When his wife asked why he was using a bride's set, Pawley became "very irritated" with her.[50] Pawley's wife was becoming even more suspicious that he had a mistress.

With her husband in Europe, Annie-Hahr took a trip of her own. Her youngest, Irene, was a bright-eyed four-year-old beauty who drew admiring looks from everyone. While she attended the Mae Rose Ballet Studio in Miami, a photograph was taken of her that Annie-Hahr entered in a *Miami Tribune* photo contest.[51] When movie producer David O. Selznick saw the photo, he contacted Annie-Hahr and invited her to bring Irene to Hollywood, where she could test for the screen role of Bonnie, the daughter of Rhett and Scarlett Butler in *Gone with the Wind*.

Having a wardrobe custom-made by her grandmother, Irene and her mother boarded a plane to Los Angeles. When the plane landed, it overshot the runway and ended up in a cow pasture. Fortunately, no one was injured. Staying at a swank

Hollywood hotel, Irene was allowed to stay up and watch guests dancing to the hotel's orchestra. An impressionable little girl, when she learned that "Bonnie" would fall from her horse, Irene thought she would have to break her neck during filming. George Cukor, the film's initial director, wanted Irene to wear a wig, but Annie-Hahr wouldn't allow it. She said she would do Irene's hair herself.

Family members offer three versions as to why Irene never got the role. One is that when Victor Fleming replaced Cukor as the director, Irene was passed over. The second is that when Irene's father heard his daughter was in Hollywood, he insisted Annie-Hahr and Irene leave immediately and come to New York. The third, and most likely, reason is that Pawley's father had died in a Miami hospital from a heart ailment. A newspaper account reported Pawley and his wife flying from New York to Miami to attend the funeral.[52]

At the end of the summer of 1937, Billy, who had graduated from Riverside Military Academy in June, entered Duke University.[53] Leaving the rest of his family behind in Miami, Pawley returned to China. Because of events taking place in China during his absence, Pawley's military aircraft business was about to expand, and he needed to be there.

On July 7, 1937, the Japanese attacked Chinese troops at the Marco Polo Bridge on the pretense of protecting their interests in China. Chennault sent the Chinese Commission of Aeronautical Affairs a telegram offering his services to help the beleaguered air force in what seemed the beginning of new hostilities between the two nations.[54] He received orders to proceed to Nanchang, where he was assigned command of the advanced combat flight school headed by Gen. Mao Pang-chu, who had tried to recruit Chennault in Miami two years earlier.[55]

Evaluating the situation, which he summarized as "a nightmare," Chennault saw immediately that he had to establish an early warning air-raid system that would give Chinese fighters advance notice of approaching Japanese bombers. A crude but effective network, which the Americans dubbed *Jing Bow* (to be alert), it involved Chinese civilians throughout the Shanghai-Hangchow-Nanking triangle calling a central station that plotted all Japanese aircraft movements.[56] Each airfield posted the information by means of a three-ball alert device that consisted of a paper- or cloth-covered bamboo frame, two to three feet in diameter, hoisted on a pole. Raising one ball meant enemy aircraft were 180 miles away, two balls warned they were 120 miles from the target, and a third ball indicated the Japanese were only ten minutes away or less.[57]

The network had another useful purpose, that is, keeping track of friendly aircraft. The network was on the same frequency as all Chinese aircraft, so if a pilot lost his bearings he could radio a nearby station tracking him. Jasper Harrington, a line chief with Chennault's American Volunteer Group (AVG) of pilots, or the Flying Tigers, recalled an instance when the network helped a straying pilot. Trackers monitoring the plane realized the pilot had missed a river turn, which would have led him back to base. Radioing the aircraft, they prevented the pilot from heading into enemy territory.[58]

After meeting Chiang Kai-shek for the first time on July 23, Chennault turned to readying the ill-equipped Chinese Air Force to enter combat against the technically superior Japanese.[59] But before he had an opportunity to train the Chinese pilots properly, Chennault received an order to attack the Japanese battleship *Idzumo*, which was shelling Chiang's troops from Shanghai harbor. The Japanese had kept the decrepit battleship afloat to serve as a floating hotel for a Japanese admiral visiting the Japanese Consulate. It should have been an easy target.[60]

Sending Chinese Air Force bombers on August 14 resulted in no damage to the *Idzumo*. Instead, they wreaked havoc on civilians when bombardiers overshot the ship and dropped their loads on Shanghai's streets. One bomb blasted a deep crater in front of the Cathay Hotel, where Pawley usually stayed, while another made a direct hit on the Palace Hotel across the street.[61] Bombers also mistook the British cruiser HMS *Cumberland* for a Japanese ship and tried sinking it.[62] Chennault-trained combat fighters fared better in their defense of Hangchow when they shot down eleven bombers from the Japanese aircraft carrier *Kaga*.

Chennault saw the opportunity to implement fighter plane tactics he long felt would be effective. The Curtiss Hawk III, assembled by Pawley's CAMCO factory, was effective against the Japanese, but it wasn't long before the Mitsubishi A5M escort plane began protecting the Japanese bombers that flew over China. A sleek monoplane with twin machine guns, the new plane was far superior to the Hawk. "Chinese pilots are most properly afraid of them," Chennault wrote.[63]

The new Japanese fighter design emphasized maneuverability, sacrificing heavy armor plating for speed, so Chennault taught Chinese pilots to lock wings with Japanese planes and tear off their lightweight wings. The first opportunity of using this tactic proved disastrous when a Chinese pilot out of ammunition tried locking wings with a Japanese bomber but succeeded only in tearing apart his own wing and tail assembly. Chennault revised his strategy by applying the maneuver only for Japanese fighter planes. Several Chinese pilots perfected the maneuver by slicing enemy wings with little or no damage to their own plane.[64]

To observe and critique his Chinese pilots, Chennault flew a fixed-gear Curtiss Hawk H75-M Special—a forerunner of the Curtiss P-36 Mohawk—that Pawley had sold to Madame Chiang in expectation of securing sales.[65] Delivered on June 8, 1937, the fixed landing gear monoplane was powered by an 840-horsepower engine and armed with four guns.[66] Although Chennault reportedly participated in combat operations—and, by his own account to a friend, even shot down Japanese planes—no evidence supports these speculations, and Chennault never made any public claims of being in combat.[67]

Chinese pilots trained by their new American commander fared well, but without a new supply of aircraft for the Chinese Air Force and as pilots were being killed in action, the total number of aircraft available for combat kept dwindling. Chennault did everything he could to stave off the Japanese bombers' constant attacks, but even his skilled tactics were insufficient. The American-trained Chinese mechanics did shoddy work, and Chinese pilots showed an inclination to go down with their planes instead of "losing face" before the enemy.[68]

As aircraft losses increased, Madame Chiang resurrected a plan formulated seven years earlier when Japan invaded Manchuria, and she employed foreign pilots to serve as combat aviators in the Chinese Air Force. Chennault opposed the plan "because the task of separating the capable pilots from the flock of would-be soldiers of fortune seemed hardly worth the effort."[69] When the Japanese destroyed all 150 Northrop Gamma 2E bombers the Chinese had, Pawley sold them thirty long-range Vultee V-11GB bombers.[70] Chennault had a change of heart, and the Fourteenth International Squadron became a reality. Each Vultee carried a pilot and two machine gunners. A single-engine, 1,000-horsepower monoplane with a 2,000-mile range, it was sufficient to disrupt Japanese shipping in the seas around China.[71]

Pawley sold aircraft as fast as he could receive the crated planes through Hong Kong. From there they went by rail to the CAMCO factory in Hengyang for assembly. The U.S. Consulate in Hong Kong tried keeping a close eye on shipments of war matériel. Paying a visit to the offices of Intercontinent China, Ltd., the American consul general Addison E. Southard felt he was getting the runaround when he inquired on the nature of the company's business. Insisting on talking to whoever was in charge, Southard was introduced to C. P. Chen, who acknowledged being head of the company. Asked about war matériel being handled by the company, Chen admitted that he received barbed wire and chemicals from England, airplanes from Italy, and "some machine guns and ammunition were coming from Sweden and Germany."[72] Southard reported that H. S. Wu of Intercontinent informed him that the number of planes that the Chinese purchased "are increasing and that transshipment is keeping Intercontinent China quite busy."[73]

Down the hall from Intercontinent, Allen L. "Pat" Patterson headed the China Airmotive Company. A Canadian by birth, Patterson was a World War I pilot who had flown as a barnstormer after the war. He also had appeared in the classic war movie *Hell's Angels* as a flier before starting his career in aviation sales. Relocating to China in the thirties, he sold military aircraft to the Chinese. When he moved into his Shanghai office, his first caller was William Pawley.

"You don't think you're going to sell any airplanes here, do you?" Pawley asked. It was more of a challenge than a question.

"Why not?" Patterson replied, taken aback by the rude encounter.

"Because I have an exclusive," Pawley fired back. "Go ask H. H. Kung or General Mao." Without waiting for a response, Pawley turned and walked out. The confrontation was just the opening salvo in a rivalry that would continue for several years.[74]

The Chinese purchased aircraft in a roundabout way, which frustrated Chennault in his efforts to secure the best equipment. Although Chennault had authority to submit requests, the Aeronautical Affairs Commission made separate recommendations. As the minister of finance, H. H. Kung would weigh both requests, confer with his personal confidants—including Pawley—and award the contracts after T. V. Soong's advisers gave them a final scrutinizing.[75] Pawley followed Kung all over Europe in 1937 and even opened a London office to help Kung with arm shipments he made during his travels.[76] During the trip, Pawley secured a $1 million order for spare parts and supplies for his factory.[77]

Selling aircraft to the Chinese meant Pawley continually had to stay close to Kung. When the Chinese government relocated to Nanking, Pawley followed. Because his factory had been bombed, Pawley moved the men and equipment with him. "I decided to sell our cars to the army and get out while we could," he wrote Annie-Hahr. "Things were getting hot there anyway—it hasn't been safe to travel by car here a long time as the Japs bomb cars every day." Pawley planned on flying back to the States for Christmas, but Kung asked him to remain. "I was the only one of the crowd that seemed to help him," Pawley wrote. Getting around China by plane was also becoming hazardous, as Pawley described:

> I went down with [Ernest M.] Allison and Juan in a Vultee bomber—all guns ready and we expected to meet Japs, but were lucky and landed just as the alarm was given. I ran for a car and went to the Wall gate and saw the Japs drop bombs on the field. Our ship was not hit, several others were. The next day we went out to take off at 7 AM, but just as we were taking off, we got an alarm and had to wait at the Wall. This happened 3 times, and at 11:30 we started. 10 minutes out we saw 3 Japs in bombers, but they didn't trouble us as they were going to bomb Nangking [sic]. We got here OK, and that's the *last time I'll do that.*[78]

Pawley's cozy arrangement with Kung was so widely known that it became an embarrassment to the Chinese minister. A report written for Secretary of the Treasury Henry Morgenthau, Jr., advised that "it is necessary to watch Kung as his decisions are fickle and very changeable." Kung was considered "the weak spot in China," but it was widely known that "Madame Kung is the real driving force" behind the Chinese minister.[79] An American newspaper correspondent described her as "a financial genius with no scruples of any sort."[80] Kung may have been considered weak, but he was intelligent enough to realize that if the gossip continued, his position could become untenable. After all, in 1933, Chiang Kai-shek had replaced T. V. Soong with Kung as Chinese finance minister and again in 1934 as chief of the Aviation Bureau.

4

Competition and War Clouds

To dispel rumors that he and Pawley had an "intimate" relationship, Kung called a meeting at his home in Hong Kong on February 11, 1938, and invited American aircraft salesmen. Attending were China National Aviation Corporation (CNAC) director Max S. Polin; Leslie A. Lewis; L. R. Dooley; W. H. Donald, Chiang's political adviser; and Pawley's main competitors: Howard "Silent Jim" Norris, the North American Aviation sales representative, and Allen L. "Pat" Patterson, who sold engines and propellers for United Aircraft, Pratt & Whitney, and Hamilton Standard.[1]

Although Intercontinent was notified of the meeting, Pawley was in the United States, and Commander Bruce G. Leighton, USN (Ret.), who was a vice president of Intercontinent, was in Hankow. It is unlikely Kung would have held the meeting without Pawley, unless Kung had planned it during Pawley's absence. Without Pawley, the rest may have felt more comfortable airing their grievances, which Kung could then relay to Pawley.

Kung opened the meeting by saying that accusations had come to his attention that an American salesman (implying Pawley) had been "using his name" and misrepresenting "his close association" to him and officials of the Chinese government. Kung then listened as the American aeronautical representatives expressed their views. The consensus was that Pawley used tactics intended "to create a monopoly of the sales of aircraft and aircraft materials to China." They felt he "appeared to be receiving preferential treatment at the expense of other American companies," adding that "this type of action was harmful to the aircraft industry."

Denying the charges, Kung stated he "was not a close personal friend of [Pawley]," and "the relations with the person in question were of a purely business nature and that he had never maintained social relations with him." A report that Pawley had paid Kung's cost of chartering a plane from Manila to Hong Kong was explained as strictly Pawley's voluntary offer "to assist by making arrangements and paying" Pan Am. Kung said he later reimbursed Pawley.

Pointing out that the Chinese government was contracted to purchase specified yearly quantities of Curtiss-Wright airplanes through Intercontinent, Kung quickly added that several aircraft orders were under consideration with other American companies and that "business would be distributed strictly on the basis of merit, delivery dates and prices." Acknowledging that China had recently purchased thirty-five Curtiss-Wright Hawk 75s through Intercontinent, Kung reminded the group that he had also bought 108 Fleet planes (trainers) from Leslie Lewis, even though Pawley "offered to manufacture the same in China for $2,000 per plane cheaper." An order had also been placed with North American Aviation for fifty trainers, "even though Pawley had offered to make the same plane in China for $5,000 less."

Referring to the Hawk 75 purchase, Kung stated that after the contract had been signed, Pawley "came to him and actually cried." Pawley also had presented Kung with a telegram he had received from the president of his company demanding his resignation because Pawley failed to include the cost of armament for the planes, amounting to a $200,000 loss to the company. Kung said it wasn't his intention "to take advantage of a salesman's mistake or carelessness." Convinced it was an innocent error, Kung allowed the contract to be modified to include the additional costs. It must have been exceedingly difficult for the Chinese minister to convince the gathered aircraft salesmen that the hard-boiled William Pawley had actually shed tears.

When it was brought to Kung's attention that Pawley had shown American aircraft manufacturers a large, autographed photo of the Chinese minister, Kung seized the opportunity to inject a bit of humor. He laughed heartily and told the group that Pawley had requested the photo while they were in Europe together. If anyone wished to have a similar or even larger photo, Kung added, he would be delighted to furnish one.[2]

Meanwhile, Pawley had already sold the Chinese sixty more Curtiss Hawks and thirty of the new Mohawk pursuit planes (delivered between May and August 1938 at $30,888 each), and the Chinese had ordered thirty Vultees when the call went out for foreign pilots to join the Chinese Air Force.[3] Just as Capt. Claire Chennault expected, the pilots answering the call were a motley crew of adventurers, out-of-work aviators looking for a paycheck, and undisciplined fliers not likely to follow orders. Some were not even qualified. One young man showed him logbooks listing 12,000 hours of flying time. Chennault ordered a solo flight, but as he approached the plane, the youth confessed, "I guess I better not. I've never flown a plane before."[4]

Notwithstanding the inept and inexperienced, among those who signed up included Jim Allison, who had seen action in Spain against the Germans and Italians; Elwyn Gibbon, a U.S. Army Air Corps training school graduate; George Weigle, an aviator from a "cow-pasture school"; and Vincent Schmidt, who had flown combat missions in Mexico, Spain, and Ethiopia.[5] There were also a German, four Frenchmen, and one Dutchman—all misfits who had been in aerial combat in one war zone or another but seemed more at home in a local bar. Assessing the group, Chennault assigned the best pilots as instructors, while the rest were sent to the Fourteenth International Squadron under Schmidt's leadership. For better or for worse, Chennault now commanded a foreign mercenary force that became the predecessor of the famed Flying Tigers.

As Chennault had predicted, the Fourteenth International Squadron was problematic and difficult to mold into an effective fighting unit. The mercenaries channeled into the squadron seemed more interested in paychecks and the $1,000 bonus for every Japanese plane they downed than the honor of fighting for the defense of China.[6] "It was the most disorganized mess you ever saw," Tommy Walker, an American pilot observed, ". . . discipline was a hollow joke."[7] Although the pilots flew for the Chinese, they were not part of the air force proper, and at any time they could walk over to the Air Ministry and quit.[8] Complicating matters even more, Chinese pilots refused to fly under the leadership of "foreign dogs" because they felt they would lose too much face.[9] Chinese ground crews were also a problem. They resisted modern methods, such as refueling planes from tanker trucks, preferring to use leaky, five-gallon tin cans hauled on an open-bed truck. Parts that were worn or on the verge of failure were not replaced as long as they passed cursory inspection.[10]

With all these problems, Chennault still managed to organize a fighting group. Julius Barr and Royal Leonard, experienced CNAC pilots, were hired to recruit pilots and managed to find a few in Manila and back in the States.[11] Barr, Madame Chiang's personal pilot, gave flight checks to several applicants. "He has had no military training and so is of little value as a pilot," he wrote of one. "Should not have come to China," he reported on another. Barr was able to give glowing recommendations on two pilots. On others he stressed they had no military training and could not handle bombers, but they might be considered for fighter pilot duty.[12]

The selection of qualified pilots was meager, but Chennault felt they were ready. Their first mission was January 23, 1938, with the airfield at Anyang as a target. Of the four Vultee bombers that participated in the strike, one crashed, two turned back to base, and the last made it to Anyang but couldn't find the target.[13]

While off duty, the Fourteenth International Squadron's foreign pilots hung out in the Hankow section they dubbed Dump Street, a seedy red-light district with opium dens, whorehouses, and backwater bars.[14] Madame Chiang, attempting to bolster her mercenary force, made regular Sunday morning visits to deliver an inspiring sermon to men recovering from a night of bar crawling.[15] Japanese agents were everywhere, and when the international pilots, who "subsisted almost entirely on high-octane beverages," gathered at Dump Street bars, loose lips provided useful information to the enemy.[16]

Security laxness proved to be the squadron's undoing when it was assigned to bomb a large enemy troop movement center at Tsinan in Shantung Province.[17] An early morning strike was planned, and to save time—or more likely to allow the pilots to sleep off their hangovers—the Vultee bombers were fueled and loaded with bombs the afternoon before.[18] In a predawn raid, Japanese bombers appeared over the air base with a surprise attack of their own. With the Vultees conveniently lined up along the runway, it took only one Japanese bomb to set off an explosion that resulted in a chain reaction that destroyed every plane. "What was left of the Chinese bombing force vanished in five seconds of flame and dust," Chennault wrote. "With it went the jobs of International Squadron pilots."[19] Chiang Kai-shek was "disappointed over the efficiency and conduct of this group of foreigners."[20] Madame Chiang's mercenary force was deemed a failure. The Fourteenth International Squadron was disbanded March 22, 1938.[21]

Complicating matters, Chennault found it frustrating to deal with the Chinese way of conducting business with airplane manufacturers. The roundabout procurement system was not to his liking. "Conditions are very bad regarding business methods out here," he noted. His selection—Curtiss Hawk III, Curtiss Hawk 75, Seversky P-35A fighter, Vought SB2U Vindicator dive-bomber, and the North American NA-16 Basic Trainer—was recommended to Madame Chiang, who, in turn, passed it on to Kung. The minister placed the orders for the trainers and the Hawks, but he had forgone the rest.[22]

The payment of squeeze had gotten so out of hand that W. H. Donald recommended to Madame Chiang that she conduct a cleanup campaign and execute the guilty. He focused his investigation solely on Pawley, hoping to catch him as a way to capture the rest. Pawley swore he never paid squeeze, despite the fact he had garnered 90 percent of the business. One source told U.S. naval attaché James McHugh that Pawley's "style is to do everything in a grand manner—if the official suggests $1,000 squeeze, P[awley] will up him to $5,000."[23] The investigation never produced concrete evidence, however, and the matter was dropped. "The Chinese have been at it too long to be crude enough to get caught at it," McHugh wrote, "and Pawley was obviously pretty cute in the way he handled it."[24]

With the competition becoming fiercer, Pawley felt it was time to bolster his roster. Although George, the eldest brother, had died in 1936, Pawley brought his surviving brothers into the business. While Pawley still maintained complete control, he gave them positions in management, not only in China but also in the United States. Eugene and Edward both arrived in China in early 1939, while Wallace worked out of the Intercontinent office in New York.

Chennault soon learned that Pawley had made certain to garner the lion's share of contracts through his cozy relationship with Kung and by constructing the aircraft assembly plant at Hangchow and later relocating to Hankow.[25] When the Japanese advance threatened his factory, Pawley loaded the machinery onto flatcars and sent them to Hong Kong, where they were sent on ships to Haiphong, Indochina. "Chiang gave us 10,000 coolies to carry our equipment on yo-yo poles to a railroad, where we loaded nearly 100 boxcars," Pawley recalled.[26] When the Japanese pressured the French to close the Indochina railroad to war matériel shipments, Pawley had the equipment hauled back to Haiphong and loaded on ships to Rangoon, Burma. Like a traveling circus, the factory's crates were unloaded on the Burmese docks, reloaded onto railroad cars for a journey to Lashio, and then taken by barge and elephant to their final destination at CAMCO's new factory at Loiwing.[27]

On a site carved out of the Burmese jungle miles from civilization, six thousand Chinese laborers built modern facilities, with electricity and running water to house U.S. personnel. The bungalows were attractive and comfortable, and the facility even had a nine-hole golf course, complete with a clubhouse built with full-length, plate glass windows.[28] Providing for his own comfort, Pawley had living quarters decorated with thick Chinese rugs, soft beds with eiderdown quilts, and blue-tile bathrooms complete with a tub, shower, and toilet.[29] In a factory worth $4 million and supervised by Americans, a thousand Chinese workers assembled and repaired almost every type of American plane. The factory also was used as a CNAC stop on the Rangoon-Chungking route.[30] The arrangement benefited the Chinese because they saved 20 percent on the cost of purchasing completely as-sembled planes from foreign countries.[31] In the three factories he operated in China, Pawley built and repaired $30 million worth of aircraft for the Chinese, resulting in profits as high as $1 million a year.[32]

The Curtiss-Wright Hawk 75 that Chennault desired proved to be a head-ache because of delays and problems encountered at Pawley's CAMCO facility. Throughout the summer of 1938, the crated planes arrived in Hong Kong, where they were shipped by rail and boat to Loiwing. After assembly, their performance didn't match factory specs. For instance, they only reached speeds of 255 miles per hour versus a specified speed of 275 miles per hour and an altitude of 8,500 feet in-stead of the contracted 10,500 feet. After isolating the problems, however, Pawley ordered the necessary parts to correct the planes' performance.[33]

Chennault also wanted to add armor plate and a way to see the rear of the plane from the cockpit without having to turn. "Right here," Chennault pointed out, "right behind the seat this should be dished out, so that I could look behind me." Using the frost-covered wing as a sketch pad—as Sebie Smith observed, "He was a darn good artist"—Pawley drew a diagram showing how it could be done.[34]

Another innovation Chennault requested was to have four machine guns mounted instead of two. The problem was that a four-gun synchronizer (to allow bullets to be shot through the propeller without damaging it) was available only from the Russians, who had developed one for their E-16 aircraft. Pawley said if they could obtain one from the Russians, he would send it to the Curtiss-Wright factory in the United States to be duplicated. Smith was assigned the task of steal-ing it and was able to bring one back from the Russians' supply depot. Pawley sent it to Curtiss-Wright, but nothing was ever heard about it after that.[35]

Contentions between Pawley and Chennault over the Curtiss-Wright Hawk 75's failure to meet specifications, compared to the performance of the demonstra-tor viewed by the Chinese, was brought to a head in a series of letters Chennault sent to the Aeronautical Affairs Commission. Chennault accused Pawley of making statements that the Hawk's performance suffered because of structural changes Chennault had recommended. Chennault's recommendations had included installing a larger battery, lowering the canopy to decrease wind resistance (possible because Chinese pilots were small), altering the wheel fairing for better drainage, and redesigning the windshield to allow better vision. Chennault claimed, however, that he had not "insisted upon or demanded modifications" but had merely offered suggestions. He refused "to take any responsibility for the decrease in performance."[36]

Chennault also blamed the Japanese advance that summer on Pawley's blocking of a contract with a rival manufacturer (Seversky) for pursuit planes that could have been used to stop the Japanese. Charging that Pawley's business tactics effectively shut out all competition, Chennault felt "convinced that even more business will be lost unless the idea that one representative should have a monopoly on all business in China is abandoned." In a letter to Curtiss-Wright, Chennault wrote, "Personally I would welcome a radical change in the methods and attitude of Mr. Pawley as I am confident that it would be for the benefit of China."[37]

Their animosity escalated further when Chennault sent copies of both letters to Pawley. However, both letters were dated December 13, 1938, and Pawley didn't receive them until January 26, 1939. He fired back a letter to Chennault noting "that the date on which your letters were written and circulated coincides with the period where it was common knowledge that I and representatives of the 'rival manufacturer' referred to in them were submitting proposals to the government." Charging that the letters "could not fail to be particularly harmful to any proposals" he might make and "distinctly helpful to the prospects of the nearest competitor," Pawley added that the delay in receiving the copies made him appear as if he had failed to respond to the complaints in a timely manner and that he "tacitly admitted their justification."

Regarding modifications to the Hawk recommended by Chennault, Pawley wrote that they had been accepted "in good faith" and dealt with accordingly. As for Chennault's point about blocking competition, Pawley charged Chennault with favoritism. "It has always been my impression that you favored the Seversky as against the Hawk 75A and that your discrimination against the latter continues down to the present date." Chennault may have had a reason for favoring Seversky. "Few people knew that Chennault was the co-designer with Seversky of the P-35," Pat Patterson recalled.[38] As for the failure to stop the Japanese because China hadn't purchased Seversky pursuit planes, Pawley dismissed the conclusion as unsubstantiated, "unless one is prepared to question the intelligence and integrity of the high Chinese official making purchases of aeroplanes for the Government."[39]

According to Chennault, his reasonable explanation for the late delivery of his letters was that he had wanted to hand them personally to Pawley. When he didn't see him on two trips to Chungking, he mailed them. As to Pawley's denial of exerting influence on Kung not to purchase the Severskys, Chennault said that Madame Chiang had shown him a telegram from Kung in which Pawley was quoted as advising the Chinese minister to investigate Seversky thoroughly before buying the company's planes. Chennault claimed he was trying to help Pawley in aircraft sales, but Pawley consistently had failed to correct deficiencies in the Curtiss planes.[40]

To further impugn Chennault, Pawley spread a rumor that Chennault was receiving a fee from the Patterson contract. While lunching in Hong Kong with several prominent businessmen, W. H. Donald heard the rumor repeated by Sir William Dodwell, head of Dodwell & Company Ltd. Donald reacted vehemently, reproving Dodwell for spreading malicious gossip and storming out. Dodwell apologized in a letter to Donald, explaining he had received the information from Pawley, whom he always had considered reliable. When Dodwell suggested he meet with Pawley, Donald replied that he didn't associate with anyone who "spread lies about innocent people." Donald then dictated a letter to Chennault describing the incident.[41]

Safe from Japanese bombs, the Loiwing factory became the lifeline for China's defense against the encroaching Japanese. Pawley was now in a position to provide warplanes and the Aeronautical Affairs Commission, which through "inertia and ignorance" had delayed making aircraft purchases, now began placing orders.[42] It gave Pawley a $5.25 million contract to provide fifty-five Curtiss Mohawks, seventy-five Vultee V-12C and V-12D light bombers, and thirty-three Curtiss-Wright 21 Demon interceptors (fashioned after a Curtiss racer), all to be assembled at the Loiwing factory.[43]

The exact number of Curtiss Hawk H75-Ms destined for China seems to be a mystery. In 1946 the Curtiss-Wright Public Relations Office issued a thirty-page report listing 112 airplanes delivered. However, the company's Sales and Contract Division lists serial numbers of only 32 planes, including the demonstrator Chennault had used. Other records reveal $557,540 of tools and materials for the Hawk H75-Ms, along with $153,132 for spares, were billed to CAMCO. With this amount in equipment and material, it is conceivable that Pawley assembled 50 more planes. If true, then at the $30,888 rate Curtiss-Wright charged the Chinese for the Hawks, Pawley managed to provide additional aircraft at a cost of $14,213 (plus labor) and realized a profit of more than $800,000 on the deal.[44]

But other American military aircraft companies wanted part of the lucrative Chinese market. American naval attaché in Chungking James McHugh was an important source of information concerning rivalries among aircraft salesmen. Madame and Chiang Kai-shek trusted and confided in McHugh, who was their staunch supporter. From 1938 to 1942, he reported on conditions in China, supplied with confidential and secret information from the Chiangs and Kung.[45]

Foreign currency reserves in China were low, and obtaining credit while under siege was difficult, but Chiang Kai-shek was apprehensive to place all aircraft purchases with one individual.[46] Chennault recommended the Seversky P-35 to the Chinese because it was "the only single seater with sufficient speed, range and fire power" to reach Japanese bases as far as Shanghai.[47] The United States had arranged a $25 million credit to China through the Export-Import Bank but specified the funds could not be used to purchase military aircraft.[48] Patterson, who arranged a $12 million credit for China to purchase aircraft, was instrumental in working with Chennault to get the Chinese to place an $8.83 million contract in March 1939. The largest aircraft purchase contract ever for China, it included fifty Ryan trainers, twenty Ryan advanced pursuit trainers, fifty North American basic trainers, twenty-five Chance-Vought dive-bombers, and fifty-four of the Seversky P-35s that Chennault desired. The order included 20 percent of their value in spare parts with 25 percent of the total contract paid in cash and the remainder in installments over thirty months.[49]

Pawley was "literally livid with rage" over the Patterson contract and set out to destroy it by any means necessary. Soon after the signing, a telegram from the Colt's Firearms Company informed Patterson it had raised its quotes on the machine guns being bought for the planes. Pawley had the Colt agency in China, and the 10 percent hike amounted to exactly what his commission would be. But it wasn't enough to defeat the contract. Patterson admitted he "would be glad to sell the planes for no profit at all . . . satisfied to break even on this deal" simply to beat Pawley and be in a position to place further orders.[50]

Patterson was desperate to get the contract; he had run up sizable office expenses and faced bankruptcy. As a result, he had allowed the Chinese to tack on multiple conditions that proved impossible to meet.[51] One provision called for Patterson to guarantee the contract with a 100 percent bond, a stipulation unheard of in any previous contracts with China. A second provision specified prices of the planes would be checked against prices that the U.S. government paid for the same aircraft. If the contract exceeded those yardstick prices, Patterson would only receive 3 percent of the contract for expenses and an additional 1 percent for profit. A week after signing the contract, Kung sought to verify the prices. His American agent was instructed to "confidentially making available this contract and the price list for spare parts to an expert or *experts* designated by the American Treasury or Government in order to ascertain whether the prices charged are aboveboard."[52] As Patterson soon discovered, he couldn't secure a bond because the prices were 20 percent higher than the U.S. government would pay and the bonding company would be held liable for the refundable difference to the Chinese.[53]

Pawley claimed he convinced Kung to lower the bond requirement to 25 percent, but Patterson was still unable to secure one. In the interim, Kung deposited the first installment of $2.2 million in the Hong Kong & Shanghai Bank. In the ensuing months, regular installments were deposited but not paid to Patterson while he tried finding a way to secure the bond. Kung even agreed to have the funds transferred to the Bank of China in New York, where they would be readily available when the bonding arrangements had been completed.[54] Six weeks after the contract was signed, with no bond in sight, the U.S. Department of State entered the fray.

Now head of the U.S. Aeronautical Chamber of Commerce, Colonel Jouett approached the State Department to look into the matter, charging "undue obstacles" prevented fulfilling the contract and that William Pawley was behind it all. The State Department instructed the U.S. Embassy at Chungking to confer with Kung and seek a remedy. The instructions emphasized that the U.S. government was completely disinterested and wanted to remain neutral in competitive aviation companies' disputes, but it hoped to see that once a contract was signed that it would be carried out. The American consul was also instructed to investigate the charge of Pawley's obstruction of the contract.[55] When interviewed by Willys R. Peck, chargé d'affaires in China, Pawley claimed he had done nothing to obstruct the Patterson contract, deeming it "unworkable," and indeed had tried to show Kung how it could be made workable.[56]

A new twist was added on July 24 when Kung sent a telegram to Patterson informing the already beleaguered salesman that if the bond was not secured by

July 31, the contract would be canceled. Adding insult to injury, Kung then appointed Dr. George Sellett, Pawley's attorney, to act as his legal representative in the matter.[57] When McHugh suggested to Madame Chiang that Sellett's appointment would be difficult for people to understand, Madame looked surprised, which McHugh interpreted to mean that it was news to her.[58]

Even Chennault was drawn into the dispute. Sellett asserted that as a member of the Advisory Board on Chinese aircraft purchases and a past member of the Pursuit Tactical Board in the United States, which selected planes from competing manufacturers, Chennault was in a position to advise Patterson that his prices were too high. Chennault countered that members of the U.S. board "were specifically told not to consider the price of the competing planes"; therefore, he wasn't in a position to counsel Patterson. He then attacked Pawley, accusing him of blocking the purchase of Seversky planes just as he had in the past. "Mr. Pawley has stated that he desires his competitors to get some small orders," he added, "just to keep them in business so that there will be an appearance of competition but that he intends to do all of the real business here." In closing, Chennault wrote, "I would resign immediately were it not for the fact that Pawley would appreciate nothing more than my resignation."[59]

McHugh defended Chennault but felt he "never should have bucked Bill [Pawley] to start with," and admonished Chennault for the letter-writing campaign against Pawley. "And he has been completely pig-headed about his stand for Severskys," McHugh added. While supporting Chennault that the Seversky was a better airplane than the Curtiss-Wright, McHugh also pointed out that the Chinese had never been offered a demonstration, whereas "Bill has demonstrated his stuff all along." McHugh's advice was that if Chennault wanted to remain in China, he might as well get used to the fact that Pawley will be the man to deal with; otherwise, "he would be well advised to go home."[60]

Patterson finally did receive the necessary bonding on August 1 and had addressed ten minor objections the Chinese had raised in the contract, but Kung decided not to go ahead with the deal. Since Kung had already made the initial deposit on the contract and three additional monthly deposits, the question now was what to do with the funds. The vultures began circling to claim the prize. The British had once negotiated to sell China some Blenheim bombers, Hurricane pursuits, and Gladiator interceptors by using part of a £10 million (US $50 million) credit the British had established to assist their companies' trade throughout the world. Fearing that Japan might object to Britain's aiding China, Parliament had held up the funds. With the Patterson contract now dead, the British hoped the deposited funds for the contract could be used to finance their own deal.

But Pawley hadn't fought the Patterson contract without having in mind a way of getting the deposited funds. He was not opposed to purchasing North American and Ryan trainers in the original contract because he had nothing to offer to compete with them, but now that the Severskys and Voughts had been excluded, he wanted China to purchase Curtiss-Wright planes. The British were no competition for Pawley, not because his planes were better, but because they couldn't even establish contact with the proper Chinese officials. During the Patterson contract turmoil, Pawley's representatives (Sellett and Leighton) were in direct contact with Kung's two aviation advisers, Col. C. F. Wang and Col. C. H. Wang. Neither adviser could write English, so Pawley's representatives had drafted every telegram concerning the Patterson deal for them.[61]

Chennault allied with T. V. Soong, while Pawley worked closely with Soong's bitter rival H. H. Kung. The feud between the two high-ranking Chinese officials stemmed from who was to have control over the Bank of China, and for the time being, it was Kung. With Pawley looking to have exclusive rights for all military aircraft sold to the Chinese, Kung served to eliminate the competition. Whether Kung's affiliation with Pawley also included some form of remuneration from Pawley, it was never determined, but Kung did everything he could to ensure that Pawley received most of the government's business. Kung's only reason for considering the Patterson contract was to demonstrate his impartiality in awarding contracts; however, he ultimately did whatever he could to scrap the deal. Pawley's charges against him infuriated Chennault, who felt they were "actuated by the fact that I will not limit my recommendations to airplanes which he sells."[62] When the dust settled, the Chinese purchased only the trainers, and Seversky was bankrupted in the process.[63]

In November 1939 the first shipment of aircraft parts left New York for Rangoon. By February 1940, the parts needed to fulfill the Patterson contract, valued at $600,000, had arrived in Rangoon for shipment to Loiwing.[64] But malaria had broken out in Loiwing, delaying assembly of the aircraft. CAMCO initiated measures to control the disease, including placing an American doctor in charge of the hospital and sanitation, but by Christmas, almost everyone at the factory had been stricken, including the general manager. Taking efforts to control the malaria,

CAMCO expected to assemble one plane a week, working toward a production target of one a day.[65]

Throughout the summer of 1939, Chennault had struggled to keep the Chinese Air Force a viable fighting unit, but the lack of skilled pilots and dwindling supplies and equipment made the mission almost impossible to achieve. When Germany invaded Poland on September 1, the United States focused on providing assistance to Europe, leaving China a secondary consideration. In December, the Chinese asked the United States to provide American aviators to serve as instructors at the aviation school in Kunming. The State Department replied that if any request for active or reserve officers from U.S. armed forces were received, "our attitude would have to be unfavorable." However, the department suggested that since Chennault was in the United States at the time, he might assist the Chinese in obtaining the services of "properly qualified persons."[66]

The concept for the American Volunteer Group—the first U.S. government–financed clandestine military operation and consisting of qualified American pilots flying as civilians under contract for China—was originally speculated as early as 1937. Chennault felt such a squadron of American pilots—not necessarily financed by the United States—would be effective against the Japanese invaders. In 1938 he and Pawley discussed forming a group, and when Chennault received a job inquiry from Elwyn Gibbon, a former pilot with the Fourteenth International Squadron, he replied there was a "project under discussion." Gibbon later received a Christmas card from Chennault with a note to "write W. D. Pawley, Intercontinent Corporation, Hong Kong, for job as a pilot in a special squadron."[67]

In May 1939, Pawley met with H. H. Kung to discuss business policy. Also attending the meeting at Kung's office were Ed Pawley and Bruce Leighton, both vice presidents of Intercontinent. After concluding the business talks, Pawley asked what he could do "that would be of the greatest benefit to China and the Chinese Air Force." Kung replied that China needed a group "such as the Lafayette Escadrille active in the Asiatic theatre." Pawley left the meeting after promising to present the idea "before various men of influence in the United States."[68] Although Pawley and Chennault had been at odds with each other since the Patterson contract debacle, they would set aside their personal feelings, for the time being, to help create one of the most formidable air combat groups ever formed, the Flying Tigers.

While Pawley lobbied in Washington, Leighton succeeded in obtaining an interview on January 17, 1940, with Chief of Naval Operations (CNO) Adm. Harold

R. Stark. Leighton outlined China's problems of mounting an effective air force against the Japanese and argued that "America's interest was to prevent Japan's gaining control of China." The plan called for the Chinese to purchase aircraft with credit established through American banks and for fifty American army and navy pilots to "be secured if not discouraged by the government." Leighton said if the United States allowed fliers to be recruited, Intercontinent would employ the pilots through a private contract with China "without any direct participation by the United States Government."[69]

Chennault was also in the United States at the time, but ostensibly he was on vacation as provided in his contract with the Chinese. After a tour of the Curtiss-Wright plant in Buffalo, he arrived in Washington, D.C., to brief an army intelligence officer on the Chinese Air Force. Even though he still held ill will toward Pawley, Chennault joined him and Leighton on a tour of aircraft plants in California. When Pawley's plane left Los Angeles on February 1, they encountered bad weather and the carburetors began icing up. As the situation became serious enough that a crash seemed imminent, Pawley casually remarked, "Well, Claire, it looks like this might be it." With a coldness that underlined the hostility between the two, Chennault retorted that his only regret was that their two bodies would be found together in the wreckage.[70] After a forced landing, the icing was cleared, and the flight continued to San Francisco, where Chennault boarded a Pan Am Clipper to Hong Kong and returned to China.

5

Money and Men for a Volunteer Group

Creating an American Volunteer Group to fight the Japanese meant solving two vital problems: first, the Chinese had to establish credit to purchase aircraft, spare parts, and provide salaries for pilots and ground crews; and second, it was necessary to convince the U.S. government to allow the Chinese to recruit active and reserve pilots from the army and navy. Both objectives were reached in circuitous routes that managed to stretch neutrality laws.

China's credit with the United States was limited, not only in the dollar amount but also on what funds could be spent. In March 1939, senior treasury official Harry D. White urged Treasury Secretary Morgenthau that "the time is ripe to propose to Congress the extension of a $100 million ten year credit to be used by China for the purpose of whatever American products she wishes."[1] Although aid to China had been curtailed once the Germans began overrunning the Low Countries in the spring of 1940, Roosevelt took a closer look at involving the United States in helping Asian countries. Because Roosevelt had always been sympathetic to China, owing to his family's fortune having been made in the Shanghai opium trade, Chiang Kai-shek saw the opportunity to press China's needs in Washington.[2]

William Pawley provided his own public relations work by sponsoring an essay contest for students enrolled in American universities. Announced on April 7, 1940, the contest offered a $1,200 first prize for a 1,500-word essay on "Our Stake in the Future of China," with an emphasis on "why it is to the interest of the United States to have a strong, free and independent China." First prize included a round trip to China "if conditions in the Far East are favorable."[3] Judges included

Pearl Buck; Henry Luce; Theodore Roosevelt, Jr.; Lowell Thomas; Frank Knox; Alexander Woollcott; and William Allen White.[4] "What I was trying to do for relatively small amounts of money," Pawley recalled, "which was about forty thousand to the cost, was to get the greatest amount of publicity on the subject."[5]

T. V. Soong was assigned the task of lobbying Washington officials for aid in the form of credits to stabilize China's currency. Arriving in Washington in June 1940, Soong, who spoke flawless English, began cultivating political friends to help. Lauchlin Currie, special assistant to Roosevelt and a sympathetic friend of China, provided access to the president and to Joseph Alsop, an influential newspaper columnist and relative of Eleanor Roosevelt. But more important, Currie introduced Soong to Washington lawyer and lobbyist Thomas "Tommy the Cork" Corcoran, who knew how to facilitate issues in Washington. Corcoran would steer the Chinese minister through the quagmire of governmental policies, both official and unofficial. Soong's initial request was for a $50 million credit against tungsten exports to purchase nonmilitary supplies and improve conditions along the Burma Road, a vital supply route to southwest China during the Japanese invasion.[6] But when Soong met with Secretary Morgenthau on July 9, the ante was raised to $140 million in credit and Soong now wanted to purchase three hundred fighter planes and a hundred light bombers.[7]

Negotiations continued throughout the hot summer months with Soong's shuffling between government agencies looking for support. Meeting with Morgenthau again on August 15, he was told that finding help for China was becoming difficult. Soong was referred to the Federal Loan Agency, where Director Jesse Jones offered a $5 million loan, or a small portion considering China's needs.[8] Undeterred, Soong kept knocking on doors, but interdepartmental resentment in which the State Department objected to the Treasury Department's involvement in a matter the former felt was its domain resulted in nothing significant being accomplished. Roosevelt often allowed departments to overstep their boundaries, and for China he permitted Morgenthau to continue handling the matter.

When Russia offered strategic minerals to the United States in return for funds to purchase war materials for China, the negotiations took another turn. In a telephone conversation with Sumner Welles, Morgenthau informed him that Roosevelt had "suggested that I work out a three-cornered deal with Russia, China and ourselves whereby we would buy certain strategic materials from Russia and they, in turn, would use that money as credit with which to sell arms to China."[9] Roosevelt promoted this idea to Morgenthau as a way around the Neutrality Act, and the "three-corner deal" concept was passed on to Soong.[10]

The State Department, possibly to regain control of foreign affairs, announced September 13 that Roosevelt had approved a $20 million purchasing credit for China. Matters came to a head when Japan, in agreement with France's Vichy government, began moving troops into northern Indochina on September 23.[11] The $20 million loan was now increased to $25 million at the urging of both Cordell Hull of the State Department and Morgenthau of the Treasury Department, and the official announcement was made on September 25.[12] Assured that more funds would be made available in the near future, Soong was told that the money could not be used to purchase war materials.

State Department policy concerning Americans serving as aviation instructors in foreign countries was viewed as a "private matter" as long as American pilots didn't participate in combat. However, in July 1940, the War Department warned retired officers that serving as instructors in foreign countries violated provisions of the Constitution that prevented them from accepting any "office or title" from a foreign state.[13] Regardless of U.S. policy, William Pawley actively promoted the AVG's creation by discussing the plan with a group of American pilots stationed in Hawaii in September 1940. Gen. Bruce K. Holloway, USAF (Ret.), who had been a lieutenant in the Sixth Pursuit Squadron at Wheeler Field, recalled meeting Pawley "under the big banyan tree in front of the Moana Hotel" and listening to him talk about forming the group.[14] Pawley may have foreseen a change in U.S. policy regarding American pilots, but it wasn't until October that Secretary of the Navy Frank Knox sought advice from Secretary of State Hull on a matter in which he had a "sympathetic interest":

> I am told there are a considerable number of American aviators who would be glad to volunteer their services to China in the present War with Japan if they could be absolved from any penalty for such action. Is it at all possible that we can handle this matter of American flyers going to China as we have handled the same situation with respect to young men volunteering for service in Great Britain in the present War there?[15]

The State Department replied in a memo quoting from the Nationality Act of 1940, that "a person . . . shall lose his nationality by . . . accepting . . . employment under the government of a foreign state," adding that Title 18, U.S. Code, provided "penalties for entry or the hiring of others for entry into the armed forces of a foreign state" if such acts were committed in the United States. The memo did state that if a citizen were to "go abroad and while abroad enter the armed forces of a foreign state" there would be no penalty.[16] The United States had already advised Americans on October 8, 1940, to leave the Far East as soon as possible, and on October 19, the State Department sent three passenger ships to expedite the evacuation.[17]

Chennault, back in China and suffering from bronchitis, met with Chiang Kai-shek on October 12 to discuss obtaining American aircraft and hiring American pilots to fly combat.[18] Also at the meeting was Maj. Gen. Mao Pang-chu, director of the Chinese Air Force Operations Division. Chiang desperately wanted the Japanese bombing of civilians stopped and asked Chennault to accompany Mao to the United States to purchase planes and hire American pilots and ground crew personnel.[19] On October 18, Chiang met with U.S. ambassador to China Nelson T. Johnson and expressed his fears that the Japanese would soon close the Burma Road, cutting off the essential supply route China needed to continue fighting. "I strongly hope that before the severance of communication facilities American planes can be procured in plentiful quantities," Chiang told him. "It is also hoped that American volunteers will be able to aid us in carrying on hostilities," he added.[20] He pressed Johnson for more economic credits and stressed the importance of having American planes piloted by American volunteers in the fight.[21]

While Chiang was seeking American help, Pawley was having his own problems. His aircraft factory at Loiwing was running out of material owing to a Burmese prohibition of reexportation of specified military materials from its ports. Although airplane parts were not banned initially, machine guns and aviation fuel were. Prior to the embargo, CAMCO procured all of its fuel from Burma, and 40 percent of imports from the United States that were reexported to China went to his factory.[22] Without fuel, aircraft could not be tested, raising the possibility that factory production might come to a halt.[23]

Instructed by the British government, Burma also added "aeroplanes and parts" to the list of banned articles. The CAMCO factory, having used up its inventory, was practically idle. To keep the workers occupied, improvements were made in the assembly plant, but with the ban, it was a matter of time before the factory would have to shut down.[24]

The ban was finally lifted October 17, 1940, and thirty trucks loaded with four hundred tons of airplane parts and engines began their journey from Bhamo, Burma, "by a one-way, rather poor road, 75 miles long," to the CAMCO facility at Loiwing.[25] Another three hundred tons of aircraft material and a hundred tons of machinery stored in Rangoon had to be shipped by barge to Bhamo and then by truck to Loiwing. The $5.5 million worth of equipment and material was to be used to construct 163 planes for the Chinese: 55 Curtiss-Wright Hawk 75A fighters, 33 Curtiss 21 Demon interceptors, and 75 Vultee V-12C and V-12D light bombers.[26]

As soon as most of the material arrived at Loiwing, the Japanese bombed the facility. Fifty-nine Mitsubishi Ki-21 Sallys (light and highly flammable, it was dubbed the Flying Zippo by Allied pilots) flew over Loiwing on October 26 and damaged the plant.[27] Anticipating attacks, the factory had closed between 10 a.m. and 3 p.m. so personnel would not be working during the expected bombing raids. The Japanese avoided the early warning network of radio stations by approaching from Burma and violating its territory. The factory had only five minutes' advance notice of the attack. Among the aircraft destroyed were several of the North American trainers assembled through the Patterson contract.[28] Casualties included thirty-five CAMCO employees and family members killed, five unidentified local natives who also died, and sixty wounded.[29] Fortunately, there were no American casualties, and temporary living quarters were erected across the border in Burma to house the forty men, women, and children who had been living at Loiwing.[30] Only one direct hit on the factory caused heavy damage, but almost all the machinery was saved, including the power plant, which continued to operate.[31]

Not to be deterred in the face of adversity, Pawley began planning to move salvaged parts and equipment to a safer location. The Japanese had also bombed bridges on the Mekong and Salween Rivers, cutting off the Burma Road supply route. Supplies began piling up in Rangoon and Lashio with no means of transporting them into China.[32]

The Chinese continued pressing the United States for planes, which were now becoming a scarce commodity in China. On October 31, 1940, Hu Shih, the Chinese ambassador in Washington, called upon Joseph C. Green, chief of the Division of Controls, to elicit suggestions on how his government could obtain the needed aircraft. Green reviewed the Chinese government's previous efforts and suggested the Chinese contact Philip Young, chairman of Roosevelt's Liaison Committee, who could advise them on how to secure "small orders of twenty-five or fifty" planes by adding to large orders already placed by the British.[33] To maintain secrecy, the Chinese delegation of Chennault, Mao, and Soong met in Young's apartment in November and discussed preparing an aid program to submit to the U.S. government for "sending of units of the American air force and American air supplies to China."[34] Young recalled, "Although she [Mrs. Young] was consigned to another room because of the secrecy, she heard most of what took place because Chennault's deafness made it necessary to talk with a loud voice."[35]

Elected for a third term, Roosevelt presented his Lend-Lease program for congressional approval, but getting it passed would be time consuming, and the Chinese needed immediate help. The Mao delegation's request for aircraft purchases was presented to the president's Liaison Committee on November 25, 1940. Instead of the small order Green had suggested, the Chinese wanted 500 planes, trained American crews to fly them, 150 trainers, 10 transports, and provisions to construct 14 airfields and 122 landing strips. They also requested a year's supply of ammunition and ordnance and $30 million to equip thirty divisions of Chinese ground troops.[36]

Meanwhile, efforts to stave off Japanese bombers decimating civilian populations in China were becoming hopeless as the Chinese Air Force continued losing planes. China's cities, especially Chungking, were subject to aerial attacks without any effective defense to stop them.[37] Seeking other avenues of approach, Soong and Chennault began wooing Morgenthau and Knox, both of whom already indicated their willingness to support China with U.S. aid.[38] As treasury secretary, Morgenthau was in a position to convince the administration to provide funds for the Chinese, but he also was determined to see that combat aircraft purchases were secured for China's fight against Japan. A cautious man, he kept tabs on American sentiment, and it was reflected in the Treasury Department's memorandums regarding letters it received concerning aid to China. "Strongly support proposal for large loan in delivery of planes to Chinese," one read. Another urged Morgenthau to "use his great influence to give financial and material aid to China."[39] At the same time, Morgenthau was receiving FBI reports on its continuing surveillance of Soong's activities.[40]

Cordell Hull was apparently taking a hawk-like position on Japan. In a talk he had with Morgenthau on the morning of December 10, 1940, Morgenthau recalled that before "I could even open my mouth," Hull said we should "get 500 American planes to start from the Aleutian Islands and fly over Japan just once." Hull added,

"That will teach them a lesson." Morgenthau was speechless. Hull continued, "If we could only find some way to have them [the Chinese] drop some bombs on Tokyo." Seizing the opportunity, Morgenthau confessed he had told Soong "we could make available to him a limited number of long distance bombers provided that they were used to bomb Tokyo." Hull responded, "Fine," but hedged by asking, "That proviso doesn't have to be part of the contract, does it?"[41]

Armed with the secretary of state's endorsement, Morgenthau next pitched the idea to Roosevelt. After a cabinet meeting on December 19, Roosevelt asked Hull, Stimson, Knox, and Morgenthau to stay. Pouring over a secret map Soong had given to Morgenthau that showed the various airfields in China, Roosevelt gave his approval. Morgenthau asked, "Should we work it out and come back?" Roosevelt said that wasn't necessary: "The four of you work out a program."[42] Meeting with Soong the next day, Morgenthau told him, "I am going to put all of my energy behind this because it has to be done at once."[43]

Allocating planes for China met resistance from Army Chief of Staff general George C. Marshall, who felt the priority of available aircraft should be to aid Britain.[44] Nevertheless, Secretary of the Navy Knox—who had been a Rough Rider under Theodore "Teddy" Roosevelt—and his military aide, Navy captain Morton L. Deyo, held conferences with William Pawley and Bruce Leighton to discuss China's ability to use planes effectively if the United States made them available. Leighton, who had served in China on the Yangtze River patrol and was now an Intercontinent vice president, expressed an opinion that unless the Chinese were furnished American "technicians" to assist in air operations, the proposed program would fail.[45] Soong had suggested creating a joint British-American air force to operate in China, but in a meeting with Nevile M. Butler, the British chargé d'affaires, Sumner Welles agreed it would be better "to take parallel action rather than joint action" in aiding China.[46]

During meetings with Knox, Pawley repeatedly said he would not participate in the program if Chennault had any part in it. Pawley suggested Gen. Tony Frank be given military command of the volunteer group. If Frank were not acceptable, Gen. Ralph Royce would be an alternative. "T. V. Soong nevertheless insisted on Chennault," Pawley said, "and Leighton and I finally capitulated in this regard."[47]

Getting the planes China needed proved difficult, but securing loans to purchase the aircraft was gaining support in Washington. Dr. Hsu Mo, Chinese vice minister for foreign affairs, told Ambassador Johnson in Chungking that China

didn't have the money to purchase planes, and Johnson forwarded the information to the State Department.[48] When Soong met with the secretary of state on
November 26, he told Hull that China needed $200 million to $300 million "for
airplanes and other weapons."[49] Four days later, Soong met with Morgenthau at
the Treasury Department to discuss receiving the loan as soon as possible. Also
at the meeting was Tommy Corcoran, who listened as Soong stressed the urgent
need of the loan because the Japanese had just recognized a puppet government in
Nanking, and "any assistance given now would have very good effect, both politically and psychologically." Morgenthau questioned how the previous loans were
being used, and Soong said they were using the Universal Trading Corporation as
the conduit. Morgenthau replied, "Good. That is a good set-up."[50]

The Universal Trading Corporation was indeed a good setup. Headquartered
at Rockefeller Center in New York City (the location of Intercontinent's office),
Universal was manned by former U.S. government employees, and its sole purpose
appeared to be China's go-between purchasing agent for war materials from the
United States and other countries. The corporation had handled the transactions of
repaying the $25 million U.S. loan in 1939, with exports of metals and minerals,
and using the funds to purchase war supplies even though Universal was forbidden
to do so by the China Trade Act.[51]

When the United States began a more aggressive program of military aid to
China, China Defense Supplies, Inc. (CDS)—a new private corporation chartered
in Delaware—was entrusted with the funds being advanced. Organized by Soong at
the request of Madame Chiang, CDS set up its offices at 1601 V Street, Northwest,
in Washington, D.C.[52] As China's appointed purchasing agent and its sole client,
CDS attracted a roster of officers that included the cream of the Washington elite.
Tommy "the Cork" Corcoran served as legal counsel and his brother David was installed as president. David served as the manager for General Motors Corporation
in Tokyo but resigned after Japan invaded Manchuria in 1931. In 1941, David,
along with Nelson Rockefeller, formed the Sydney Ross Company, a subsidiary of
Sterling Drugs that supplied CDS with medical drugs throughout the war, and later,
quinine, caffeine, and drugs to South America.[53] Frederic A. Delano, FDR's uncle,
was named a director of CDS; William Brennan was its congressional liaison; and
Whiting Willauer, a reserve officer in naval intelligence (and Chennault's future
partner in the postwar Civil Air Transport, which evolved into Air America) was
the corporate secretary. Others serving CDS included Gordon Tweedy, William

Youngman from the Federal Power Commission who acted as general counsel and a go-between for Chiang Kai-shek, and Quinn Shaughnessy, a Harvard lawyer and Marine Corps intelligence officer who had worked for the Reconstruction Finance Corporation's legal division.[54]

By November 1940, State Department–issued export licenses for aircraft for the entire year showed China had received only four combat planes, and the rest—mostly trainers and transports—totaled forty-seven aircraft.[55] The secretary of state was pressing to "make available to the Chinese Government as promptly as is possible a few planes," but finding them from available production runs was difficult.[56] Soong admitted that the Chinese had relied on the Soviets to supply combat planes but "had been disappointed in the number of planes furnished"; now China depended on the United States.[57] Fortune smiled on Soong's request when the Curtiss-Wright Corporation announced that production of its P-40 Tomahawk combat fighter was exceeding demands, and the company would have an additional hundred planes available for the summer of 1941 and another ninety-four by the fall. If the United States or Britain, both of whom had current orders placed with Curtiss, would agree to defer deliveries and take delivery from the extra planes, China might receive some planes from current production.[58]

Now Morgenthau had to find a source of funding to make the purchase possible. The question arose as to which agency would handle the loan because a guarantee of China's repayment was risky.[59] After the inquiry was presented to the Federal Loan Agency, Director Jesse Jones informed Roosevelt that "if China proposes to use the proceeds of our loans for war materials, we will have to ask Congress to modify the [Neutrality] law."[60] Jones told the president that a guarantee of additional credits of $100 million would be provided easily by purchasing strategic materials—such as wolframite, antimony, and tin—from China.[61]

On November 30 Roosevelt announced a $100 million credit to China. Half was earmarked for currency stabilization with the balance for "general purposes," which the Chinese understood could be used to purchase war materials, especially planes.[62] Concurrent with the announcement, State Department adviser on political relations Stanley K. Hornbeck advised Soong that the United States would be "making a substantial additional number of airplanes available as soon as possible." Touching on the subject of allowing American aviators to serve in China, Hornbeck was careful to point out the penalties involved, but he added no laws prevented U.S. citizens from going abroad to serve in a foreign country. The

State Department would probably issue passports for those who served as "aviation instructors."[63] The framework for the American Volunteer Group was being implemented.

In a secret memorandum that Chiang Kai-shek endorsed and Chennault submitted to Morgenthau on November 30, a program was outlined for the formation of a "Special Air Unit" composed of "200 modern bombers and 300 pursuits" to be assembled in Rangoon or India, "or transported by water from Rangoon to the Chinese frontier and assembled there [at Pawley's Loiwing factory]." It also proposed that "personnel from the British and American Training Centers should be drawn upon" for pilots and mechanics.[64] While riding in a car after a White House luncheon on December 8, Morgenthau asked Soong if he would pass along something to Chiang but to no one else in Washington. "Absolutely," Soong answered. "Well, his asking for 500 planes is like asking for 500 stars," Morgenthau said. Then he asked what Soong thought of the United States' providing long-range bombers to be used on Tokyo and other Japanese cities. In his notes on the conversation, Morgenthau wrote, "Well, to say he was enthusiastic is putting it mildly."[65]

Chiang Kai-shek was also pressing for immediate help. In a telegram to Roosevelt on December 12, Chiang mentioned the air force proposal, writing that he would "be grateful if in view of the urgency of the situation you could indicate to [Soong] your views on these grave matters as soon as possible."[66] FDR was willing to help Chiang and asked Morgenthau, "Is he still willing to fight?" Morgenthau assured the president he was. "Wonderful," Roosevelt responded.[67]

The plan to supply bombers to strike the Japanese homeland was discussed once again, this time at Morgenthau's home with Soong, Chennault, Maj. Gen. Mao Pang-chu, and Philip Young attending. Asked about the bomber crews required, Chennault said, "Each bomber would need an American pilot, an American bombardier, and about five mechanics." Morgenthau told them, "The Army would release enough men from active duty at $1,000 per month to help the Chinese." When he asked if that was enough pay, both Soong and Mao agreed. When Mao asked about the possibility of getting pursuit planes, Morgenthau replied, "China would have to have at least a hundred as ten or twenty would not do any good."[68]

Army Chief of Staff George Marshall, who felt England needed those planes more than China did, questioned the advisability of the bomber proposal. He felt, however, Britain "might better give up some of their pursuit ships rather than these bombers."[69] Secretary of War Stimson thought that "China should get pursuit ships before she got bombers."[70]

Meetings away from the treasury office continued when Soong, Chennault, General Mao, and Young gathered at Morgenthau's home. On New Year's Day, Morgenthau told them "it looked very doubtful" that China would receive bombers, but to protect the Burma Road "there was a good possibility of getting some P-40 pursuit ships." Delivery would come from a British order, Morgenthau told them, but the process was "a very complicated one" because replacements at a later date would have to be arranged.[71] Chennault had already visited the Curtiss-Wright plant in Buffalo, and Burdette Wright had informed him that another assembly line could be added to increase production. To further the swap proposal, it was pointed out that the Colt factory had on the shelf 132 machine guns of an odd caliber—for which the Chinese had ammunition—thus the British wouldn't have to release the armament for the planes.[72]

During Treasury Department meetings held the next week, Morgenthau told those present a story he found quite amusing. The anecdote arose during a discussion of leaks to the press of the department's policies. It prompted Morgenthau to quote the following:

Morgenthau: As you know, Mr. Soong, if what I am saying to you now ever appears in the paper or you ever say you talked to me about it, I will just say I never saw you.

Soong: Well, Mr. Secretary, I want to tell you that I can't tell you how disturbed I was when that story appeared in the paper about the Chinese planes and what they needed. General Mow [Mao] talked to a newspaper man and after I saw it, I sent for General Mow [Mao] and I said, "General, you are a military man. You go back to China for court martial" and he said, "You know in war times what that means." General Mow [Mao] should be very, very grateful that you received him so graciously, because now he does not have to go back to be court martialed.

After the meeting, Chennault stayed behind, and Morgenthau questioned him:

Morgenthau: Well, what is all this? He didn't tell it half to me.

Chennault: Do you really want to know what happened?

Morgenthau: I would love to.

Chennault: The true story, after this appeared in the paper, General Mow
[Mao] shot his mouth off. Soong sent for him, and he says, "General,
here is a pistol. You are a soldier. Go to your hotel room and shoot
yourself." I said, "You mustn't do that, Soong. Think of the bad press
that you will get."

Morgenthau delighted in repeating the story to visitors. He also told it to
Roosevelt, who enjoyed it so much that he said he might use it himself.[73]

The negotiations for credit loans to China and the permission to use them for
military aircraft purchases had taken a year. Washington had become more receptive to aiding the Chinese, possibly with the thought that the Chinese keeping Japan
at bay in the Far East would allow the United States time to prepare for the coming
war and assist England in its war with Germany. But purchasing the Curtiss-Wright
planes still had an obstacle to overcome, namely, William Pawley.

The Curtiss P-40 deal passed the first hurdle of coaxing Britain to give up
the hundred planes for three hundred planes to be delivered in May, June, and
July.[74] When Morgenthau apprised FDR of the British decision, he said the president "gave it his Blessing."[75] Morgenthau recently had sent a letter to Cordell Hull
notifying the State Department of the transaction when he received a confidential
letter from Philip Young detailing a "snag" that had developed between Curtiss-
Wright and the Intercontinent Corporation. According to Young, "Inter-Continent
Corporation has a legal contract for the exclusive agency for Curtiss Wright in
China, to which Curtiss Wright is legally bound. Thus, if Universal Trading purchases the 100 planes from Curtiss Wright, under the contract a commission should
be paid to Inter-Continent. Inter-Continent has taken the position that it will not
waive this commission fee in this instance."[76]

Young added that since Intercontinent was the only company that could assemble and maintain the planes in China, it should receive a service charge for its
services but not a commission. Another solution suggested was for China to buy
the planes directly from Britain, sidestepping the contractual relationship Curtiss
had with Intercontinent, but as Young pointed out, that arrangement would raise
problems on the British side. Morgenthau instructed Young to contact Curtiss directly and explain the urgency of starting deliveries "regardless of the negotiations
between the parties."[77]

While Pawley was playing hardball with the U.S. government on the Curtiss commission, he also was negotiating with the British to move his Loiwing factory to India and assemble planes for the Indian government. He also wanted to produce aircraft at the new facility for export to China. The British welcomed the proposal but with stipulations. Military aircraft produced in India could not be fitted with bomb racks or guns, thus preventing them from engaging in combat en route; planes could be assembled but not manufactured in India for export to China; and "no publicity should be given to the matter and that the site of the factory in India and all details of the scheme should be kept secret for as long as possible." If agreed, the British would allow Pawley to negotiate directly with India and make arrangements with the Burmese government to assemble planes at Rangoon.[78]

While the Curtiss negotiations dragged on, Pawley continued supplying the Chinese. To keep the business functioning, his brother Edward leased land adjacent to Mingaladon Airport in Rangoon. Defended by the Royal Air Force (RAF), it was an improvement over the unprotected Loiwing facility.[79] By January 8, Pawley received permission to assemble at Rangoon the training planes provided by the Patterson contract, including thirty-four planes salvaged from the October 1940 bombing of the Loiwing factory. Sixty-six other planes provided by the contract were being assembled at the Rangoon airport using ninety Chinese workers transferred from Loiwing.[80] Pawley was showing he was capable of overcoming adversity in delivering any product he had promised to the Chinese.

As the U.S. representative in the Curtiss P-40 deal, Philip Young was beginning to show signs of exasperation with the parties involved. In the interim, Curtiss-Wright sent a letter dated January 16, 1941, to Intercontinent, "confirming the obligation to pay Intercontinent 10% of the purchase price of the aircraft." Pawley's lawyers felt the Treasury Department was unreasonable in wanting Pawley to waive his commission, "despite the fact that no objection was raised to the profit that Curtiss-Wright would receive."[81]

Keeping in contact with the three companies—Universal Trading, Curtiss-Wright, and Intercontinent—Young took the position "that as this was a Government arranged transaction there was no reason why Intercontinent should receive any selling commission over and above the price of the planes." Intercontinent claimed the 10 percent was necessary because the company couldn't calculate the cost of services it would be performing in China, and it didn't care who paid the commission, either the Chinese or Curtiss-Wright. Young attempted "a separate deal with the Chinese Government for actual services rendered in China," but Intercontinent still argued its contract with Curtiss entitled Intercontinent to the fee. "At this point we can either back out of the deal and let the three of them fight it out between themselves or we can insist that Intercontinent justify the fee which it proposes to charge," Young wrote to Morgenthau. Although Curtiss was showing good faith by moving the planes to Weehawken, New Jersey, in preparation for overseas shipment, Young felt that since the deal had originated with the U.S. government, "it could be insisted that neither Curtiss nor Inter-Continent take any profit."[82]

In an all-day meeting with the Chinese and representatives from Curtiss-Wright and Intercontinent on January 29, 1941, Young hammered out a compromise from all parties involved. The discussions may have been heated as indicated by a note Pawley sent to Young. "I enjoyed the opportunity of making your acquaintance," he wrote, "although I am sorry it had to be under the circumstances of our last week's meeting."[83] Young reported the results to Morgenthau at a meeting the next day at the Treasury Department.

"We reached a tentative agreement last night," Young told the gathering, which included Tommy Corcoran, ". . . which will save the Chinese somewhere between a hundred and fifty and three hundred thousand dollars on the deal."

"Wonderful," Morgenthau replied.

"In the service charges," Young continued, "a hundred thousand of which is going to be paid up by Curtiss-Wright, rather against Guy Vaughn's [president of Curtiss-Wright Corp.] feeling about it."

"You mean he is contributing that?" Morgenthau asked in amazement.

"What it amounts to is they will cut the British price by approximately a hundred thousand dollars on the planes," Young explained.

"And it saves them how much?" Morgenthau asked. "How much will these— will they still get their 10 percent?"

"No," Young told him. "I cut the 10 percent down—the 10 percent amounted to 450 thousand dollars and I cut that down to 250, which represents just about the best estimate of the actual service charges that this fellow [Pawley] will perform in China for erecting and transporting planes and that sort of thing."

"What you saved them pays more than the freight," Morgenthau asked, "doesn't it?"

"It probably should if they have done it the original way—if they had, they would have paid the 450."

"In behalf of the three Soong sisters, I thank you," Morgenthau chided, which brought a round of laughter from the group.

"Of this 250 service charge," Young added, "Curtiss-Wright is paying a hundred and the Chinese are paying a hundred and fifty."

"They should now 'Sing a Soong of Six Pence,'" Morgenthau joked, bringing more laughter.[84]

According to Archie Lochhead, president of Universal Trading, a determining factor in the settlement centered on the aircraft engines. Since Allison Motor Company of General Motors supplied the P-40 engines, it was felt that Pawley was not entitled a commission for that portion of the sale.[85] The final contract price for the P-40s was $8.9 million, which Universal Trading paid, and the ship carrying the first thirty-six planes left for Rangoon on February 19.[86]

In his memoir, *Way of a Fighter*, Chennault offers a different version on the settlement of Pawley's commission:

In February the planes were on the New York docks ready for shipment to Rangoon. At this critical stage William D. Pawley, Curtiss-Wright salesman in China, entered the picture. . . .

Pawley's role in the A.V.G. project began with his demand that Curtiss-Wright pay him a 10-per-cent commission on the $4,500,000 purchase price of the one hundred P-40's being sold to China. He produced his contract with Curtiss, which called for the commission on all planes sold by Curtiss in China, and threatened to get an injunction against shipment of the P-40's unless he was paid. Curtiss-Wright refused to pay Pawley alleging he had nothing to do with the sale. Months were lost in futile negotiations until there was acute danger that the Chinese would lose the planes. Rather than pay Pawley, Curtiss-Wright was ready to sell them back to the R.A.F.

Secretary Morgenthau called a conference on April 1, 1941, for a showdown. The fight lasted all day. The Chinese were so desperate for the planes they offered to pay Pawley out of Chinese funds. Morgenthau refused to let them and concentrated on wearing Pawley down. Morgenthau threatened to take over the Curtiss contract as a war emergency, but Pawley didn't scare. Finally the Chinese suggested a compromise whereby Pawley would be paid $250,000—considerably less than the $450,000 he wanted—in return for which Central Aircraft Manufacturing Company would assemble, test fly, and service the P-40's in Burma and China. CAMCO then had an assembly plant at Loi-Wing just across the Burmese border in China that was ideally located as a heavy maintenance base. Late in April, the planes were shipped aboard an old slow Norwegian freighter. The first plane was lost when a cargo sling broke, depositing a P-40 fuselage in the waters of New York harbor.[87]

Chennault claimed the P-40 shipment was held up until late April. The first thirty-six planes left New York on February 19, long before the April 1 "showdown" Chennault described. In fact, the April 1 meeting he described might never have taken place. Morgenthau was a stickler for keeping notes, transcripts of phone conversations, dispatches, and letters within the scope of his job. Pawley's commission is detailed in the minutes of the January 30, 1941, group meeting.

Morgenthau's notes record two meetings with Chennault: December 21, 1940, and January 1, 1941.[88] Nothing concerning Pawley's commission was discussed. Both meetings were held, not in Morgenthau's office but at his home. Morgenthau would have been cautious about receiving Chennault at his office because the talks centered on supplying China with military aircraft, a violation of the Neutrality Act. The meticulous *Morgenthau Diaries* do not have any record of a meeting held April 1, 1941, in Morgenthau's office as described by Chennault.

Finally, during a telephone conversation on January 3, 1945, U.S. senator Claude Pepper asked, "Do you know the man personally?" Morgenthau replied that he had "never met him [Pawley]."[89]

6

Those Willing to Take the Risk

After the problem of getting combat planes for Chennault's suggested Chinese air defense program had been solved, the ticklish situation of finding American pilots and ground crews still remained. Whoever hired them would violate the Neutrality Act forbidding the recruitment and employment of American servicemen in the service of a foreign nation. After exploring the proper route to take, Gen. George Marshall informed Acting Secretary of State Sumner Welles on February 15 that someone was willing to take the risk—William Pawley.[1]

Being a cautious man, before agreeing to use his company as a "covering organization," Pawley consulted with his legal counsel to determine what Neutrality Act penalties he was exposing himself to if he recruited men. "I advised Bill that the program was in violation of the Neutrality Act and that he was running the risk of fine and imprisonment," Pawley's attorney Paul R. Scott recalled. "He replied that he believed the program was vital to National Defense and that he was willing to go to jail, if necessary."[2] Pawley's lawyers wanted the law amended, but when this suggestion proved impractical, they advised him to go ahead. Arthur Young summed up the government's position in a January 29 memorandum: "In practice the American authorities are prepared to close their eyes if it is possible to avoid raising issues with which they will be forced to deal."[3]

Chennault, who promoted the idea of a civilian company doing the hiring, balked at the thought of having to work with Pawley, but since the majority stockholder in the Central Aircraft Manufacturing Company was the Chinese government, T. V. Soong endorsed using CAMCO as the front. Pawley was willing to drop out of the scheme if Chennault couldn't bring himself to work with him, but wiser heads prevailed. Pawley's administrative skill, coupled with the fact that his company was already in place and could provide the necessary facilities, was a deciding factor. Pawley declared Chennault was "indisputably among the informed few who know just about all there is to know concerning aerial warfare against the Jap" and was the logical choice to head the military aspects of the mission. So the partnership, which would result in further animosity between the two, was formed.[4]

Anticipating President Roosevelt's approval, on February 18, 1941, Pawley instructed Octavio Cuevas, treasurer of Intercontinent in New York, to send the following telegram to Pawley's brother Ed in China:

Negotiating extensive training program requiring employment by CAMCO of approximately 250 [stop] 100 pilots 150 technical including mechanics clerks radio operators doctors nurses [stop]. British asked to cooperate[stop] Air Vice Marshall [John] Slessor (spell in code) now Washington notifying Royal Air Force Far Eastern Commanding Officer Singapore to contact you through British Embassy Chunking regarding any local information he may require[stop] Royal Air Force London requested furnish several pursuit squadron leaders to instruct American pilots[stop] Possibly will arrange for several weeks squadron training in Burma[stop] P. T. Mow [Mao Pang-chu] possibly familiar with part of program[stop] Diplomatically ascertain progress he is making in providing facilities such as quarters fields but do not disclose any information[stop] 100 P-40's purchased 35 being shipped immediately balance soon[stop] Intercontinent signed contract covering assembly and flight test Rangoon[stop] Special revolving fund being arranged New York payment of expenses this program[stop] British showing excellent cooperative spirit[stop] You can discuss this telegram with British Ambassador[stop][5]

Although he supported aiding China by providing aircraft, FDR was not warm to the idea of using American pilots as mercenaries. Lauchlin Currie, who had given the president a report on China, had recommended allocating planes but did not mention supplying American pilots.[6] The president seemed to be fence-straddling and hoping for a better solution—possibly amending the Neutrality Law—but China was desperate and needed immediate help. Aware of the problem,

Soong asked Tommy Corcoran, the Washington "fixer," to "wrangle for him with the Army and with the Navy to have them practically order certain men to enlist in the Chinese Air Force." Corcoran attempted to persuade Roosevelt that the concept and critical timing were right.[7] He sent him a copy of A. E. Housman's poem "Epitaph on an Army of Mercenaries":

> These, in the day when heaven was falling,
> The hour when earth's foundations fled,
> Follow'd their mercenary calling
> And took their wages and are dead.
> Their shoulders held the sky suspended;
> They stood, and earth's foundations stay;
> What God abandon'd, these defended,
> And saved the sum of things for pay.[8]

Roosevelt may have been swayed by the poem commemorating the British army (whose professional soldiers the German press had labeled "mercenaries" for taking pay) in the dark days at the beginning of World War I, but there is no record of his thoughts. However, Roosevelt did sign a secret, unlisted executive order on April 15, 1941, authorizing a private corporation holding a contract with a foreign government to hire U.S. military officers.[9] Following the precedent the Canadians had used in establishing the Dominion Aeronautical Association to hire American pilots in late 1940, a private corporation would be used to implement U.S. policy in a war in which America was not a belligerent. It became a forerunner of CIA operations in the postwar years.[10]

Recruitment of pilots and ground personnel could not begin until Pawley and Soong reached an agreement as to which company would be signing the personnel's contracts. Pawley wanted Intercontinent, but Soong wanted closer control. With Corcoran mediating, CAMCO was selected.[11] Signed on April 15, 1941, the agreement between CAMCO and the Chinese government outlined CAMCO's responsibilities:

> to engage the personnel for "three advanced training and instruction units," hiring them by contract and paying them;
> to obtain reimbursement from a revolving fund of $400,000, which would be replenished when it fell below $250,000;

to furnish technical assistance for assembling, maintaining, and repairing equipment of the units; receive material shipped to Rangoon; and "send technical personnel to assist in operations of the 'training and instruction units'";

to accept the instructions of the "American supervisor" of the units; and

to not be required to break any laws of any country in which it operated.[12]

The contract, listing Chennault as the "American supervisor," was signed by Bruce Leighton, vice president of Intercontinent, and T. V. Soong.[13]

CAMCO drew up a contractual agreement form to be used in signing pilots from air bases across the United States. It stated:

CAMCO would pay $600 a month "to render such services and perform such duties as the Employer may direct."

Employment was for one year and would begin when the employee reported in person at a designated port of departure from the United States.

All reasonable travel expenses would be paid by CAMCO "to the place in China" where the employee would be assigned. Expenses included: first-class railroad fare and berth, the cost of a passport and visas, the reasonable cost of hotels and meals "while awaiting ocean transportation," transportation to China, $100 for "contingent expenses," and "actual expenses" incurred on the trip to destination in China.

CAMCO would pay $500 in lieu of employee's return transportation costs from China to the United States upon termination of the contract.

CAMCO would have the right to terminate the contract "in the event of misconduct" of the employee for: insubordination, revealing confidential information, habitual use of drugs, excessive use of alcohol, illness or disability not incurred in the line of duty as a result of employee's own misconduct, and malingering.[14]

With blank contracts in hand, CAMCO representatives prepared to fill the roster of the First American Volunteer Group in China. Chennault wanted experienced P-40 pilots, but they were in short supply. He requested that the recruiters look for pilots between the ages of twenty-two and twenty-eight, with at least two years' experience.[15] Pawley, on the advice of Capt. C. C. Moseley, contacted Richard

Aldworth to help recruit pilots from the services. Aldworth, a former army pilot, was recovering from an ailment at Walter Reed Hospital in Washington, D.C., but after Pawley called him and then met him in New York, Aldworth agreed to act as a hiring agent.[16] Assisted by Capt. C. B. "Skip" Adair, Rutledge Irvine (a retired navy commander), Harry C. Claiborne, and Fenton L. Brown, they scoured military air bases throughout the country to find willing and able pilots.[17]

As a way around Neutrality Laws, Oscar Cox of the Office of Emergency Management (OEM), Division of Defense Aid Reports, drafted an amendment to a 1926 act allowing the president to let applicants assist American hemisphere governments and the Philippines. The amendment would add China to the list, but it was deemed best if FDR used his executive power instead. Roosevelt ordered that enlisted men would be allowed to reenter U.S. military service at their former rank after completing their CAMCO contract, and he issued instructions to the secretaries of the War and Navy Departments to advise U.S. training centers to cooperate in the endeavor.[18] At the same time, the State Department issued denials that servicemen were being released for duty in China. George Bookman's story on the front page of the *Washington Post* June 1 said American pilots signed by a Chinese recruiting agency in Washington would not lose their citizenship, but the State, War, and Navy Departments all denied involvement.[19]

Even with presidential approval, base commanders would not cooperate with recruiters (officers at Hamilton Field told Chennault to leave or they would put him in the stockade), but after given a Washington phone number to call, they reluctantly acquiesced and allowed pilots to be interviewed.[20] Maj. Gen. Henry "Hap" Arnold opposed the plan, but Secretary of War Stimson ordered him to relay the executive order authorizing the bearers of "certain letters" to enter bases and actively recruit military personnel.[21] Maj. Gen. George H. Brett, chief of the U.S. Army Air Corps, told Pawley, "You're trying to steal the top of my batting order."[22] Unaware of Roosevelt's endorsement of the project, U.S. attorney general Francis Biddle threatened Pawley with imprisonment, but recruitment of pilots continued.[23]

Recruitment was not limited to pilots. The AVG also needed skilled aviation civilians. Walter W. Pentecost, an Allison engine specialist at North American Aviation in Inglewood, California, answered a *Los Angeles Times* ad for "aviation people, for work overseas, call this number—." He was told to report to A. J. "Andy" Sargeant and Murph Gerald at the CAMCO office at Vail Field in

Alhambra. He was told that a military organization was recruiting for various personnel, including pilots, ground crews, and administrative, intelligence, and other positions, but he was not told where he would be going. That information came later when Pawley and his brother Ed treated those who were accepted to a dog and pony show one evening in Los Angeles, complete with color pictures of Burma showing scenes of pagodas, water buffalo, peasants, and the beautiful countryside. Pawley was selling the glamour of adventure (minus the dust, heat, and filth), but Pentecost didn't need the sales pitch. "I'd already made up my mind to go; I didn't care what they showed me. It was something different, and I was ready," he recalled.[24]

Sgt. Robert Moody Smith received an honorable discharge from the U.S. Army Air Corps "for the convenience of the government" after signing a CAMCO contract. He noted in his diary that "$300 a month plus expenses sure beats the $84 I got as a sergeant-air mechanic first class . . . I would have signed up for $100 a month."[25] As children of the Depression, others signed up for the money, but it was only part of the complex reasons why men from thirty-nine states joined. Navy pilot James H. Howard's "overriding reason was my yearning for adventure and action." Although the pay was high, other governments paid more. Spain offered up to $1,500 a month for pilots with a $1,000 bonus for kills, and Britain paid $1,500 a month to ferry bombers to England with a $2,500 ten-trip bonus.[26]

Recruitment was slow, even with a $500 incentive bonus for each Japanese plane shot down (approved April 2 by T. V. Soong).[27] By May 3, 73 applications had been received, but only 18 pilots were accepted. At the end of the month, the pilot total was 55, and only 58 of the 170 who applied for ground crews were accepted.[28] Salaries offered to pilots varied according to experience and training, with $750 a month going to first-class pilots and $600 to others. Enlisted men in ground crews and support groups received an average of $300 a month,[29] although all who signed were required to take out a $10,000 government life insurance policy with the premiums deducted from their paychecks.[30] CAMCO agreed to pay six months' salary to anyone disabled in the line of duty and to defray transportation costs back to the United States. It would pay the same amount to the designated beneficiary of anyone killed in action and provide a decent burial.[31]

Those who signed contracts traveled to California, staying at hotels and other billeting spots (including the exclusive Jonathan Club in Los Angeles) until enough personnel were recruited to form the first group. They were then put up at the

Bellevue Hotel in San Francisco, where they awaited further orders. At the hotel, Aldworth gave a speech welcoming "all of you who are about to embark on a mission to the other side of the world to defend American interests in that part of the globe." He then introduced Pawley.

James Howard recalled Pawley's speech:

"As president of CAMCO, I welcome you to San Francisco where you will start the first leg of your trip to Burma. I have spent many years in the Orient where we established an aircraft manufacturing plant. Because of the constant advances of the Japanese army, we have been forced to move our factory several times until it is now located in the town of Loiwing on the Burma-China border."

"When do we get our P-40s?" an anxious pilot asked.

"I have a branch of my factory in Rangoon which is assembling the planes from crates that are on the Rangoon docks. By the time you arrive in Burma your planes will be ready to fly," Pawley replied.

As events later proved, either Pawley withheld information that all was not ready as he said, or he was optimistic that contingency plans in progress would prove him correct about the planes being available. Chennault also attended the briefing and assured the men that their American citizenship was not in jeopardy "as long as we fight for a country that professes democratic faith."[32]

While the first volunteer contingent gathered on the West Coast, Pawley sent his brother Ed to China to prepare the group's reception. Arriving in Chungking, Ed discovered the Chinese hadn't made the necessary arrangements. Bill Pawley suggested that he contact the British military authorities in Burma to arrange for training facilities there.[33] CAMCO had permission to assemble and test planes in Burma, but now the company also wanted to conduct combat training exercises there. Group Captain E. R. Manning, the senior RAF officer in Burma, looked upon the mercenaries as a threat to his peaceful domain because of the Japanese presence in Indochina.[34] Air Chief Marshal Sir Robert Brooke-Popham, British commander in chief of the Far East, felt otherwise. Burma was vulnerable, and he welcomed the presence of an air group to defend the area.[35]

Bill and Ed Pawley, along with Chennault and General Mao, met with British military and governing authorities in Rangoon to work out an agreement. Mao pointed out that because the Japanese had refused to acknowledge officially that they were at war with China, the AVG "could not legally be considered belligerents," and their presence in Burma would not violate British neutrality.[36] Brooke-Popham received permission from the British War Office for CAMCO to use the Kyedaw Airfield at Toungoo, 175 miles north of Rangoon, as long as the group did not use the airfield as a base of operations to attack the Japanese.

Carved out of the jungle, six miles from Toungoo on the Sittang River, and an all-day trip by railroad, the Kyedaw Airfield had a four-thousand-foot paved runway, but conditions were primitive. The Americans soon learned that the British abandoned it during the monsoon season as it was "unfit for habitation by Europeans due to its foul, stinking climate and infuriating insects."[37] Ed Pawley provided CAMCO's twin-engine Beechcraft for Chennault to inspect the facilities, but the tough, battle-hardened colonel was appalled with what he saw.[38] He wrote, "The runway was surrounded by quagmire . . . rotting vegetation carpeted the jungle . . . dampness and green mold penetrated everywhere," and "torrential monsoon rains and thunderstorms alternated with torrid heat to give the atmosphere the texture of a Turkish bath."[39] Built with teak and bamboo, the barracks featured a long veranda on one side, and each bed had a sticker affixed reading "On His Majesty's Service."[40] Bathroom facilities were in a primitive shack with only cold water, and the men had to "step over snakes along the way." Lighting was provided by kerosene lamps and "an unreliable electric lighting system."[41] But Chennault had his air base, the first volunteers were ready to set sail, and Pawley promised the P-40s would be ready by the time the pilots arrived.

While a hundred Curtiss P-40s were being shipped from Weehawken to Rangoon, Walter Pentecost was on his way to Burma as a CAMCO employee hired to assemble the planes, ready them for combat, and get them to the airfield at Toungoo. Intercontinent (the name being now interchangeably used with CAMCO) had arranged his passage through Thomas C. Cooke Co. "We did nothing in these arrangements," he recalled. "They told us where to be, they got the tickets, we just got on a ship."[42] Arriving May 23 in Rangoon, Pentecost learned only part of the shipment had arrived; meanwhile, a half dozen had been unloaded and were sitting uncrated at the Mingaladon Airport in Rangoon while nine others were still on the freighter. Chennault arrived two months later and found "most of the AVG P-40s still sitting in crates on the docks where they had been unloaded late in June."[43] Part of the backup problem stemmed from a British custom that permitted clearance of a shipment only after accounting for every article listed on the bill of lading.[44] The shipment had been split up among three freighters, so Pentecost had to stay at the Strand Hotel, across the street from the Brooking Street wharves where the two remaining freighters would arrive and around the corner from the Intercontinent offices at 42 Phayre Street.[45]

Pentecost soon discovered facilities were primitive or nonexistent for assembling planes. "There were no tools or forklifts of any kind, and this being Burma, with large numbers of expendable laborers, everything was done by hand," he recalled.[46]

Test pilot Bryon Glover also answered the CAMCO *Los Angeles Times* ad and arrived in Rangoon shortly before Pentecost did. He was the first to realize that the Pawley brothers hadn't made proper arrangements to assemble the planes. Seeing that a local contractor had constructed the assembly hangar with brick and bamboo thatch, he ordered steel trusses to shore up the flimsy building and had an outdoor hoist erected to use in assembling the P-40s.

The crates containing the parts presented another problem. The fuselage and motor were crated in one thirty-five-by-ten-by-six-foot box that weighed a little less than eight thousand pounds. The wing crate was forty feet by ten feet by five feet, and weighed eighty-three hundred pounds. None of the available trucks in the area were capable of transporting such crates from the Rangoon docks to the assembly area. Fortunately, several truck body manufacturers were in Rangoon, all busily assembling trucks to handle the Burma Road traffic. One truck body builder solved CAMCO's problem by constructing two large truck trailers in less than a month.[47]

Using the plentiful laborers available, Pentecost began assembling planes as the hot sun bore down on them. "I don't mind hot weather," he said, "but the Burmese summers are more than hot. They're hell. All your pep leaves you, as if somebody had opened a valve and let it leak out."[48] The laborers had to take each fuselage from its crate and push it by hand until it was under the hoist to be lifted. They carried the wings on their shoulders and lifted them in place. After bolting them on securely, they lowered the plane's landing gear so that the plane rested on its own weight.[49]

The crated planes arrived with "only iron sights, no ammunition or boresighted guns," and there were no bomb racks or radios.[50] When Robert Smith arrived August 16, he began the job of tearing out the P-40 radio wiring, which had been fitted for British transmitters at the Curtiss-Wright plant. In their place he installed RCA-7-H transceivers, which were designed for use in Piper Cubs and not tested under combat situations.[51] Pawley also provided workers from Loiwing to help assemble the P-40s at Mingaladon, but the facilities were such that radios, oxygen equipment, and guns had to be installed at Toungoo.[52]

Arthur Young arrived June 18 and saw uncrated planes piled on the docks. Concerned they were vulnerable to sabotage, he had them moved to safe places until they could be assembled.[53]

Finding experienced pilots was difficult enough; filling the headquarters' staffing slots proved to be even a harder task. Getting staff officers released from active duty was virtually impossible, so Chennault improvised by hiring men he hoped would grow into their jobs. He recruited his chief of staff, Harvey K. Greenlaw, in Hong Kong and even hired Greenlaw's wife, Olga, to serve as part of the administrative force. A West Point graduate, Greenlaw had resigned his commission and gone to China in 1933 to become part of the Jouett mission. After Olga joined him, they remained until 1936 and then returned to the United States. Two years later, they were back in China, where Harvey worked for North American Aviation, supervising the assembly and testing of planes sold to China. A competitor of Pawley's, Greenlaw also knew Chennault from the early days when China was building an air force.[54]

Paul Frillmann, a Lutheran missionary hired as the unit's chaplain, was pressed into filling the lists of supplies needed for the anticipated three hundred American volunteers. "Write out what you think we Americans, or a group of Americans of this kind, will need in the way of food, which we cannot get in China," Chennault told him. With the list, Frillmann ran around Washington and filled orders with wholesalers.[55] Although he had purchased a military uniform, Frillmann also bought civilian clothes of a style that he hoped would make him look less like a missionary. "I guess I overdid this," he recalled. "I got the loudest suit I ever had, a regular racetrack model with stripes and padded shoulders plus a floppy Panama hat and some screaming neckties." When Frillmann showed up in Los Angeles, Eugene Pawley took one look at the outfit and said, "Holy Smoke! You can't be the Frillmann we're expecting."[56]

Frillmann and the first group of volunteers staying in San Francisco—mostly mechanics and staff—boarded the SS *President Pierce* for the trip to China. Also on board were reinforcements for MacArthur's troops in the Philippines. They made a stopover in Honolulu before heading to Singapore, where they stayed for sixteen days in the famed Raffles Hotel. From Singapore, they sailed on the freighter *Penang Trader* to Burma, arriving July 28 in Rangoon.[57] Chennault met them on the docks and informed them they wouldn't be going to China right away. Instead, the mechanics would help assemble planes at Mingaladon while the rest would wait in local hotels until the pilots arrived. Chennault again pressed Frillmann into service to pick up supplies. "It was a long list . . . plane and auto parts and tires," Frillmann recalled, "then tapering off in a miscellany of musical instruments, screen doors, typewriters, coffins, hunting rifles." Chennault told him, "Get the money from the Pawleys and bring the stuff up to Toungoo when you come."[58]

The second group—thirty-seven pilots, eighty-four technicians, and two nurses—sailed July 8 from San Francisco to Rangoon via Singapore aboard the *Jagersfontein*, an antiquated Dutch ship.[59] CAMCO paid $490 per person.[60] Although the mission was supposedly a secret, *Time* magazine described "tall, bronzed American airmen . . . quietly slipping away from east- and west-coast ports, making their way to Asia."[61] Pilot Erik Shilling heard a Tokyo Rose propaganda radio broadcast that the Japanese knew about their mission and "they intended to sink our ship."[62]

Fearing the Dutch ship was vulnerable to enemy attack, Lauchlin Currie suggested to Roosevelt that the U.S. Navy should offer some protection. Secretary of the Navy Frank Knox and CNO Adm. Harold Stark proposed "splitting the contingent up into smaller units," but this recommendation was considered unfeasible.[63] Since American servicemen were aboard and "essential to U.S. support of China," Admiral Stark decided to dispatch the cruisers USS *Salt Lake City* and USS *Northampton* to escort the liner while at sea.[64] From July 17 until August 6, the cruisers sailed with the *Jagersfontein* until they reached the Torres Strait between New Guinea and the northern tip of Australia, where the Dutch cruiser *Java* escorted the ship through the mined channel to Singapore.[65]

Chennault and Pawley once again became embroiled in their differences, this time over CAMCO hiring practices. Chennault wrote to T. V. Soong that pilots complained about being misinformed as to the type of combat they would face. Recruiters said they would be fighting bombers, not pursuits, and there would be no night fighting.[66] Gregory "Pappy" Boyington, who would earn fame as the commander of the U.S. Marine Corps' Black Sheep Squadron operating out of Guadalcanal, recalled that a recruiter said, "The Japs are flying antiquated junk

over China. Many of your kills will be unarmed transports." He added, "The
Japanese are renowned for their inability to fly. And they all wear corrective glass-
es." When he also said that several of the American pilots had "twenty years of
combat experience," Boyington silently wondered—given his knowledge of aviation history—how that was possible.[67] Chennault also accused Pawley of hiring
many inexperienced pilots, to which Pawley countered, "In all my experience I
have never seen a finer aggregation of pilots. . . . This force is so superior, in my
judgment, that even inferior leadership cannot destroy its effectiveness."[68] The hostility between them continued throughout the war, resulting in petty arguments that
affected the performance of the Flying Tigers, and Chennault remained bitter over
their relationship for the rest of his life.

The State Department listed creative occupations on the volunteers' passports. One was a "retired acrobat," W. D. McGarry was an "artist," and others were
described as "Presidents-in-training," or simply "tourists."[69] "I think I was supposed to be a Plantation Manager," R. T. Smith recalled, "of what I don't know."[70]
Boyington's passport listed him as a "member of the clergy," which amused him
since he considered himself "a whiz at a cocktail party."[71] Walter Pentecost saw
a group "all dressed up in pea-green slacks and chocolate sports jackets," posing
as jazz musicians. "They were carrying empty violin and cornet cases, and saxo-
phones they couldn't play if their lives depended on it."[72] Chennault's passport
application listed him as a "farmer," but when a State Department clerk became
skeptical, he replied, "I own land in Louisiana and I make a living from it. That
makes me a farmer."[73]

The first shipment of thirty-six Curtiss P-40s arrived May 23 in Rangoon,
having taken three months at sea, and thirty-two more came in July 12.[74] By July
14, only ten had been assembled, but they still needed machine guns and radios.[75]
Spare parts and ammunition were in short supply, prompting Lauchlin Currie to
ask the War Department for help. Chief of Staff George Marshall informed him that
ammunition was "one of the critical problems" for the army and navy, and the request could not be filled.[76] The first plane assembled at Mingaladon was delivered
to Toungoo on August 3, 1941, having taken three weeks to finish.[77] As planes were
completed, the air base at Toungoo was notified, and Chennault sent the required
number of pilots to Mingaladon to pick them up. The pilots were usually ferried
in Pawley's Beechcraft and required to sign an Intercontinent-prepared form stat-

ing how many hours of flying time they had in a P-40 and whether they had a map showing them the route back to Toungoo.[78] Pawley left nothing to chance when it came to maintaining a paper trail.

Although the world focused its attention on Europe, on July 7 Sumner Welles wrote to Lend-Lease program administrator Harry Hopkins, pleading "to do all we can to make available to China urgently needed supplies," and sent a copy of the letter to George Marshall and Admiral Stark.[79] In September, Lauchlin Currie reported to FDR that shipments to China were still "quite small."[80] Although many Americans, including influential advisers to the president, shared concern for China, Winston Churchill felt supporting China was based on a policy of "grand illusion" and should be abandoned.[81] To placate the Chinese, military attaché to China Brig. Gen. John Magruder led a military mission to Chungking to determine what was needed.

In the meantime, Pawley's CAMCO continued to ready P-40s for combat. By the end of August, twenty-two planes had been assembled and delivered to Toungoo, most being used to train pilots and ground crews.[82] Trying to whip his group into a disciplined fighting unit—the men described him as "tough, and he kept driving them, but he always led them, like a teacher"—Chennault found that some men felt deceived by the Pawley brothers' promises when recruited.[83] After dining with polished silverware and waited on by stewards tending to their every need aboard a Dutch ship, the men arrived August 16, 1941, in Burma and took a seven-hour train trip to the Kyedaw Airfield, where they encountered totally different accommodations.

It was not an exotic Kipling setting. Torrential rains created a pestilent quagmire, followed by intense, suffocating humidity that rotted tires on planes. The muck of steaming jungle vegetation harboring every imaginable type of insect greeted the recruits upon their arrival at Toungoo. "Shoes were a favorite hiding place for scorpions," recalled Erik Shilling. "One only had to put his shoes on once without inspecting them to learn this painful lesson."[84] Five pilots decided they had enough of "rats that chewed the buttons off their clothes at night" and resigned. Those who remained could only laugh as they recalled the CAMCO recruiter telling them, "As much as possible, we'll try our best to parallel the living conditions you have here over there, wherever we send you."[85] Some who quit were accused of having used their volunteering as a way to get out of the army or navy, whereupon they could return to civilian life and get jobs with airlines.[86]

On August 1, 1941, Chiang Kai-shek issued General Order No. Hi Sy 05987, which formally established the First American Volunteer Group under Chennault's command.[87] The Magruder mission had been in China for almost three months, but it had accomplished very little. His instructions, "to consult with the Chinese military authorities on the extent and forms" of aid to be adopted should America and China find themselves "engaged in hostilities with a common enemy," were dissected in a series of discussions between the War and State Departments until it was finally decided that Magruder would act as a liaison between the United States and China in implementing the Lend-Lease program to obtain necessary military supplies.[88]

Global war was approaching reality in the autumn of 1941, but China was desperate to defend itself against the encroaching Japanese and couldn't wait for the United States to enter the conflict. The Curtiss P-40s in Rangoon were being assembled—not as quickly as Pawley had promised—but they were there. Although Chennault viewed Pawley as an opportunist concerned only with receiving his commission and continuing to do business with the Chinese, Chennault had to focus his attention on training the mostly inexperienced pilots to fly the planes when they became available. With one eye on Pawley and the other on trying to make his pilots into a formidable fighting group, Chennault had his work cut out for him. Although he would achieve his goal of shaping the unit into one of the most successful mercenary combat forces, contentions with Pawley over supplying the planes and keeping them in service would continually plague him.

Out of the hundred P-40s shipped to Rangoon, only ninety-nine were assembled and sent on to the AVG. One had dropped in New York harbor during loading. "The salt water didn't do it any good," Walter Pentecost said, "so it was dismantled and used for replacements on other planes."[89] As planes were being assembled, Chennault played a dual role; he trained pilots while trying to work with Pawley on getting planes and needed supplies. He spent most of his time in Toungoo but had to make the trip to Rangoon to discuss delays and problems arising from the lack of supplies and to deal with the men who wanted to go home.[90] Meanwhile, Pawley was trying to get planes readied in Rangoon while reestablishing his bombed factory at Loiwing.

In a letter to Chennault, Pawley outlined his concerns that when Japanese intelligence discovered that the Loiwing facility was back in operation, the bombers would appear again. To offset the threat, Pawley suggested Chennault provide a radio station network using staff from the AVG to maintain and operate the system. Pawley wanted "eight or ten additional stations" networking with the base station "on a twenty-four hour basis" as an early warning system. In addition, he wanted eighteen of the Curtiss P-40s to be stationed at Loiwing to protect his factory, which he described as "one of the main repair bases" for the AVG. Pawley was also assembling twenty-nine Curtiss-Wright 21 Demon Interceptors he had sold to the Chinese, which he felt "would be extremely valuable in this defense program."[91]

Chennault, however, could ill afford to split his group before training had been completed. Pawley's factory would have to be left exposed for now.

7

The Tiger Roars

Training American Volunteer Group pilots became increasingly difficult not only because of the shortage of aircraft but also because of the pilots who had never flown the P-40, let alone shot down an enemy plane in combat. While Chennault was away in Chungking on September 8, 1941, two pilots collided in a routine flight over the jungle, and John Armstrong became the first AVG casualty. Since there were no caskets at Toungoo, Ed Pawley had one sent up from Rangoon, along with a load of flowers. Armstrong was buried at St. Luke's cemetery with full military service.[1] By December, three pilots had been killed in training, and one had crashed five planes during the course of his instruction. This accident-prone pilot even painted five American flags on his sixth plane, signifying he qualified as a Japanese ace in downing his own planes.[2] On one particularly black day, Chennault watched six pilots crash on landing, and a seventh plane was damaged when it collided with a ground mechanic who was busy watching the crashes on a bicycle.[3]

As more pilots arrived—the last contingent docked in Rangoon on November 25, 1941—Chennault knew he couldn't devote sufficient time to train them personally, so he assigned the best pilots as squadron leaders and left the training of newly arriving pilots in their hands. Split into three squadrons called Adam and Eve, Hell's Angels, and the Panda Bears, the pilots painted distinctive squadron emblems on the planes. They also borrowed an idea from the RAF P-40s in Africa and painted tiger sharks on the nose of the planes, complete with eyes and a row of menacing sharp teeth along the open cowling.[4] Chennault recalled that one of the pilots had seen an illustration of the shark design in the *Illustrated Weekly of India*, but he also mentioned that the Luftwaffe painted shark's teeth on some of their

95

Messerschmitts.[5] Walter Pentecost claimed he saw the magazine cover and showed it to Raymond L. Hastey, one of the pilots.[6] "We made the teeth a bit larger because we had heard that the Japs had poor eyesight," said Kenneth Sanger.[7]

The name "Flying Tigers" (*Fei Hu* in Chinese) came later, and its origin varies by several accounts. Credit seems to belong to the China Defense Supplies office in Washington, where the painted shark face was not known. In an effort to come up with a distinctive emblem, the proposed idea of a flying dragon was discarded because it was thought to symbolize a favorable sign to the Japanese. The eagle would have been fitting for the American group, but it wouldn't tie in with its Chinese mission. T. V. Soong may have quoted a Chinese proverb, "Giving wings to the tiger," as a more fitting symbol, and Whiting Willauer, a graduate of Princeton, where the tiger was the mascot, may have endorsed the idea. American ingenuity then took over. Disney Studio in Hollywood was assigned the task of designing a logo and developed a winged Bengal tiger with outstretched claws, vaulting from a *V* for victory.[8] The name caught on and was promoted in *Time* magazine on December 29, 1941, but Erik Shilling recalled United Press correspondent Robert L. McGrath in Rangoon filing a news report on December 26 using the soon-to-be-famous name.[9]

By October 10, the thirtieth anniversary of the Chinese Republic, the AVG had not mounted any air missions—offensive or defensive—and T. V. Soong was still pressing the United States for more help. In August he had complained that after his being in the United States for fourteen months, China had not received a single plane "sufficiently supplied with armament and ammunition" and characterized the 100 P-40s as only "training ships."[10] Promised more aircraft, Soong reminded the president in an October 24 memo that none of the planes had been delivered. Roosevelt penciled in the margin of the memo "HH—Speed up!" before passing it on to Harry Hopkins for disposition.[11]

While Soong was concerned about future aircraft deliveries, problems mounted with those that the Chinese already had received. Shortages of fuel, spare parts, and ammunition restricted Chennault's efforts to train his mercenary group properly. He advised Washington that twenty-three planes were out of service owing to the lack of replacement engines, and another twenty-six were waiting for flat tires to be changed.[12] Even with these seemingly insurmountable obstacles, in his report on the aviation situation in China, General Magruder stressed that Chiang Kai-chek had told him, "The American Volunteer Force was the only one that counted" in the Far East.[13] He added, "If Chennault's force does not fight it will be considered a breach of faith by the Chinese."[14]

In contrast, newspaper correspondent Vincent Sheean visited Toungoo on November 1 and a somewhat pessimistic report to the Office of Coordinator of Intelligence (OCI) when he returned to the United States near the end of November:

> I do not think their morale is very good and I am very much afraid that in a clash with the Japanese they would come off badly. The chief reason for this is, of course, that they are a mercenary force. They all went out there because they were offered a lot more money than they can get in our own army and navy. They tend to complain a great deal of everything and seem to be on the worst possible terms with the British and Australians of the R. A. F. Their equipment consisted at this time of 64 P-40's with no spare parts. They crashed one of the P-40's and were taking it apart for the spare parts when I was there.

Despite the grim report, Sheean felt Chennault was "a remarkable man and he may be able to turn them into coherent and efficient forces."[15]

Acting on Lauchlin Currie's recommendations, Roosevelt gave approval for 269 combat fighters and 66 bombers along with a military mission for pilots and ground crews to operate in China. Working with Soong, Pawley began planning for a second AVG, calling for a mixture of American bomber and Chinese fighter pilots. Although CAMCO began hiring on November 1, Pawley found it difficult to find trained bomber pilots.

Worried that he would receive more unqualified (and misinformed) pilots, Chennault wrote to the CAMCO's New York office and requested that "nothing should be omitted" in the sales pitch about the expected duties of pilots: "Far from merely defending the Burma Road against unaccompanied Japanese bombers, the AVG will be called upon to combat Japanese pursuits; to fly at night; and to undertake offensive missions when planes suitable for this purpose are sent out to us. These points should be clearly explained. . . . I prefer to have the employment quotas partly unfilled than to receive pilots hired on the principle of 'come one, come all.'"[16] Pawley, however, seemed more concerned with filling the roster and ignored the letter. CAMCO had hired the needed ground maintenance personnel, who then set sail for China on November 25, but when the Japanese attacked Pearl Harbor, the forty-nine men were stranded in Australia.

When the British ambassador to China warned that the "situation in China was very grave," Pawley supported a proposal that British bombers be made available to operate alongside the AVG's force.[17] However, because of aircraft shortages and pressing needs in Europe and North Africa, deliveries were delayed. The AVG alone defended China.

Shortages of parts and supplies continued to plague Chennault, so he sent men throughout the Far East to search for them. Assigned to see Air Chief Marshal Sir Robert Brooke-Popham about acquiring spare parts from the RAF, Joseph Alsop was told none were available. Hearing that General MacArthur in the Philippines might have P-40 parts, Brooke-Popham gave Alsop a letter of recommendation. Before departing for Manila, Alsop met with Pawley, who said Chennault had given him authorization to negotiate with MacArthur and took the letter from Alsop.

When Alsop returned to Toungoo, Chennault was furious because he hadn't said any such thing to Pawley. Firing off a telegram to China Defense Supplies, Chennault advised, "Pawley not authorized to negotiate by me."[18] Although Pawley managed to obtain tires from MacArthur, Chennault felt, "Pawley did not understand our situation clearly," because P-40 spare parts were also of grave importance and he failed to get them.[19]

Pawley wrote that when he arrived in Manila, "they offered every possible assistance, but they had no supplies for P-40's. I did manage, however, to secure 75 tires and tubes, engine parts, radio equipment and some ammunition."[20] Chennault refutes this claim, stating Pawley obtained only tires, and maintains that he had "to send Alsop on to Manila to get the spare parts Pawley had failed to obtain."[21] John King Fairbank's later memorandum to Currie noted that Chennault had sent a cable on December 4 stating, "Pawley had got many spare parts in Manila and had them flown by the Navy to Singapore in 3 PBY flying boats."[22] Pawley seemed to have muddled his recollection, because in a 1971 interview he stated that MacArthur's Philippine base "had more P-40 parts than they could use in five years."[23]

Privately, Chennault accused Pawley of going to Manila under the guise of representing the AVG so that he could conduct private business.[24] Chennault always harbored the feeling that Pawley thought the AVG wouldn't last three weeks in combat.[25] In any event, Pawley continued offering his services through CAMCO and was in Rangoon on November 12 to greet the arrival of the ship bringing more pilots on their way to Toungoo.[26]

As pilot training continued, resulting in more crashes and wear and tear on planes, Chennault's patience with Pawley was wearing thin. The CAMCO contract called for assembly and maintenance of the P-40s, but Chennault accused Pawley of keeping technicians and factory workers at Loiwing to work on the trainers Pawley had sold to the Chinese instead of using the personnel to keep the flow of P-40s moving. After the late November delivery of P-40s, Chennault kept pressing for repairs on disabled planes. Although advised by the Loiwing manager that he would offer his "facilities for the good of the cause," Chennault felt the factory workers were just dragging their feet. He interpreted their reluctance to work on AVG planes as another case in which Pawley had chosen the course that offered the greatest personal profit.

Chennault also complained that the volunteers were not being paid on time and fired off cables to Intercontinent in New York to have the matter rectified. Chennault may have been frustrated when it replied that delays in cables were part of the problem, but Intercontinent defended Pawley by adding that "conflicting and erroneous information" sent from the AVG was causing more confusion. The bickering even went as far as Chennault's complaining about AVG money being spent on groceries for CAMCO employees at Loiwing, and he ordered it stopped.[27]

In December, Chennault reported having sixty-six operational planes with ninety trained pilots and a ground crew of 180 Americans, but he still contended Pawley kept the AVG from achieving its full potential.[28] With seventeen planes disabled due to lack of parts, Chennault met with Pawley December 3 at the Intercontinent office in Rangoon. The discussion became so heated that the secretary was unable to keep up with her notes, and Chennault was still angry when he left. Pawley informed Soong that it might be best if he withdrew from his contract with the AVG and let Chennault take charge of everything. He cited a "continuous stream of telegrams and letters condemning me and CAMCO for everything that appeared to be going wrong."[29]

On the other side of the international dateline, Pearl Harbor was attacked on December 8, 1941, in the Far East. The news was first heard on Japanese-controlled radio stations in China and later confirmed by station KGEI in San Francisco.[30] When handed a telegraph message from RAF headquarters in Rangoon reporting the attack that morning, Chennault responded, "I bet they were all sleeping."[31]

Pilots at Toungoo were still asleep when Harvey Greenlaw, the AVG executive officer, roused them to get out of their bunks. He wanted them to get their planes in the air as soon as possible because he feared an attack. Without airfield lighting facilities, pilots jumped into their planes in pitch-black darkness and began taking off without sufficiently warming them up. Some made it into the air but failed to stay aloft. Others stopped short at the end of the runway, tipped over, and bent their propeller blades, or damaged their landing gear in the mud. When it appeared the Japanese were not going to attack, the airborne planes were brought back.[32]

Feeling his group was not combat ready, Chennault recommended to Madame Chiang that they move the unit to Kunming, where they could protect the Burma Road. Chiang Kai-shek vetoed the plan and ordered the unit to remain at Toungoo and to coordinate defense efforts with the British. Pawley remembered the situation differently. "Chennault intended to take all of the planes to China immediately," he recalled. "I didn't want that, because 17 vessels loaded with Lend-Lease supplies were waiting to discharge their materials on the Rangoon docks." Pawley said he convinced Churchill to intercede and had Chennault ordered to leave part of the group to defend Burma.[33] There is no record, however, of Churchill having participated in the decision, and it is highly unlikely that Pawley would have had access to the British prime minister.

Concerned that Toungoo had no early warning system, Chennault split the unit and sent the Third Squadron to the Mingaladon Airfield at Rangoon.[34] The AVG still hadn't flown a single mission, but that situation was about to change. Three pilots—Erik Shilling, Allen Christman, and Ed Rector—took off from Rangoon on December 10 and headed for Bangkok, four hundred miles away. Their mission was to conduct photo reconnaissance of Japanese air strength in the area.[35] The crisp, clear photos exasperated Chennault when he viewed close to a hundred enemy planes sitting on the ground. If he had had bombers under his command, he could have easily destroyed them.[36]

Pawley's reaction to the Pearl Harbor attack was to immediately begin consolidating his widespread aircraft enterprise. He closed the Mingaladon assembly plant just as the last P-40 was being pieced together from parts salvaged from planes wrecked during training. The P-40 dropped in the harbor was loaded on a flatbed truck and sent to Loiwing with assembly plant workers following behind. Betting the escalating war would result in the formation of more fighter squadrons, Pawley still maintained his office at Rangoon in expectation of garnering a lucrative maintenance contract for the additional aircraft.[37]

While Pawley was occupied in Rangoon, his brother Eugene wasn't faring too well. The Japanese had also bombed Hong Kong, and Eugene was trapped, along with columnist Joseph Alsop. They couldn't get a flight out. Eugene managed to leave later and during the war headed the China desk for the OSS.[38]

Fearing the AVG might be caught by surprise as had the U.S. planes in the Philippines and Hawaii, Chiang changed his mind and ordered Chennault to keep one squadron at Mingaladon to fight alongside the British and to move the rest to Kunming.[39] "We are going to abandon Toungoo!" Robert Smith wrote in his diary on December 11, although Chiang didn't issue the order until the fifteenth.[40] On December 20, the squadrons at Kunming received word through the early warning network that ten Mitsubishi Ki-21 Sally bombers were heading in their direction.

Sending fighters to intercept the bombers thirty miles from Kunming, Chennault's AVG finally had its first taste of combat. Seeing the bombers unescorted by fighters, the AVG pilots attacked the formation. They shot down six bombers, and the remaining four jettisoned their bomb loads and scurried back to their base in Hanoi. Although one plane ran out of fuel and landed in a rice paddy, not one AVG plane was lost to the enemy. The Flying Tigers had only begun to prove their worth in the China skies.[41]

With the world enveloped in a global war, Pawley became more involved in the business of maintaining planes for the American Volunteer Group while considering his next move, relocating his aircraft factory as far away as possible from advancing Japanese forces. Traveling in his private plane, Pawley stayed in Toungoo one day before heading to Rangoon. The busy Burmese city was still the unloading point for tons of matériel destined for China, but the Japanese hoped to close the entry port.

The AVG had another taste of combat on December 23, 1941, when fifty-four Japanese bombers, this time escorted by twenty pursuit planes, attacked Rangoon with the objective of destroying the docks crammed with Lend-Lease material waiting to be shipped to China.[42] Going up against the formidable attacking force, the AVG had fourteen combat-ready P-40s but only twelve pilots. Against all odds and outnumbered by the approaching enemy force, the Flying Tigers took to the air to defend Rangoon.

In the heat of battle, many forgot the combat tactics Chennault had taught them, but their courage compensated for forgetfulness as they attacked the bombers. Japanese bombs resulted in more than a thousand deaths, but the AVG downed five bombers while losing only two pilots.[43] After his plane was hit, Paul J. Greene bailed out and was strafed by Japanese fighters. "You want to see my 'chute," he told O. D. Gallagher. "It's got more holes in it than the nose of a watering-can."[44]

The Japanese won that day, but the American volunteers vowed to get even. Christmas Day that opportunity presented itself when the Japanese sent sixty bombers accompanied by eighteen pursuit planes to bomb Rangoon. AVG ground crews had frantically worked long hours to patch together as many damaged planes as possible, but by Christmas, with temperatures reaching 115 degrees, only thirteen were combat ready.

The Japanese bombers did considerable damage, including knocking out the power plant, leaving Rangoon without electricity. In an air battle, which lasted an hour and a half, the Flying Tigers acquitted themselves admirably by shooting down twenty-five enemy planes.[45] Two AVG planes made forced landings—the only extent of the group's damage that day—but the British lost six pilots and nine planes in the battle while downing seven enemy aircraft.[46]

Pawley watched the air battle from a vantage point under a grove of banyan trees near the Mingaladon Airfield, along with his secretary, Edna Earle Cadenhead; his brother Edward; and his Lockheed pilot, Roger Reynolds.[47] To celebrate the AVG pilots' performance in their valiant effort to defend the city, Pawley ordered food supplies from the CAMCO stores to be sent out to the airfield so the men could have their first good meal in three days.

Chennault, who wasn't in Rangoon at the time, wrote in his memoir that Pawley "apparently suffered a slight change of heart in his attitude toward the A.V.G." in providing the dinner.[48] Whatever his motive, Pawley gave the men ham, roast chicken, fresh vegetables, cake, pies, cold beer, and Scotch whiskey for their Christmas dinner. Setting up trestle tables in the open, the men were joined by Maj. Gen. George Brett and British general Sir Archibald Wavell, both of whom had arrived in Rangoon minutes before the Japanese attack.[49]

Chennault's critical assessment of Pawley may have been merited because soon after the Christmas Day attack, Pawley closed his Rangoon office and left a skeleton crew of Chinese mechanics at the Mingaladon Airfield to repair damaged planes. On December 28, thirty Vultee P-66 Vanguard fighters arrived by freighter in Rangoon. They were supposed to replace damaged P-40s, but Chennault didn't like them and turned them over to the Chinese Air Force. The reassignment was moot anyway, because Pawley had closed the CAMCO assembly factory. The crated aircraft remained aboard the freighter, finally ending up in India.[50] Operating out of Loiwing, Pawley concentrated on assembling Curtiss-Wright 21 Demon interceptors that had been sold to the Chinese.

If his relationship with Chennault hadn't deteriorated enough, on January 1, 1942, Pawley notified the AVG that CAMCO would no longer make repairs on the damaged aircraft. Stationed at Kyedaw Airfield to test repaired P-40s, Robert "Buster" Keeton remarked, "I think it is a dirty trick for [Pawley] to pull out after getting the organization set up."[51]

The contract Pawley had with the Chinese called for CAMCO to repair all damaged AVG P-40s. In September 1941, Pawley and Chennault had met with the director of the Chinese Commission of Aeronautical Affairs general Chou Chih-jou. The contract was modified, and the CAMCO facility at Loiwing was assigned responsibility for only repairing aircraft damaged west of the Salween River. The repair facility run by the Chinese Air Force at Kunming would handle any aircraft in need of repair east of the Salween.[52] As planes needing repair came into Kunming, it was decided that the heavily damaged ones would be sent by rail to Lashio and by truck to Loiwing, but with Pawley's work crews busy assembling the Demons, the incoming P-40s began piling up.[53]

Labeling Pawley's attitude as "a remarkable lack of cooperation," Chennault argued that repairing combat-proven P-40s took precedence over assembling "experimental fighters" he considered second rate. Chennault went to plea his case before Chiang Kai-shek, who was in Chungking.[54] The generalissimo agreed with Chennault and ordered Col. Chien Chang-tso, the Chinese manager at the CAMCO Loiwing facility, to work on the damaged P-40s. Chennault then began an all-out attack on Pawley, writing letters and cablegrams to T. V. Soong and the China Defense Supplies office in Washington. On January 11, 1942, he wrote, "I am convinced, after a long trial, that Mr. Pawley will not cooperate in any work which does not provide a generous profit or other award for Mr. Pawley. I have also come to the conclusion that he should not be given control of the revolving fund unless close supervision and frequent audits are made of his financial operations."

Arguing that Pawley had ignored several requests for a complete audit of expenses charged to the AVG account, Chennault went on to accuse Pawley of black market activities: "Mr. Pawley directed the delivery of a large portion of the groceries and sales articles, which I had purchased in New York for the use of the AVG, to Loiwing, and there authorized the sale of a considerable number of these articles. I have requested a full accounting for the articles sold, but have not been able to obtain one."[55]

But Pawley was not a man to have serious charges hurled at him without fighting back. In a letter to Chennault on January 11, 1942, Pawley accused the AVG leader of "repeated efforts to place me in a very bad light with Chinese government officials," adding that Chennault was "depriving us of even a small portion of the credit" of the AVG's success.[56]

Pawley then began a campaign to discredit Chennault, sending letters and cablegrams to CDS and anyone else he felt might listen. Chennault received word from the CDS office in Rangoon of "W. Pawley making severe criticisms of your handling of AVG and minimizing your part in AVG performance." The attack only widened the gap between the two, which was becoming hostile. Pawley's counterattack also included a letter sent to Chennault in which he chastised him for remaining in Kunming during the Rangoon Christmas Day battle. Criticizing Chennault for being absent when he could have offered his leadership, Pawley added that the squadron performed magnificently without Chennault's "assistance or support."[57]

Always the enterprising and astute businessman, Pawley decided it was time to move on. When Chiang Kai-shek ordered repairs on the P-40s at Loiwing, Pawley saw his chance and sold his interest in CAMCO to the Chinese. "Pawley has turned in his suit in a huff," McHugh noted, "and has even disassociated himself from any further connection with CAMCO."[58] Pawley may have had another reason to leave. Sam D. Irwin, vice president of Curtiss-Wright, said his company had canceled all contracts with overseas sales representatives when the United States entered the war.[59]

The battle of Rangoon lasted seventy-five days with the Flying Tigers' performance exceeding all expectations, but in the end, the advancing Japanese proved too formidable for ground troops to contain.[60] Singapore fell on February 25, 1942, and the airfield at Mingaladon was evacuated on February 27, forcing the Flying Tigers to move their operations to Magwe, an airstrip "hacked out of scrub land close to a peanut farm" 250 miles north on the Chindwin River.[61] From Magwe in Burma and from Loiwing and Kunming in China, the AVG was assigned to protect western China and keep the Burma Road open.

In early March, the Japanese had four divisions in Burma, two having been transferred from Malaya and the Dutch East Indies after the fall of Java on March 12. Pushing the Allied forces deeper into Burma, the Japanese proved to be unstoppable. Chinese troops managed to delay the Japanese near Toungoo for a short time, but when it fell, the Burma Road was open for the Japanese to advance their troops northward. When Lashio fell to the Japanese on April 29, the Burma Road was effectively closed and the airlift of supplies from India over the Himalayas ("The Hump") began. That same day the AVG was ordered to evacuate Loiwing and relocate to Baoshan farther north in China. The Allied defense of Burma was collapsing, leaving them with little choice but to retreat into China and India. By May 26, the Japanese had effectively driven the Allies out of Burma. Although the AVG continued to harass the Japanese, especially their airbases set up in Indochina, Chennault redeployed his units to provide air defense for China. On July 4, the AVG was officially disbanded. Although fifty-five volunteers stayed an extra two weeks, only five pilots accepted commissions in the newly formed 23rd Fighter Group of the China Air Task Force under Chennault. Many of the pilots wanted out and chose duty elsewhere, and several distinguished themselves during the war in other theaters of operation.[62]

While operational only seven months, the AVG amassed an extraordinary combat record. The Flying Tigers were credited with downing 286 enemy planes in the air, with destroying an additional 40 on the ground, and unofficially with another 200 probable kills. Of the pilots, only four were lost in air combat, nine killed on the ground, and three taken prisoner. Labeling them mercenaries, *Newsweek* reported that the pilots collected $150,000 in bonuses for downing 300 Japanese planes.[63] They were highly paid for their services, but the Flying Tigers had proven themselves one of the "deadliest groups of fighter pilots ever assembled," owing in part to the training and combat tactics Chennault had provided them.[64]

Thirty-nine pilots became aces during their Flying Tiger tenure or later, and many went on to prove that their training and experience in China had been invaluable. For example, Pappy Boyington flew for the Black Sheep Squadron and was awarded the Medal of Honor. Charles Older, an AVG ace, attended law school after the war and became a superior court judge in Los Angeles, where he presided over the Charles Manson trial.[65]

What were the reasons for their success? Number one: "Their morale was the highest." They were willing to volunteer for combat. Number two: "Every man was hand-picked." No one with bad habits or ill tempers was allowed, and they had to be physically fit. "You were out if you had a half-rotten tooth." Number three: "We only want the men who want us." Anyone who wanted to be regarded as a hero was sent packing. Number four: "The AVG gave its members the chance to retain their individuality." Number five: "The group's honestly democratic way of running itself." Any ideas from the ranks that would improve performance were heard and given full attention. Number six: "Money." Being well paid, as compared to what they had been earning in the States, helped bring out the best performance in each man.[66]

For William Pawley, the war in China was over, but the battle with Chennault continued for years. Although their feud had begun in the late thirties when Chennault first locked horns with the aggressive aircraft salesman, it renewed in intensity when Pawley sought credit for his part in creating the American Volunteer Group. A 1942 *Time* magazine article dubbed him the "China Swashbuckler" and described his contribution "to help sell the U.S. Government on the idea of the now-legendary A.V.G.," starting when "he began touting the scheme in 1939." In closing, the article quoted Pawley as unabashedly saying, "Unquestionably I have been one of the prime contributors to China's defense."[67]

When the *New York Times* ran a feature article on Chennault, a letter to the editor stated regrets that it "did not also include a few words of praise for William D. Pawley. For it was this energetic and patriotic American who, as early as 1937, emphasized the importance of defending the Burma Road." The letter was from Melvin D. Hildreth, who failed to mention he was Pawley's attorney.[68]

Hollywood contributed to the war effort by churning out low-budget films depicting U.S. fighting forces battling the evil warmongers of Japan. Among these patriotic-based films—many of which were produced to help raise morale on the home front—was a Republic Pictures production called *Flying Tigers*. Filmed between May and July 1942 and starring John Wayne in his first of many war films, the movie was a romanticized and totally inauthentic story of the famed volunteer group.

Kenneth Sanger and Larry Moore, two former AVG clerks who were mustered out for suspicion of homosexuality, were hired as technical advisers.[69] In the credits at the end of the movie, acknowledgment for assistance in the production was given to Curtiss-Wright and "William D. Pawley, co-founder of the American Volunteer Group." No mention was made of Chennault, who had objected to the AVG's hiring of Sanger and Moore.[70]

Near the end of the war, Pawley commissioned Raymond P. R. Neilson, a member of the National Academy, to paint portraits of twenty-seven Flying Tiger pilots, who gave their lives in the cause of freedom. Pawley wanted the oil paintings exhibited in a countrywide tour and eventually to place them on permanent display at a future "West Point of the Air." Working from old and sometimes in-adequate photographs, Neilson produced "photographic canvases, all alike in their flattering prettiness," but with "little artistic distinction," according to one news-paper account.[71] Art magazines were highly critical of the paintings. "Practically all the subjects look ill at ease," one wrote, "many indulging in America's great juvenile grin, unbeautiful but humanly appealing."[72] *Art Digest* characterized the portraits as being "necessarily conventional in treatment" but applauded Neilson for giving "living personality" to the subjects.[73]

After being exhibited at the Grand Central Art Galleries in New York City, the portraits were shipped to the Smithsonian Institution in Washington. On October 4, 1945, the paintings were hung in the Natural History Museum to be exhibited for a month.[74] The Chinese ambassador to the United States attended the opening, along with an embassy delegation. Pawley sent out invitations to a virtual who's who list of famous people—Pearl Buck, New York mayor Fiorello LaGuardia, Supreme Court justice William O. Douglas, Eleanor Roosevelt, and David O. Selznick—and an extensive grouping of military, State Department, and business notables.[75]

Years later, Dudley A. Whitman, a former World War II pilot who flew the "Hump," or the route over the Himalayan Mountains to supply the Chinese war effort, acquired the paintings. Having never been cleaned or varnished, they had deteriorated from neglect, and several had severe damage. Whitman hired Jana Justan, an art restorer from Macon, Georgia, who had worked for several years at the Smithsonian, to restore them. On September 11, 1998, the paintings were displayed for the first time in fifty years in an exhibit at the Museum of Aviation at the Robins Air Force Base in Georgia. There they remain on display as part of the permanent collection.[76]

Pawley also commissioned the publication of a booklet containing copies of the paintings, titled *Americans Valiant and Glorious*, in which he described Chennault as a "great man" who deserved praise for his AVG accomplishments. In the preface of the booklet Pawley included an excerpt from the official history of the U.S. Army in World War II that credited Pawley as the man "who was willing to take a chance on recruiting pilots . . . in spite of existing neutrality legislation."[77]

Chennault was not so obliging in returning the praise Pawley may have been seeking. When several AVG veterans discussed forming a Flying Tiger Association, Pawley offered a $10,000 donation for its initial funding. When Chennault heard about it, he sent a telegram to George Paxton, an original Flying Tiger who helped organize the veterans' group: "Will not accept membership in any organization with Pawley who was never member of AVG and who failed to serve us in the most critical hour. Best wishes to all others."[78]

In his autobiography, Chennault recalled Pawley's offer "was flatly rejected by the membership, who apparently felt that a few repaired P-40's during the dark days of 1941–42 would have been more valuable to them than a postwar check."[79]

PART III
Postwar Adjustments

8
Divorce and Remarriage

Pawley was on a Pan Am Clipper to China in 1940 when he met Walchand Hirachand, an Indian financier who told him the Indian government needed an aircraft factory. Applying the same deal-making techniques he had used in establishing his businesses in China, Pawley looked for government backing. Negotiations for building the factory in India led to a contract in which the Indian government would own one third; the state of Mysore, where the factory was to be located, would have one third; and Pawley and Hirachand would share the remaining third. Capitalized at $12 million, with India contributing half, construction in Bangalore began February 1941. Pawley was installed as chairman of the board.[1]

With Burma and China both hot war zones, Pawley simply moved his operation to a safe haven far beyond the reach of Japanese bombers.[2] Four supervisory employees from Pawley's Chinese operation oversaw the construction of the factory in India.[3] The contract also called for India's purchasing fifty military aircraft annually built by Pawley's Hindustan Aircraft Company at a cost of $2.8 million.[4] Using material kits from Curtiss-Wright, the factory was constructing forty-eight Hawk 75s for India, but only five were completed before the contract was canceled.[5]

In early 1942, Pawley's aircraft industry career was coming to a close. He had constructed a $500,000 airplane factory adjoining the Miami Airport on LeJeune Road in November 1940.[6] The first of its kind in the area, the factory designed, manufactured, and tested planes to be sold abroad. Part of the Intercontinent Aircraft Corporation that Pawley and Bruce Leighton founded, the plant also supplied parts to Vultee and other aircraft manufacturers. The largest war plant in Florida, it was eventually taken over by the government through the Defense

111

Plant Corporation. On July 17, 1942, Pawley sold his interest in the Intercontinent Aircraft Corporation to Vultee Aircraft.[7]

He still owned Hindustan Aircraft in India, which repaired a variety of aircraft including Lockheed Hudsons and Consolidated PBY Catalina flying boats.[8] The factory held a contract to repair U.S. Army Air Corps planes and another for maintaining and overhauling planes for the Royal Air Force and British Fleet Air Arm. The plant worked on fourteen types of engines and more than sixteen different types of aircraft. In addition, Pawley was starting to construct gliders for use in the war effort.[9]

After "cost and inefficiency" complaints were reported at the Mysore plant, Pawley's interests were bought out, and the government made arrangements between July 1942 and September 1943 for the Tenth Air Force to acquire the rights to direct the factory's operations.[10] Maj. Gen. Clayton Bissell used his authority as commander of the Tenth Air Force to force Pawley out despite Pawley's "vigorous objections" that "loss of efficiency would be inevitable."[11]

While making arrangements in Delhi in September 1943 to turn Hindustan Aircraft over to the U.S. Army Air Corps, Pawley received a call from India's secretary of supply. During a meeting lasting several hours, Pawley was asked to construct a 50,000-ton ammonium sulphate (fertilizer) plant and was told he would be making a great contribution to the war effort. Instructing Intercontinent's New York office to investigate the project's feasibility, Pawley went to the Indian state of Travancore to inspect industrial projects already under way. After seeing the rapid industrialization of the area, Pawley agreed to build the factory.

Manufacturing fertilizers was important to India because it grew rice, a major staple, at a meager production rate per acre. India imported most of its rice from Burma and Siam, but because of the war, imports were curtailed, resulting in widespread famine and more than a million deaths. Although India urgently needed the project to begin, Pawley found himself running into obstacles from the start.

India had to approve the project and then approval was needed from the London–United States Dollar Control Board to authorize funds used from a U.S. source. Travancore had ample British sterling funds but not U.S. dollars. Because Pawley would be purchasing equipment in the United States, $3.5 million had to be released, but Pawley learned officials in London were procrastinating. They were not eager for the Americans to establish businesses in India and were looking ahead for postwar investments to revitalize their economy. Indian officials also balked because they felt if a plant were built in Travancore, other states would demand similar facilities.

In mid-1944, Pawley was in Washington with a legal team to help him, but he was already talking about retiring and letting one of his brothers assume control of the project.[12] Famine in India continued taking lives as the project was delayed. Although many were sympathetic to India's need, Pawley received no support and finally gave up the project. A year after signing the agreement to build the plant, Pawley learned London had finally approved the dollar exchange but for a British company, Imperial Chemical Industries.[13] In his agreement with India, Pawley was guaranteed protection against any losses, a provision he had perfected in his dealings with China. When the venture didn't pan out, he claimed a $750,000 loss because the Jawaharlal Nehru government repudiated the original agreement. After gaining independence, the Indians decided to build the plant themselves, and Pawley's business interests in the Far East came to an end.[14]

His marriage was also coming to an end. Pawley and Annie-Hahr's fairy-tale romance had degenerated into an acrimonious relationship. Much of the blame for the deterioration was Pawley's fault. He wanted to control everything, including his wife and children. On one occasion, as they visited friends, Pawley paused at the doorstep, drew out his handkerchief, spat on it, and rubbed off the makeup Annie-Hahr was wearing. "Dad was never affectionate in any way," his daughter Irene claimed. "A hug was given very lightly. He never asked how you were, he only 'held court,' and everyone gathered around to listen to his stories."[15] Aside from Pawley's lack of affection, there was another reason for the downfall of the marriage.

Annie-Hahr had long suspected another woman had taken her place, but now she had a name, Edna Cadenhead. Arriving in China as Bruce Leighton's secretary, Edna had stayed as Pawley's secretary when Leighton returned to the States. Handling correspondence and accounts, Edna was constantly with Pawley. "Bill Pawley broke the monotony by appearing with a blond," Olga Greenlaw had noted in her diary on December 15, 1941. "She turned out to be his secretary."[16]

Although thousands of miles apart, Annie-Hahr and Edna were beginning to develop a feud as illustrated in a telegram Annie-Hahr sent to Intercontinent in New York:

Dear Carl [Dolan] see what you can do to stop Miss Cadenhead from writing those foolish letters to Miami about my accounts. The credit bureau

knows what Bill makes, and the heads of all business firms have tele-
phoned me to express their surprise at his conduct. The letters are not
hurting me at all but by leaps and bounds with the appearance in Miami
and Miami Beach of each letter, Miss Cadenhead is tearing down Bill's
good reputation of fifteen years standing.[17]

Annie-Hahr was convinced that Edna was trying to break up her marriage. She
pleaded with her husband to pay more attention to her and the children, pouring out
her feelings in a cable sent to Pawley's Hong Kong office:

Children and I do not understand why we have never heard one word
from you. It has made me so ill that I have not been able to go on a much
needed trip. We love you and miss you, why don't you believe it, why do
you want to hurt us by such a long silence. You know how much I love
you. In heavens name please answer.[18]

Pawley did not respond to his wife's pleas, leaving Annie-Hahr to worry about
her future. What she didn't know was that her husband was already making plans
to divorce her.

In 1941, Pawley began constructing a home on Sunset Island in Miami. The
twenty-room, six-bedroom mansion was magnificent in detail, complete with a
winding staircase, a formal dining room, and a swimming pool off the back ter-
race.[19] It was opulently furnished, Pawley sparing no expense to have a home that
reflected his fortune. Annie-Hahr and the children continued to live at the Pine Tree
Avenue home, and she never set foot in the Sunset Island house.

Pawley decided to file for divorce in Cuba to lessen the chances Annie-Hahr
would contest it, but first he had to establish residency. Although he had lived in
Cuba as a boy, he had not been there for years and didn't own any property on the
island. In setting up a legal residence to satisfy the Cuban courts, Pawley turned for
help to Mario Lazo, an attorney in Havana.

Lazo owned undeveloped land in a desirable section of Havana and agreed
to sell Pawley property to establish residency. The agreement, according to Lazo,
was that Pawley would pay the same low price Lazo had paid several years before
but with the proviso that if Pawley did not construct a personal residence on the
property, he was obliged to resell it to Lazo for the same price. To further the cha-
rade, the transaction was made a matter of record with Spruille Braden, the U.S.

ambassador to Cuba. As an added touch, Pawley began showing photographs of his Miami home, stating he intended to duplicate the house on his newly acquired Havana property.

Ten years later, after having the property as proof of Cuban residency but never building a home on it, Pawley resold the property to a different buyer than Lazo. The attorney labeled Pawley a crook for not living up to their agreement, claiming the transaction netted Pawley a $30,000 profit.[20]

Officially declaring his Cuban residency on July 26, 1942, Pawley initiated the Cuban divorce suit on September 28, 1942. The suit claimed Annie-Hahr had refused to live in China with him "where for business reasons he found it advantageous to live." Based on this separation, Pawley asked for a divorce on the ground of desertion. He offered Annie-Hahr a $250,000 settlement if she would grant him a divorce or at least "recognize the validity of the Cuban divorce." She turned down the offer.[21] On May 6, 1943, the judge of the first instance for the western district of the city of Havana issued the final decree granting the divorce.[22]

During the Cuban proceedings, the sheriff of Dade County made two attempts to serve Annie-Hahr notice of the pending suit.[23] On advice of her Miami attorney, William Ward, each time service was attempted, Annie-Hahr refused to accept it. "It was a horrible experience for my mother," Annie-Hahr McKay recalled. "The sheriff waited outside our home, and when my mother drove up in her car, the sheriff threw the papers at her."[24]

Despite the upheaval in her life, Annie-Hahr tried keeping her family together. Her son Billy was in the U.S. Army Air Corps, having graduated from flight school at George Army Air Field in Lawrenceville, Illinois.[25] He was eventually stationed in India, where he flew a Curtiss-Wright C-46 Commando over the Hump and was made an instructor. After India he was stationed in Dallas and Long Beach until the war ended.[26]

While her son was in the service, Annie-Hahr did her best to support the war effort. RAF pilots were being trained at a nearby base in Clewiston, Florida, and billeted at private homes. When Annie-Hahr inquired as to how many hadn't been placed, she was told eight to ten men were without housing. "I'll take all of them," she replied. Clearing out a large playroom in her home, Annie-Hahr set up bedding for the British pilots.

At Christmastime, Annie-Hahr erected a second tree in the pilot's quarters. Her children decorated the tree with small packets of razor blades and three cigarettes tied with ribbons as gifts for the men. Although strict rationing was in effect,

Annie-Hahr went to stores without having the required ration stamps. She pleaded with store owners to provide her with groceries to prepare a traditional Christmas dinner for the pilots. Loaded down with turkey and all the trimmings, Annie-Hahr returned home to cook the meal.[27]

Although Annie-Hahr contended the Cuban divorce was invalid, William Pawley married for the second time. Relying on the validity of the Cuban divorce, he married Edna in India on June 30, 1943.[28] A thirty-seven-year-old striking blonde at the time, Edna would prove invaluable as a supportive spouse when her husband began a new career working for the U.S. government.

Annie-Hahr refused to accept her husband had divorced her. She wrote a lengthy letter to Franklin Roosevelt on August 7, 1944, pouring her feelings out and asking for his help. Addressing FDR as "Commander-in-Chief," she pleaded for official action to "establish her standing as the lawful wife of Pawley, not only in her own interest but those of her children." The letter was turned over to the Secret Service to "determine the mental condition of the writer." After interviewing Annie-Hahr and her attorney, agents concluded, "Mrs. Pawley is sane but under severe mental stress."[29]

On September 7, 1946, Annie-Hahr filed a bill for alimony "unconnected with causes for divorce," attacking the Cuban divorce because no provision had been made for alimony or child support. The suit claimed Pawley was making more than $1 million a year, but he contributed only $800 a month for Annie-Hahr to maintain a home and provide for the children. "He is a man of virtually unlimited resources," she declared.[30] "In view of the defendant's position and wealth," the suit noted, she and the children were entitled to $5,000 a month.[31]

Pawley answered the suit by asserting that his ex-wife's claim of his having unlimited income was "absurd and ridiculous." He claimed his 1945 income was a little less than $60,000, and his estimated 1946 income would be around $36,000.[32] This reported income is suspect because Pawley had established a $500,000 irrevocable trust in April 1944 for Annie-Hahr and their four children.[33] Annie-Hahr filed an amendment to her brief asking the court to declare that a divorce existed in her favor and listing the grounds as desertion, extreme cruelty, and adultery.[34]

On June 1, 1948, Florida circuit judge George E. Holt upheld the Cuban divorce, ruling Annie-Hahr's suit for divorce "came too late." In an eleven-page decision, Judge Holt also dismissed her request for $5,000 monthly maintenance.[35] Holt said evidence showed that Pawley had given her an average of $25,000 a year after the divorce and contributed "generously" to his children. Holt also criticized Annie-Hahr for "contending that she is still the wife of defendant, branding him as an adulterer and casting a serious cloud upon the marital status of his present wife."[36]

On April 6, 1950, a Supreme Court of Florida appeal decided 7–2 in favor of Pawley. Florida Civil Code provided that a wife was "required to follow her husband to the place where he fixes his residence," which she had failed to do since 1936. Annie-Hahr contended she had received money for "support and care and maintenance of the large home and for the education, care and support of the minor children," but that "said funds are not adequate even to maintain the home." The court's appointed special master found sufficient evidence that Pawley had "contributed to their support almost luxuriously," and the court accepted his conclusion as fact.

The court ruled the Cuban divorce was valid and, furthermore, that Annie-Hahr was not entitled to share Pawley's wealth, "which was acquired not with, nor by, the appellant's assistance but in spite of her lack of cooperation, for she obviously insisted that he give up his business in the Orient and find employment in or near Miami Beach in which city she preferred to live and she refused to make her home with him in China."[37] Still not satisfied, Annie-Hahr filed an appeal with the Supreme Court of the United States. On October 23, 1950, the Supreme Court refused to grant a writ of certiorari, effectively ending the legal battle between Pawley and his ex-wife.[38]

While fighting to nullify the divorce, Annie-Hahr had resorted to desperate measures. In a letter to President Harry Truman on April 25, 1945, she discussed personal issues and the "fake" divorce granted to her ex-husband. She questioned his activities in China, including his failure to pay income tax and the possibility of his involvement in black market activities. A Truman aide scribbled a handwritten note on the letter that reads: "S. S. [Secret Service] has a file on this lady. She is a mental case."[39]

Various U.S. government agencies already had confidential files on Pawley's activities, and Annie-Hahr's letter was added to the pile. A confidential note dated September 23, 1942, in Pawley's CIA file accused him of transmitting by open mail secret War Department documents entrusted to him. Pawley had sent them to George Sellett, his legal adviser at the Intercontinent office in New York. The envelope was marked Secret and Confidential, which alerted the Office of Censorship.[40] No further disposition of the incident was reported. Another report dated January

15, 1945, from New Delhi, India, described Pawley as having "lots of good commercial business contracts" and being "a clever politician and good organizer but quits when money runs out and organization monopoly fails." It also said that he was "not of good character or reputation and engaged in shady deals."[41]

Throughout the period when she was trying to restore her marriage, Annie-Hahr did her best to maintain her dignity, but it seemed even society turned against her. Each year she was listed in the *Society Register of Greater Miami*, but in 1944, her application was denied because she wanted to be listed as Mrs. William Douglas Pawley. The Blue Book Publishing Company of Miami, which issued the *Society Register*, suggested she be listed instead as Pawley, Mrs. A. H. Dobbs (Annie-Hahr Dobbs). She pleaded with them to reconsider but was turned down. The register's secretary, Mary Jane Sertel, wrote to Annie-Hahr, offering her sympathy: "I've never done anything I hated so much to do as this. I know you're right, and that right is on your side. I know, too, that you will win out because the things you are fighting for are only the things that belong to you. The very best of luck in everything."[42]

Despite the sympathy of others and the moral support provided by her children, Annie-Hahr was devastated when the last court decision was handed down. Her hair turned white, "almost overnight," and she took to her bed. Irene said her mother didn't recognize who she was for almost three years. Annie-Hahr was eventually hospitalized in a mental institution, where she remained until her death on April 30, 1986.[43]

Shortly after Roosevelt was elected to his fourth term, he advised Robert E. Hannegan, chairman of the Democratic National Committee, that he would appoint Pawley to a foreign diplomatic post.[44] Hannegan, a close friend who would later vacation with his two sons at Pawley's Sunset Island home, agreed he would make a fine diplomat.[45] A staunch Roosevelt supporter, with contributions to the Democratic Party to match, Pawley was surprised when FDR asked, "How would you like a change of pace from business to diplomacy and public service?"

Pawley replied he would serve if called, but he was taken aback when Roosevelt wanted to appoint him as the ambassador to Czechoslovakia. Pawley said his background in China and Latin America, plus a lack of knowledge in European affairs, suggested otherwise. Roosevelt dismissed those arguments, saying he needed a "strong Ambassador in Prague," and Pawley was the one.[46]

Hannegan asked Treasury Secretary Henry Morgenthau for a background report on Pawley, with an emphasis on any income tax problems arising from his business in China. When Pawley got wind of this investigation, he sent an emissary to Morgenthau and complained that the Treasury Department was holding up his nomination. Morgenthau called Secretary of State Edward Stettinius, Jr., to complain that Pawley was "throwing the entire blame onto me."[47] Two days later, Lauchlin Currie, special adviser to FDR, sent a memorandum to the president: "I understand that some material exists in government files that raises some question as to Pawley's integrity and therefore eligibility for a government post. Pawley knows there is something but doesn't know what the specific charges or allegations are. He would like to have a thorough investigation made and I think he is entitled to that." FDR responded with a short note to Morgenthau: "Will you do this and let me have a report?"[48]

Currie also wrote to Morgenthau expressing his opinion that Pawley was being denied a position based on accusations. "Both you and I feel he is entitled to a thorough investigation," Currie wrote.[49] On the same day, FDR also sent a memo to Morgenthau, asking the Treasury Department "to send me as promptly as possible a summary of whatever material is available in your Department concerning Mr. William Pawley."[50] Morgenthau responded with a copy of the investigation report that the State Department had given to him.

Written by Department of State chief special agent T. F. Fitch on December 19, 1944, it noted that Pawley was "a genius at grasping opportunities and converting them to profit for himself." The agent suggested that Pawley be denied any position with the government for several reasons:

1. Because he is under investigation by the Treasury Department in connection with income tax returns, and for the reason that he will be investigated by that Department for black market operations in China, money transactions resulting in inflation, and for furnishing material under Lend-Lease which is said to have passed into the hands of the Japanese.

2. Because his appointment would bring into the open the fact that he divorced his wife in order to marry his former secretary, such divorce being based on a decree obtained in Cuba, culminating in a marriage in India.

3. Because of the strong possibility that any Government position sought by him would be for the future business gain it presented, or for the protection from past actions which such appointment might guarantee.[51]

At this point, FDR seemed to be having second thoughts. Stettinius asked FDR if he was still considering Pawley. "Well, it's all right, but you'd better have a word with Henry [Morgenthau] because I understand that there's something about income tax," he replied. Morgenthau confided to Stettinius he was getting the impression that FDR wasn't too happy about what he had heard. "I've got some bad reports from State, Justice and Treasury," FDR had told Morgenthau. Morgenthau concluded that FDR "thought Pawley wasn't up to being a representative of the President of the United States out of this country."

There were other concerns about Pawley that Morgenthau discussed with Stettinius. "Now, there's a question of residency, you see?" Morgenthau told the secretary of state. "The way it stands now, he claims residence out of the country, then he wouldn't have to pay taxes from what he earned in China. On the other hand, when he entered the country through Customs, he claimed he was a resident of the United States. Now, there's a definite conflict there."[52]

Heading into the New Year, Pawley tried political pressure to force his appointment. He asked U.S. senator Claude Pepper to put in a good word. "Pawley's been a good friend of mine for several years," Pepper told Morgenthau and launched into a recap of his friend's career. When Pepper touched upon the commission Pawley had received for the Curtiss P-40s, Morgenthau cut him short. "That has nothing to do with this," Morgenthau said, adding that someone was "trying to spread this thing that this is something that is sort of a personal issue with me."

Morgenthau rehashed the questionable customs declaration Pawley had made upon entering the United States. If Pawley stated he was an American resident, then how could he claim being a foreign resident when it came to paying income taxes? "We've got in the Treasury two signed statements from him in direct conflict," Morgenthau said. But there was a third possibility.

"Now, what he had to gain by declaring himself in Customs—whether he was able to bring in some stuff free that way—I don't know," Morgenthau offered.

"Well, I can't—the man is quite well off," Pepper said. "I think he's worth a considerable sum of money and I can't imagine that he—I don't believe on account of saving a pay for Customs duties or something like that."

"Well, you'd be surprised what some very rich people will do to save a few pennies," Morgenthau countered.[53]

Pepper followed up his conversation with Morgenthau by forwarding several letters from prominent people attesting the character, ability, and integrity of W. D. Pawley, two of whom had represented Pawley in the past as legal advisers.

Pawley cooperated in the investigation. He spent $10,000 of his own money for lawyers to go back as far as 1932 and obtain the required records for the Treasury Departments report.[54] The Treasury Department's inquiry was thorough, delving into three aspects: "first, whether his domestic relations were such as might be cause for scandal; second, whether his income was secured in an honorable manner, and, third, whether his tax record shows any irregularities."[55]

The issue regarding Pawley's Cuban divorce was raised, but investigators found no reason not to consider it valid. The report covered "marital difficulties" Pawley had with his first wife, "which the President knows about," Morgenthau remarked, "and either the President or somebody else says that somebody, a Treasury man in Miami, is keeping company with his first wife." The rumor of Annie-Hahr's infidelity was totally false, and Pawley may even have started it. When asked if the matter should be looked into, Morgenthau said, "I am not interested in the first Mrs. Pawley, and I don't think it is any of my business." The question of Pawley being a bigamist was discussed, but after determining he wasn't, the matter was dropped. The Treasury Department's investigation indicated Pawley "made an awful lot of money in the past ten years dealing with the Chinese" and only paid taxes on one-fourth of it, but no tax case could be made.[56]

A 1954 FBI report on Pawley referred to the earlier treasury investigation. According to a confidential informant, the Internal Revenue Service (IRS) delved into Pawley's finances for the years 1934–1943. It determined "most of Pawley's fortune was derived from operations abroad during periods when he was a nonresident citizen." Nonresident income was tax exempt, so Pawley's earnings were not taxable. A "technical violation" was found for three tax years amounting to $1,200, but since no fraud was involved, Pawley was allowed to pay the money.[57] Morgenthau attached a memo to the report for FDR saying, "Although his income in recent years has been very large no information available to us indicates that he has not met his tax obligations."[58]

With the treasury investigation completed, Pawley then had to submit to vetting by the State Department. The assistant secretary of state for European affairs asked Pawley why he felt he was qualified for the position. "I'm *not* qualified for this particular post," he replied, "the President has asked me to accept it." Believing the interviewer resented him because he wasn't a career diplomat, Pawley left with a feeling that forces within the State Department were working against him.[59] He soon discovered Roosevelt's wishes were being ignored.

In his syndicated column, *Washington Merry-Go-Round*, Drew Pearson reported that Pawley had been promised the ambassadorship to Czechoslovakia, but the State Department had "upset the apple-cart" by transferring Laurence Steinhardt from his diplomatic post in Turkey to be the ambassador to Czechoslovakia. The last-minute switch had been made to make room for Leland Harrison to be appointed the ambassador to Turkey.[60]

With his wife Edna, Pawley attended Roosevelt's fourth inauguration, which was held on the White House grounds in a snowfall. "I realized that he was so dedicated to the proposition that he alone could secure from the Russians some semblance of peace for the World," Pawley recalled, "that he agreed to continue in the presidency."

When Roosevelt died in April 1945, Truman had been in the White House only a few weeks when Pawley received a call to see him. According to Pawley, Truman began by confessing he was "so ignorant of many serious problems facing our country," and he had "little or no experience in world affairs to prepare me for a hot seat like this."

Pawley suggested to Truman that with the war almost over, an unprecedented opportunity in history now existed for the United States to establish long-lasting peace. Echoing sentiments of Gen. George Patton, who was criticized for his views, Pawley suggested that Truman should announce that "the armies of the United States will proceed to Moscow and beyond to Vladivostok." He was convinced Soviet generals despised Joseph Stalin's police state and would "lay down their weapons" in order for people to "freely choose their own government."

"Bill, I can't risk it," Truman responded. "If I took your advice, I might start World War III, and I don't believe Congress would go along. Anyway, our men would never hold still for it. They've just finished fighting magnificently, they're sick of war and they want to come home."

"But what I'm saying is they wouldn't *have* to fight," Pawley insisted. "Russian soldiers are sick of fighting too."

"I wish I could agree with you," Truman said, effectively dismissing the idea, "but the United States just can't risk it."[61]

The fact that more than 2 million Soviet armed forces were in Germany and Poland and supplied with six thousand tanks and forty thousand artillery pieces indicated that Pawley's plan would have been costly if the Russians didn't lay down their arms as he predicted.[62] Seeing that his drastic plan would not be implemented, Pawley waited patiently for Truman to get around to the reason he had been called.

In a display of the no-nonsense style that marked his handling of the highest political office in the land, Truman got straight to the point. "You know Latin America and you speak their language," Truman said. "I need someone who can handle a specific problem that I'm faced with in Peru. I'm asking you to be my Ambassador in Lima."[63]

9

Peru and Brazil

"I want to help Peru get on her feet," President Truman told Pawley. "We owe her a debt of gratitude for being the first Latin American Republic to break relations with the Axis powers." He was referring to a meeting of ministers of foreign affairs held in Rio de Janeiro shortly after Pearl Harbor and Peru refused Japan access to its ports and fuel oil. "She's going to need financial aid from the U.S. Government and an economic climate favorable to direct private investment," Truman added.[1]

As the new ambassador to Peru, replacing John Campbell White, who had served less than a year, Pawley faced problems requiring immediate attention. Peru's economic problems were even greater than Truman had imagined. Mining was its prime revenue source, and although the war had provided an outlet for copper, lead, and zinc exports, Peru now had huge surpluses. The U.S. Commercial Company, which purchased ores from Peru during the war, now recommended cutting back. Mining companies that prospered during the war had not invested their profits to modernize or improve their facilities. The minerals attaché in Peru felt it was time to seek "private marketing channels" for the transition to a peacetime economy. "To underwrite the economy of Peru and other Latin American countries is beyond even the financial capabilities of even an over-generous Uncle Sam," he concluded.[2]

Miami newspapers hailed the appointment of "Ambassador Bill," calling him "an industrious and ingenious man" with "native and experience-acquired capacities."[3] Pawley spoke briefly at his swearing-in ceremony, pledging to work for better relationships with Peru. Guests at the ceremony included friends Mao Pangchu, James Doolittle, Bruce Leighton, and high-ranking military officers such as

125

Gen. Alexander Vandergrift (USMC) and Maj. Gen. Pete Quesada and Lt. Gen. H. S. George from the U.S. Army Air Force.[4]

Not being a career diplomat had its disadvantages. Speaking the language was a plus, but lacking knowledge of protocol was a drawback. Before he and Edna left the States, Pawley spent a month in Washington making the rounds to State Department officials. "Just use common sense," he was told during a briefing with a protocol officer.[5] The State Department timed his arrival in Lima on July 14, 1945, to present his credentials to the outgoing president of Peru and attend the inauguration of the newly elected Dr. José Luis Bustamante Rivero.[6]

Pawley's first problem as a noncareer diplomat came from a member of his own American Chancellery staff. As distinguished from the embassy residence, his office was at the chancellery and supported by a staff of career Foreign Service officers. His office was unattractive and cramped in comparison to the others. He felt his presence was not needed, an impression that was fortified when Chargé d'Affaires Edward G. Trueblood informed him "everything had been running smoothly" since Pawley's predecessor had departed. If Pawley would pass on economic or political information garnered at cocktail parties, Trueblood assured him, it would be included in the daily reports to Washington.

Accustomed to hands-on dealings, Pawley was not about to change while serving his country. He ordered every important document, including dispatches, telegrams, and mail, placed on his desk so he could be familiarized with what was required of him. The next day, Pawley's personal secretary Catherine Alford, who had accompanied him to Peru, greeted him at work. "You have a big surprise in store for you," Alford said.

Opening the door to his office, he couldn't believe his eyes. His desk overflowed with the contents of eight mailbags that had been dumped unceremoniously and allowed to spill onto the floor. Pawley summoned Trueblood. "Get all this stuff out of here," he ordered, "and remove it personally." Trying to gain Trueblood's cooperation, but to no avail, he shopped for a new assistant. He phoned Walter Donnelly, the chargé d'affaires in Panama, who that same day was offered an ambassadorship in Central America. After some thought, Donnelly decided to join Pawley, and the chancellery staff problems stopped.[7]

Dealing with the State Department meant going through proscribed channels, which were complicated by red tape and slowed requests to a snail's pace. The State Department authorized him to spend $3,600 out of his own pocket for embassy office furniture, but getting repaid took more than two years. He also had problems receiving his ambassador's salary and wasn't fully compensated until after leaving Peru.[8] Unlike most Foreign Service officials, Pawley didn't have to depend on his $25,000 stipend, because he was making a reported $750,000 a year from his aircraft factories.[9]

Before addressing problems relating to Peru, Pawley had to face the political situation. After ruling more than ten years as a dictator, previous president Manuel Prado y Ugarteche had acquiesced to holding free and democratic elections. Bustamante, a former ambassador to Uruguay, a poet, and a university law professor, was elected by a 2–1 majority over the conservative candidate.[10] His victory was the result of a coalition between the liberal party, the Peruvian Communist Party, (Partido Comunista Peruano), and the radical Alianza Popular Revolucionaria Americana (American Popular Revolutionary Alliance, or APRA). APRA controlled both houses of Congress, but members refused to accept positions in the new government in order to have freedom to criticize its policies.

Among the policies Bustamante supported was the abolishment of censorship. "There will be freedom of the press here," he promised. He wanted Peru to create schools of journalism and to support "existing or newspaper enterprises that practice journalism in the true sense of the word." He also hoped to encourage private capital investment, eliminate the multitiered tax system by implementing a direct income tax, and seriously attempt to balance the budget.[11] But without APRA's cooperation, any legislation would be defeated.

Victor Raúl Haya de la Torre, a charismatic and dynamic politician who came from a well-to-do family that had fallen on hard times, led APRA. Haya attended law school, where he immersed himself in Marxist teachings. He organized a textile worker's strike, but during a 1923 student protest, police fired upon the crowd, killing three people. Haya went into hiding but was later arrested. He was "deported after leading a mass demonstration protesting the dedication of Peru to the Sacred Heart of Jesus."[12] In Mexico he organized APRA as a movement against any program in Peru that did not embrace socialist ideas.

In 1924 he attended the Third World Congress of the Communist International in Moscow and became influenced by Soviet doctrine. Five years later he was studying the political tenets of Nazism in Germany. Returning to Peru in 1930, he ran for president and lost. APRA members became targets of harassment after the election, and many were imprisoned, including Haya. In retaliation, his movement's adherents, the Apristas, rioted in the streets and assassinated the Peruvian president. During World War II, Haya supported Roosevelt's Good Neighbor Policy, opposed Nazism, and distanced himself from Moscow theology. By the end of the war, he emerged as the leading APRA spokesman.

Pawley knew that to serve U.S. interests effectively he had to establish a friendly relationship with Haya. Beginning with meetings and social gatherings he attended with the heads of both houses of Congress who were close friends of Haya's, Pawley was soon invited to visit Haya at Chosica, a small town outside Lima. Going out of his way to meet the leader of Bustamante's opposition would pose a delicate situation, so Pawley suggested that Haya have lunch with him at the American Embassy instead. When Haya declined, Pawley then arranged—at Bustamante's suggestion—a small dinner party at the Peruvian minister of the interior's home with Haya as guest of honor.

Pawley didn't have detailed protocol instructions from the State Department, but from his upbringing in Latin America, he knew the custom that no food or drink was served until the guest of honor arrived. At 10:45 p.m., Haya sent word he wasn't coming because of car trouble. Reiterating to the leaders of Congress that it would be fruitless to suggest measures to help Peru without meeting Haya, Pawley was encouraged to make another attempt. He sent another invitation for Haya to dine with him at the American Embassy and discuss "matters of importance to our two countries." Haya accepted, but when he hadn't appeared at the embassy by two o'clock, Pawley ignored Latin custom and decided to dine without him.

Before he made it to the dining room, Haya suddenly appeared with the president of the Senate and Speaker of the House. In his late forties, the five-foot-six, slightly fat, but energetic Aprista leader wasted no time in expressing his displeasure. "Why did you refuse to come and see me in Chosica?"

"If you were President of Peru," Pawley countered, "would you want the American Ambassador to go visiting a political opponent of your administration?"

Haya paused, taken aback by the directness of Pawley. "That is a good answer," Haya said, shaking Pawley's hand. "I think we can be friends."[13]

After lunch, they delved into those issues that the United States might be able to offer assistance to Peru, with an emphasis on settling the bond debt. Peru had borrowed $100 million in the late twenties, but with the Depression and the collapse of raw material prices, the country had been in default since 1931. "Peru owed $150 million to Americans who had bought that country's bonds," Pawley recalled, "and nothing had been paid on these bonds in 20 years."[14] Complicating matters were Peru's petroleum laws, which restricted oil sales, and a monopoly that made the price of salt higher than the price of fish.[15] Through Pawley's efforts, Peruvian petroleum laws were rewritten to allow American companies to develop "what appears to be one of the greatest oil reserves in this hemisphere." He also induced Peru to invalidate the salt monopoly laws and procure assistance from the United States to help the ailing fish industry rise from "practically nothing up to $6 million per year."[16]

Through Pawley's mediation efforts, Haya agreed to participate in the government and allowed three Apristas to be included in a reorganization of the cabinet, filling positions in the Finance, Public Works, and Agriculture Ministries.[17] After months of debate, both houses of the Peruvian Congress approved the program of debt settlement that the United States had offered.[18]

Peru faced another crisis with political repercussions when it began running short on wheat. In late January 1946 Foreign Minister Enrique Garciá Sayán told Pawley that Peru would run out of wheat by March. Pawley notified the State Department, urging immediate approval of a 40,000-ton shipment.[19] Peru had expected 150,000 tons from Argentina, but political difficulties between the two countries, crop shortages, and demand from the United Nations stalled shipments. One flour mill had closed and the largest one was down to nine days' supply. Pawley was concerned a panic would give APRA increased strength.[20]

On his own initiative, Pawley personally investigated the problem, arriving at an ominous conclusion. Unless the United States began immediate emergency shipments, starvation and riots would ensue. Pawley warned the State Department that "closing of mills will exaggerate crisis in public mind with grave consequences in markets and to Govt."[21] Wheat and flour began arriving from the United States and Canada, but Peru was still 25 percent short meeting its needs. Argentina took advantage and required Peru to purchase wheat by selling Argentina sugar, petroleum, coal, and rubber—all below market prices.[22]

As Pawley predicted, Apristas used the wheat shortages to gain popularity. What Pawley didn't know until after leaving his post was that secretly Haya had sent emissaries to Argentina to bargain with Juan Perón. Argentina publicly agreed to ship 150,000 tons of wheat to Peru while secretly agreeing to provide milk, frozen beef, and lard. Haya had been openly anti-Perón, and although he continued to speak out against the Argentine dictator, the Aprista newspaper, *La Tribuna*, suddenly stopped criticizing Perón.[23]

On February 23, 1946, the Medal for Merit Board recommended to Truman those individuals who should be cited "for exceptionally meritorious conduct in the performance of outstanding services in connection with the prosecution of the war." Among those selected were Dr. Edwin P. Hubble, J. Edgar Hoover, David Sarnoff, and William Pawley.[24] The citation credited Pawley "with keen foresight" in urging "the strategic importance of defending the Burma Road as early as 1937." It described his contribution to the Flying Tigers, and "when air action proved impossible because of damaged planes, without hesitation he assumed leadership and at great personal risk brought from other fronts the needed material. In spite of danger, he joined them in the field, and by procuring necessary supplies and providing maintenance and repairs made possible the heroic resistance which the American Volunteer Group offered in defense of Rangoon."[25]

The continued U.S. military presence in South America, meanwhile, was a priority as a bulwark against Communist advances. In Peru, the United States had constructed the Talara Air Base on property owned by International Petroleum Company, a Canadian corporation in which U.S. citizens—mainly Standard Oil shareholders—had 90 percent control. A formal agreement was never made, but the United States repeatedly assured Peru it would abandon the base completely "no later than six months after the termination of the war." Given that the Apristas were an "anti-Yankee imperialism" group, permanent occupation of the base by the United States would cause heated opposition. In addition, the land was a proven oil field, and although the Canadian company would have liked to resume drilling operations, it genuinely feared Peru would expropriate the property.[26]

Bustamante suggested a hemispheric defense program whereby Peru and the United States would jointly share the facility. He wanted an Inter-American Conference convened so all interested American republics could consent mutually to the joint use of all bases instead of Peru negotiating a unilateral agreement with the United States. Pawley knew "even if the suggestion appeared feasible to the other American republics," it would take time to reach an agreement. Talara needed repairs, and the U.S. government would not expend funds until an agreement was made. Since its purpose at Talara was to provide technical and maintenance support to the Peruvian Air Force, and not to maintain a U.S. military presence, Pawley felt the base should come under joint control.[27]

At a May 1946 State Department meeting in Washington, Pawley reported that Bustamante, as well as Haya, felt the emergency establishing Talara no longer existed, and Peru now wanted a Peruvian base commander with the U.S. presence limited to technical and operational personnel.[28] Pawley came under fire after suggesting in an interview that the United States was staying in Peru. Denouncing the U.S. military presence as serving "imperialist and capitalist interests," Communist newspapers demanded that the United States withdraw its forces and return the base to Peru.[29] At the end of May, Truman and the State Department instructed Pawley to negotiate turning over Talara to Peru and establishing a technical commission composed of three members from both countries to oversee the air base but with a Peruvian having direct command.[30]

Negotiations dragged on as Peru insisted the agreement be terminated and the air base turned over to Peru, but Pawley had a time constraint, having been appointed ambassador to Brazil.[31] He returned to Washington to brief the new ambassador to Peru, Prentice Cooper, and to attend briefings on his new posting in Brazil. Pawley and his wife left for their Miami Beach home and prepared to depart for Brazil when a call came from Truman.

"I'm sorry to have to change your itinerary, Bill, but I need badly for you to go to Peru tomorrow," Truman told him. "You know all those air bases we had for the defense of the Canal? Well, it seems that we've given them all back. But we're still going to need Talara."

"But I've just given them back to the Peruvians on your instructions," Pawley reminded the president.

"I know that," Truman replied, "but we're going to need it for another two or three years for the main defense of the Canal."

Pawley's concern was that Bustamante would find it difficult to survive politically if after receiving public acclaim for regaining control of Talara he had to reverse his position. Gen. George Marshall, who was with Truman at the time, told Pawley to remind Bustamante that defending the Panama Canal was also important to Peru.[32]

Arriving in Lima on June 3, 1946, Pawley and Edna stayed at the country club because former president Herbert Hoover had taken up residence at the embassy. Talking to Bustamante, Pawley knew he had a slight advantage because Peru could not afford to maintain Talara. He proposed that Peru would retain ownership of Talara, but the United States would provide a joint training and maintenance program with a substantial payroll funneling dollars into Peru's economy. Bustamante and his cabinet worked on the proposal into the late hours for four consecutive days so that they could hand Pawley a copy before his departure for Brazil, but they wanted the base turned over before the Peruvian Congress convened on July 28.[33] As the new ambassador to Peru, Prentice Cooper continued the negotiations until an agreement was made in which the United States relinquished control of Talara, and the Pawley proposal remained intact.[34]

Appointing Pawley as ambassador to Brazil was part of a shifting of Latin American postings within the State Department. He replaced Adolf A. Berle, Jr., who had held the post from January 1945 to February 1946.[35] Ambassador to Argentina Spruille Braden became assistant secretary of state in charge of Latin American Affairs. (Pawley felt Braden was a Communist sympathizer and later testified against him before a Senate committee.) George S. Messersmith, ambassador to Mexico and a career diplomat since 1914, succeeded Braden as ambassador to Argentina.[36] Joseph Flack, another career diplomat, became ambassador to Bolivia.

At the Rio de Janeiro Airport, the Brazilian protocol officer and fifty members of the American Embassy staff met Pawley and Edna. The diplomatic contingency in Brazil was much larger than its counterpart in Peru was, and Pawley knew directing a staff of eight hundred civilians and a military mission of the same size would require much of his time. "In the most strenuous of my years as a businessman," he wrote of his duties in Brazil, "I never worked so hard."[37] If he felt accommodations in Lima were sparse, Pawley couldn't believe what he saw in Rio.

There were no carpets, no paintings or wall decorations, and no chandeliers. "In fairness to my predecessor," Pawley wrote, "the rugs he had been expecting had gone to the bottom of the South Atlantic . . . prey of a German U-boat." Never allowing adversity to slow him down, he arranged for a shipment of personal furnishings from Miami while Edna purchased chandeliers at a local store.[38] Staff offices, each with its own duplicate filing system, were in seventeen separate buildings. Pawley convinced Washington to allocate funds from Brazil's repayment of its Lend-Lease debt for the construction of a modern twelve-story chancellery, including apartments to house newly arrived personnel until they could find permanent residences.[39]

The political situation in Brazil mirrored Peru's. President Getúlio Vargas had ruled for fifteen years and agreed prior to Pawley's arrival to hold free elections.

Opposing Vargas were air force commander Eduardo Gómes, leader of the Liberal Party, and Gen. Eurico Gaspar Dutra, a conservative. Ambassador Berle had publicly stated that Vargas would keep his promise to hold elections, which immediately brought cries against U.S. intervention and "Yanqui politics." Dutra won the election, and Vargas blamed Berle for his defeat, vowing to oppose U.S. policy in Brazilian affairs from then on.[40]

As he did in Peru, Pawley set out to meet the opposing party leader and to encourage Vargas to work with the present Brazilian administration. Through former foreign minister Oswaldo Aranha, a close friend of Vargas's, a luncheon was arranged at an out-of-the-way restaurant to avoid press coverage. Knowing business in Latin America is conducted in a leisurely and relaxed manner, Pawley spent the afternoon getting to know Vargas. In follow-up meetings, he was able to gain Vargas's respect and to convince him that the United States looked upon him as a patriot who had the best interests of his country at heart. Impressed by Pawley's sincerity, Vargas chose an inopportune moment to show his desire to cooperate.

While delivering a Fourth of July speech as the official representative of the American community, Pawley was informed that Vargas, dressed in formal wear, had presented his card at the embassy. Realizing the visit was a gesture indicating Vargas's desire to mend relations with the United States, Pawley contacted President Dutra and elicited his opinion on whether he should accept the visitor. "By all means," Dutra said. Pawley then visited Vargas's apartment to return the courtesy. "I saw prominently displayed a handsome record player that had been presented to Vargas by FDR," he recalled. An autographed photo of Roosevelt was conspicuously placed on top. The two men had a "warm chat," and Pawley felt assured that Vargas had good intentions. Vargas eventually regained the presidency and established friendly relations with the United States.[41]

As ambassador, Pawley was required to receive and make courtesy calls. Protocol demanded he call on close to seventy-five other embassies in Rio and with the ministries of the Brazilian government. "In most cases as tedious as they were time-consuming, and although they may have served a useful purpose in a more leisurely era," Pawley wrote, "such courtesies, in my opinion, might well be dispensed with for the benefit of all." He also was required to entertain guests who dropped in at the embassy during visits to Brazil. His first guest at the furniture-bare embassy was former president Hoover, who arrived two days after Pawley did. During his two years as ambassador, Pawley played host to a parade of guests, including President Truman; his wife, Bess; their daughter, Margaret; General and Mamie Eisenhower; Adm. William "Bull" Halsey; W. Averell Harriman; and *Time* magazine publisher Henry Luce.[42]

Pawley was also obligated to attend every national holiday celebration given by the other foreign embassies. Described by one Brazilian official as "a fascinating and mature lady," Edna was always by her husband's side. "Whatever Bill does," she told a reporter, "he puts his whole heart and soul into it and it's my job to keep up with him."[43] The American Embassy held formal dinners several times a month. With the entertainment budget soon depleted, Pawley dipped into his own pocket to continue the lavish gatherings. Spending his own money to entertain guests was a practice he had begun in Peru. "We heard that Pawley spent $70,000 of his own money during his ten months' tour of duty in Lima," a *Time* magazine reporter wrote. "That, on top of his $25,000 salary." Ever the gracious host, Pawley sometimes loaned his private Douglas DC-3 for guests to take an excursion into the Brazilian interior.[44]

Among dignitaries Pawley entertained, General Eisenhower visited in August 1946, and the men developed a lifelong friendship. It was Eisenhower's first trip to South America, and Pawley was determined to show the general and Mamie how well liked he was in Brazil. During their stay, the Eisenhowers were assigned a personal aide and interpreter, Maj. Vernon A. Walters, who was Pawley's assistant military attaché. Walters spoke eight languages fluently and became an invaluable asset to Pawley because he not only spoke Portuguese (Pawley did not) but also was well versed in protocol.[45]

The reception Eisenhower received from Brazilians was overwhelming. As Pawley recalled, "Thousands of people would line the streets as far as the eye could see and would applaud and shout his name as he passed."[46] During the visit Pawley arranged an embassy reception, giving his staff strict instructions to limit the guest list to seven hundred, but when seventeen hundred people showed up in a torrential rain, Pawley reversed his order and admitted everyone. The cost was more than the annual entertainment budget, so Pawley paid the extra expense from his own pocket. With the reception line stretched beyond proportions, the Eisenhowers greeted guests for hours until Pawley and Edna rescued them for a quiet dinner in their private apartment.[47]

In an unprecedented gesture, political parties in Brazil set aside their differences to welcome Eisenhower in a joint session of the Senate and Chamber of

Deputies.[48] He endeared himself to the Brazilians when he expressed his gratitude for the Brazilian army division that fought in Italy long before other Latin
American republics joined the fight. The embassy hosted a farewell reception for
the Eisenhowers before they left Brazil that was attended by four hundred guests.
Eisenhower expressed his appreciation in a personal letter to Pawley:

> I am quite sure that I have never before, on such short acquaintance, ad-
> dressed any individual by his nickname. However, as Mamie and I look
> back on our five days in Rio, we find they have been so crowded with in-
> teresting events, in all of which you and Edna have figured so prominent-
> ly, that definitely we feel the existence of a friendship that can scarcely be
> measured in matters of days or hours. . . . I hope that you will never hesi-
> tate to communicate with me instantly on any matter of common interest,
> whether the subject be official or personal.[49]

Pawley took up Eisenhower's offer when Dutra complained about U.S. military bases in Brazil flying the American flag, which was a direct protocol violation
because the bases were on Brazilian soil. Issuing a directive to cease the practice,
Pawley met resistance from an air force general who insisted on displaying the
flag. Pawley notified Eisenhower, and the commander was recalled to the States
within twenty-four hours. Before Pawley could express his gratitude, Ike thanked
Pawley for bringing the matter to his attention.[50]

Shortages of wheat supplies also plagued Brazil, and just as he had done in
Peru, Pawley set out to resolve the problem. He attended a meeting with former
president Hoover and Brazilian foreign minister João Neves da Fontura who informed him that Brazil had less than two weeks' wheat supplies and Argentina was
taking advantage by charging $3.50 a bushel. An agreement between the United
States, Brazil, and Argentina called for Brazil to sell rubber to Argentina and
Argentina to sell wheat to Brazil. The United States would not guarantee the supply of rubber, only its allocation, to Argentina, and Brazil was coming up short. The
United States also artificially supported prices—it paid Brazil sixty cents a pound
and resold it to American manufacturers at twenty-three cents—and the contract
would not end for another year. Brazil wanted Argentina to pay the same price, but
President Juan Perón felt Argentina was "being held up by Brazil." Complicating
matters, Perón had a supply-and-demand play of his own by purchasing wheat at

twenty pesos a ton from Argentine growers and reselling it to Brazil for thirty-five
pesos a ton.

"I have no desire that the United States continue to be Santa Claus," Pawley
wrote, "but wherever we have a bona fide contract, even though it be unfavorable
to us, we must carry it out to the letter."[51] Unlike his tearful pleading with Dr. Kung
to cover a mistake Pawley had made in a contract with the Chinese, when it came
to U.S. government funds, Pawley had no problem in this instance suggesting that
Washington should pay for it. The United States agreed to ship rubber to Argentina
and fulfill Brazil's obligation, but Brazil asked that the United States hold up the
shipment until Argentina shipped the wheat.[52] Meanwhile, Argentine tire companies were reaching a critical shortage of rubber and would be forced to close their
factories if supplies didn't reach them in time.[53]

Pawley next suggested the State Department authorize Brazil to sell rubber
directly to Argentina and negotiate the wheat price. "Through this process we
would be relieved of paying 60 cents for Brazilian rubber," he wrote, "that would
ultimately reach Argentina after paying freight to the United States and back."[54]
The State Department and Pawley finally seemed to be thinking along the same
line, that is, getting the tripartite agreement canceled. Realizing the United States
wanted to bail out, Brazil began negotiations with Argentina on a rubber-wheat
swap accord. The United States continued shipping Brazil's allocation of rubber
to Argentina during negotiations and Argentina sent wheat to Brazil. In September
1946, Brazil agreed to cancel the tripartite agreement, and the following month
Argentina released the United States from further commitments.[55]

Brazil's wheat problems didn't end, however; Pawley was in the middle of
another crisis, this time between the U.S. Commerce Department and Brazil.
Argentina and Brazil's pact called for 120,000 tons of wheat to be shipped monthly
for Brazil's needs. When Argentina abruptly stopped shipping wheat, Pawley requested a temporary allocation from the United States until the matter was resolved.[56] The Department of Agriculture met with Brazilian officials in Washington
and said that many European nations were in short supply of wheat as well and
would suffer if the United States gave its wheat to Brazil. Even when a new crop
was harvested in June, Brazil still would have little chance of receiving an allot-
ment.[57]

Brazil tried substituting flour for wheat in its request but ran into a bureaucratic snag. The Department of Commerce, which administered export licenses,

had imposed an embargo on flour shipments. It could place Brazil on a priority list if the State Department felt an extraordinary need for flour existed, but the latter determined that "the need does not appear to have been established in this case."[58] Complicating matters, Brazil had withdrawn from the International Emergency Food Council (IEFC) to receive a better price on its rice exports.

Pawley encouraged President Dutra to rejoin the IEFC, and he agreed, if he could do so without "losing face." Pawley also noted to the U.S. secretary of state that if Brazil ran out of wheat, "the political difficulties of the Dutra Government would be indeed serious." He reminded Secretary Marshall that the situation had taken on diplomatic overtones, and if the United States failed to offer aid, the Brazilian Communist Party would be in a position to embarrass Dutra's administration.[59] The State Department still did not want to intervene. Instead, it suggested to Pawley that the best approach would be for Brazil to rejoin the IEFC and submit a request through it for additional wheat. The department would "support it strongly," even though sources indicated "that situation is not as critical as represented by you."[60]

Pawley faced another critical issue after a telephone call from President Dutra.[61] In August 1947 the Brazilian Army purchased a half million bags of flour from the Overseas Trading Corporation, a company that had never been a flour exporter and now sought permission to ship the flour. When the flour reached New Orleans, it began deteriorating and amassing storage charges while awaiting the export license to ship it to Brazil. Dutra, who needed the Brazilian Army's support, failed to inform Pawley that one of the top army officers had received a sizable kickback on the deal.[62]

Acting on Dutra's request, Pawley contacted Secretary of the Treasury John Snyder, who said the problem was not in his bailiwick, but at the next cabinet meeting he would raise the issue. Pawley's second call was to Secretary of Agriculture Clint Anderson, who said, "We would be delighted to issue an export license." Support also came from Secretary of Commerce Averell Harriman, Bill Batt (who oversaw wheat exports), and Undersecretary of State Robert Lovett, who told Pawley: "I will get you an export license." Thinking it would be a coup for Truman to take credit, Pawley contacted Matt Connelly at the White House. He was informed the president "is delighted that this Government will issue an export license for the 40,000 tons of wheat for the Brazilian Army," and that "there will be no need to take the next month's allocation for civilian consumption."[63]

Pleased his government acted swiftly to solve the matter, Pawley notified Dutra that the flour would soon be shipped. Washington bureaucracy then ground the greased wheels to a halt. The Commerce Department notified the State Department it was "impossible to license this flour because not bought from regular exporter."[64] Dutra summoned Pawley to the Presidential Palace to ask: "Does your President have no authority?"[65] Because the flour sitting in New Orleans was about to rot, Brazil had no choice but to sell it. Mexico purchased one-third at a reduced price, and the State Department announced it would "cooperate . . . in seeing if remainder cannot be disposed of . . . to avoid possible spoilage with resultant complete loss."[66]

Livid that Truman's promise had not been honored, Pawley flew to Washington to find the root of the problem. With the cooperation of Undersecretary Lovett, an immediate investigation was started, but in the end the culprits turned out to be "a sort of self-appointed sub-cabinet of eager beavers from the State, Treasury, Commerce, Agriculture and other Departments—most of them fairly senior officials—who were in the habit of meeting weekly to decide what was best for the United States. These worthies had seized upon a few irregularities in Brazil's past wheat transactions to block the license on the grounds that its issuance would establish a precedent for laxity by other countries."[67] Although Pawley tried to get to the bottom of the mishap, he found himself mired in the closed-ranks mentality of Civil Service employees who protected their fiefdom.

When the wheat episode came to light during Senate hearings in 1961, the *Brazil Herald* applauded Pawley's efforts while chastising American bureaucracy. "We have been insisting that the ablest U.S. ambassadors abroad cannot carry out their missions without complete and understanding support from Washington," the article stated. "It is utterly illogical to maintain a first class diplomatic corps if unauthorized junior pipsqueaks can make their will prevail over the decisions of their chiefs."[68]

Butting heads with bureaucrats became a Pawley trademark, and they continually frustrated his attempts to get the job done. "Pawley does not approach us as a protocol-minded stuffed shirt," Brazilian Embassy secretary Fernando Saboia reported. "He came to us like a practical business man," Saboia added.[69] "He's the best we ever had," a U.S. businessman in Rio labeled Pawley, but diplomatic maneuvering was not his forte.[70]

10

Latin American Diplomacy

Unstable Central and South American governments provided Communists fertile ground to foment unrest among those seeking freedom from dictators and U.S. influence. Pawley was a fervent opponent of the "Red Menace" and became upset when he learned the FBI's Latin American agents were being withdrawn and replaced by an intelligence service formed within the State Department. "This actually makes the Ambassador a secret service agent in the minds of the people in the country to which he is accredited," Pawley wrote to Attorney General Tom C. Clark.[1]

Writing to J. Edgar Hoover, Pawley said, "I did everything possible while in Washington to assist in maintaining the service . . . and to express the view that the U.S. cannot afford *at this time* to lose the services of this organization and these men."[2] Attorney General Clark told him "the FBI will stay in temporarily," but eventually agents would be replaced by a new organization independent of the State Department, namely, the CIA.[3] When that transition occurred, Pawley persuaded Hoover to place the two FBI agents stationed in Brazil on leave of absence, and both were then put on Pawley's personal payroll.[4]

In January 1945, George Michanowsky, a Russian-born, naturalized U.S. citizen, had been appointed executive secretary of the Committee of Latin American Affairs of the Congress of Industrial Organizations (CIO), a trade union federation. He immediately began a public relations campaign to promote the career of U.S. ambassador to Cuba Spruille Braden. Through his American press contacts, he let it be known that the CIO wanted Braden to be ambassador to Argentina, a post Braden received later that year. But Michanowsky had a higher goal in mind for

Braden, Nelson Rockefeller's job as assistant secretary of state for Latin America. When Rockefeller was dismissed from the State Department in September 1945, Michanowsky intensified his pressure campaign by informing Secretary of State James Byrnes and Assistant Secretary Dean Acheson that "the 6,000,000 voters of the CIO" were backing Braden. Truman nominated Braden in October 1945, and the appointment was made in April 1946.[5]

The Braden-Michanowsky connection was documented in a paper prepared by a U.S. Military Intelligence undercover agent. The man who wrote it handed a copy to Pawley while he was in Washington in 1946. Realizing its importance, Pawley showed it to Eisenhower, then chief of staff of the army. It documented Michanowsky's influence in State Department matters; his Communist leanings because of the people he associated with; and his job in a powerful labor union, the CIO. The document then went to Attorney General Clark, who let J. Edgar Hoover look at it. The following morning Pawley received a call from Matt Connelly that President Truman wanted to see him at once.

"Bill, why in hell didn't you bring a document of this importance directly to me, instead of Ike or anyone else?" Truman asked.[6]

Pawley explained that since the report also detailed Eisenhower's attempts to mend relations with Argentina through Argentine general Carlos von der Becke, he felt obliged to confer with Eisenhower first. According to the report, von der Becke had written to Eisenhower and suggested that he should visit Washington to discuss U.S.-Argentine political differences. Braden knew about the letter and had disclosed its contents to Michanowsky, saying he had advised Eisenhower not to answer it. "I never wrote to General Eisenhower," von der Becke claimed. "In my opinion, 'my letter' was forged . . . when it became evident that Perón would win the presidential election, to which Braden contributed unwillingly."[7] Pawley also told Truman that when von der Becke had visited Miami in April 1946, Braden had ordered Pawley not to see him, even though they had been friends for years.[8]

Acting on the intelligence report and Pawley's input, Truman fired Braden in June 1947. Truman also felt he should let Ambassador to Argentina George Messersmith go, but Pawley believed that move was a mistake. Although Truman said he fired Messersmith because of his long and repetitious letters, which had earned him the tag "Forty-Page George," Pawley felt the real reason was that Truman wanted to placate the CIO and keep its 6 million votes.[9]

Michanowsky surfaced again, this time at Pawley's business office at Rockefeller Center. Recalling the man's name from the Braden report, Pawley invited him in without revealing he knew him by reputation. Pawley described him as "a striking-looking young man, bright as a Hollywood agent and filled with an air of self-importance to match." He wasted no time getting straight to the reason for wanting to see Pawley.

"Mr. Ambassador, I represent the CIO Political Action Committee and the Latin American Division. We like the cut of your jib. I'd like to know if we can work out some arrangements whereby you would be willing to cooperate with us."

"What in the world could I do, Mr. Michanowsky, that would be useful to you?"

"We are trying to keep abreast of all the labor problems in Latin America and we are trying to keep abreast of the Communist problems as they develop. We have to know all about these matters. That's where you come in. We could assist you if you assist us."

"In what way could you assist me?" Pawley asked, leading the man on.

"We could probably make you Assistant Secretary and we probably could make you Under Secretary."

"It is my understanding that the President of the United States and the Secretary of State are in the habit of making those appointments," Pawley declared.

"Are you forgetting, sir, that we have six million votes? That's quite a bit of political muscle in this country."

Pawley had heard enough. Threatening to throw Michanowsky out the window, Pawley advised him he should consider leaving the country as soon as possible. He also informed the CIO influence peddler that he would report their entire conversation to J. Edgar Hoover and the president. Although Pawley didn't resort to physical violence, he did follow through and reported the incident to Hoover and Truman. Three days later, Hoover phoned Pawley to advise him that Michanowsky had taken his advice and left on a six-month vacation in Mexico.[13]

Truman may have had no difficulty in making the decision to fire Braden. The previous year Braden had caused controversy concerning Argentina, which almost cost the diplomat his job. On January 26, 1946, the CIO had published a "White Book" outlining Perón's activities in Argentina and the Nazis' infiltration of Latin America. In February 1946, two weeks before the presidential elections in Argentina, the State Department published a similar volume authored by

Braden, *Consultation among the American Republics with Respect to the Argentine Situation*, which became known as the Blue Book.[11] In this detailed document, Braden accused Perón of being a Nazi sympathizer during the war. Serving in Peru at the time, Pawley said the only Lima newspaper commenting on the Blue Book was the APRA paper *La Tribuna*. "Silence of major periodicals is considered as deliberate avoidance of [a] controversial issue," Pawley informed the State Department, adding that "publication of the Blue Book was a mistake, ill-timed, and if anything may have done more harm than good."[12]

Truman wanted to arrange an inter-American conference to negotiate mutual assistance treaties, but he did not want to include Argentina. Braden opposed giving arms to Argentina until it had rid itself of the "stronghold of Hitlerism," but the Pentagon was determined to supply weapons to all Latin American republics, including Argentina.[13] "For Heaven's sake don't send us arms," a former Venezuelan cabinet officer reportedly told Braden. "The Communists are likely to take over one of these days, and if they do they'll turn them against us."[14] When Perón gained the presidency in June 1946, Messersmith took a position opposed to Braden's and urged continued support for Argentina, and both Democratic and Republican foreign policy watchdogs in Congress endorsed Messersmith's stance.[15]

Members of Congress and top U.S. Army brass began pressuring Truman to get rid of Braden, but Secretary of State Byrnes told reporters "that the Assistant Secretary of State had his full confidence and he knew that Mr. Braden also had the full confidence of Mr. Truman."[16] Publicly, Pawley said he saw "eye to eye" with Braden on Argentina, but behind the scenes he was maneuvering against him.[17]

"Sometime late in 1946, as I recall, the rumor mills had it that Pawley was gunning for my job," Braden wrote in his memoir.[18] As far back as January 1946, Braden labeled a rumor that he was resigning as "wishful thinking on the part of certain elements in Argentina," but the gossip continued.[19] Columnist Drew Pearson reported that Braden would resign before July 15, "a clear-cut victory for William D. Pawley," who "has been sniping relentlessly at Braden for months and is now slated to succeed him."[20] In October, the press reported Braden had threatened to resign in protest of the Argentine policy that Messersmith had formulated (and Pawley had endorsed), but again, Braden dismissed the rumor.[21]

Pearson reported the controversy differently. He wrote an entire *Washington Merry-Go-Round* column on the Pawley-Braden affair titled "Miami's Ambassador

Bill Pawley Denies He's after Braden's Job." According to Pearson, Braden called a staff meeting with Pawley present.

"I have invited you all in here," Braden said, "because Mr. Pawley has something to say to you."

"I want you to know," Pawley said, "that I am loyal to Mr. Braden. He's my superior, and I take my orders from him. I don't want his job, and I'm not after it."

Pearson claimed that Pawley met with Truman after the showdown, and the president promised Braden's job to him.[22]

The controversy surfaced again in November in *Newsweek* magazine. The article said Braden confronted Pawley and asked if he was seeking his job. "No," Pawley replied, but added "if Braden resigned and he were called he would of course respond." When Braden asked if Pawley had testified before the Senate Foreign Relations Committee attacking his Argentine policy, Pawley said no but added that "when questioned he had declared it unreasonable."[23]

After seeing the *Newsweek* article, Pawley "reacted violently," demanding a meeting to discuss it, and he wanted twenty diplomatic officers in Braden's section to attend. "The matter was between him and me," Braden wrote. "However, realizing how silly he would look, I conceded." At the meeting, Pawley demanded Braden write to *Newsweek* denying the story.

"That kind of letter would enlarge and extend the controversy," Braden told him. "You say you want to avoid publicity. The best thing is to ignore the article as I intend doing."

Pawley protested, saying he had never expressed his thoughts on the matter to anyone, but Braden was ready to counter. "I said that Henry Wallace had revealed Pawley's statements to me earlier and they duplicated *Newsweek*'s story." Pawley was still not satisfied.

"Bill, you told some of the senators on the Foreign Relations Committee the same intention. You should have known that one of the best ways to make something public is to talk as you did with those particular senators."

Realizing he had painted himself into a corner, Pawley stormed out, forgetting his hat. The confrontation didn't end. Years later, Pawley would resurrect his animosity toward Braden in testimony before a Senate subcommittee hearing.[24]

If Pawley was gunning for Braden's job by means of a smear campaign, that goal was short lived. Braden was a career diplomat, Pawley was not, and the State Department frowned upon anyone within its ranks using the print media to further his or her ambitions. Pawley had also been the target of adverse publicity from Drew Pearson, whom Pawley described as "a left-wing columnist of more influence than integrity."[25] Pearson claimed that, while ambassador to Peru, Pawley "applied pressure to collect the old Seligman National City Bank loan of $100,000,000 to Peru . . . , including a bribe to the son of [former] President [Augusto Bernardino] Leguia." Pearson had a prediction: "So, if Pawley takes over the key job of administering Pan-American policy, Latinos will interpret it as the end of the good neighbor policy and a reversion to the old days of when the marines did the bidding of Wall Street."[26] Pawley was irate, claiming the loan, including the reported bribe, originated long before he arrived in Peru. He went on the offensive by writing to Henry Luce, *Time* magazine publisher. Luce did not answer the letter. Instead, the editorial director of *Time*, John Shaw Billings, replied: "We do our best to counteract Drew Pearson's misinformation whenever we can, but the clipping you enclosed just seemed so inane and far-fetched that we decided to ignore it."[27]

After the war in Europe ended, Truman turned his attention to combating aggression while solidifying world peace. In Europe it came in the form of the Marshall Plan, designed to get nations back on their feet following the devastation of war. It included forming the North Atlantic Treaty Organization (NATO) to guarantee protection of U.S. allies. Latin America, although not having been a significant part of the war zone, was still looked upon as a potential breeding ground of rising nationalism, and there was concern that communism would make inroads with America's southern neighbors. Held February 21 through March 8, 1945, in Mexico City, the Inter-American Conference on Problems of War and Peace resulted in the Act of Chapultepec, which established solidarity and cooperation among the twenty-one nations. But more was needed, specifically, a mutual assistance and common defense pact.

Another conference was to be held in Rio in November 1946 that would strengthen ties between the United States and Latin American republics, but Argentina was proving to be a spoiler. When Perón assumed leadership, the Argentines still hadn't agreed to anti-Nazi provisions in the Mexico City pact, and without their ratification the new conference could not be scheduled. "There must be deeds and not merely promises," Braden told Latin American republics when Perón submitted the question to the Argentine Congress without adding his recommendation.[28] Both Pawley and Messersmith, feeling the United States should be patient and allow Argentina time to comply, recommended that no date for the conference be fixed until then.[29]

By December 1946, the conference date still had not been set, and Pawley decided to discuss the matter directly with Brazilian president Dutra. He asked if Brazil had changed its view of Argentina concerning the conference—it hadn't— so Pawley talked about Truman's bill to provide Latin American republics military aid. Pawley told Dutra that in discussing the arms bill with the Brazilian chief of staff, he was asked if Brazil might receive arms before the other republics and was questioned about the "advisability" of Argentina getting arms.[30] Secretary of State Byrnes immediately fired off a telegram to Pawley advising him that the State Department disapproved of his "initiative" and "that no further conversations along that line be undertaken without such instructions."[31]

Frustrated that his efforts to recognize problems facing Latin American countries were being ignored, Pawley sought Eisenhower's advice. After speaking with him by phone on January 13, 1947, Pawley followed up with a long letter outlining his reasons for wanting to resign as ambassador to Brazil. He would delay his decision until Marshall had succeeded Byrnes as secretary of state, but he wanted Eisenhower to know the reasons for his wanting to resign.

Pawley claimed Assistant Secretary of State for Latin America Braden was hostile toward Argentina. "Well-advised Latinos" told Pawley that Braden's policy had "contributed in a great measure to Peron's election as President." Pawley also felt the new ambassador to Argentina, George Messersmith, was not convincing the State Department that a friendlier approach would encourage Argentina to meet its obligations. If a sound, realistic policy was not formulated, "in righteous indignation, Peron may be found rapidly moving into alliances which will cause the United States many headaches for years to come."[32]

Not one to keep secrets from his boss, Eisenhower showed the letter to Marshall, who had recently been sworn in as secretary of state. Eisenhower told Pawley, "This gave me a good opportunity to tell him that it was my conviction that you were in the State Department merely because of the belief that you could serve your country and that you happened to be in such position financially that you could afford to sacrifice something in order to render such service."

Pawley wanted the State Department to call together the heads of missions for a seminar to discuss their problems, but Eisenhower suggested tabling the idea because Marshall "must concentrate very seriously on the problems that will confront him at Moscow." He advised Pawley to "sit tight for the moment" and wait until Marshall eased into his new job, but in the meantime, he should "develop logical and decisive answers."[33]

For several years, Pawley had been having stomach problems that he had been able to keep under control, but his condition began to worsen. In addition, he began to suspect his efforts in Brazil were being compromised. "I have not been able to work effectively," he wrote Attorney General Clark, "because, only too frequently, matters of top-secret nature coming from me were permitted to reach either the press or sometimes members of the Brazilian Embassy in Washington . . . usually in a form discrediting my work here."[34]

On May 31, 1947, Pawley typed a letter of resignation to Truman. Pawley expressed his regret but found it necessary to resign because of his health.[35] Instead of submitting it directly to the president, however, he sent it unsealed to Attorney General Clark, asking him to read it before sealing and passing it on to Truman.[36] Two weeks later, Pawley changed his mind and frantically tried contacting Clark, but he had left on a trip to San Francisco. Pawley asked Clark's secretary to destroy the letter to Truman, but word of its existence had already leaked. The White House was able to deny it had received the letter, because Clark hadn't delivered it.[37] Clark had chosen to show the letter to Marshall first, so Truman had not seen it.[38]

Although he had second thoughts about resigning, Pawley still felt he needed rest. "I am not feeling at all well," he wrote to Clark, "and I may find it necessary to either drop out or request a leave of absence of sufficient time to try to get myself in shape." Knowing how important the upcoming Rio Conference was, and by this point Braden was out of the State Department, chances were good that Argentina would take its place in cooperating with other countries in the hemisphere. "I spend much time trying to convince Brazilians of the desirability of seeking friendly relations with Argentina," he wrote, feeling that "these countries can do much toward bringing about better relations and understanding." Pawley's decision to "get myself in shape to hold on" was based on the hope that the Rio Conference would take place soon. He added, "If I do not see any material improvement within a month or so, I may find it unavoidable to step out."[39]

Whatever physical shape he was in, Pawley had managed to shuttle between Washington and Rio four times already for consultations with Truman about the conference.[40] It was scheduled to open August 15, 1947, and as ambassador to the host country, Pawley was responsible for many of the preparations for the long list of delegation members and their staffs. Pawley quoted even Truman as being "very anxious to go." The president's visit, however, was scheduled at the close of the conference to avoid adverse publicity in the event it "became involved in serious difficulties and . . . unable to reach its goal."[41]

The United States sent a strong delegation headed by Secretary of State Marshall. Among the delegates were two U.S. senators—Texas Democrat Tom Connally and Foreign Relations Committee chairman Arthur Vandenberg—UN representative Warren Austin, and a group of political and military advisers.[42] In the event Truman did attend, Pawley offered—and Truman accepted—the services of Major Walters as interpreter.[43] Marshall had his own interpreter, a senior ambassador acquainted with most of the foreign ministers, but as Marshall made the rounds to call on delegates, the interpreter monopolized most of the conversation.[44] Marshall had been criticized in Moscow for "not mingling," so Pawley assigned Walters as his interpreter.[45]

The Rio de Janeiro Conference for the Maintenance of Continental Peace and Security would be deemed a success, as it resulted in a treaty to "provide for effective reciprocal assistance to meet armed attacks against any American State." An armed attack against any of the countries would be considered an attack against all. Each nation formally condemned war, agreeing to settle controversies between them peacefully and to refer disputes to the United Nations.[46]

Pawley's strong suit as a host who provided top-notch housing facilities and lavish social functions was fully tested, and he lived up to his reputation. Aside from providing living quarters for the delegates and their wives, he arranged for high-level communications and transportation. He secured the use of a private estate in the western part of the state of São Paulo where Marshall and his guests could relax, hunt, and fish.[47] During the conference, Marshall received an invitation to attend a formal ball in Rio to honor Eva Perón, but he declined in order to prepare a speech he was giving the next day. He asked Pawley to attend and represent the United States.[48]

Accompanied by his wife, Bess, and daughter, Margaret, Truman arrived aboard the president's plane *Independence*, landing at Galeão, an island airport in the bay of Rio. Pawley, Edna, Marshall, and his wife, Katherine, greeted the president as he and his family stepped off the plane. Taking a launch across the bay, the group was enthusiastically welcomed by crowds lining the streets (Truman estimated it was more than a million people). Brazil issued a postage stamp for the occasion, banners lined the route, and everywhere there were huge posters of Truman.[49]

The following morning, the party drove the forty-five-mile trip through winding mountain roads to Petrópolis, where Truman was scheduled to close the conference. After his speech, which was warmly received, Truman returned to Rio to receive five hundred guests aboard the battleship USS *Missouri* in the harbor. Fog and heavy winds dampened the occasion, but Truman managed to greet delegates and Brazilian officials and receive accolades from the Brazilian foreign minister.

Despite the foggy and rainy weather over the next two days, Pawley's tightly planned but pleasurable schedule ensured Truman made the most political mileage possible from the visit. Pawley even provided entertainment for Margaret Truman and arranged an evening at the opera. With her Secret Service escort and Pawley's niece Anita, Margaret, who envisioned an opera career of her own, attended a performance of Beniamino Gigli in *Tosca*. After they had left for the opera, Truman said to Pawley, "I'd like to go there myself and hear some real music." During his stay in Brazil, Truman had been bombarded with repeated strains of the "Missouri Waltz," which he hated. "I don't like the damned thing," he later confessed, "but I've had to listen to it over 40,000 times because people think I do."[50]

Without alerting the Secret Service (at Truman's request), Truman, Pawley, and Chief of Staff Adm. William Leahy sneaked out of the embassy and entered the opera house through a side door. Using a private elevator, they reached the unoccupied governor's box and watched the remainder of the first act and part of the second.[51] The cast took six curtain calls until the members discovered the tumultuous ovation was for Truman. When he stood to acknowledge the greeting, the Secret Service men in Margaret Truman's box were mortified to see the president had no escort of his own. Truman quietly left during the second act and returned to the embassy.[52]

Not everything went smoothly during Truman's visit. He was invited to a luncheon at the home of Ernesto Gonzales Fontes, a wealthy Brazilian banker who had entertained Roosevelt during his 1936 visit to Brazil.[53] The home, Gaveo Pequena (Little Crow's Nest), in the Tijuca Mountains could only be reached by a corkscrew road.[54] Pawley and Leahy were in the car with Truman when it suddenly veered on the wet-clay road and skidded to a stop. The car's left rear wheel was hanging over the retaining wall, two feet from a sheer drop into a deep ravine.

Despite pleas from the Secret Service escort, Truman refused to get out. While he and Pawley sat in the car, Leahy joined the Secret Service men and Brazilian military police who pushed and heaved until the car gained traction. "I'm all right," Truman responded when asked about the incident. "I have done the same thing myself many times on country roads." With everyone back in the car, the entourage continued on to the luncheon.[55]

After celebrating Brazil's Independence Day and attending a luncheon at the American Embassy, Truman boarded the *Missouri* for the trip home.[56] Senator Vandenberg praised the Rio Conference as being "one thousand percent worthwhile," and *Time* magazine praised Pawley for "his thorough background job in advance of the Conference," noting he "had done a lot to pave the way for the most successful hemispheric meeting in years."[57] As Senate Foreign Relations Committee chairman, Vandenberg considered the Rio Treaty "to be of vital security value" and pressed his fellow senators to approve it. After four days of hearings, it was ratified by a 72–1 vote.[58]

Pawley's stomach problems, meanwhile, worsened to the point where he could no longer ignore them. On September 28, 1947, he flew to the United States for treatment.[59] "The stomach troubles that had plagued me for so long forced me into the Mayo Clinic," Pawley wrote.[60] Physicians ran a battery of tests, and after a thorough examination they determined he had ulcers. He was advised to take an extended leave of absence, but against their wishes he returned to Rio in December.[61]

Having withdrawn his letter of resignation and with his hosting obligations for visiting dignitaries out of the way, Pawley turned his attention back to his ambassadorial duties. Many concerns with Brazilian-U.S. relations still needed to be faced, and although continuing to suffer from stomach ailments, Pawley poured his energy into keeping abreast of the problems.

11

El Bogotazo

Back in the United States to "undergo health treatment," Pawley worked on a new U.S.-Brazilian trade agreement.[1] Shuttling between his homes in Miami and outside The Plains, Virginia, he also visited the Lahey Clinic in Boston. His doctor told him to get complete rest and slow down his schedule, but Pawley couldn't conceive of relaxing.[2] He tried altering his diet by eating soft foods, but he still had difficulty digesting them. Work was the only activity taking his mind off his medical problems.

The Rio Conference had strengthened Washington's military ties with Latin America, and now the Truman administration turned its attention to formalizing its political and economic relations at the Pan-American Conference to be held in Bogotá, Colombia, in April 1948. Headed by Secretary of State Marshall, the U.S. delegation would include Secretary of Commerce W. Averell Harriman; Secretary of the Treasury John W. Snyder; Hawthorne Arey, president of the Export-Import Bank; and a strong contingent from the diplomatic corps. Pawley was selected to help Marshall in the preparatory work.[3]

The dominant theme stressed in Bogotá would be the "role which private capital might play in the economic development of Latin America . . . through governmental development corporations financed by foreign and local government capital." This effort was to be accomplished by chartering a new agency within the United Nations called the Organization of American States (OAS). Latin American countries attending the conference wanted to establish an inter-American development bank with funds provided by the United States. Truman hoped to avoid having to offer direct U.S. aid, but he did announce he would ask Congress to target an additional $500 million for the Export-Import Bank specifically for Latin American loans.[4]

Months before the Bogotá Conference, Pawley went to see Secretary Marshall to tell him that things were going badly in Latin America. The *latinos* were sore because they felt that the United States was neglecting them in favor of Europe. Pawley expressed his opinion that "it is essential that we be prepared at Bogotá to offer a very constructive program of assistance," and he had a plan.[5]

Secretary Marshall's answer was prompt. "O.K., Bill," Marshall told him. "You're elected." The first part of his plan was to conduct a public relations campaign directed toward Latin American countries to show that funds channeled into the European Economic Plan would result in money being spent in Latin America for $1.9 billion of food and minerals for Europe. The second phase was to establish an Inter-American Bank for industrial development. Although Pawley wanted the United States to finance the bank, he didn't know that Washington had already decided against it.[6]

Pawley's first stop was at the State Department, where he presented his thoughts at a roundtable discussion on an economic program for Latin America. He felt these nations had put "tremendous pressure" on the United States to provide economic assistance, and by the United States not taking a more "positive line," it was confirming their belief that U.S. interests lay in Europe, not Latin America.[7] He reminded those present that an Inter-American Bank project had been proposed in 1940, but never ratified, "and still is pigeonholed in Senate committee."[8] Seeking to revive the program and to provide $2 billion for economic development, Pawley felt it was important enough even "if this requires the creation of a special agency to handle it."[9] After dinner at the White House with the group that had accompanied Truman to Rio the previous September, he outlined his proposal to Chief of Staff William D. Leahy. While he thought it was "a very interesting study," Leahy did not offer any thoughts on how to accomplish it.[10]

Pushing for the Inter-American Bank proposal, Pawley contacted William McChesney Martin, Jr., chairman of the Export-Import Bank. Martin thought establishing a separate entity for Latin American loans was "unwise and of doubtful practicability," but he did suggest an increase in the lending authority of the Export-Import Bank to assist in making loans to Latin American countries.[11] Sensing a compromise, Pawley wrote to Truman about it and suggested "it would go a long way in creating a much more favorable climate for the negotiations at

Bogotá." Pawley's original proposal to Martin for $300 million was increased to $500 million when he presented it to Truman.[12] However, when the announcement was later made at the Bogotá Conference, "there was not a single handclap or other reaction." Latin representatives may have felt it was "small potatoes" compared to funds being poured into the European recovery effort. The U.S. delegation reportedly "sat in uncomfortable silence" until the session ended.[13]

While preparing for the Bogotá Conference, Pawley wrote a letter to Secretary Marshall and offered a proposal he felt might improve State Department objectives. He suggested amending the Foreign Service Act of 1946 to create a new position of career ambassador. "The suggested amendment would make it possible to give to men . . . a title which would add official prestige to their personal prestige." Pawley was convinced it would improve the financial position of those asked to serve their country at low salaries. The new title would alleviate political pressure to appoint unqualified persons whenever a post became vacant, he wrote, adding there would still be a place for political appointees. "A well fitted man from outside of the ranks of the Foreign Service can bring to it new ideas and, often, special qualifications not usually found in the career service."[14] His proposal may have seemed sound to Marshall, but it never took hold.

Pawley also doubted the Bogotá Conference would be as successful as the Rio Conference unless the United States offered "a massive blood transfusion of dollar assistance." Feeling the conference should be postponed until a monetary policy could be worked out in advance, Pawley met with a group of prominent financial and industrial leaders on February 11, 1948, at the State Department. The meeting focused on two issues—should the conference be held on schedule, and what should be done about Latin American credit problems?

Although the majority felt the conference should be delayed until the United States developed a sound financial aid policy, the participants were divided in their recommendations. Expanding the lending authority of the Export-Import Bank, establishing a special Inter-American Bank, and creating a development corporation with equal contributions from the United States and the Latin American republics were all suggested, but all Congress would approve was a $500 million increase in the Export-Import Bank's lending authority.

Before the Bogotá Conference, Pawley also had submitted his resignation as ambassador to Brazil on February 5, 1948. In his letter to Truman, Pawley asked that the resignation take effect March 30 because of his health, but he offered to assist Marshall with the conference.[15] Truman accepted Pawley's resignation "with reluctance." The president credited him with his "indefatigable labors" at the Rio Conference and closed with a personal note thanking him for the "charming hospitality and innumerable kindnesses" that he had extended to Truman's family during their Brazilian trip.[16]

Appraising Pawley's tenure as ambassador to Brazil, *Time* magazine noted that "often he lost patience because Brazilians did not buy his ideas as quickly as he would have liked." The article said, "He had little to show for his two years," except for background work on the Rio and Bogotá Conferences, "and often his rear was harassed by confusion (or worse) in the State Department."[17]

Despite *Time*'s critique, others felt differently about Pawley. The Brazilians awarded him the Grand Order of the Southern Cross, an honor accorded to ambassadors with at least two years of service in Brazil. Because of Pawley's "outstanding service," the foreign minister of Brazil said he "was most happy to make an exception in this case." President Ralph E. Motley of the American Chamber of Commerce for Brazil, an organization of American businessmen, asked Truman to appoint someone "as close as possible to 'Bill Pawley' specifications"; a man with "broad business experience and international background." Truman replied, "I sincerely hope we can get an Ambassador who will fill Bill's shoes—that will be a hard job."[18] His replacement was Herschel V. Johnson, deputy U.S. representative in the United Nations Security Council.[19]

Before going to Bogotá, Pawley and Edna stopped in Rio to bid farewell to Brazilian friends and arrange to ship their personal belongings to the United States. While in Rio, Pawley contacted Ambassador to Colombia Willard L. Beaulac to inquire about suitable housing while in Bogotá. He found them a house at $4,000 a month, and Pawley accepted it even though he felt the rent was outrageously high. They spent Easter in Caracas, Venezuela, with Walter Donnelly and his wife and traveled with them to Colombia. Upon arrival, Pawley found the house he had rented was not only cramped and uncomfortable but also decorated in a hideous purple. Donnelly's wife, a native of Colombia, found them more suitable accommodations and at a more reasonable $600 a month.[20]

George Marshall and his party arrived in Bogotá on March 29, the day before the conference began. The CIA office in Colombia had received word that terrorists planned to bomb Marshall's car en route from the airport. The message was sent to

Washington, but through a bureaucratic mix-up at the State Department, it never reached Marshall. The Colombian chief of national security wisely arranged for a circuitous route, and Marshall arrived without incident.[21]

While Pawley was laying the groundwork for a successful conference, others were preparing to disrupt the proceedings. Latin American Communist leaders planned a threefold attack: embarrassing the United States by demonstrating against the conference; overthrowing the democratic government of the host country, Colombia; and assassinating political leaders, including George Marshall. What resulted was chaos and anarchy, costing millions in property damage and the loss of several thousand lives. Among the participants in the uprising, which came to be known as el Bogotazo in the Latin American press, was a relatively unknown follower of Marxism from Cuba who was attempting to make his views heard in the political arena: Fidel Castro.

Colombia had two major political parties. President Mariano Ospina Pérez led the Conservative Party, while Jorge Eliécer Gaitán, a rabble-rousing orator who had made unsubstantiated charges against Ospina, led the Liberal Party, the majority in Congress. With a free press and a highly educated and patriotic citizenry, Colombia's political arena was active and sometimes volatile. Adding fuel to the fire, when Ospina announced the bipartisan coalition delegation representing Colombia at the conference, Gaitán's name was not on the list. Liberals threatened to boycott the conference and called for dissolution of the National Union, the coalition under which Ospina held office.[22]

Two months earlier, Ambassador Beaulac reported to the State Department evidence that Communists planned to disrupt the conference. His report said systematic outbreaks of violence and protests were clear indications that the Communists had organized efforts to wreck the conference. The report included incidents of President Ospina's car being attacked in downtown Bogotá and of workmen, whose employment was ending after completing public works, stoning members of Congress.[23] The CIA representative in Colombia also filed detailed reports warning of an insurrection being prepared, including a particular caution that a plot to assassinate George Marshall had been revealed.[24]

Days before the conference, students from several Latin American countries arrived in Colombia to hold an anti-imperialist, student-led counterconference that was scheduled to coincide with the Bogotá Conference and demonstrate against it. Rafaél del Pino and Fidel Castro checked into the Hotel Claridge, while two other

Cuban students accompanying them, Enrique Ovares Herrera and Alfredo Guevara (no relation to "Che"), stayed at a rooming house.[25] "I conceived the notion of making the students meeting simultaneous with that of the OAS," Castro recalled, "and in the same location, Bogotá. The idea for organizing the congress was mine."[26]

As the opposition leader, Gaitán saw an opportunity to embarrass the administration. When he heard of the students' plans, he invited them to meet and discuss their ideas. Castro and del Pino arrived at Gaitán's law office April 7 at 10:30 a.m. and were warmly received. Eloquently explaining the objectives of the student congress, Castro so impressed the Colombian leader that Gaitán's daughter later recalled, "My father was going to give them a *salón de asamblea* in one of the public buildings for their student congress." Gaitán gave them copies of a selection of his speeches and scheduled a second meeting April 9 at 2:00 p.m.[27]

On the day he was to meet again with Castro and del Pino, Gaitán left his office for a scheduled luncheon with Rómulo Betancourt, leader of the radical, socialist Democratic Action Party in Venezuela. On the way, Gaitán was fatally shot several times by Juan Roa Sierra, a shabbily dressed, unshaven Colombian who had once been in an insane asylum. Sierra may have had a personal motive for the assassination. As an attorney, Gaitán had argued for and received a not guilty verdict for the killer of Sierra's uncle.[28] When policemen pursued Sierra as he fled the scene, an angry crowd cornered him. Bootblacks used their shoeshine boxes to smash his face to a bloody, unrecognizable pulp, despite efforts by police to stop them. Swelling in size and intensity, the mob dragged the bloodied corpse through the streets of Bogotá shouting, "*Al palacio* . . . To the Palace! Let the bosses see the barbarian assassins hired by the Government!"[29]

A police report detailed Castro and del Pino's activities during the Bogotá Conference. Filed a year later by Colombian "Detective #6" to the chief of the Intelligence Services, the report is noteworthy because it links Castro, who was not well known, with the assassination of Gaitán. Assigned to protect President Ospina while attending a play at the Colón Theatre on April 3, Detective #6 apprehended Castro and del Pino as they threw propaganda leaflets to the audience. Taking them into custody, Detective #6 brought them to the Hotel Claridge, where he found more pamphlets and papers in their room, including a letter of recommendation from Betancourt.

Denied permission to lift their passports, Detective #6 ordered the Cubans to report to the National Police the following Monday. When they failed to appear,

Detective #6 went to their hotel room. Castro and del Pino were there, and the detective noticed a photograph of Gaitán sitting on a table. The next day, the chief of the Alien Section informed Castro and del Pino that their activities could be considered illegal. After promising to cease, they were released. Detective #6 reported that on the morning of the assassination he saw Castro and del Pino seated at a table in a café. "Moments later," he reported, ". . . I saw del Pino standing in the door of the Colombia Cafe, talking with a shabbily dressed individual whose photograph would later appear in the newspapers as the murderer of Dr. Gaitán."[30]

Other investigations, including a Scotland Yard report, concluded Castro may not have been involved in Gaitán's death. "We dismiss, on the evidence before us," the report stated, "as untenable any theory that contact which the two Cubans [Castro and del Pino] may have had with Roa was part of any premeditated conspiracy. . . . The behavior of the Cubans . . . was scarcely that of men privy to a desperate plot demanding the utmost secrecy and reticence." The report concluded Juan Roa Sierra had acted alone, and there was no evidence he had previous contact with Communists.[31]

Mob hysteria reached frenzied proportions after reports circulated of Gaitán's death. The uprising stemmed from a combination of Communist-organized disruption and the lower classes' dissatisfaction over living conditions and anger over the death of their hero. The mixture unleashed looting, killing, and property damage that shocked the world in its magnitude. "Almost everyone had a weapon of some kind in his hand," Willard Beaulac wrote. "The looting was organized and systematic."[32]

Joining a crowd entering a police station, Castro, like others, looked for weapons. All the rifles had been taken, so he walked out with a shotgun and a cartridge belt with tear gas shells. When a police officer began forming a squad of men, Castro joined them. The officer gave Castro his loaded rifle to replace the shotgun. Leaving the station, Castro separated from the squad and joined a crowd heading toward the palace.[33]

Even the police, the only armed force in Bogotá, joined the revolutionaries "almost to a man," giving the mob increased strength. A directing hand behind the mob became evident when the only buildings targeted for destruction were the Chancellery, the Palace of Justice, and the offices of the conservative newspaper, *El Siglo*. Even the historic home of Simón Bolívar, a national shrine, was torched.

All radio stations were overrun and occupied but not destroyed, as well as every place of recreation, such as cinemas and theaters.[34]

During el Bogotazo, riots, demonstrations, and attempted coups broke out in several South American countries. They were seemingly linked to the Bogotá uprising and coordinated to offer support to the attempted overthrow of the Colombian government. Police in Paraguay arrested Communist leaders and confiscated a radio transmitter along with five thousand pamphlets detailing a planned revolution in the country. University students in Ecuador organized a demonstration protesting their government. Police in Santiago, Chile, arrested ten persons implicated in a Communist plot against the government scheduled for May 1.[35]

Rioters in Bogotá poured through the downtown district, upending trolley cars and looting stores. The city was under a state of siege while residents hid for protection and bodies of the dead lay in the streets for hours. Priests at Our Lady of Carmen Church armed themselves with rifles to protect the French nuns residing there. Rebel snipers took up positions in high towers to fire on loyal troops attempting to restore order.[36]

"When this started," Edna Pawley wrote, "we had planned to go to the Plaza Bolivar to do some shopping. . . . Fortunately, Secretary Marshall drove by the house for a visit . . . otherwise, we would have been in the midst of all the rioting."[37]

Hearing of Gaitán's death, Ambassador Beaulac asked Second Secretary Roy Rubottom, who lived close by, to accompany him to the American Embassy. As Beaulac reported,

> We were within a block of the building when we saw approaching us a mass of frenzied humanity that filled the street solidly. There was no going against such a current. We started to turn down a street to the right but stopped when we saw that it also was blocked by a crowd of people who likewise were approaching us. We turned and retraced our steps, keeping well ahead of the advancing mob but being careful not to hurry.[38]

They never made it to the embassy; instead, they headed to an apartment building housing most of the American delegation's staff. Beaulac called the embassy and was told the staffers there were virtual prisoners and fearful of leaving.

Pawley, Walter Donnelly, Edna, and Marshall were having lunch, unaware of the trouble brewing in the heart of the city. After Marshall left, Grady Matthews and

Jerry Grimes, Pawley's pilot and copilot, arrived at the house to report the distur-
bances. Donnelly and Pawley immediately headed for the conference headquarters,
but they came upon a mob of several thousand people tearing down the flags of the
twenty-one nations attending the conference that lined the street. Realizing it was
futile to continue, Pawley ordered the driver to return to his residence. Listening to
the radio for any news, Pawley heard a voice say, "This is Fidel Castro from Cuba.
This is a Communist revolution. The President has been killed, all of the military
establishments in Colombia are now in our hands. The Navy has capitulated to
us, and this revolution has been a success."[39] The name meant nothing to Pawley
at the time, but it stuck in his mind because he recalled having known a family of
photographers named Castro when he was a boy in Cuba.[40]

Pawley is the only person who claimed to have heard Castro's radio broadcast,
and he never reported the incident through official channels. Ambassador Beaulac
did report that the National Radio Broadcasting Company had been seized by "a
group of day students."[41] In an interview thirty-four years after the uprising, Castro
said, "We decided to go and help the students who were at the National Radio
Broadcasting Company. . . . We did not know exactly where it was located. . . .
When we reached there, they [soldiers] began to fire at us. . . . We could not do
anything to liberate the radio, and we decided to go to the University." Castro
claimed he gave a speech to a group of soldiers from a bench opposite the Ministry
of War building.[42]

Radio stations continued broadcasting, filled with rabble-rousing speeches inciting mobs to more violence. An announcement proclaimed President Ospina had
been killed (untrue) and the Presidential Palace completely destroyed (also false).
Verbal attacks were leveled against the United States, blaming it for Gaitán's death,
and one rebel-controlled station gave instructions on how to construct Molotov
cocktails.[43]

With Gaitán's assassination and Bogotá's ensuing riots, most Americans sought
cover and were afraid to wander out until help arrived. "Our cook left the first
night," Edna Pawley wrote, "and never did come back." Over the next three days,
the Pawley household made do with tinned goods, rice, and potatoes, which eventually ran out, and the family was "reduced to Champagne and pâté de foie gras."[44]

Concerned that President Ospina's life was in grave danger, his advisers
begged him to leave the city. "I gave the order consequently to defend the Palace
inch by inch," he said. "I observed that I would remain at the presidential desk be-

cause I wished, at the supreme moment, to die in the place of my usual activities."[45] Liberal Party leaders demanded his resignation, but Ospina refused. During an all-night conference, he finally agreed to a coalition government with Darío Echandía, Gaitán's successor as Liberal Party leader, as the minister of state and another liberal, Gen. Germán Ocampo Herrera, as minister of war.[46] Ospina's refusal to bow to the mob may have been a deciding factor in quelling the revolution.

With the Bogotá police siding with the mob, the only hope to end the killing and looting was to call in the army. The uprising coincided with most of the Colombian Army engaged in military exercises far from the city, but by 11:00 a.m. on April 10, enough units were mustered for troops and tanks to enter the city. The American Embassy had been set ablaze with many of the staff personnel still inside. Fortunately, because of lack of oxygen in the high altitude and a steady rain, the fire only reached the third floor.[47]

Food supplies were running short, and it looked as though it would be days before the city would be safe enough to get trucks through. Pawley was not one to stand by idly. He dispatched Major Walters to the airport to find his pilot, Grady Matthews. Wearing his uniform to facilitate passing through army barricades, Walters found the pilot and returned. When they arrived, Pawley took a wad of money from his pocket and counted out $5,000. He told Matthews, "I want you to fly to Panama. Buy about twenty hams, twenty turkeys, twenty pots of caviar, and twenty pots of foie gras."

"What are you going to do with all this, Pawley?" George Marshall inquired.

"General, these delegations are living on Army rations. They think they are in a state of siege. If I can get them some of the luxuries of life, they will settle back and vote to keep the conference here."

When Matthews returned from Panama with the supplies, Pawley made the rounds to visit each delegation and distribute the food.[48]

While the city was in ashes, half of the conference delegates met at the quarters of the leader of the Honduran delegation to decide if they should stay. Argentina and Cuba both urged leaving, but Marshall was adamant on continuing.[49] The decision was made to carry on at a local high school library, where twenty-five folding chairs were set up for the delegates.[50] Conference staffs installed telephone and telegraph equipment and trucked in necessary files for the sessions. "I think that most of the Delegates are now fully aware of the sincerity of the American Delegation's desire to reach an agreement," Pawley wrote Truman.[51]

When Pawley applied to the State Department for reimbursement for the food he had purchased, his request was denied since no disbursement officer had approved it. The IRS refused to consider it a bad debt because doing so would mean the State Department would be rated a poor credit risk. He was never reimbursed. When Marshall heard the Colombian troops were not properly dressed for the cold and rain, he had four thousand raincoats flown in from Panama. Receiving a $16,000 bill for the raincoats, Marshall sent it to the American Red Cross for payment. When he became head of the Red Cross in 1949, Marshall found the unpaid bill and routed it to the Department of Defense. When named secretary of defense in 1950, Marshall found the same unpaid bill coming across his desk. "Hell," the general said, "I guess we will have to pay it."[52]

Although the riots' death toll reached several thousand and a third of Bogotá was destroyed, many felt the conference achieved its goals. In addition to establishing the OAS, the treaty provided for safeguarding foreign investments against expropriation. Before the conference, few delegations supported an anti-Communist resolution, but the riot was instrumental in changing their position.[53] "I would be glad to challenge any one who would attempt to define the Bogotá Conference as anything but a magnificent success, a great achievement, and in the spirit of solidarity," Pawley declared.[54]

Others disagreed. "The basic trouble is that we really have much less in common with these people than we like to pretend," a nondelegate observed.[55]

With Colombian police after them, Castro and del Pino hid in the Cuban Embassy until Dr. Guillermo Belt, ambassador to Washington, made arrangements to get them out of the country.[56] "We heard the President of Colombia announcing over the radio that Fidel Castro and Rafaél del Pino were responsible for the riots," del Pino said in an interview ten years later, "and we drove immediately to the Cuban embassy without our baggage."[57] The revolution in Colombia had failed, but Castro would be heard from again.

With his tenure in South America over, Pawley could look back with pride at his involvement in Latin American affairs. As one writer summarized, "By the end of 1948, the Closed Hemisphere was complete as a formal system. The Rio Treaty provided the military framework for the system, while the OAS Charter and the Economic Agreement of Bogotá provided the political and economic framework. All non-American military and political power had been successfully excluded from the hemisphere."[58]

After the conference, the Pawleys left for Los Angeles to visit Pawley's mother, stopping along the way in Guatemala and Mexico City. Back in the United States, they stayed at their farm in Virginia's hunt country for a well-deserved rest. "We are *FREE* people now though," Edna wrote to a friend, "and that is a wonderful feeling."[59]

PART IV
World Traveler and Miami Transit

12

Spain, a Movie Star, and India

The euphoria of feeling free may have been a bit dramatic for Edna because she and her husband would continue to lead an active life filled with responsibilities. On the home front, Pawley took time out to attend the wedding of his son Clifton to Eugenia Yang DePass on June 17, 1948.[1] President and Mrs. Truman received an invitation but regretfully declined.[2] At an Indian Creek Country Club (Miami) reception, Pawley presented Eugenia with a platinum wristwatch with diamonds. The bride's father, a U.S. Army colonel on duty in Peking, couldn't attend, but he gave the couple a honeymoon trip to Europe and India. The couple returned to Atlanta, where Clifton was in his senior year at Georgia Tech.[3]

When Truman decided to seek another term in the White House, Pawley became part of the election campaign team. During the summer of 1948 one of the problems the members faced was money, specifically, where to get it and who was to be in charge of the finance committee. "People didn't think that Truman was going to win so why back a losing horse," Matt Connelly recalled.[4] Small contributions were coming in, but checks from big contributors were not.

A White House meeting was held July 22 to select committee members and determine the use of the limited funds.[5] Pawley attended and listened as Cornelius V. Whitney's name was mentioned for finance chairman. Members seriously considered Assistant Secretary of the Air Force Whitney, but they dropped his name when they determined it would be difficult for him to carry both positions at the same time.[6]

No one seemed to want the position, so Connelly arranged for "some of the leading fund raising boys" to meet with Truman. Pawley suggested he be given the position but a few days later changed his mind. "I believe Mr. Pawley started reading the Gallup polls," Connelly recalled. "I think he began to think that the chances for him raising the dough were a little dim and he didn't want any part of it."[7] Attorney General Clark recalled Pawley "didn't enjoy the confidence that the people put out for publication. I don't think that he was asked."[8] In the end, Louis Johnson received the nod.

The committee still counted on Pawley, however, for personal contributions and to solicit funds from wealthy friends. In a telegram to Pawley, Johnson wrote, "What we need are contributions to finance this campaign. Still counting on you."[9] But that same day, referring to Pawley, Johnson informed Connelly, "This bird has not produced anything yet. Thought you ought to know this because we are going to keep on needling him."[10]

When Pawley learned of the letter, he fired off a telegram to Johnson and let him know "your request for Ed to needle me is thoroughly out of place." He added, "If you will check the records you will find there are many others whom you might needle."[11] Two days later, Truman was in Miami to address the American Legion, and Pawley told him, "I had already personally advanced $15,000 toward the campaign." He then said that he had "had very little opportunity to do anything further," owing to his trips to Spain.[12]

George Marshall had suggested the trips to Spain and invited Pawley to serve as an adviser at the Third Regular Session of the United Nations General Assembly in Paris. Heeding the call, Pawley and Edna left August 4, 1948, for a few days in London first.[13] Marshall asked Pawley, once he arrived in Paris, to visit Spain and have an informal talk with Spanish leader Francisco Franco. He wanted Pawley to sound him out on the possibility of Spain forming a military treaty with the United States or the future-planned NATO, with the objective being to secure military bases within Spanish territory.

Spain had already made overtures through its Foreign Office regarding the possibility of allowing the United States to establish military bases in the Canary and Balearic Islands or even within Spain itself.[14] The unofficial visit would be confidential, and Pawley would not be traveling as an accredited diplomat or be allowed to carry any papers concerning the purpose of his visit. "I was to memorize the questions . . . ," Pawley recalled. "Nor was I to disclose the nature of my assignment to anyone but Franco."[15]

The mission was a delicate matter because the free world community was treating Spain as an unruly child. During World War II, Franco supported the Axis powers because they had aided him during the Spanish Civil War; however, Franco limited Spain's participation to one legion fighting alongside the Germans in Russia. Churchill stated he was looking "forward to increasingly good relations with Spain," but he was defeated for reelection and replaced by a Labor government that was hostile to Franco.[16] France was also opposed to Franco and had joined the United States and Great Britain in a UN resolution to exclude Spain's membership until Franco was ousted. Eleanor Roosevelt, still commanding a presence in the Democratic Party, was an avid supporter of Spanish Republican exiles.

With this scenario and equipped with nothing more than his skillful ability to negotiate and his fluent Spanish, Pawley set out to do the impossible. Presenting his card to Alberto Martín Artajo, the Spanish foreign minister, Pawley took his time during the conversation, adopting the Spanish way and talking around the subject of his visit while waiting for the right moment. Artajo seemed pleased with the respectful approach and soon extended an invitation to meet Franco.

On the evening of September 11, 1948, Pawley arrived at the San Sebastián hilltop home of the generalissimo, expecting an audience with the Spanish leader of no more than a half hour. The meeting lasted three hours, during which Pawley broached a variety of subjects. They discussed Spain's policy toward political prisoners and religious freedom for foreigners, with Franco's offering that neither presented a problem with him. Pawley asked if Franco would join NATO or some other bilateral military pact with the United States. He had no interest in joining NATO, but Franco would allow troops in the country to defend it against Communist aggression if they were commanded by Spanish or American officers, not French or British officers.[17]

"All I can give you is bases and men," Franco stressed. "You will have to furnish all military equipment, transportation, supplies, and modern weapons."

It was a generous offer, Pawley thought, but he said he needed to know what Franco wanted in return. It was a simple request: He wanted Secretary of State Marshall to use his influence to repeal the UN resolution branding him "an enemy of world peace." Pawley suggested that Franco send a team of diplomats to Paris with that objective in mind, and he in turn would speak to Marshall. Franco reminded Pawley that Truman opposed his regime, to which Pawley remarked that with the upcoming election, all indications pointed to Thomas E. Dewey becoming president. Pawley expressed his feelings that Marshall would be able to convince the new administration of the wisdom of their discussed military arrangement.

Before seeing his guest off, Franco had one last question: "Are you a Cuban?" Pawley explained that his accented Spanish was a result of the years he had spent in Cuba as a youth.[18]

After a brief side trip to Italy and Switzerland, Pawley reported to Marshall. They dined with John Foster Dulles at the American Embassy in Paris and discussed Franco. Dulles, who supported Dewey for president and expected to become secretary of state, went to the United States to inform Dewey of a possible agreement with Spain. Returning to Paris, Dulles told Marshall and Pawley that Dewey would favor a fundamental change in U.S. relations with Spain.[19]

When Dewey lost, Dulles had to wait four more years to be appointed to the coveted post. In the meantime, Marshall announced his retirement from government service effective January 1949. In a congratulatory telegram to Truman on his victory, George Baker Long, a Republican from Brookline, Massachusetts, suggested the possibility of Pawley being a "wonderful" secretary of state.[20]

Although Pawley's visit with Franco was to have been secret, news of the meeting leaked to the press, and the reaction was not favorable. In an article titled "U.S. Diplomats Abroad Deplore Private Envoys," unnamed career diplomats expressed their hope "that the growing habit of sending private envoys to foreign capitals will be terminated." The "flock" of unofficial visitors was blamed for confusion among the visited governments "and sometimes irritating to those diplomats whose function it is to represent the official Washington attitude at their stations." Pawley was reported in the article as not having seen Franco, and whatever discussions Pawley had with Foreign Minister Artajo were never relayed to Paul Culbertson, the chargé d'affaires at the American Embassy in Madrid.[21] At least the visit with Franco had remained secret, although Pawley felt the only distasteful part of his mission had been instructions from Marshall not to discuss anything with Culbertson, whom Pawley considered a friend.[22]

After the November elections, Pawley returned to Paris, this time as an official member of the U.S. delegation to the United Nations. Although the Truman administration was in favor of admitting Spain to the United Nations, Pawley knew that securing the necessary votes would be difficult. Assuring Franco that progress was being made, he called upon his old friend Guillermo Belt, the Cuban ambassador to Washington. With Belt's vote, a repeal of the anti-Franco resolution could pass, paving the way for Spain to be a member, but Belt was hesitant in supporting the measure.

"I intend to run for the Presidency of Cuba," he told Pawley, "and I think I can win . . . unless I am accused of being a *Falangista* [Franco supporter]." Belt did offer a way to secure his vote. If Pawley could convince the newly elected president of Cuba, Dr. Carlos Prío Socarrás, to write a letter instructing the Cuban ambassador to vote for repeal, then Belt would have proof he acted under orders. But Pawley knew there wasn't time to contact Prío, so the measure failed.

Pawley became concerned that the United States was "not consistent" in its foreign policy and felt it had come to the point where it was "almost childish." With no one in Washington to listen, Pawley expressed his opinions to Marshall: "We need Spain in the technical organizations of the United Nations, and I can't see for the life of me why Spain could not be a member of the United Nations. We should not penalize the people of Spain because we do not like the head of their Government. If that were the case, we might not like to have Argentina as a member, or Russia, or Poland."[23] Pawley also expressed his disappointment to Franco. Pawley also assured him that the United Nations eventually would see clear to repealing the resolution, which it did in 1950.[24]

Meanwhile, health problems continued to plague Pawley, resulting in frequent visits to clinics for diagnostic examinations. Matters came to a head in April 1949 when he complained of intestinal pains. An examination at Jackson Memorial Hospital in Miami determined that he needed an operation. The surgeon found "four or five fairly bad adhesions, which were partially blocking the intestinal tract."[25]

The abdominal pains persisted, but they gradually subsided after ten days in the hospital. Truman sent a telegram advising Pawley to "keep your chin up."[26] Attorney General Clark sent his best wishes and hoped Pawley could make it to Washington for Truman's birthday party.[27] Pawley hoped to recover enough to travel to his Virginia farm and then drive in for the party, but his doctor advised against it. After his resting a month in Miami, the pains finally disappeared.

Never one to shy away from publicity, Pawley may have been surprised in the summer of 1949 when the media focused its attention, not on him, but on his son William Pawley, Jr. A decorated World War II pilot who had earned the Distinguished Flying Cross and the China Medal for flying 138 missions over the Hump from India to China, Bill was ruggedly handsome and six feet tall, with jet-black hair and bright blue eyes. A founder of the Miami Bachelors Club in 1940, Bill had been working for his father's company Intercontinent.[28]

While in Miami, Bill received a call from Dick Reynolds, an old friend and heir to the R. J. Reynolds Tobacco fortune. "Bill, a young friend of mine is in town from California. She's a young starlet and she's having a birthday party, which I'm giving for her at the Villa Venice. I was wondering if you would be her escort for the party."[29]

Reynold's friend was seventeen-year-old Elizabeth Taylor, who had recently returned from England after filming *Conspirator* and was staying at the estate of Howard Young, the uncle of Elizabeth's father, Francis Taylor. Bill had no idea who she was, but he agreed to be her date.

Upon arriving at the Villa Venice, she was approached by a crowd of people asking for her autograph. Grabbing Bill's hand, Elizabeth pushed through the fans and led him into the restaurant and to the table where her parents were sitting. She made the introductions, which impressed Bill as a sign of good breeding. He was beginning to like this young Hollywood actress.[30]

"We went well together under the palm trees," Liz would say in later years. "We looked nice on the dance floor."[31] Elizabeth and her mother, Sara, even moved into the Pawley's Sunset Island home. As the romance blossomed, Bill decided to marry Elizabeth. Flying to New York, he bought a 3½-karat, blue-white diamond, setting him back $16,000. Under a Miami moon, Bill proposed and Elizabeth accepted.

"Elizabeth won't be graduated from Metro-Goldwyn-Mayer high school until next February," Sara told the press, "and that's why we'd like to wait until spring for the wedding."[32] Sara proclaimed young Pawley as "brilliant, understanding, strong, poised, but also boyish and full of fun," hoping that the groom-to-be would help bring out "some hidden domestic talents" in her daughter.[33] At the press conference held poolside at the Pawley Miami estate June 7, 1949, Liz flashed the diamond ring Bill had given her.

"Nice piece of ice," she remarked to the reporters, "that's what Bill calls it." Both Bill and Liz took a backseat during the interview as Sara Taylor said the couple would wed in Beverly Hills right after her daughter's eighteenth birthday on February 27.[34] When asked whether Liz would continue her film career, Bill gave noncommittal answers, but Liz declared they would live in Miami Beach "because we like the climate better here."[35]

Elizabeth was scheduled to begin filming *Father of the Bride*, and Bill was being considered to play opposite her. A casting director's dream, the make-believe image of an engaged couple preparing for a wedding would be mirrored in real life with an actual wedding. Bill told his fiancée, "I don't know if I can act or not. You'd better make the decision." Liz thought about it and said, "Well, maybe it would be better if you didn't."[36]

Jackie Park, who later became a mistress to Jack Warner, recalled the feelings of the Pawley family at the time:

I had been dating Claude Karin, a wealthy partner and associate in the Pawley family oil business. According to Claude, the family wanted nothing to do with Elizabeth Taylor. They wanted Bill to marry a debutante, not an actress. They didn't care whether she continued acting or not. The family wielded considerable political power, and they didn't feel Elizabeth would fit into their circle. Her low-cut dresses, her avaricious parents, her link to Hollywood—Elizabeth Taylor wasn't good enough for their son.

She was most upset about the Pawley family's judgment of her. They threw a big bash aboard a yacht in Miami while Elizabeth and Bill were still together, and you could feel the undercurrent. All the well-connected members of southern society showed up and viewed Elizabeth in one of her patented Hollywood gowns. Her breasts were hanging out. The Pawleys wanted somebody more demure and subtle for Billy, and they eventually forced him to end the relationship.[37]

The couple continued seeing each other and made plans to attend Jane Powell's wedding in September. By then the engagement was over, but they decided not to make the announcement until after Powell's wedding and Bill had returned to Miami. On September 19, Bill announced he and Liz had "mutually agreed" to end their engagement.[38] Over the years, Pawley and Taylor kept in touch by phone. "It took me a long time to get over it," he said in a 1997 interview.[39]

William Pawley had more important matters than his son's romance with a movie star to consider. He desperately wanted to get back into government service and felt by supporting the Democratic Party financially he might be noticed. Opportunity came when the Democratic National Committee held a fund-raising dinner for the upcoming 1950 midterm congressional elections.[40] Renting a suite at the Waldorf-Astoria Hotel in New York, where the dinner was to be held on December 2, 1949, Pawley hosted a pre-dinner cocktail party. He personally shelled out the $100-a-plate contribution for more than forty people to attend the dinner.[41]

Throughout the following year, Pawley continued to call on government officials to keep his name in their thoughts. He talked on several occasions to Dean Acheson, Averell Harriman, and General Marshall. He also saw William M. Boyle, Jr., Democratic National Committee chairman, who felt Pawley should be an ambassador-at-large, "assigned either to the President or Secretary of State." Boyle advised the White House that Pawley was "available immediately," recommending "this appointment be made at once."[42]

Appointed by Truman in 1950 as supreme allied commander, Europe (SACEUR), Eisenhower had suggested that Pawley be appointed ambassador to Spain. "I did not fail to voice my sentiments around Washington that you would have made an ideal representative at Madrid," Ike wrote Pawley.[43] Instead of being posted to another country, however, Pawley was made a special assistant to Secretary of State Dean Acheson.

With the rank of ambassador, Pawley was given the vague task of "review and appraisal of various departmental programs," but his assigned missions went far beyond those of a mere adviser.[44] "I have no immediate assignment," he told a reporter. "I am just opening a desk at present."[45] Widely considered a Latin America expert, Pawley could be tapped also for his Far East experience. A *Miami Daily News* editorial applauded the posting, saying he was at the "peak of his career," and "he is certain to be of real value to the State Department."[46]

Two weeks prior to being sworn in, Pawley attended the wedding of his eldest daughter, Annie Hahr, to Hobart Boomer McKay. Because McKay's father had recently died, only family and a few close friends attended the church wedding and reception at the Pawley Sunset Island home. After the honeymoon, Hobart, an air force captain, was called to active duty.[47] The mother of the bride was still under care at a mental institution and did not attend.

Tom Clark had conducted the small ceremony for Pawley's swearing in, and Secretary of Defense George Marshall was a guest. No sooner had Pawley been sworn in when Undersecretary of State James E. Webb, who later became NASA Administrator, invited him to lunch. Not knowing what was in store for him, Pawley sat with Webb, who was about to spoil the day for the newly appointed assistant.

"I don't want to make you feel badly," Webb began, "but at a meeting in the Secretary's office this morning, to which we purposely did not invite you, it has been decided that you are to see no document dealing with the Far East, you are to participate in no conference that is held in the Department of State or anywhere else in Government dealing with this matter, and as a favor to the Secretary just don't discuss Far East matters."

"Jim, am I considered a subversive?"

"No," Webb replied. "Let's say reactionary. We have our views on what ought to be done, and they do not coincide with yours and therefore we don't want any trouble."

Considering his Far East experience, he was at a loss as to why the State Department wouldn't call upon him for advice, even as a devil's advocate. After lunch he immediately went to see Marshall. As Pawley recalled, "He wanted to take it to President Truman but I asked him not to." Marshall then assured Pawley that any paper coming out of the Policy Planning Board had to cross his desk, "and I certainly will take advantage of your experience . . . and give you an opportunity to criticize or comment on it."[48]

The posting in Spain went to former ambassador to Argentina Stanton Griffis, who asked Pawley to visit him in Madrid, but Pawley was now wary of interfering in State Department matters if he was not officially invited. Acheson approved the visit through the American Embassy in Madrid, and Pawley requested that the press be informed that his visit was purely personal. The State Department responded by declining "to say what Mr. Pawley's assignment was or to divulge the nature of his position with Secretary Acheson."[49] Press releases reported only where Pawley was but never the nature of his visits, and Pawley's response to inquiries was that his presence in foreign countries was "purely a friendly one," with "absolutely no ulterior motive."[50] During the visit to Spain, Griffis, who did not trust embassy interpreters and knew of Pawley's good standing with Foreign Minister Alberto Martin-Artajo Álvarez, wanted Pawley to accompany him when he visited the emissary.[51]

On his way to Madrid, Pawley stopped in Paris and was invited to dinner with SACEUR Eisenhower and Gen. Alfred M. Gruenther. The gist of the conversation was that "political obstacles" blocked the Pentagon's desire to rearm Spain and something had to be done to change policy.[52] They wanted Pawley to secure an affirmation that Spanish troops could be called upon for Western Europe's defense and to ascertain if Spain wanted to be in NATO. With that in mind, Pawley flew to Madrid in Ike's personal plane, and he and Griffis called upon Artajo on June 13.

Two days later, Pawley filed his report to U.S. Embassies in London, Paris, and Madrid:

> Franco does not object to the use of Spanish troops in Western Europe, but the subject requires negotiation. He would want to know how they would be used and who would command them.
>
> Franco is willing to make available to U.S. air, naval and other bases by means of a negotiated bilateral treaty, and he would have no objection to Spain's ultimate integration into NATO, although he does not necessarily prefer membership in NATO (to a pact with the U.S.).
>
> Franco . . . [does not] agree with the theory of England and France that there is no hurry with reference to Spain. Time is running out and the potential power of a completely anti-Communist nation may be useless unless something is done soon.
>
> [Artajo] emphasized that the only positive help to be strongly counted on in case of disaster would be a rearmed and well-equipped Western Germany, Turkey and Spain.[53]

Returning to Paris, Pawley met again with Eisenhower and Gruenther, along with Ike's political adviser, Douglas MacArthur II. "I recommended a major commitment of our European defense resources . . . in Spain," Pawley later wrote. "I also recommended a substantial transfer of European expenditures from France to Spain."[54]

Strongly pro-French, MacArthur disagreed. In his opinion Spain was unreliable. He felt France would suffice as the anchor for Western European defense. The U.S. Navy had the final word. Adm. Forrest P. Sherman, chief of naval operations, was determined to acquire a Sixth Fleet base near Cádiz. Truman acquiesced, and the navy negotiated for the base, which was followed by successful arrangements for U.S. Air Force bases as well.

Lifting the boycott against Spain resulted in the U.S. government pouring billions of dollars into the Spanish economy. Through Pawley's efforts, "we acquired the Air Force bases at Torrejon, Zaragosa, and Moron; the Navy complex at Rota; and the pipeline across Spain from Seville to Madrid and Zaragosa."[55] While

Pawley could take pride in starting negotiations resulting in the United States having a forward defense line in Europe against Communism, he could not prevent Communism from gaining ground in a country he was more familiar with, namely, China.

He pleaded with Truman on several occasions to back the Nationalist government with arms and financial aid; he even suggested appointing a special advisory commission of old China hands to offer recommendations. Opposition came from a State Department Foreign Service officers' clique that steadfastly blocked support of Chiang Kai-shek. Pawley realized Truman would remain loyal to his subordinates, and any attempt to dissuade him from policies they formulated on the China situation would result in a staunch, defensive position.

In his unpublished memoir, Pawley wrote that matters came to a head in December 1949, or six months before the North Koreans invaded South Korea. During a meeting with Truman he warned that the continued U.S. position on China would result in disaster and Communism would gain a strong foothold in Asia.

"Unless we go all out, right now, to back up the Nationalist movement in China, in which Chinese will do their own fighting for their freedom," Pawley told Truman, "you've lost China."

Having twice appointed Pawley to ambassadorial posts, the president did give the man an opportunity to air his views even if Truman failed to act on them.

"On top of that," Pawley continued, "you'll have a war on your hands in Burma, Indochina or Korea within a year . . . most likely Korea, where the Reds are strongest. That will leave you a choice of committing America to a ground war, or you will lose all of Asia."

"God damn it, Bill!" Truman shouted as he pounded the desk with his fist. "I will *never* commit an American ground soldier to a war in Asia!"

"I repeat, sir," Pawley emphasized, "that within *one year* you are going to be in a bind where you'll *have* to make that decision."[56]

Although Pawley's prediction came true, the man who foresaw the end results of America's Asian policy did not relish being right. Meanwhile, the State Department, in the famous *China White Paper* given to the president on July 29, 1949, had advised Truman that "the ominous result of the civil war in China was beyond the control of the government of the United States. . . . We will not help the Chinese or ourselves by basing our policy on wishful thinking."[57] Pawley felt the defeatist attitude of the document was "untenable at the time" and did everything in his "power to block its publication, including protests to Truman."[58]

Citing U.S. support of Greece and Turkey, Pawley felt helping Chiang would further the U.S. policy of containing Soviet-influenced aggression in Asia. His sentiment that Communist-influenced State Department officials should bear responsibility for America's failure in China was echoed by first-term congressman John F. Kennedy: "Our relationship with China since the end of the Second World War has been a tragic one, and it is of the utmost importance that we search out and spotlight those who must bear the responsibility for our present predicament."[59]

Even when the Chinese Nationalists were driven to Formosa, Pawley continued to press the State Department that the situation was not hopeless. He sent a memorandum to Secretary of State Dean Acheson dated November 7, 1949, pleading for a policy change:

> The Chinese Nationalist government, deeply concerned with the urgency of halting the advance of aggressive communism in Eastern Asia and the West Pacific . . . [and realizing] that United States policy is opposed to sending to China American advisory missions that would include military officers on the active lists . . . the Chinese desire themselves to employ . . . a small group of American civilian, economic, industrial, agricultural and [retired or ex-officers] military advisors. . . A number of civilians and retired officers have signified their willingness and desire to serve, provided this project is not disapproved by the United States government. They feel . . . that with the help of relatively small number of able assistants the situation in Formosa and possibly in Hainan can be saved. . . . Our information is that the Chinese government would work very closely with the advisors so employed. . . . The officers would advise and assist in the training program and in maintenance of equipment. They would also provide operational and training advice. . . . Assurance can be given that these men would not engage in any activities inimical to the interest of the United States. . . If this small group of advisors can be as successful as we feel it possible that they may be, the holding of Formosa and Hainan would contribute greatly to a Nationalist government being able to maintain its consulates and embassies throughout the world, friendly to the United States.[60]

If Roosevelt could support a sub rosa organization like the American Volunteer Group, Pawley felt Truman could do likewise to help Chiang. He was not alone in his support of the Nationalist Chinese. Gen. Douglas MacArthur was feeding information to pro-Taiwan Republicans and encouraging veteran Japanese pilots to go to Taiwan and support Chennault's proposed plan in which volunteers would attack mainland China.[61]

Acheson had left for Paris that day, so Pawley gave the memorandum to Undersecretary of State Webb. Five weeks after receiving the memo, Webb replied that he "did not want to receive the paper as an official proposal," but he "would be willing to look it over and consult with" him.[62] Sensing the Washington run-around, Pawley began drafting a response to Webb's letter to express his views in stronger terms. A more pressing development occurred, however, that he felt needed his immediate attention: the State Department was about to recommend recognizing Red China.

Philip C. Jessup, special assistant to the secretary of state, was embarking on a tour of Asian countries bordering on or adjacent to mainland China. His mission was to meet with U.S. ambassadors in those countries and encourage them to recommend immediate recognition of the Mao Tse-tung government and bring China into the United Nations. Apparently, Acheson hoped if the United States stopped harassing Red China, it would "follow Tito in stopping active abuse of us."[63]

When Pawley heard of Jessup's mission, he asked to meet with him on December 10, 1949. He talked for an hour and a half, attempting to dissuade him from this policy. "I continued to strongly urge him not to follow this course of action," he recalled. "I found myself up against a stone wall."[64] Determined to prevent the U.S. government's recognition of Red China, Pawley next enlisted the help of George Marshall who was president of the Red Cross at that time. After Pawley presented his case, Marshall suggested the three of them meet at Marshall's apartment the following day.

Pawley wrote, "Jessup refused to reveal what his mission in Asia was on the grounds that he could not disclose government secrets to private citizens." Considering that Marshall was a former chief of staff and a former secretary of state, labeling him a "private citizen" may have been an affront. Nevertheless, Marshall made it clear that if the State Department went ahead with this policy change, he would personally take up the matter with the president.

Pawley never did learn if Marshall carried out his threat to raise the matter with Truman, but the results were that Red China remained outside and the United States continued recognizing Formosa as the legitimate Chinese government.[65] In October 1951, Jessup testified at a Foreign Relations Committee hearing considering his appointment to the UN General Assembly staff and told a different story. According to Jessup, "the Department of State had at no time considered the possibility of recognizing Red China."[66]

Meanwhile, during World War II, the best-kept military secret was America's construction of the atomic bomb. Production of fissionable uranium relied on obtaining rare ores containing the coveted material. Aside from uranium, thorium was sought as a commodity because it was capable of augmenting production of fissionable uranium. Thorium is found in monazite sand, a phosphate with thorium oxide (up to 18 percent), which is concentrated in deposits formed from the weathering of rocks. Minor deposits were discovered in the Piedmont region of the Carolinas, as well as in Australia, Ceylon, the Netherlands, East Indies, and Malaya. One of the richest sources of monazite sands was in the Indian state of Travancore.[67]

Securing monazite sands from India proved a difficult undertaking. In 1946, Nehru's government imposed an embargo on shipping any to the United States, but in early 1951, Pawley felt he had a solution. While Nehru may have viewed the United States as an imperialist nation, evident in his repeated attacks on Washington's foreign policy, he was not above accepting aid in the form of wheat shipments to feed his starving population. Many in Congress felt if Nehru continued to "bite the hand that fed him," then aid should be withheld. Pawley's proposal was simple: the United States would provide wheat to India in exchange for monazite sands. Pawley invited Foreign Relations Committee members and Senator Brien McMahon, chairman of the Joint Congressional Committee on Atomic Energy, to dine with him and discuss what he had in mind.

Instead of giving wheat to India, Pawley proposed that the U.S. government should give India a loan to purchase American wheat and use the additional funds to develop an agricultural program to provide Indian farmers with tools, seed, fertilizer, and technical assistance to increase their own wheat production. He reminded the senators that if the United States gave the wheat as an outright gift, shipping costs alone would be higher than the price of the wheat. If aid were provided, Pawley felt confident he could crack India's embargo on monazite sands. Warming to the idea, the senators suggested Pawley appear before the Senate Committee handling the Indian wheat problem. Following his testimony, a bill was introduced and quickly passed the Senate.[68]

The bill was passed to the House of Representatives, but as debates carried on, Nehru dropped a bombshell: he refused to negotiate India's "self-respect or freedom of action even for something we need so badly." His remarks resulted in the House postponing further action on the bill.[69] Pawley felt Nehru's real purpose was to derail the proposal of joint power over control of the funds. "What he wanted, I was sure," Pawley wrote, "was sole control over these vast funds for his own political ends."[70] Nevertheless, he felt the United States could not allow politics to compromise a situation in which millions of Indians could die of starvation. A new suggestion was made to give India a fifty-year loan without strings attached, and the Senate Foreign Relations Committee quickly agreed.

But Nehru would have the last word. An hour before announcing the new agreement to the Indian Parliament, he released a press statement that "Russian ships with wheat have started for India." Prominence was given to the 50,000-ton Russian shipment, ignoring the monthly 100,000-ton shipments already coming from the United States and the proposed 2 million tons promised with the new legislation.[71] "While Moscow got the credit, *we* averted the famine," Pawley observed.[72]

The Emergency Food Aid Act gave India a $190 million loan to purchase U.S. wheat.[73] Representative Mike Mansfield noted in the *Congressional Record* that "Ambassador Pawley is a quiet, effective worker who gets things done, and done right. . . . His testimony before the Joint Atomic Energy Committee was so convincing that every House member of that committee spoke in behalf of the measure when it was before us for consideration."[74]

Pawley arrived in New Delhi on June 18, 1951, accompanied by his assistant V. Lansing Collins and J. Bruce Hamilton, a State Department atomic energy expert. U.S. ambassador to India Loy W. Henderson had left for the United States and had not notified the embassy that the group could stay at the chancellery. As a result, Pawley's group stayed at a hotel with no air-conditioning. Even their offices at the chancellery offered no relief, "the air-conditioning system consisted of grass mats hung from the ceiling . . . watered all day like a 'desert cooler,' in the 110-degree heat." With his own money, Pawley purchased three air-conditioners for the chancellery so they could at least work in comfort.[75]

Negotiations for monazite sands proved difficult. Pawley did secure an agreement, however, for India to ship 500 tons of monazite concentrate to the United States, ostensibly for "medical research."[76]

13
Troubleshooting

At dawn on Sunday, June 25, 1950, after a heavy barrage of artillery fire, units of the North Korean People's Army (KPA) crossed the 38th parallel dividing North and South Korea. The invasion was purportedly a counterattack against a South Korean raid. Two days later, the Soviet Union alluded in a message sent to the U.S. government that it would not make a move against U.S. armed forces in Korea. That same day, President Truman committed the navy and air force to help the South Koreans. The KPA pressed deep into South Korea, but in September, after the landing at Inchon, UN forces crossed the 38th parallel, taking the war into North Korea. In late October, China entered the conflict by sending troops across the Yalu River into North Korea. By the summer of 1951, a stalemate had developed around the 38th parallel, with neither side gaining territory.

The CIA asked Pawley, once he completed his mission in India, to visit the Far East in the summer of 1951. While on stopovers in Hong Kong, Formosa, Japan, Burma, and Siam, he was to appraise CIA activities in those countries and obtain information on Chinese activities.[1] While in Taipei, he was the guest of Chargé d'Affaires Karl L. Rankin and discussed the possibility of supplying Formosa with military supplies from Japan and Korea if truce negotiations went well in Korea.[2]

Pawley felt Washington had overlooked a source of manpower that would have greatly reduced the Americans' presence on the battlefield. "It seems most unfortunate that it is necessary to sacrifice large numbers of American and other allied troops in the fight in Asia when there are millions of Asiatics who are willing and anxious to fight Communism in defense of their own freedom." As added benefits, it would destroy the myth that the war is "between Western capitalistic forces and the peoples of Asia" and allow the United States to hold its forces in readiness against the Russians in other parts of the world.[3] General MacArthur shared Pawley's sentiments and urged the military to use Chinese Nationalist troops to attack South China and create a "second front."[4] Pawley would express these same sentiments—use Asian troops to fight Asian troops—two decades later when U.S. armed services fought in Vietnam.

After the tour, Pawley received word that his son Clifton was seriously ill. Clifton, who lived in Havana, had joined uncles Edward and Eugene Pawley in their import-export business in Mexico City.[5] He had taken his baby son swimming and had come down with a cold. When hospitalized, he was diagnosed with bulbar polio, a deadly form of the disease.[6]

After making arrangements for a doctor to be sent from Boston's Lahey Clinic, Pawley and his wife flew from Washington and reached his son's bedside shortly before he died.[7] Pawley had also arranged for a Miami physician and a respirator to be flown to Mexico, but the plane arrived too late.[8] Married only three years, Pawley's twenty-five-year-old son left a wife and infant son.

"Fate . . . dealt me a blow to which there is no counterpunch," he wrote. Although dedicated to serve his country, Pawley needed time away from his duties: "I took a leave from the State Department and returned to the sanctuary of my home in Miami Beach."[9] Truman expressed his sorrow in a telegram to which the grief-stricken father replied, "The loss of my younger son has been the most serious tragedy of my life and for a time it seemed too great a burden to bear."[10]

Pawley never fully recovered from Clifton's death, but he knew that remaining in his Florida sanctuary would do him no good. He had to return to an active life. The opportunity came at the invitation of Secretary of Defense Robert Lovett. Written on the day before Clifton's death, Lovett sent a letter that included a note of support concerning the illness of Pawley's son. What Lovett wanted, however, was to avail himself of Pawley's abilities as a negotiator:

> For some time both General Marshall and I have felt the need of having readily available a "trouble-shooter" on whom we could dump any particularly nasty problem that did not normally fall into appropriate staff channels, or to whom we could look for assistance and guidance and <u>action</u> on a complicated matter involving delicate negotiations. I have in mind such things as searching out and recommending remedial action on oc-

casional industrial bottlenecks or production slowdowns, special projects possibly involving personal liaison with some of my opposite numbers in other countries, and, in general, keeping me out of trouble in certain areas where my regular staff would not normally operate. I don't know whether this sounds attractive or not—in any event I can assure you it will be varied and certainly not dull.[11]

Pawley sent a copy of Lovett's offer in a letter to SACEUR Eisenhower, telling him he had "considered dropping out of government work altogether" but felt he should accept the job. Eisenhower supported the decision: "The ramified activities of the Defense Department reach into so many nooks and crannies of American and international life that there will never be any lack of opportunity for a devoted, intelligent public servant in that Department to find plenty to occupy his entire attention," he wrote Pawley.[12]

The friendship that developed between the two men since Eisenhower's visit to Brazil had continued as each man furthered his career. When Eisenhower was to become president of Columbia University, Pawley sent him a watch. "Even more than I value such a handsome present," Eisenhower wrote his friend, "I treasure the thought that led you to bring it to me." Pawley was in Europe at the time with Edna, about to return by boat, but altered his plans and flew to New York to attend Eisenhower's installation ceremony.[13] When Mamie and Ike sailed for Europe in 1951, Pawley had orchids and roses sent to their stateroom. "Just how you figured out that Mamie and I would be on the Queen Elizabeth I don't know," Eisenhower wrote him.

Ike and Mamie were frequent visitors to Belvoir House, Pawley's farm in Virginia. There, Eisenhower could relax and enjoy the graciousness of his host. Eisenhower trusted Pawley because they seemed to have identical political ideologies. "I cannot tell you what both of us wouldn't give this minute to be able to sit leisurely there a week or two, on the back porch of your home," Eisenhower wrote his friend, "with no thought of going farther astray than the bass lake to see if the big ones are rising to fly."[14] Eisenhower was drawn to Pawley's farm and looked forward to going "down to your Virginia farm for a couple of hours of bass fishing."[15]

Still on active duty to the State Department, Pawley submitted his letter of resignation to Dean Acheson, who was in Italy at the time. Noting he would have preferred to resign in person, Pawley added that his new assignment met with

Truman's approval. Asking that his resignation take effect November 30, 1951, Pawley also offered to complete the negotiations he still had pending with India. Acheson said he deeply regretted Pawley's leaving. "You have been a tremendous help to me," he wrote, noting that if it became necessary he would ask him "to participate in the completion of the negotiations with the Government of India."[16]

Pawley's first assignment from Lovett was to examine problems that resulted in bottlenecks in manufacturing arms for the Korean War effort; specifically, Lovett wanted to know why machine tools were not "cutting enough chips."[17] Lovett was particularly concerned with the lead time between orders and the delivery of machine tools. He cited surface grinders as an example, noting that in 1950 a grinder was delivered within six weeks after being ordered, but it now took thirty-six weeks.[18] Pawley was required to visit major defense contractors in the United States and devise a more efficient production program.[19] After less than a month on the project, though, Lovett pulled Pawley to work on a more important assignment.

"I am greatly concerned about the responsibilities of the Department of Defense in Western Europe," Lovett wrote, "with particular reference to France." Outlining specific areas needing attention, Lovett wanted assurances "that our politico-military efforts in that area are so organized and so executed as to produce the maximum result and at the same time get the maximum possible return for the U.S. defense dollar expended." Lovett had two concerns—tactical airfields in France and Germany to support NATO ground forces, and providing and building facilities for logistic support of combat forces in those countries.[20] Pawley had to negotiate cost-sharing arrangements with the French construction firms being used, covering "all extremely technical, sensitive areas involving many aggressive personalities."[21]

Pawley and Edna flew to Paris on April 14, 1952, and set up quarters at the American Embassy.[22] He conferred with U.S. ambassador to France James Clement Dunn and U.S. ambassador to NATO William Henry Draper, Jr., on how to approach the French to strengthen agreements with the Military Facilities Negotiating Group, which was constructing air bases in France under a joint venture using American and French construction contractors. Eight airfields being built in France were falling behind schedule, and Lovett wanted them completed before the year ended.

Pawley was given authority to assign contracts directly to American firms for purchasing and construction "totaling not more than $50,000." In addition, regarding any project assigned to the French that lagged behind schedule thirty days after work started, Pawley was empowered to "assume direct supervision and management of the project" and reassign it to another French contractor jointly associated with an American firm. If that move didn't resolve the problem, he was authorized to use American military engineering troops stationed in France to complete the project.[23] In short, he was to get the air bases built, even if it meant upsetting people.

Before Pawley arrived, junior American officers handled the negotiations with equally ranked French officials. He immediately put an end to the stalemate by elevating the negotiations and dealing directly with cabinet-level French officials. As in China, Pawley surrounded himself with the best technical advisers, including George Giles, a no-nonsense engineer who waded through the morass of designs and specifications before making recommendations.

Meeting with Eisenhower, who headed the Supreme Headquarters of Allied Powers Europe (SHAPE), Pawley showed him the instructions from Lovett. Surprised that Pawley had been assigned the project because the Joint Chiefs of Staff had failed to find a way to proceed, the SACEUR offered his full support. After months in Paris working on the plans, Pawley was ready to request bids on projects to complete the bases.[24]

Facing congressional attacks over the waste and delays in constructing bases in Europe, Lovett felt establishing a unified command of U.S. forces in Europe was the solution. If the U.S. European Command, the U.S. Naval Forces Eastern Atlantic and Mediterranean Command, and U.S. Air Forces in Europe could be placed under one commander (Eisenhower was Lovett's choice), duplicated efforts might be prevented. Pawley discussed the possibility with Eisenhower, who thought combining the commands would be detrimental but did feel "some action of this type" would be desirable.[25] Eisenhower requested that an ad hoc committee of military command leaders study the problem, and Pawley asked to meet with top officers of the U.S. commands to solicit their opinions.[26]

Although each service branch jealously guarded its fiefdom, Pawley managed to persuade the commanding officers of the army and air force European groups to attend a meeting to discuss a unified communication line; however, the navy's Adm. Robert B. Carney was a no-show. Pawley sent a strongly worded telegram to Carney requesting his presence at the next meeting, and he personally met the admiral at the airport and escorted him to the rooms reserved for him and his staff at the Hotel George V.

The second meeting took place as scheduled, and after listening to the army and air force representatives offer their support for the plan, Admiral Carney rose to make the navy's presentation. With an assortment of organizational charts and diagrams tacked on the wall, Carney outlined his reasons for not wanting to co-operate in the joint venture. Having heard enough, the SACEUR suggested they discuss the situation on a more informal basis.

"Mick, you're rocking the boat," Eisenhower told Carney. "We've got to have *one* line of communication. That's all there is to it, and the navy will have to co-operate."

As supreme commander in Europe, Eisenhower held the strongest position, and the navy soon fell in line. With everyone agreeing to a unified plan, Pawley went to work on the details that would result in financial and manpower savings for the armed forces in Europe. The day after the meeting, Eisenhower notified the Joint Chiefs of Staff that indications pointed "quite definitely to a more central-ized system of control."[27] After Eisenhower left SHAPE, his replacement, Gen. Matthew Ridgway, continued the reorganization plan and made it a reality.[28]

Mission completed, Pawley was ready for his next assignment, which turned out to be an old one—that is, negotiating with India to establish a monazite process-ing plant. The Department of Defense had the responsibility to secure an agreement with India, and Lovett called upon Pawley's prior experience to get the job done. Lovett advised him that $1.4 million had been made available and "may be used, in your discretion . . . as investment capital or as partial and participating aid in setting up the proposed monazite processing plant . . . for the purchase of thorium oxide . . . and for the purchase of or option to purchase monazite sands." Pawley was also instructed to "obtain from the Indian Government a commitment to prevent ores and compounds of uranium and thorium from reaching Iron Curtain countries."[29]

Pawley's mission didn't get off to a good start. Meeting with U.S. Navy rep-resentatives, whose department was handling the monazite contracts, Pawley soon learned that the two Indian officials he was supposed to talk to were not available. He contacted Nehru who told him that he had not been informed in advance of Pawley's visit. The two men Pawley wanted to see—Dr. H. J. Bhabha, chairman of the Atomic Energy Commission of India, and Dr. S. S. Bhatnagar, a cabinet member in charge of scientific development—were on missions in Moscow and London, respectively. Nehru also informed Pawley that India would not export thorium to the United States or the Soviet Union because he thought the material might be used in atomic weapons.

"We have no intention of making nuclear weapons from any Indian raw materials," Pawley informed Nehru, "and I will be happy to give you that assurance in writing." He told the Indian leader that the monazite would be used solely for medical and experimental purposes. Nehru's staunch position seemed to have softened, and he suggested Pawley meet with Bhatnagar in London. Five days later Pawley was in London to initiate negotiations.[30]

In a meeting at India House in London, Pawley opened the discussions by referring to the correspondence he and Dr. Bhatnagar began in 1951, all dealing with the United States securing monazite shipments from India. Pawley also reminded him of the meetings the two had held in Washington after which monazite shipments from India became easier to secure. The present mission, Pawley said, was to formulate plans for a joint venture to establish monazite-processing facilities in India and increase exports for the U.S. market. It was his understanding, Bhatnagar replied, that present needs could be satisfied from existing production facilities. If the United States wanted India to construct new processing plants, then he wanted assurances that the additional quantities would have a market.

Pawley was not in a position to render an opinion on future demand for monazite, yet "it appeared reasonable to expect that technology would develop further new uses for these valuable materials." When asked if India had studied the marketability of increased production, Bhatnagar said that government-owned Indian Rare Earths, Limited, which operated the present monazite plant, had done so, but he had not brought the report with him. Before the meeting adjourned, Pawley reiterated his conversation with Nehru, from which these exploratory talks had been initiated to "smooth away whatever obstacles were found."[31]

At a second meeting, Pawley continued pressing for the construction of a second monazite-processing plant in India. The United States wanted 2,500 tons annually of unprocessed monazite, but given the allowance now being granted, that amount could be reduced to a 1,500-ton guarantee. The Indian delegation was hesitant to commit since its government's current policy was not to export the valuable ore, but Bhatnagar promised to present his findings and recommendations to Nehru for consideration. When it was suggested that Pawley return to New Delhi to negotiate an agreement at the top level, he hesitated. He had hoped to wrap up the deal in London but was told "a favorable decision could not be looked for unless the Prime Minister could be convinced that the proposal was an economically attractive one." Delaying the decision to return to India, Pawley turned next to the construction and management of the proposed facility.

They discussed a possible location for the new plant and who would construct it. Now that he had the Indian delegation talking about the details of a new facility, Pawley raised the question of financing. Bhatnagar estimated that one-third would be in dollars, one-third in sterling, and one-third in rupees, while Pawley expressed a desire to see half in dollars. When management of the new plant was broached, Bhatnagar once more informed Pawley that such discussions should take place in New Delhi. Steering the conversation away from returning to India, Pawley asked about providing technical assistance. He expressed his government's desire to use private industrial enterprises rather than government agencies, but again, the Indian delegation said this issue could only be settled in New Delhi. They did agree that a provision should be made whereby India would have an option to purchase the Americans' interests after a specified period of time.[32]

Before the talks concluded, Pawley convinced the Indians to continue negotiations in Washington instead of New Delhi. A problem arose when it was revealed Dr. Bhabha, who would be participating in the meetings, had been a Communist as a youth. He required a special dispensation from the State Department so he could enter the United States. The Washington meetings were time consuming, "but we finally reached agreement with India." As a result of Pawley's mission, India agreed to export "all of her surplus thorium and substantial quantities of her rare earths" to the United States.[33]

Having served two ambassadorial posts, a position with the State Department, and one with the Department of Defense—all under a Democratic president— Pawley now felt the country needed a change of administration. To support his choice for president—Dwight D. Eisenhower—Pawley would have to switch his party affiliation.

While preparing to run for reelection in 1948, Truman had been concerned by rumors that Eisenhower might throw his hat in the ring. Although Eisenhower had made several statements that he wasn't interested, Truman felt the possibility still existed that the popular general might be swayed if a grass-roots campaign endorsed him. Truman wanted Eisenhower to make a definite "I'm not a candidate" statement to quell the rumors.

"Bill, you are a close friend of Ike's," Truman said to Pawley during an informal meeting held one evening on the porch Truman had added to the White House. "Would you mind calling him tomorrow and making a date? Ask him to make a really strong statement, just as strong as the one made by George Marshall, that he's not interested in running in 1948." Truman added that if Eisenhower made such a statement, then he would support him for the presidency in 1952 "and that he will very likely be elected."

At the time, Pawley was residing at Belvoir House, his Virginia home one hour from Washington. The sprawling estate had three bedroom-parlor suites and a separate cottage with three small bedrooms and three baths. The property included a small lake (dredged under a plan provided by Eisenhower) and a horse stable. In addition to fruit trees dotting the landscape, the farm had a herd of sixty white-faced Herefords. A full-time butler and his wife, who was the cook, and a resident gardener maintained the estate.[34]

The 880-acre estate, which Pawley's children called "the farm," was bordered on all sides by properties owned by families who had held them for generations. The neighbors did not look upon the newcomer too fondly, especially when he decided to dredge for a lake. Although the locals informed him that there wasn't any water within miles to fill a lake, he went ahead with the project anyway. He sent his three nephews, Edward's sons, out to scour the property for a source of water, and they found one.

After running a ditch from the natural spring to fill the lake, Pawley had a local hatchery stock the lake with brim and bass. The bass were supposed to feed on the brim, but somehow the hatchery miscalculated the mixture. "After a while, you could row out in the middle, throw your line and haul in a five-pound brim," Irene Pawley recalled.[35] The bass became more and more difficult to catch and a sore subject to mention in Pawley's presence. Still, as noted earlier, whenever Eisenhower visited the farm, he enjoyed the challenge of snagging the elusive bass.

Pawley made arrangements with Virginia authorities to have his farm declared a game preserve. Constructing large pens on the estate, he raised pheasant, chukar partridge, and quail. More than one hundred acres were planted in feed for the game birds. Shooting was permitted from the beginning of October until the last day of March.

Meanwhile, acting on Truman's instructions, Pawley picked up Eisenhower at his Fort Myer, Virginia, residence and drove him to the farm for dinner. Waiting for the proper moment, Pawley finally popped the question.

"I'm afraid the answer has to be 'no,' Bill. I'll begin to look pretty foolish if I keep repeating that I am not a candidate, don't intend to be, and that I'm not interested in the Presidency."

Pawley told Eisenhower that Truman wanted the public statement from him so badly that he was willing to support him in 1952. Pawley added he would offer his support whether Eisenhower ran as a Democrat or Republican.

"By the way," Pawley asked, "*are* you a Republican?"

Eisenhower replied with an anecdote on that very same question put to him by a friend. The man walked into Eisenhower's office, pulled a thousand-dollar bill from his wallet, and dropped it on the desk, telling Eisenhower he wanted to ask a question and the answer was worth that much to him. He then asked with which political party Eisenhower was affiliated. Eisenhower said he might have answered if the money hadn't been put on the desk.

After hearing the story, Pawley replied, "Well, I suppose that, even though I'm not offering a thousand, I won't get an answer to that question, either."[36]

"I would like for you to know now," Pawley would write to Eisenhower on November, 16, 1951, "that you have a very strong, loyal friend and supporter, who believes in you and what you stand for—and that support carries with it no strings."[37]

Years later, near the end of Eisenhower's second term, Pawley tried coaxing the president to visit the Virginia farm again. Knowing Eisenhower enjoyed shooting but that he had been going to Georgia and North Florida for game, Pawley felt Belvoir would be ideal for him. Reminding him that Belvoir "is only an hour's drive from Washington," Pawley wrote, "and you might fit in some relaxation and exercise on a much easier schedule."[38] Later, Pawley also would invite Vice President Nixon to the farm for shooting. Bagging several pheasants with a gun Nixon had loaned him, Pawley sent some of the birds to the Nixon family.[39]

14

Ike and Guatemala

By 1952, the political landscape had changed. Truman was not running for reelection, the Korean War was a campaign issue, and Senator Robert Taft was the leading Republican Party candidate for president. Eisenhower was still mulling, even though a Draft Ike Committee had formed. A lifelong Democrat, Pawley wanted him nominated and elected. He solicited Dewey to endorse Eisenhower but received a negative response. He invited Arthur E. Summerfield, a key member in Michigan politics, to visit him in Paris to discuss the matter with Eisenhower. Recuperating from an operation, Summerfield also declined. Two weeks later, Edna and Pawley were invited to dinner with Ike and Mamie, and Pawley was pleasantly surprised to see Summerfield there.

Once his man was nominated, Pawley spent considerable time and funds to get Eisenhower elected. "I organized the first big meeting of 'Democrats for Eisenhower,' inviting about 1,500 people from every part of Virginia to spend the day at 'Belvoir.'" Hiring a caterer to serve guests under a large tent, Pawley and Edna hosted a gathering featuring George M. Humphrey, who would later serve as Eisenhower's secretary of the treasury, as the main speaker. Earl Butz, who would serve under Nixon as secretary of agriculture, also spoke. The fund-raiser proved successful, but Pawley wanted to do more. "We built an Eisenhower-for-President organization for Northern Virginia on a county and precinct level," Pawley wrote, "and worked to get out the vote with telephone volunteers, car transportation and even baby sitters—the works."[1]

Although still in the midst of negotiations with India on a monazite agreement, Pawley took time to attend a rally for Eisenhower in Miami. He was in the delegation greeting him at the airport and later at a Roney Plaza Hotel reception and a rally at Bayfront Park. Interviewed by reporters, Pawley insisted he still considered himself a Democrat, even though he intended to be a "vigorous supporter" of Eisenhower's. "You don't always have to be for a party," he said. "You can be for a man." Acknowledging he supported Truman in 1948, he said, "Mr. Truman is not running this time. Mr. Stevenson is."[2] Pawley later admitted he hadn't remained a Democrat. "I changed parties in 1951," he said during an interview in 1960. "I could see what was happening in China and the Democratic administration refused to pay any attention to my warnings."[3]

Garrett L. Smalley, a staunch Democrat and newspaper reporter, provided Truman with details of Eisenhower's Miami visit, including Pawley's role in the arrangements. "They had quite a squabble here over TV arrangements. First, television was 'OK'—then it was called off. Then it was finally announced that the Eisenhower speech would be televised. Who made the final arrangements? It was Mr. Pawley. Who guaranteed the payment? Mr. Pawley. Who paid the bill? Mr. Pawley." During the Bayfront Park rally, Pawley was introduced on the dais as a "great Democrat who is supporting Ike."[4] Truman was "hurt and angry" that a man who had served under him would support Eisenhower.[5]

Virginia and Florida went for Eisenhower in the election, and Pawley looked forward to a State Department housecleaning. When John Foster Dulles was appointed secretary of state, Pawley couldn't have been happier. He wrote to Dulles, "I have been deeply gratified to see the caliber of men that [Eisenhower] has selected for his cabinet . . . and have read with a great deal of pleasure the announcement that you have accepted."[6]

As for a role in the Eisenhower administration, Pawley wrote he "stayed away from the New York Republican headquarters and from the Washington headquarters because I am seeking no position with the new administration. I worked like the devil for their success and I am again proud to say I am an American."[7]

Pawley wanted to participate in policymaking, especially when the president held similar thoughts on combating Communism, but getting to see Eisenhower in the Oval Office became difficult. The new White House chief of staff, former New Hampshire governor Sherman Adams, tended to isolate the president from people wanting to see him. "On the few occasions that I managed to see Ike in the Oval Room," Pawley wrote, "Adams first endeavored to sidetrack me by asking that I tell him what was on my mind, so that he could inform the President."[8] But

Eisenhower always managed to see his friends. "Bill Pawley just came in for a short talk," he wrote to Robert Lovett. "I'll be seeing more of him."⁹

The relationship Pawley enjoyed with Eisenhower even extended to helping the president find a private residence outside Washington. In July 1953, he wrote that he had found a five-hundred-acre Virginia property "considered one of the outstanding farms in this general area." He offered to purchase the property and hold it until Eisenhower decided to move in. "In talking to Mamie," Eisenhower wrote Pawley, "I have come to the conclusion that her heart is really set on the [Gettysburg] Pennsylvania farm." Eisenhower regretted "we cannot look forward to having you and Edna as neighbors—but, after all, we won't be too far away for frequent visits."¹⁰

A frequent guest at the White House, Pawley often expressed his candid opinions to the president. Eisenhower was equally forthcoming. "Your understanding is not quite what I *think* I said at the dinner," Eisenhower wrote on a matter discussed at a White House stag dinner. "I think it would be very unwise to repeat anything publicly that was said at a private dinner. While in this case I see the logic of your suggestion, still this could lead to the most dangerous of practices and would eventually eliminate informal personal affairs for any President."¹¹ Eisenhower valued Pawley's opinions because he believed they were neither self-serving nor politically motivated. Pawley may have represented an extreme, conservative viewpoint, but Eisenhower always listened to his friend.

Mamie and Ike often visited Belvoir to relax in a rural environment far from Washington politics. Pawley also offered to host the president at his Miami home following Eisenhower's heart attack in 1955. The invitation originated with the mayor of Miami Beach who asked if Pawley's home could be made "available for a High Government official, should a vacation in Florida be possible." After agreeing, Pawley was "surprised and delighted" when he learned it would be the president. "Mamie and I were deeply touched by your extraordinary kindness in offering to us the use of your house on Miami Beach," Eisenhower wrote.

The planned Florida vacation, however, didn't occur. "The fact is," Eisenhower wrote, "that with the emphasis we are now giving to preparatory work for the coming session, I cannot go that distance from Washington. . . . So much as I should like to sit on your dock and fish, I simply cannot take advantage of the opportunity."¹² Although Eisenhower hadn't accepted Pawley's offer of hospitality this time, the president never hesitated to call upon his friend to serve his country.

One such opportunity came in May 1954 when Eisenhower called upon Pawley to help out in a delicate Central American situation. Guatemala had become a democratic nation in 1944 when it held its first ever free elections, but during the Truman administration there were rumblings that Guatemala had come under the influence of a Soviet-dominated regime. On March 15, 1951, Jacobo Arbenz Guzmán became the second democratically chosen president of Guatemala. His predecessor, Juan José Arévalo, barely survived his term of office owing to uprisings and attempted assassinations. Arbenz proposed elevating Guatemala from a quasi-colonial country, dependent on foreign corporations, through economic development and agrarian reform. He wanted to compete with foreign-owned corporations instead of nationalizing them, but he faced two powerful groups—wealthy landowners (2.2 percent of the people held 70 percent of the arable land), and the United Fruit Company, which employed more workers than the entire Guatemalan industrial sector.[13]

Land reform began June 27, 1952, with the passage of an act allowing the government to expropriate uncultivated tracts of plantations and distribute small plots to landless peasants. True to his word, Arbenz announced plans to construct an Atlantic Coast port to compete with the privately owned Puerto Barrios of United Fruit. In addition, a new highway to the coast would be an alternative to the only railroad, which United Fruit also owned.[14]

In 1953, Walter Turnbull, a retired official of United Fruit, approached General Miguel Ydígoras Fuentes, the candidate Arbenz defeated in the election. Turnbull introduced Ydígoras to two CIA agents who would "lend their assistance" to overthrow Arbenz if Ydígoras would "favor" United Fruit and its railroad and would repay any expenses incurred during the takeover. Ydígoras wanted time to consider, but the CIA was anxious. It turned next to exiled rebel leader Col. Carlos Enrique Castillo Armas, who agreed to head the movement.[15] He was convinced "Arbenz was elected by assassination" and that "Communists had political control of Guatemala."[16]

Protecting its investment in Guatemala was reason enough for United Fruit to seek a change in the country's government, but the idea had to be sold to Washington and the American public. With Senator Joseph McCarthy ranting about "pinko" sympathizers, the choice was clear; it could paint Guatemala as under control of the Communists and demand that something had to be done. United Fruit sponsored a massive public relations campaign that labeled Arbenz a Communist and painted

Guatemala, which is close to the Panama Canal, as Moscow's selected target to gain a foothold in the Americas.

Arbenz may have even unwittingly helped UFC's cause with his public statements. He viewed Communism not as a threat to Guatemala but also saw anti-communism as a tool of foreign powers. Since Communists controlled the labor movement, Arbenz accepted them as the legitimate voice of the working class.[17] The State Department, monitoring the Arbenz administration, concluded that "Communist elements had consolidated their economic and political bases" in Guatemala.[18]

Meanwhile, Nicaraguan president Anastasio Somoza had visited Truman in April 1952 and offered to overthrow Arbenz. "Just give me the arms," he offered, "and I'll clean up Guatemala for you in no time."[19] Truman directed the CIA to investigate the possibility, out of which grew the plan code-named PBFORTUNE. The operation would supply Castillo Armas with $225,000 and weapons, while Nicaragua and Honduras would provide air support for an invasion of Guatemala. PBFORTUNE also had a proposal to assassinate "top flight Communists whom the new government would desire to eliminate immediately." Even Dominican dictator Rafael Trujillo offered his support if four Dominicans residing in Guatemala were killed prior to the invasion. A month before the U.S. presidential election, the CIA determined that PBFORTUNE had been co-opted, which should not have come as a surprise considering all the different parties involved.[20]

To begin with, United Fruit offered one of its ships to be refitted to carry the arms shipment. Because the crates were labeled "agricultural machinery," two officials of the stevedores union in New Orleans were let in on the secret. After the ship had sailed for Nicaragua, a CIA agent went to Edward G. Miller, Jr., assistant secretary of state for Inter-American Affairs, and asked him to sign an authorization request on behalf of the State Department's Munitions Division. Miller showed the document to Deputy Undersecretary of State Freeman Matthews and Undersecretary of State David Bruce. The three confronted Secretary of State Dean Acheson, who in turn went to see Truman. The president immediately aborted the plan and had the ship redirected to Panama, where the weapons were unloaded.[21]

When Eisenhower assumed office, advocates wanting Arbenz overthrown had someone who would listen. Committed during the campaign to thwart the spread of Communism, Eisenhower readily agreed action was needed in Guatemala. The question was, what should be done? Assigned to Mexico near the end of Truman's administration, the CIA's Howard Hunt learned through his contacts that "Arbenz might be vulnerable to some type of paramilitary operation."[22]

Before committing to a covert military operation, though, Eisenhower wanted assurances that other avenues had been explored. John Moors Cabot, newly appointed assistant secretary of state for American republic affairs, toured Caribbean nations and met with Arbenz. Cabot wrote, "President Arbenz had the pale, cold-lipped look of the ideologue and showed no interest in my suggestions for a change of course. . . . He had obviously sold out to the Communists and that was that."[23]

U.S. ambassador to Guatemala John E. Peurifoy also felt Arbenz might be trouble. After a six-hour dinner in December 1953, with only the Guatemalan president and their wives present, Peurifoy filed a five-page report to John Foster Dulles, concluding, "I am definitely convinced that if the President is not a Communist, he will certainly do until one comes along."[24]

Covert action against foreign governments was nothing new to the Eisenhower administration. Acting on a British proposal on August 19, 1953, the CIA had ousted Mohammad Mossadegh, the democratically elected prime minister of Iran, and restored power to the exiled shah, Mohammad Reza Pahlavi.[25] By the fall of 1953, methods were being discussed on how to eliminate Arbenz. Out of these meetings, the National Security Council authorized the CIA to formulate a covert operation. Working with the State Department, the CIA drew up plans for PBSUCCESS, which involved removing "covertly, and without bloodshed if possible, the menace of the present Communist-controlled government of Guatemala."[26] John Foster Dulles was in charge of the overall operation, and he advised the president to establish an informal special committee to deal with procedures. "I suggested that this committee should consist of Dr. Milton Eisenhower, Walter Donnelly and Bill Pawley. The President agreed to the last two names." Eisenhower thought his brother, Milton, would not have time to devote to the task, but Dulles said it would only require "an hour or so a month."[27]

At home in Miami Beach, Pawley received a call on May 16, 1954, from Eisenhower, who asked him to come to Washington immediately on a confidential and urgent matter. Assistant Secretary of State for Latin American Affairs Henry F. Holland and Walter Donnelly, U.S. Steel representative in Latin America, met Pawley at the airport when he arrived the following evening. Not knowing what his assignment was, Pawley invited them to his suite at the Mayflower Hotel, where they talked until two o'clock in the morning.[28]

The project was Guatemala and how the United States could offer assistance to the Castillo Armas–led rebels who sought to overthrow the government. Before joining the committee, Pawley wanted Eisenhower's assurances that "we would commit ourselves to seeing the operation through to success." Eisenhower agreed and planning began. The president's brother withdrew from the group when he learned his wife had cancer. Walter Donnelly also withdrew after U.S. Steel advised him that his value to the company in Latin America might decrease if he participated in the plan. Forging ahead, the rest of the Guatemala group set up offices in the State Department and received the CIA's full support and resources.[29]

The plan called for establishing a powerful radio station (Voice of Liberation) to "coordinate the planning and execution of PBSUCCESS" and override the Guatemalan national radio. Later, when the airwaves were bombarded with propaganda, Arbenz became convinced that U.S. armed forces supported the invading army, when in fact the rebel force consisted of only two hundred men and mercenary pilots staging a few bombing raids.[30] The group set up operations at a secret military base at Miami's Opa-Locka Airport and trained rebels for the invasion. "We had these black flights coming in," Howard Hunt recalled, "practically around the clock, bringing in people for training."[31] Allen Dulles showed up, "resplendent in a tweed sport coat and puffing on his pipe," to give a pep talk and exhorted everyone to do their jobs in stopping the spread of Communism.[32] In addition to supplying arms and training, "K" groups, or assassination teams, were being trained for assassinations on known Communists once the invasion began.[33]

Allen Dulles summoned Al Haney, the CIA station chief in Seoul, to head up the Opa-Locka operation. Taking charge, Haney began increasing his role in PBSUCCESS, much to the chagrin of Frank Wisner, who ran the overall operation from Washington. "It was a system of double headquarters that led to a lot of squabbling," Richard M. Bissell, Jr., later said. "It was a mistake that we avoided in the Bay of Pigs operation; Opa-Locka was used again, but there was only one headquarters—Washington, period!"[34]

Even though planning was carried out in secrecy, word began leaking that the United States was contemplating the overthrow of Arbenz. Phil Graham, publisher of the *Washington Post*, told Pawley about the planned invasion after they played a game of tennis. Pawley listened as Graham revealed detailed information he had received. "I might as well have been listening to a top secret briefing at State," Pawley wrote. Although his role in the planning wasn't mentioned, Pawley learned the source of the leak, a high official in the CIA covert operations division. He reported his finding immediately to Eisenhower, whose response surprised him: "I want you to conduct a thorough investigation of the covert side of CIA operations for me."

Although flattered by Eisenhower's confidence in him, Pawley knew realistically he was not the man for the job. Citing a possible breakdown in the special relationship Pawley had with the Dulles brothers, Pawley suggested Eisenhower appoint someone else to head the investigation. Mulling it over, Eisenhower agreed. He appointed James Doolittle to lead, but Eisenhower still wanted Pawley to be part of the investigation. Later, after the Guatemala operation, the Doolittle Commission would delve into the CIA's operations and organization and make recommendations to the president.[35]

Meanwhile, diplomatic measures were also tried to lend legitimacy to the overthrow. At the March 1954 Tenth Inter-American Conference at Caracas, John Foster Dulles attempted to secure a resolution calling for action against Communism in Latin America "without prior consultation." Only U.S.-supported dictatorships— Nicaragua, El Salvador, Peru, Venezuela, and the Dominican Republic—endorsed the resolution.[36] Watered down with an agreement to "consult" with member nations before taking any action, the resolution passed with sixteen votes.

For his part, Pawley arranged a social gathering on June 13 at his Virginia farm and invited ambassadors from several Central and South American countries to discuss their views and opinions. A week later, he held another luncheon attended by Latin American ambassadors and their wives, along with several U.S. diplomatic and military officials.[37]

The United States also sought legitimacy for the operation from outside Latin America. In 1953, the British were about to sell military vehicles to the Arbenz government when British minister of state Selwyn Lloyd sent Prime Minister Churchill a memorandum outlining a quid pro quo proposal with the United States. It said Britain would ban military equipment shipments to Guatemala if the United States withheld any military support of Egypt during Britain's Suez crisis. After the Guatemalan coup, when Arbenz attempted to elicit help from the United Nations, Britain abstained (along with France) from a Security Council motion to place the issue on the agenda. British deputy prime minister Anthony Eden wrote in his memoir that "the United States had encouraged the overthrow of a Communist-influenced government [Guatemala]. . . . We had understood her action there and done what we could not to hamper her in the Security Council."[38]

The meticulous planning was completed, the training and arming of the rebel forces had been accomplished, and the diplomatic policy to provide the right for intervention was in place. All that remained was finding a catalyst to initiate the invasion. On May 15, 1954, the Swedish freighter *Alfhem* docked at Puerto Barrios and began unloading cargo. Except for stevedores and military officials, the port was off-limits while the crates labeled as optical and laboratory equipment were unloaded. What they actually contained was more than a million dollars' worth of military weapons and ammunition purchased from Czechoslovakia. "Having been refused arms purchases by the United States . . . Guatemala turned to the Iron Curtain for arms."[39] Arbenz was mistaken in thinking the arms shipment was secret, because the CIA had known about it for almost a year. When it sailed from Szczecin, Poland, on April 17, 1954, the CIA and the U.S. Navy tracked the *Alfhem* until it arrived in Guatemala.

Dulles contacted British ambassador to the United States Roger Makins to seek assurances that British vessels would cooperate when U.S. Navy ships detained any boat suspected of having arms. "Whatever the law may be," Dulles said, he hoped Deputy Prime Minister Eden "would, in practice, agree to whatever action was necessary in order to prevent further arms reaching Guatemala." The thought of U.S. naval forces boarding British ships horrified the Foreign Office. When Dulles refused to back down, the British acquiesced. Superintending Undersecretary Richard Speaight felt that Dulles seemed "to think that the 'cold war' justifies the setting aside of the law and one might suppose from his attitude that the United States was directly threatened by Guatemalan aggression."[40]

Nevertheless, Dulles knew Britain would remain an ally, as it was counting on the United States to support its efforts in Egypt. On May 16, Allen Dulles convened a meeting of the Intelligence Advisory Committee, which determined that the arms shipment on the *Alfhem* posed a threat to the Panama Canal. The following day, he urged the National Security Council to take appropriate action. With its backing, Dulles set the invasion date for mid-June.[41]

Based upon his American Volunteer Group experiences in China, Pawley was concerned that the aircraft needed for the operation had been grossly underestimated. Nicaraguan president Somoza suggested it needed ten planes, and Pawley agreed. In a heated debate with Allen Dulles, who insisted three were sufficient,

Pawley finally yielded "against my better judgment." Anti-aircraft fire shot down two planes, and the third was disabled during the first two days of the invasion.[42] Immediate action was needed to support ground troops for the operation to succeed. With Castillo Armas pleading for replacement aircraft, Allen Dulles conferred with Assistant Secretary of State Henry Holland on how to get more planes to the rebels.

"It's not quite that simple, old boy," Holland told him. "We were in the clear when we originally supplied the arms to Nicaragua for use by Castillo Armas' forces. But now that a civil war exists in Guatemala, it's a new ball game—we're bound by treaty not to intervene."[43]

Pawley and Allen Dulles sought out Acting Secretary Robert Murphy, who was in charge of the State Department while John Dulles was out of town. Listening to both men and hearing Holland's dispassionate legal stance, Murphy decided to lay the decision on the president's desk. Granted an immediate audience, the group entered the Oval Office.

"Henry," Eisenhower said when he saw Holland carrying three large volumes under his arm, "put away the law books. Let's discuss this from a practical viewpoint."

Asked what the chances were if the planes were not replaced, Allen Dulles replied, "Nil."

"And if we supply them?" Eisenhower asked.

"Perhaps twenty percent."

Eisenhower knew "the important psychological impact of even a small amount of air support" and ordered Pawley to get the planes.[44] Although Eisenhower's decision to support the Guatemalan operation, which "only succeeded by the narrowest margins," is presented as a historic moment, chances are it would have succeeded anyway since the Guatemalan Army was convinced the United States would invade if the overthrow failed.[45] As for Guatemalan aircraft, most of them never left the ground because the airport administrator, a relative of a top military strategist to Castillo Armas, had given orders to have them sabotaged.[46]

Writing about the meeting in his memoir, Eisenhower stated that only Holland and Dulles had come to see him. Pawley asked Eisenhower about the recollection. "He told me that he had deliberately omitted my name," Pawley wrote, "because he felt that the practice of mentioning people who held no official position in affairs of this sort could have undesirable repercussions."[47]

Leaving the Oval Office, Pawley rushed to his office and told his secretary to get Nicaraguan ambassador Guillermo Sevilla-Sacasa, a personal friend, on the phone. He informed the ambassador of Eisenhower's decision and asked how quickly he could come up with $150,000. "I've arranged with the Defense Department to have a bill of sale ready for the purchase of three aircraft [Republic P-47 Thunderbolt fighter-bombers] by your government." When Sevilla-Sacasa said it would take two or three days to raise the money, Pawley replied, "That's too long. I'll have to advance it to you."

While his secretary emptied his briefcase, Pawley called an officer of the Riggs Bank in Washington and arranged to have the cash ready when he arrived in a half hour. Accompanied by Sevilla-Sacasa, Pawley drove to the bank, stuffed the money into his briefcase, and headed for the Pentagon. It was an unorthodox transaction, but Department of Defense officials complied by signing the contract and transferring title of the planes to the Nicaraguan government. The three planes were in Puerto Rico, and Pawley put in a call to get them in the air. Arriving in Panama that evening, the planes were turned over to Guatemalan rebel pilots who flew into combat the next morning. A few days later, Pawley received a letter from Sevilla-Sacasa expressing his government's appreciation "for the immediate cooperation which you so graciously gave us in the purchase of the three airplanes."[48]

Although the overthrow of Arbenz was a success, the regime of Castillo Armas provoked civil unrest because of its repressive and corrupt policies. The regime suspended the Constitution, put the secret police back in power, and granted Castillo Armas authority to rule by decree. Insisting that Castillo Armas had helped stem the "Red Tide," the Eisenhower administration received him on a state visit and sent him to Denver to confer with Eisenhower, who was recovering from a heart attack.[49] "Deep down everyone in Guatemala knows that Communism was not the issue," Daniel Graham reported. "Feudalism was the issue, and those who profited from feudalism won."[50] For United Fruit's efforts to replace Arbenz, the restored properties and privileges they previously enjoyed were worth less than before, with profit margins dropping from 33.4 percent in 1950 to 15.4 percent in 1957.[51]

In 1957, Castillo Armas was assassinated, and Guatemala plunged into a long, protracted civil war. A military junta held elections for a successor, but after reports of blatant fraud, another election was held. Gen. Miguel Ydígoras Fuentes was elected, but it did little to stem opposition of the working classes. Having a change of heart about cooperating with the CIA, Ydígoras Fuentes later allowed Guatemala to be used as a staging ground for the Bay of Pigs invasion. When reports of his involvement surfaced, Ydígoras Fuentes was forced to impose martial law.

When former president Arévalo announced his candidacy for the 1963 election, strongman Col. Enrique Peralta Azurdia seized control and canceled elections. In 1966, Julio Mendez Montenegro, the Revolutionary Party candidate, won a plurality, and Peralta Azurdia allowed him to become president on the condition that the military would continue to maintain its independence. A reign of terror followed when the army began eliminating guerrilla groups opposed to the military and used the opportunity to silence anyone who protested government policies. When Col. Carlos Arana Osario assumed the presidency in 1970, very little had changed. Backed by the U.S. and Guatemalan landowners, the people suffered poverty, social injustices, and economic instability for more than thirty years under a government of military rule bent on stamping out dissidents by means of terror and repression.[52]

Operation PBSUCCESS might have been a success, but the patient lingered in ill health for decades. Eisenhower drew heavy criticism for America's role in the takeover, and the controversy would shape U.S. foreign policy against the spread of Communism in Cuba and Vietnam in the years to come.

For his participation in PBSUCCESS, Pawley received a warm letter from John Foster Dulles expressing his thanks for cooperating in the planning of the operation.[53] Eisenhower wanted to appoint Pawley to a post, but Dulles felt "he was better qualified for special missions than for a steady desk job," mentioning "his useful work in connection with Guatemala."[54] As a result, Pawley was back to work as a troubleshooter, specifically as a State Department consultant on Central America.[55]

15

Buses and Trolleys

In 1941, Pawley purchased the Miami Beach Railway Company from Florida Power and Light, beginning a long and sometimes troublesome business venture lasting twenty years. At the time of the purchase, the company had a $1.2 million deficit, but over time (except when it lost $36,000 in 1951), it began showing a profit every year and wiped out the huge deficit.[1]

On April 3, 1947, George B. Dunn, majority stockholder of the Miami Transit Company, died. He had started the Dunn Bus Company in 1915, servicing Miami south of Flagler Street into Coconut Grove. In 1925, he bought several small jitney services and reorganized the streetcars into the Miami Transit Company. By 1940, he had taken over the city-owned bus lines and merged them with Miami Transit Company, which had a fleet of 208 buses covering 193 miles of routes.[2] A year after Dunn's death, Pawley purchased Miami Transit.

Adding a neighboring bus system to one he had been operating successfully seemed a wise move, but Pawley soon learned his acquisition was fraught with problems. "It appears that under the old management," Pawley wrote to George Marshall, ". . . the head of the local labor union was actually running the company and permitting many payments of extremely substantial sums to be made to personnel, not provided for in the contract."[3] Calling the Miami Beach system a "model of efficiency," with "praise for the fine equipment, frequent schedules and courteous drivers," a *Miami Daily News* editorial felt Pawley was "taking up a Herculean task" to revamp Miami Transit.[4]

Labor problems plagued Miami Transit for several years, despite Pawley's efforts to improve relations with the bus union. In addition, the company continu-

203

ally sought relief from the City Commission for fare increases. Bus transportation jurisdiction in Dade County was divided among various municipalities and the state's Railroad and Public Utilities Commission. Pawley offered Miami Transit and Miami Beach Railway to the city of Miami for $4 million, nothing down, and ten years to repay, but the city turned it down. Union leaders were "dead set" against public ownership because they would lose a basic bargaining chip; strikes against government-run utilities were forbidden.[5]

In 1955, the Miami Chamber of Commerce proposed giving the Dade Port Authority power to "take over, own and operate" a unified, countywide bus system. The outcry against the plan came from the bus union and the mayor's office, but not from Pawley, who viewed it as an opportunity to get out of the bus business.[6] Calling the plan "a midnight scheme to unload the [Miami and Miami Beach] bus companies to the county," a bus union attorney charged Pawley with trying to dump his bus companies before the union contract expired. Miami mayor Abe Aronovitz said the city would lose $250,000 a year in taxes from the bus company. Although not commenting directly on the plan, Pawley let it be known he was willing "to accept a sales agreement with the county which would call for no down payment," adding he would "never oppose any move that will in the last analysis result in the good of the community."[7]

Expecting a confrontation between Pawley, the mayor, and the bus union, the *Miami Daily News* published a two-part article written by staff writer Jane Wood, mother of future attorney general Janet Reno. "A festering boil is getting bigger. . . . This boil is bus service," the article began. After recapping Miami's bus history, Wood wrote that "the nub of the whole matter" was whether Pawley was honest about his company losing money, or if Mayor Aronovitz's charge that "the loss is all done with fancy bookkeeping" was the true picture.

The second article featured a cartoon depicting Pawley in a top hat and tails, similar to the Monopoly game character, storming city hall as buses wearing feathered headdresses encircle him. Outlining Pawley's diplomatic and business career, Wood noted, "The only two failures in his record of business operations around the world have both been in Miami"—his 1920s real estate venture and the bus company. After buying Miami Transit and "realizing that he had bitten off more than he could chew," Wood wrote, "he began trying to sell the city the bus line within a year."[8]

Pawley made two offers for the city to purchase his bus company. The first was a cash price of $1.5 million, with the city assuming the $2.5 million of company debts. The second was a "no down payment" offer for $2.2 million. Whichever offer the city chose, it would still have to assume Miami Transit's debts and the contract problem with the union was still unresolved.[9]

"We're not going to take the city's word, or anybody's word for that matter," union president W. O. Frazier declared vehemently, "that the union will be taken care of." Pointing out that the union had agreed to a profit-sharing plan in the last contract, and "everybody promised us then that they would help in making sure there were profits to share," Frazier charged that after the contract was signed, the union was forgotten. "This time we want to be sure that the union doesn't get kicked around."[10]

Taking the initiative, Pawley negotiated a new union contract. He had already signed a new union contract for Miami Beach Railway that gave the 150 employees a nineteen-cent raise spread over three years.[11] Miami Transit drivers would receive higher wages but only if the city agreed to abolish the franchise tax.[12] Aronovitz challenged Pawley to prove Miami Transit was losing money. With the City Commission in favor of granting Pawley a new bus franchise, Aronovitz stalled the vote. He hired Herbert Pope, director of the Chicago Public Administration Service, to analyze Miami Transit's books and asked Pawley to pick up the tab. The City Commission went along with the survey, even agreeing to pay for Pope's services if Pawley refused.[13]

Pawley wrote to the mayor and countered that Miami Transit had already hired three experts to go over the books. He was willing to pay for another review, up to a maximum cost of $5,000, if he were allowed to appoint an accountant, the city another, and the American Transit Association a third. "If this suggestion is agreeable to you," Pawley wrote, "we respectfully suggest that the three experts visit Miami at the same time and work jointly on the matter."[14]

During a radio talk show, Aronovitz agreed to Pawley's proposal, but he felt it "a mistake" to allow the American Transit Association to appoint a member. "I think the Miami Chamber of Commerce Committee, or the Greater Miami Development Committee should name the third party." He then accused the bus company of "unfair principles" by submitting one copy of its returns to the federal government and a different one to the city.[15] The mayor offered two ways to solve the problem. The city could grant a twenty-year franchise to the bus company, "based on its unfair and unreasonable demands," or it could work out a plan based upon what is "right and wrong" in a nebulous, undefined alternative that he didn't explain.[16] The mayor also accused Pawley and Frazier of collusion to force the city to avoid a strike.[17]

Miami hired Dr. John Bauer, a New York public utilities expert, to determine if Pawley's bus company was losing money. He wanted the union and bus company to negotiate a contract not dependent on a favorable city franchise. "Make your contract with the city," he offered. "Then let the company go to court and force the city to allow a reasonable earnings schedule."[18] A public utilities expert, Bauer was working on bus franchise cases in three other cities when he agreed to come to Miami for $100 a day plus expenses.[19] Pawley offered his own plan, a program guaranteeing a 3½ percent profit of gross revenue, and avoided any worries of collecting rebates at the end of the year. Acknowledging Dr. Bauer as an "extremely able and competent person," Pawley added regrets that the transit expert "was closeted with the city commission and didn't check the other side."[20]

In the summer of 1956, Pawley expanded his bus empire by purchasing South Miami Coach Lines, intending to dovetail South Miami Coach with his existing lines.[21] In September, he purchased the Red Adams Bus Lines, a company that operated chartered and sightseeing tours. His plan was not to merge Adams with his other bus lines; instead, he wanted to rent idle Miami Transit buses to the tour company during slack periods. "We'll now be able to get more use, and therefore more revenue from our buses," he said.[22]

Pawley also owned Key Island Transit, a ten-bus fleet servicing Key West that he had purchased in 1956. Four years later, Pawley announced he was shutting it down and gave city commissioners one month to buy him out. Because the city had no authority to purchase the bus line, city officials scurried to find private investors. Pawley had set a price of $25,000 for the company, plus all assets and liabilities. As the deadline approached, former Texas oilman and Key West resident Ernest Brooks stepped up and met Pawley's offer.[23]

Meanwhile, as the Miami metropolitan area continued to grow, providing adequate public transportation became a problem. Eleven bus systems and five jitney companies serviced Dade County, in most cases operating within restricted limits. Pawley's lines accommodated 84 percent of county riders. Studies to unify all bus lines into one system had existed for several years, but no progress had been made.

During the spring and summer of 1959, the dream of a unified bus system seemed about to become a reality, with Pawley's interests at the core of the deal.

Under an operating authority named Miami-Dade Metro, the area was in a position to acquire the bus lines and place them under one system. Pawley agreed to sell all three of his bus lines to Metro for $8,113,000. He would take the bulk in tax-free 5 percent bonds, yielding him more than $300,000 a year until the bonds were retired.[24] After an audit placed the appraised value of the three bus companies at $8.4 million, Pawley upped the price to $9.4 million. He said the extra million would cover taxes or claims against his company during the transition. "Why should I be stuck for the taxes if the county owns the business?" he asked.[25]

Dade County then established the Metro Transit Authority, a commission empowered to submit proposals on how best to bring about a new bus system.[26] Working with citizen groups, Pawley applied pressure on the commission to purchase his bus lines. Metro Transit Authority agreed in principle to buy Pawley's bus companies for $8.2 million, payable over ten years with 5 percent bonds. When the proposal was presented to the Metro Commission, it voted to exercise an option only on Miami Transit. The deal called for the county to pay Pawley $1.5 million in cash and to assume the company's liabilities of an additional $4.3 million.[27]

Negotiations continued between Pawley and the union over further wage increases, but they made little headway. With Metro looking to purchase the bus lines from Pawley, he felt little need to resolve the issue. Once Metro took over the system, drivers would not be allowed to strike. With only a bond validation hearing holding up the bus system's transfer to Metro, preliminary measures were taken to assure a peaceful transition. When the union contract expired at the beginning of 1962, Metro sent out job application forms to union bus drivers. An accompanying letter said, "If such forms are not returned, it will be assumed that you do not wish to work for Dade County." Out of 780 employees, only twenty-five drivers and eighteen other bus line employees signed on.[28] The union had advised workers not to return the forms, setting the stage for a battle between the union and the county.

When the courts validated the bond issue to purchase Pawley's bus lines, the union still hadn't reached an agreement on a new contract. Leaders wanted a thirty-seven-cents-an-hour wage increase, but negotiations had come to a halt. Because Pawley still legally owned the bus system, even though the real fight was against the county, the union still considered Pawley at fault. "We charge that Pawley is depriving us unfairly of bargaining rights," the union contended. It accused him of conspiring with Metro "by agreeing to transfer the status of employer to Dade County even though Pawley continues to have all the benefits of ownership."[29]

The only matter left to settle was the legal transfer and purchase arrangement between Pawley and Metro. A May 1962 referendum secured Metro's right to take over the system.[30] By November terms of the purchase were settled. Pawley received $7 million for the bus lines and another $2 million in bonds at an interest rate "a shade below" 5 percent. Spread over fifteen years, the total cost to the county, including interest, was more than $13 million.[31]

Having owned the bus lines for two decades, Pawley was finally able to sever most of his business ties with Miami, but he still maintained one last connection to his former employees. After Metro took over the system, twenty-one drivers lost their medical insurance coverage because they had never been county employees. Without publicity, Pawley personally assumed the premiums for his former workers.[32]

Meanwhile, having spent his childhood in Cuba, Pawley returned in 1950 to oversee his newest acquisition, the Havana trolley car system. Outdated and badly in need of major repairs—"an average of seventy were breaking down each day"—the electric tram system ran on steel rails through narrow, winding streets and crammed up to sixty passengers in a conveyance designed to hold twenty.[33] A tangled, tattered maze of overhead wires provided power to the dilapidated rolling stock, creating an eyesore on Havana's streets.

The Havana Electric Railway Company operated the system owned by the Electric Bond and Share of New York until it defaulted on a mortgage loan. When the bank holding the note foreclosed, the Cuban government purchased the assets. Installing its own management, Havana hoped to see some improvement, but service deteriorated and the company continued operating at a loss. Seeing an opportunity, Pawley made an offer for the trolley system.[34]

Already a seasoned owner of the Miami Transit Company, Pawley felt the best solution would be to junk the entire Havana system, tear out the rails, and replace the rattletrap electric trams with modern buses. In an $11 million package deal, he offered to settle bondholder claims with a $1.5 million payment. As new owner, he would put up $1.2 million for operating capital and arrange financing for 720 modern buses. To win over the labor unions, he agreed to assign 25 percent of the company's stock to the worker's retirement fund.[35]

The Cuban cabinet had to approve the plan, but before it could act on the offer, Havana newspapers began opposing the deal. Local business interests felt they should be allowed to present a proposal, but no one seemed to know what that would be. Protesting the Pawley offer, trolley workers walked off the job. Calling the strike illegal, the government jailed six union leaders and ordered soldiers and the national police to operate the streetcars. The one-day strike ended when President Carlos Prío Socarrás released the labor leaders, who ordered workers back on the job.[36]

The Cuban Council of Ministers awarded the franchise on March 10, 1950 to Pawley, who had the financial resources to back the project and a proven management team.[37] Forming a new corporation, Autobuses Modernos de la Habana, Pawley installed himself as president and general manager, heading a team he brought from Miami to organize and operate the new system. Although the team remained in Havana only long enough to get the company running, Pawley and Edna decided to move to Havana and take up residence while he supervised his new enterprise.[38]

After purchasing 100 buses from a Philadelphia company, Pawley sought financing for more. "First we made the rounds of every possible source in the United States," Assistant General Manager T. E. Lewis recalled, "but the banks and bus companies all turned us down."[39] Eleven U.S. banks, including the Export-Import Bank, wanted no part of the deal. He tried the British Export Credits Guarantee Department, hoping postwar England would relish the opportunity to provide the capital. It established a $7.7 million line of credit, provided that Pawley purchase the buses from England. He placed an order for 620 modern buses with Leyland Motors, Limited, and put up 10 percent in cash, with the British government carrying the rest on credit.[40] "I'm so impressed with the quality of the Leyland," Pawley said, "that it's very likely that the next order placed for buses by the Miami Transit Co. will be for the same bus."[41]

Cuban newspapers again tried to block Pawley's deal with their government. Leading the attack was *El Mundo*, which was principally owned by Amadeo Barletta, who also held distribution rights in Cuba for General Motors (GMC). "Behind this deal is a rapacious promoter internationally known for his misdeeds and crooked deals," *El Mundo* proclaimed, "a buzzard who presents himself to us disguised as the Holy Ghost, a speculator in shady business, a knave with hands of silk." Pawley ignored his critics and pressed ahead, but *El Mundo* would not relent. "Pawley came to Havana and said: 'I have come to exchange the old streetcars for modern buses to benefit the population.' But what he really intends to do is exchange the goat for the cow."[42]

Realizing he would be labeled a foreign capitalist seeking to take control of Havana's transportation system, Pawley placed several Cuban nationals in the company, including Jorge Vila, lieutenant to the late president Machado.[43] Enlisting the aid of the trolley conductors by promising to keep them on the job, Pawley gained support of the trolley union, which in turn promoted the new company to Havana's straphangers. The weekly *Bohemia*, in contrast to other Havana newspapers, called Pawley "one of the most distinguished figures in the U.S., whose various enterprises, including aviation firms in India and China, make his biography a true teaching in industry and social service."

Despite media pressure, President Prío awarded the bus franchise to Pawley's company. The twenty-five-year contract gave him 4 percent interest on the $3 million he invested, and he would "be well paid by the company as president and manager." But he had competition. Omnibus Aliados, the other Havana bus company, had made arrangements to purchase 300 GMC buses, "thanks to the cooperation of General Motors."[44]

Pawley's honeymoon with the labor union also ended. "We needed only 2,200 men to operate the system," Pawley recalled, "but the union insisted that we retain all the 5,500 employees we had inherited."[45] While operating costs soared—monthly losses were $240,000—labor relations did not improve sufficiently to warrant continuing the enterprise.[46] Pawley threatened on several occasions to abandon the operation until President Prío stepped in and nationalized the bus franchise for the second time.[47] Dr. Antonio Silio y Gutierrez, legal consultant of the Ministry of Education, was appointed company manager and instructed to "take such measures as he deems desirable." Problems continued, however, even when Fulgencio Batista y Zaldívar reseized power in Cuba.[48] "The government reimbursed me for my investment—but not for my headaches," Pawley recalled.[49]

PART V
Dominican Republic and Cuba

16
Batista

Pawley's investment in Cuba went beyond the Havana public transportation system; he also wanted to buy a sugar plantation. A group of friends held 150,000 shares of a Cuban company, and in 1954 they wanted Pawley to buy another 250,000 shares so they could gain control. It was a vast operation with three sugar plantations, eight thousand head of cattle, and a wholly owned railroad to ship the product to market. Working assets were $5 million in cash, $4.5 million in negotiable securities, and $4 million of market-ready sugar. Physical assets—plants, buildings, railroads, and land—were approximately $13 million, while the debt side listed $7 million in loans and accounts payable, $1.5 million in taxes owed, and capital and earned surplus of $17 million.[1]

Book value of the stock was $26 a share, but it was selling at $11.[2] Pawley was "somewhat strapped" for cash, having recently laid out close to $5 million in other investments, but he wanted to put in $400,000. "We can in a very short length of time get our investment back," he wrote to friends, "and still retain a very substantial part of this company's assets."[3] When Republicans lost control of Congress in the 1954 elections, some of the friends Pawley had been urging to invest in the sugar company backed off for fear that U.S. support of the Batista government would diminish. But Pawley was "going ahead," because he felt Democrats would work with Eisenhower.[4] Having a considerable amount of his personal fortune tied up in Cuban investments, he knew it was imperative that the island government remain stable.

Batista had controlled Cuba since the early 1930s, but his political power was exercised behind the scenes. Batista allowed free elections to be held in 1944, and

213

Ramón Grau San Martin, an enemy of Batista's and a social reform advocate, was elected president. Following World War II, Grau faced rising prices, food supply shortages, and increasing black market activities. He was succeeded in 1948 by Carlos Prío Socarrás, whose government became graft ridden and corrupt. Backed by the military, Batista staged a coup and took control in March 1952. He faced resistance from opposing political organizations, including Fidel Castro's Movimiento Revolucionario 26 de Julio.[5]

The United States supported Batista with military hardware and the CIA helped establish the anti-Communist intelligence-gathering agency called the Buró Para Represión de las Actividades Comunistas (Bureau for the Repression of Communist Activities [BRAC]). "I was the father of the BRAC," U.S. ambassador to Cuba (1953–1957) Arthur Gardner revealed. But sympathy for Castro began softening the State Department hard-line position. Led by Assistant Secretary of State for Latin American Affairs Roy Rubottom and Director of the Office of Caribbean and Mexican Affairs William Wieland, hopes that Castro might offer a liberal government began forming U.S. policy. When *New York Times* reporter Herbert Matthews wrote a series of Castro-friendly articles, American public opinion began supporting the rebels.[6] But Pawley wasn't convinced Castro would be the savior of Cuba.

"In four or five meetings with Eisenhower during those years," Pawley recalled, ". . . I warned him of a Communist takeover if Castro ever came to power."[7] Eisenhower suggested that Pawley should be considered for the position of assistant secretary for Latin American affairs, but John Foster Dulles told the president he "recognized his ability but had some reservations."[8] Wieland had served as press attaché in Rio when Pawley was ambassador, and Pawley had "a squirmy feeling regarding his activities." With Wieland in a position to formulate U.S. policy in Cuba, Pawley went to see Eisenhower and Vice President Nixon to inform them of his misgivings. Eisenhower made arrangements for Pawley to meet Douglas Dillon at the State Department and transmit his information. At the meeting, Pawley said,

> I would like to do something that I know you people don't particularly like but I think it is important that I do it. I have great misgivings of the wiseness to have had and to continue to have William Wieland in a critical post. His close association with Herbert Matthews of the New York Times and the activities having to do with this whole Cuban episode in which

he is in charge, and has a great deal to do with the policies that come out, this man should not be there, and he should not have been there for a long time.[9]

Pawley was told in no uncertain terms that Wieland would remain at his post. Pawley was unaware that the president's brother, Dr. Milton Eisenhower, who acted as an adviser on Latin American affairs—but had never visited Cuba—received information on Cuba from Eubottom and Wieland and supported them both.

Pawley, along with several career diplomats, always had misgivings on how State Department policy was formed. "I believe that the policies are determined in the lower echelon," former ambassador to Cuba Earl Smith testified, "and by the time the higher echelon receives them, policies have already been made, and they have to live by them."[10] Smith would later be more specific: "I think 'The Fourth Floor,' the lower echelon of the State Department, was interested in seeing the revolution succeed—for the overthrow of the rightist dictator."[11]

Pawley offered an even more detailed assessment of the procedure during his tenure at the State Department:

No one ever puts his name on a document. You can never pin anything down. . . . A policy paper develops, let's say, for the sake of argument, on Cuba . . . I will get word one day there will be a policy paper discussion in room 427 at 3 o'clock. . . . There will be 30 people sitting around from many branches of Government and they will hand you a mimeographed document . . . There are no names or anything on it. You don't know where it came from or who did it or anything else and you will sit down and the senior men will say, "let's start, read page 1." . . . you go through the whole thing, they will change words, and change paragraphs and they will debate back and forth, but nobody ever debated whether this policy paper itself had any justification or whether the thing they were driving at made sense.

. . . When it was all over, all of those people would sign this document on this margin. Then it would go to the Under Secretary and he would see all these signatures on here, and obviously he is a very busy man, so he puts his on it. It goes up to the Secretary. That becomes a policy paper, a U.S. Government policy paper, and it is made by a man of very junior position and not only junior, but very questionable judgment on whether this thing is right or wrong.[12]

This common manner of formulating policy at the State Department was, in Pawley's opinion, the reason why the U.S. government supported Castro. Democratic senators James O. Eastland of Mississippi and Thomas J. Dodd of Connecticut, who were on the committee investigating the reasons for Castro's rise to power, agreed: "American foreign policy is not made in the office of Secretary [Christian] Herter on the fifth floor of the State Department. It is made on the fourth floor, by the unknown policy planners and memo makers who fill the Secretary's 'in' basket."[13]

Nevertheless, the damage was done, and Batista lost U.S. support, beginning with an arms embargo in March 1958. This restriction "caught the Armed Forces [of Cuba] with obsolete equipment," Batista said, and placed "the United States in a position of neutrality between the constitutional government and the groups who developed their illegal terrorist plans."[14] At the same time, Pawley was aware that federal authorities were "closing their eyes" and allowing illegal arms shipments to leave Florida bound for Castro forces in the mountains of Cuba.[15]

Although Roosevelt had said Batista was a "son-of-a-bitch, but he was our son-of-a-bitch," it was apparent that Eisenhower did not hold the same opinion.[16] Critics pointed out that millions in military aid given to Batista for hemispheric defense had been used in the dictator's struggle against Castro.[17] Batista was a liability and expendable, but was Castro an acceptable substitute? Pawley urged Eisenhower to keep Batista or replace him with a military junta acceptable to the United States, but under no circumstances should he allow Castro to gain control.

Eisenhower listened, but he wanted State Department approval. He sent Pawley to see Rubottom and Wieland to convince them on this approach. "Knowing that I was licked before I started," Pawley wrote, "I nevertheless followed Ike's instructions." Citing "mountains of evidence" that Castro was a Communist, Pawley warned the two men: "If you permit this man to seize power, you're going to invite more trouble than you've ever seen in your life."[18] His pleas fell on deaf ears. They were convinced that Castro was not a Communist and indeed was key to Cuba's future.[19]

Time was running out. Pawley saw that he had to convince Eisenhower to replace Batista with a hand-picked military junta and prevent Castro from gaining power. What Pawley didn't know at the time was that the idea of replacing Batista

William Douglas Pawley and Annie-Hahr Dobbs in Marietta, Georgia (photo taken in 1919). *Courtesy of Annie-Hahr McKay*

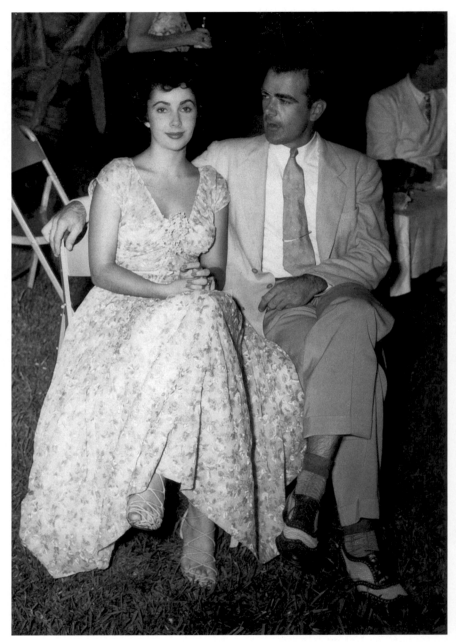

Elizabeth Taylor and William Douglas Pawley, Jr., at lawn party at the home of neighbor Julio Sanchez (photo by unknown guest—1949). *Courtesy of William Douglas Pawley, Jr.*

Mother Annie-Hahr Pawley (photo by Murnor—Miami, 1934). *Courtesy of Annie-Hahr McKay*

Dedication of Rancho Boyeros Airport, Cuba, February 24, 1930. Left to right: Capt. Mario Torres Menier, Cmdr. of the CAEC (Cuerpo de Aviacion Ejecito de Cuba, or Cuban Army Air Corps); Capt. Gustavo Alfonso, director of CAEC's Flight Academy and chief air instructor; William Douglas Pawley; Col. Jose Aire, head of the Cuban Secret Service; Gen. Alberto Herrera Franchi, Chief of Staff; Gerardo Machado, president of Cuba; Carlos de la Rosa, vice president of Cuba; Commodore L. Llaneras, Cuban Navy; Dr. Pablo Carrera Justiz, lawyer and vice president of Escuela Curtiss Flight School. *Courtesy of Annie-Hahr McKay*

William Douglas Pawley in Shanghai in Chinese garb (date unknown). *Courtesy of William Douglas Pawley, Jr.*

General Eisenhower's visit to Rio de Janeiro, Brazil (August 4 10, 1946). Left to right: Marshal João Batista Mascarenhas de Moraes (in front); Col. Jose Bina Machado; William Douglas Pawley; General Dwight David Eisenhower; Mamie Eisenhower. *Courtesy of William Douglas Pawley, Jr.*

had already made the rounds of the State Department. In April 1958 former ambassador to Brazil Adolf Berle and Puerto Rican governor Luis Muñoz Marín had
submitted a plan to the State Department that called for Batista to step down and
allow free elections. Batista had rejected the plan and another that would replace
him with a candidate submitted by President José María Hipólito Figueres Ferrer
of Costa Rica.[20]

In late November 1958, Pawley moderated a public forum in Miami with ambassadors and officials from several Latin American countries. Among them were
American officials from the State Department and the CIA, including former assistant secretary of state for inter-American affairs Henry Holland, Deputy Assistant
Secretary of State for Inter-American Affairs William Pennell Snow, and Chief of
the Western Hemisphere Division of the CIA's Directorate of Plans J. C. King.[21]
After the forum, the Americans, who were staying as Pawley's guests, held their
own meeting and discussed the Cuban situation until three o'clock in the morning.

"I told them that we should now, to try to save the place, to see if we can go
down there to get Batista to capitulate to a caretaker government unfriendly to him,
but satisfactory to us, whom we could immediately recognize and give military
assistance to in order that Fidel Castro not come to power," Pawley recalled. After
discussing issues and possibilities, the group felt Pawley should go to Washington
with them and attend meetings at the State Department and CIA to hammer out a
course of action.[22] "I hated to phone [John Foster] Dulles, who was desperately ill
[with cancer] in Washington," Pawley wrote, "but I considered that his approval
was essential before I made any other move."[23] Dulles liked what he heard and
called Eisenhower, asking him to hear Pawley out on the proposal.

Pawley was a salesman at heart and had no difficulty in convincing Eisenhower
the plan had merit. Since Pawley spoke fluent Spanish and was a longtime friend of
Batista's, Eisenhower selected him to make the pitch to the Cuban dictator. Before
heading to Havana, Pawley spent several days at the State Department, working
out details of the offer he would make. "I have a lot of influence with Batista,"
Pawley boasted, "and I'm going to use it. I'll lay it on the line."[24]

The first step would be to provide a sanctuary for Batista, his family, and
closest friends. The Cuban dictator owned a home in Daytona Beach and it was
suggested he reside there. Next, a caretaker regime composed of anti-Batista supporters would be appointed as an interim government until free elections could be
held eighteen months later. Third, the caretaker government could take no reprisals

against Batista's followers. After a duly elected government was installed, how-ever, the courts would be free to prosecute anyone of crimes committed during the Batista regime. Finally, the U.S. government would recognize the caretaker government immediately and grant $10 million in military aid to prevent Castro from gaining power.[25]

The list of names being considered as interim caretakers included Col. Ramón Barquín, Gen. Martín Díaz Tamayo, Col. Enrique Borbonnet, José Pepin Bosch, and a fifth man Pawley couldn't recall. Barquín had received training at the U.S. Army Strategic Intelligence School and had served as the military attaché at the Cuban Embassy in Washington, but at the time of Pawley's visit, he was imprisoned in Cuba for conspiracy to overthrow Batista. Held incommunicado, he didn't know he was being considered (and later he would split with Castro when he saw Cuba was becoming a Communist country). In any event, it seemed doubtful Barquín would have worked with Tamayo since it was Tamayo who had sentenced Barquín to prison. Borbonnet was also in prison with Barquín on the Isle of Pines. Bosch, a member of the family that owned the Bacardi rum company and former finance minister under Batista, had been financing Castro.[26]

Feeling confident he could sell Batista the plan, Pawley packed his bags and stopped at the White House for a last-minute conferral with Eisenhower. "As I was leaving the White House," Pawley recalled, "J. C. King told me that acting Secretary Herter wanted me to see Rubottom before my departure."[27] Pawley knew some-thing was wrong, but he couldn't ignore the call. Arriving at the State Department, Pawley was ushered into a conference room where Herter, Rubottom, and Wieland were gathered with several other officials familiar with Latin American policies.

As expected, Pawley was informed of a "modification," as Rubottom phrased it, to the proposal being made to Batista. "I felt the point of a knife being thrust between my shoulder blades," Pawley later wrote. The overall plan was fine, but Rubottom gave Pawley a "categorical order" forbidding him to mention anything to Batista that he was speaking for Eisenhower. Pawley was to tell Batista that he was acting as a private citizen without White House approval, and if Batista was amenable to the plan, Pawley would then seek U.S. approval.

"Has the President, personally, approved this alteration in my instructions?" Pawley asked, knowing fully well what they would say.

"The President has delegated full responsibility in this matter to us, or we wouldn't be here" was the expected response.

Pawley now faced a decision. He could double back to the White House and plead his case, but that move would pit Eisenhower against his own State Department. He could refuse the mission on the ground that his hands would be tied, but he felt someone had to approach Batista. Realizing his only chance was to convince those officials in the room that their "modification" would take the punch out of the proposal, he tried in vain to reverse their decision. It was no use. Any argument he offered was met with stiff opposition, and he was told the decision was irreversible. Disillusioned and wary of State Department politics, Pawley felt he had no other choice than to give it his best effort and sell the program to Batista.[28]

"If he falls flat on his face," Rubottom said after Pawley had left the room, "he won't embarrass anyone in government." Knowing the necessity of keeping a tight ship, he told Wieland, "Anything in this room does not go beyond this room to *anyone*. Do you understand? Absolute silence."[29] But the State Department was a leaky ship, and it couldn't contain the news of Pawley's secret mission.

As soon as Pawley had presented his plan to Eisenhower in late November, Mario Lazo, a prominent attorney in Havana, had received information about the mission from a "responsible and confident source." Not only did Lazo know about the Pawley mission, he also learned that the State Department hadn't informed U.S. ambassador to Cuba Earl Smith of the plan and that the department intended to summon Smith back to Washington prior to Pawley's departure. Having a high regard for Smith, and likely harboring resentment toward Pawley because of their real estate deal, Lazo debated whether he should tell the ambassador. "On Thanksgiving Day 1958, at the Havana Country Club, I informed [Smith] of the decision to send a secret emissary to Cuba to negotiate with Batista. I also gave him the names of the men who were to be suggested for the caretaker government."[30] Although Smith made no comment "as this was all news to me," the revelation did surprise him.

Lazo's source had been accurate, and on December 4 Smith was called to Washington. Kept in the dark, Smith didn't meet with State Department officials until the day after Pawley had visited Batista. Held in Undersecretary Robert Murphy's office on December 10, the meeting with Smith included the usual cast of characters: Rubottom, Wieland, the CIA liaison with the State Department, and William Snow, who had attended the November late-night meeting at Pawley's home in Miami Beach. Smith disclosed to Rubottom the information he had received from Lazo and asked if it could be confirmed. Silence. Not knowing who had been sent on the secret mission, Smith asked Rubottom (later in a cable) if Batista had been approached. Silence.[31]

Meanwhile, Nixon was being continuously briefed on the Cuban matter. His connection to Cuba began before he became vice president. He and his wife, Pat, visited Havana shortly after their marriage; he even talked about practicing law there. One of his close friends was Charles "Bebe" Rebozo, the son of Cuban expatriates. During several subsequent visits to the island, Nixon frequented its casinos, and the Mafia reportedly picked up his tab. On an official visit in 1955, Nixon viewed Batista's Cuba as a land that "shares with us the same democratic ideals of peace, freedom and the dignity of man." In a report to the cabinet, Nixon proclaimed Batista would "deal with the Commies."[32]

But the bottom was about to fall out. On December 5, 1958, Nixon received a cryptic message from Arthur Gardner, the former ambassador to Cuba: "The Miami matter . . . should be started at once. Also, outside of ordinary Embassy channels, in an extremely confidential and personal manner, a check should be made of the situation, and probably the Head Man should be seen and given a little moral support that might save the situation for the time being, offering time for our own judgment as to what is best to do."[33] Nixon and Eisenhower anxiously waited to see if Pawley could succeed in Havana.

On December 7, Pawley and Edna flew to Havana and checked into the Country Club. Since officials at the U.S. Embassy were unaware of his mission (although CIA Havana station chief James Noel was apprised), Pawley avoided contact with them.[34] Instead, he spent four hours with Cuban foreign minister Gonzalo Güell, trying to convince him that he urgently needed to see Batista. Güell recommended that Pawley should send a telegram to Batista and request an interview. Pawley received a reply that Batista would see him the following evening at six o'clock, but then the meeting was postponed for twenty-four hours. Returning to the Foreign Ministry, Pawley urged Güell to convince Batista it was important he see him sooner.[35]

Wearing a white suit and a wide-brimmed, plantation-style straw hat, Pawley received a three-hour audience with Batista at the Presidential Palace on December 9.[36] Batista had left dinner guests to see Pawley, who felt pressured to make his presentation before the Cuban dictator became restless. "Speaking to me as a friend," Batista recalled, "he suggested the convenience of forming a government composed of elements of the opposition." Batista told Pawley he had been holding conversations with members of the opposition, but they ended because Castro had threatened them with prison or death if they continued their contact with Batista's representatives.

"Who could be those political enemies to whom you refer?" he asked Pawley.[37]

Pawley listed the names of acceptable opposition leaders but added he had not spoken to any of them. "I'm positive it's the only way to save Cuba," Pawley pleaded. "If you accept, I'm confident that I can go back to Washington and get the plan approved as United States policy."

"Your State Department has turned down every suggestion for compromise which my administration has offered. So why should they endorse *your* plan? If I accept, and the news leaks out to Castro and his sympathizers, it will be interpreted as weakness on my part. And if I show the slightest weakness at this moment, I promise you, my family and I will never leave Cuba alive."[38]

Batista added that none of the names on Pawley's list "would dare to make a pact" without Castro's consent, which seemed unlikely since the rebel leader wanted absolute power. But Pawley felt that opposition leaders could be convinced to lead a caretaker government, and then "Fidel Castro would . . . have to lay down his arms or admit he was a revolutionary fighting against anybody only because he wanted power, not because he was against Batista."[39] Batista felt certain that Pawley was trying his utmost to prevent Castro from gaining control, "but in fact he did not give me any proof that he was acting in an authorized connection."[40] The State Department's restriction hampered the negotiations, but Pawley refused to give up. He asked Batista if it would be possible to meet with him the following day and continue discussing the plan.

"We will waste time for nothing," Batista replied. "I must carry on. But by all means return to Washington and ask your people to permit me to remain in power until March, when a new president will succeed me. It is crucial that Cuba not fall to Castro before March."

"Your Presidency can't last much longer in any case, and I think your best choice is to leave, now that Cubans have lost confidence in your ability to maintain order."

"I have a duty to remain at my post," Batista replied proudly. "And that I intend to do."[41]

Pawley returned to Washington and reported to Eisenhower that Batista had refused the offer. The day after Pawley's visit with Batista the United States reaffirmed its noninterference policy in the Cuban rebellion.[42] On December 14, Ambassador Smith, who had been patiently waiting in Washington, finally received instructions. During a meeting with Foreign Minister Güell, he broke the news: "It is my unpleasant duty to inform the President of the Republic that the United States will no longer support the present government of Cuba and that my government believes that the President is losing effective control." Güell arranged for Smith to see Batista the night of December 17, and the meeting lasted more than two and a half hours.

Batista made suggestion after suggestion of ways to solve the volatile situation, with some including his remaining in power. He pleaded with Smith to ask the U.S. government to lift the arms embargo but to no avail. The dictator wanted to hold on until the newly elected president, Dr. Rivero Aguero, took office on February 24, but Smith thought it unlikely.

Two years later, Batista revealed what Smith said next:

At the end he surprised me greatly by practically repeating Pawley's words, in the sense that a provisional government could establish peace through negotiations with the leader Castro, or confront him with arms, duly supported, if the Communist leader rejected to consider the negotiations; that . . . I should avoid great bloodshed if I abdicated, adding that my family could go directly to Daytona Beach, and I also, if I wished, although the Government Officials with whom he had spoken in the United States preferred, for political reasons, that I should go to Spain, or some other country for three or four months, at the end of which I could rejoin my wife and children . . . in Daytona.[43]

"He breathed like a man who had been hurt," Smith recalled, "and both he and I knew he had." Smith reported back to Washington and offered his opinion that some form of mediation was necessary to stop the fighting. He suggested that the Catholic Church might be helpful in this effort, but the State Department was not receptive to his recommendation.[44]

From December 10 to December 27, the *New York Times* was not published due to a strike by the delivery unions. Although accustomed to their own newspapers being shut down, the *Times*'s absence caused great concern among the Cubans.[45] Batista was also worried, not because of the lack of newspapers, but because Castro's rebel army had swelled from five thousand to fifty thousand men since summer.[46] Cuban army chiefs were beginning to panic, fomenting plots. The consensus was that Castro should be contacted to "discuss the feasibility of an understanding."

Using a church emissary, a meeting was set for December 28 between Castro and Gen. Eulogio Cantillo, chief of operations in Oriente Province to arrange for the creation of a military junta to take over the government. Cantillo asked that Batista, his cabinet, and several army and police officers be allowed to leave the country. Fidel's counterproposal was direct: Batista would not be allowed to leave the country, and the Cuban army should join his rebel forces and march on Havana. Delivering the message to Batista the following day, Cantillo was first chastised for having met with Castro but then implored to hold on until the end.[47]

Every New Year's Eve, Batista hosted a party at his enclave at Camp Columbia, but this year he invited only a handful of intimates and their wives, high-ranking government officials, and military chiefs. Mingling among the seventy guests, Batista engaged in light conversation before joining his military chiefs in an adjacent room to discuss the hopeless situation. Talk centered on the possibility of holding on until the new president's inauguration, but no one present held out any promise. After the guests departed, Batista informed President-elect Aguero and former prime minister Jorge García Montes that he was leaving Cuba. Inviting them to join him in his flight (Montes declined), Batista tendered his official resignation at 2:00 a.m.[48]

Boarding a plane with his wife and son Jorge, Batista was joined by staff members, their families, and other Cuban officials who feared for their lives if they remained. When the pilot informed Batista they had left the jurisdictional waters of Cuba and were en route to Florida, Batista said, "Turn around and head for the Dominican Republic."[49] Landing at Ciudad Trujillo, Batista tipped the pilot and copilot $1,000 each. His arrival in the Dominican Republic was a complete surprise to the government, which had no advance knowledge of Batista's plan to seek asylum there.[50] "In the first days," Batista wrote in his memoirs, "the Dominican Republic was courteous to me."[51]

But it was not so, according to a British diplomat's report filed in a dispatch to London. It stated that Trujillo "extracted about $3 million from Batista. . . . Just what . . . for I could not elucidate—perhaps Dominican expenses for military operations, present or future, against Fidel Castro. Anyway when Batista jibbed at paying up after the first couple of million, the Saviour of the Fatherland threw him into a dungeon and tipped in a box of hungry rats for company, and after 24 hours, Batista's purse strings soon loosened again."[52] This account may have merit because the U.S. State Department had received previous reports from its embassy in the Dominican Republic on the relationship between the two leaders. In an embassy report filed July 30, 1959, the State Department was informed that

> in separate conversations with the two men both denied to Pawley any difficulty between them or any pressure on Batista for extortion or other purposes. Batista also denied that he had any apprehension of physical harm to himself.
>
> The Embassy suspects this change was brought about by Batista's making or committing himself to make a substantial contribution to Trujillo. . . . This theory is supported by the allegation that Mrs. Batista had withdrawn large sums of money from US banks and had visited Miami at the same time as one of the officials of the Trujillo regime.[53]

Batista eventually settled in Spain and Portugal, living a quiet, comfortable lifestyle. He owned a villa overlooking the sea in the resort of Estoril near Lisbon, a chalet near Marbella on the southern coast of Spain, and an apartment in Madrid. Seldom making public appearances, he was constantly surrounded by bodyguards. Having written four books during his exile, Batista was working on his memoir when he died in 1973 at the age of seventy-two.[54]

While Pawley may have helped ease Batista's exiled stay in the Dominican Republic, he could do nothing to prevent Castro from taking control of Cuba. Eisenhower would later characterize Pawley as having "a pathological hatred for Castro," which Pawley held for the rest of his life, and in the meantime he would sponsor plots to overthrow Fidel.[55]

17

Castro

Pawley's Havana mission wasn't made public until February 1961 when the Senate Subcommittee to Investigate Internal Security released his testimony of September subcommittee added no comment to the testimony, Pawley and others furnished enough information to capture headlines for several weeks.[1] Pawley was candid and forthcoming during his subcommittee appearance after being told his testimony would be kept secret. "When I was first called," Pawley said, "I was told specifically that it would not be released, that it was for the benefit of the committee and that it was for their use only. I talked quite freely . . . named names." Evidently, the committee members changed their minds.

According to Pawley,

> First they said they were now going to release this testimony . . . one time they said during September and we got them to hold it off until after the election. Now they said they were going to release it on January 10th and Senator Dodd is insisting that they do it on January 9th. If this is released now it is going to put me in an awful spot. I named many names . . . I did not think it was for public consumption.

Pawley's concern was not for himself: "I don't mind what they do to me . . . I am working on something right now for the President and the Vice President knows about it. The things I am helping to do would be jeopardized if this testimony is released right now. The release of this material at this time would completely disqualify me as a person who could keep up this kind of work."[2]

As Pawley feared, the explosive testimony set off controversy and resulted in other investigations being conducted of those people Pawley had named.

In his testimony, Pawley chastised Roy Rubottom, who had become ambassador to Argentina in the interim, for two decisions—for his not allowing Pawley to tell Batista the U.S. government had approved Pawley's plan for the dictator to step down and for "bringing down the curtain on Batista" by cutting off arms shipments. Gen. Francisco J. Tabernilla, commander in chief of the Cuban armed forces under Batista who also fled Cuba that fateful New Year's Eve, confirmed Pawley's belief by stating that when U.S. aid was cut off, "Cuban people shifted to support Castro."[3]

Pawley had characterized another target, William Wieland, as having "tendencies" that were "serving the cause of our enemies." When the Senate subcommittee asked if he felt Wieland had demonstrated them "wittingly, intentionally," Pawley replied, "I have got to say that he is either one of the most stupid men living or he is doing it intentionally."[4]

Pawley wasn't alone in his opinion of Wieland. Arthur Gardner, ambassador to Cuba from 1953 to 1957, who testified before the subcommittee a week before Pawley did, felt Wieland played a part in Castro's rise to power "just because I know the way he thinks."[5] Earl E. T. Smith, who succeeded Gardner as ambassador to Cuba, also testified. Smith revealed Wieland had instructed him to receive a briefing on his new Cuba posting from Herbert Matthews, the *New York Times* reporter who had told Gardner it would be "in the best interests" of the United States if Batista was removed from power and depicted Castro as a modern-day Robin Hood. When the subcommittee asked Gardner to name those State Department officials who were "slanting the news . . . telling falsehoods; that were pro-Castro," Gardner hesitated. "I do not want to get people in trouble," he replied. After Senator Eastland pressed him, he gave one name—Wieland's.[6]

Wieland later came under congressional attack, based partly on the testimony of Pawley and Smith, for having some responsibility in shaping State Department policy that allowed Castro to gain power. Placed on limited duty while an advisory panel investigated his case, Wieland was eventually "restored to full status as an active senior Foreign Service officer." Defended by President Kennedy when labeled a security risk, Wieland was not cleared until July 1965, when the panel reported he had "honestly exercised his judgment over the years including the period of the difficult and highly complex Cuban situation." The State Department approved the panel's recommendation and announced that Wieland was "completely cleared and his case closed."[7]

Pawley's third target during his testimony was Spruille Braden. After blaming him for blocking his appointment as ambassador to Argentina in 1946, he accused Braden of being "involved in a program which appeared to be helpful to the Communist Party in Latin America." He claimed Truman fired Braden as assistant secretary of state in 1947 for that reason.[8] A firestorm began when Pawley's testimony was released. "Pawley makes one true statement," Braden said, "that I blocked his appointment as Ambassador to Argentina."[9] Braden offered to testify under oath and have the Department of Justice review the results, along with Pawley's testimony. Truman, vacationing in Bermuda at this time, had awarded Braden the Medal of Freedom, and his only comment was that "Spruille Braden did a good job."[10]

Newspapers carried editorials on the Pawley-Braden clash, some even condemning Pawley for his accusations. Labeling his testimony "maundering . . . omnifarious," the *Washington Post* called Pawley "an exceedingly disgruntled man . . . reckless enough, moreover, to impute bad motives, even disloyalty, to anyone of whose opinions he disapproved."[11] The *Chicago Daily Tribune* called Pawley's testimony "the hottest information on the perversities of state department personalities and method since the exposure of Alger Hiss," and asked that it be discussed in Congress.[12] Senator Kenneth B. Keating agreed and called for hearings to permit those accused in Pawley's testimony to testify.[13] The *Washington Post* targeted the Senate subcommittee for "issuing one-sided, half-the-story, unevaluated reports of limited testimony of men overly intent upon finding a villain whenever foreign events have gone wrong."[14] The same paper noted that Pawley was a "long-time friend of the deposed Batista" and that he "maintained close relations with the Dominican Republic dictatorship of Rafael Trujillo."[15]

A *Miami Herald* editorial by John S. Knight, who called Pawley and Braden "personal friends," placed the controversy in another light. He felt Pawley had presented his views to the Senate subcommittee "as he should have" and was not to be blamed. He wrote, "Why the Senate Committee released Pawley's testimony without giving Spruille Braden the opportunity to defend himself is beyond comprehension." Knight added that Braden's offer to testify should be accepted and "let Bill Pawley and Spruille Braden put an end to their personal feud."[16] In a letter to the newspaper Pawley denied having a personal feud with Braden, stating he had testified to events long ago and "have made few if any statements regarding them in the interim." He ended his letter by adding, "I think it is lamentable that your editorial did not deal with the general subject of America's security rather than one individual."[17]

Shortly after Pawley's testimony was released, Batista, who was living in the Madeira Islands, broke his silence regarding Pawley's visit to Havana in the closing days of his dictatorship.[18] In his memoir, which he completed in 1960 but it was not published until 1962, the exiled dictator only mentioned Pawley's visit in footnotes and referred to Pawley's testimony before the Senate Subcommittee.[19] In a letter to George Beebe, managing editor of the *Miami Herald*, Batista verified the meeting with Pawley. "Speaking to me as a friend," Batista wrote, "he suggested the convenience of forming a government composed of elements of the opposition." Rambling on about fast-moving events at the time, Batista added that Pawley "did not give me any proof that he was acting in an authorized connection."[20]

In his unpublished memoir, Pawley claims that after Batista had been in Ciudad Trujillo a week after fleeing Cuba, the deposed dictator called and invited Pawley to visit him. Flying to the Dominican Republic the same day, Pawley met Batista at his hotel. After former Cuban foreign minister Güell left the room, Pawley said, "I am now in a position to tell you something that I couldn't reveal in Havana. . . . I came as the direct representative of the President. He had authorized my proposal." Pawley said Batista "remained silent for a moment" before replying in a hushed tone: "If only you could have told me."[21] Who said what was not important, according to syndicated columnist George Sokolsky: "Who, in the State Department, authorized Pawley or Smith to order a government to go out of existence?"[22]

Meanwhile, as Castro consolidated his rebel group to assume control of Cuba, he became fearful that the CIA might attempt to assassinate him. In reality, the CIA was receiving mixed signals on Castro, leading them to a "do-nothing" policy during the Cuban insurrection:

There were reports as early as June or July 1958 during the period that U.S. Navy sailors from Guantanamo were held by Castro forces which indicated beyond a reasonable doubt that the U.S. was up against an individual who could not be expected to be acceptable to U.S. Government interests. Admiral [Arleigh] Burke [U.S. chief of naval operations] also made reference to the fact that he had been in at least one meeting with

Colonel King [chief of Western Hemisphere affairs of the CIA] on or about 29 December 1958 in which officials of the Department of State, except for Under Secretary Robert Murphy, appeared to feel that Castro was politically compatible to U.S. objectives.[23]

It was a choice of allowing Castro to take power or sending in U.S. troops. Admiral Burke and probably CIA director Allen Dulles favored military action, while King felt "thorough consideration [should] be given to the elimination of Fidel Castro," but nothing was done.[24]

But Pawley knew what he wanted to do. "Find me one man, just one man who can go it alone and get Castro," he told a Miami newsman shortly after Castro's takeover. "I'll pay anything—almost anything."[25] And he wasn't alone in his thinking. One of the first actions the Cuban revolutionaries took upon entering Havana in January 1959 was to shut down the Mafia-controlled casinos. Meyer Lansky was infuriated that the gambling empire he had helped create would be lost. He made a deal with Castro for the casinos to reopen, but the cash-cow paradise would never be the same.

Castro had Lansky's brother, Jacob ("Jake"), manager of the Hotel Nacional de Cuba in Havana, jailed, then expelled from the country.[26] In the end, Castro reneged, closing the casinos forever and further outraging Lansky, who reportedly placed a million-dollar bounty on Castro. "Meyer indicated to the CIA," said Joseph Stacher, a longtime friend of Lansky's, "that some of his people who were still on the island, or those who were just going back, might assassinate Castro."[27] Among those in Cuba was John V. Martino, who had been installing security systems in the casinos. Jailed when Castro took over and later released, Martino teamed up with Mafioso Johnny Rosselli to sponsor Cuban exiles to overthrow Castro.[28]

And there was Richard Nixon. The American Society of Newspaper Editors invited Castro to speak in Washington a few months after he assumed power. Hoping to meet Eisenhower during his visit, Castro was shunned when the president went to Georgia to play golf. "They sent me Nixon. . . ," Castro complained. Under strict conditions, "the two of us would talk alone," Nixon stated, "without members of his staff or mine present," and there would be no "attempts made to exploit our conference for publicity purposes."[29] The meeting did not go well. "That son of a bitch Nixon," Castro exclaimed, "he treated me badly." After their talk they posed for TV cameras. "We're going to work with this man," Nixon said with his patented forced grin, but privately he told his aides the bearded rebel was an "outright Communist and he's going to be a real danger."[30]

Cuban exiles in Florida sought ways to get rid of Castro, and several turned to Pawley for help. On September 24, 1959, Fabio Freyre, a well-born Cuban who was organizing an invasion of Cuba, visited Pawley at his Miami office. Pawley had heard several of these "pipe dream" ideas before, but Freyre was serious. He told Pawley he had already received permission from a Col. Morris Hill in the "secret division" in Nassau to use a small Bahamian island as a training base and staging area for aircraft and boats needed for the invasion.[31] Alluding to acquiring aircraft and boats, Freyre tried enlisting financial assistance from Pawley, who avoided making a commitment but agreed to discuss the matter in subsequent meetings.[32]

Pawley contacted CIA White House Division chief J. C. King and repeated as much of the conversation as he could remember. Saying he was receiving an increasing number of visits from exiled Cubans, and that he no longer had a retentive memory, Pawley suggested that a recording device be installed in his office. King contacted Joseph Langdon of the CIA's Support Branch and asked him to send an agent to Miami to make a survey of Pawley's office and arrange for the installation of a recording device "to be used only for callers in person, and not by telephone."[33]

Over the weekend of October 15–16, a Revere Model T-700 recorder-reproducer was installed in Pawley's office. A BK-6 microphone was fitted into the front of Pawley's desk, along with an automatic relay system to allow remote operation of the unit. Wiring running from the desk under the wall-to-wall carpet led to a monitoring post in an adjoining conference room closet. A switching device mounted under the middle drawer of Pawley's desk controlled the entire recording package.[34] Pawley's CIA Miami Station contact would be Bernard I. Reichhardt, who would retrieve the recordings and forward them to King at the White House.[35]

Before the recording apparatus was installed, Pawley received another visit from Freyre, who brought members of his Cuban exile group. They dismissed the idea of waging any counterrevolution in Cuba and proposed that "economic action" was the only means of deposing Castro. They focused on stopping the upcoming sugar harvest, thinking that once Castro got the crops to market, he would have hundreds of millions of dollars at his disposal. Burning crops would be ineffective; instead, the sugar mills had to be targeted. Blowing up the mill chimneys would temporarily put them out of action and hopefully long enough to delay processing the harvest.

After the visitors left his office, Pawley contacted Reichhardt, asking him to come to his office to discuss the matter. Reichhardt, in his report, related that "Pawley while discussing this, decided that he felt it was so serious he put in a call, in my presence to Rubottom. Rubottom was at lunch so he talked to Bill Snow and passed him this information, again not identifying his sources. I noted that Pawley also took the time to preach Snow a little sermon about the dangers to US interests which would accrue if something isn't done to change Castro's ways."[36] The CIA issued covert security approval for Pawley to "assist WH Division by making available to them reports of conversations held by Mr. Pawley at Miami, Florida, with his contacts among Caribbean revolutionary groups, especially anti-Castro Cuban exile leaders."[37] Pawley was now knee-deep in activities of Miami-based Cuban exile groups. While reporting on them to Washington, at the same time he contemplated what he could do to help these splintered groups.

With the recording device fully operational, Pawley began toning down his opinions to the point where he now acted as a sounding board, allowing the Cubans to speak freely while he interjected comments as to the feasibility of their plans. This modified approach became evident when two men—one unidentified but believed to be a member of a group of wealthy anti-Castro Cubans and the other being a Cuban journalist "of operational interest to [CIA] station Habana"—visited him in October. They told Pawley they were in contact with Gen. José Eleutorio Pedraza, leader of Cuban revolutionary groups in the Dominican Republic. Pawley, well aware that Trujillo wanted to see Castro ousted, told his visitors he would hate to see the Dominican government get involved. Playing to the hidden recorder, Pawley said, "The Dominican Government hasn't given [the Cuban exiles] a dime," which he knew wasn't true. When the two Cubans mentioned they needed financial backing, Pawley offered no encouragement, telling them that without unity among the anti-Castro groups, it would be like "putting money down a rat-hole."[38]

The recorder's reels were also turning when former Cuban minister of education Jorge García Montes, who headed yet another Miami anti-Castro group, visited Pawley. García represented lay religious organizations that were fearful that Castro would close their schools in Cuba. Their movement against Castro would originate from within Cuba, but they needed money for arms and ammunition. Garcia also hoped to establish a "propaganda mechanism," specifically a news broadcast system outside Cuba, to expose Castro's failure to carry out promises he had made. Getting weapons into Cuba from Miami would be difficult, Pawley told him: "It might be possible to take them to some Central American country and then to Cuba," but "the radio can be financed."[39]

Two days later, Pawley discussed with Fabio Freyre and his uncle Julio Sanchez methods and operational plans among anti-Castro groups. Pawley stressed that any movement against Castro must come from within Cuba as he did "not believe that any invasion from abroad will succeed." Pawley's conviction would change eventually, and he would evolve into one of the more aggressive hawks advocating a U.S. invasion of Cuba. For now, however, he recommended pursuing a propaganda campaign and "getting as many people as possible back into Cuba who are willing to take chances." When Freyre and Sanchez said they already had propaganda material prepared but lacked the money to get on the air, Pawley steered them toward finding "Cubans . . . who would be interested in financing this sort of thing." He added it wouldn't be necessary to purchase a radio station because radio time could be bought, and "the U.S. government would not interfere since there was nothing illegal about it."

Pawley managed to get the two Cubans to talk about the subject that interested him the most, that is, the Dominican Republic's support of anti-Castro groups. They obliged by reading to him a memorandum signed by General Pedraza outlining his entire plan:

1. A junta of fifteen to twenty people would be formed to act as a provisional civilian government once Castro was toppled.
2. An intensive propaganda campaign would commence in the Dominican Republic, outlining an ideology neither for Batista nor for Fidel.
3. Means of altering transmissions would be employed to cut off Castro's voice and to insert programs designed to spread the new ideology.
4. Castro and the principal figures of his government would be physically eliminated.
5. The Cuban Air Force and the sugar mills would be destroyed.

Pawley asked if Pedraza was offering financial support. The Cubans replied that a letter of credit for $1 million had been opened for them in New York.[40]

Pawley's involvement with anti-Castro groups went beyond recording conversations for the CIA. Together, Freyre and Pawley visited Trujillo and General Pedraza in Santo Domingo. "We had found that Generalissimo Trujillo was in a position more than willing to cooperate in all ways possible to him so that the

Cuban opposition would be organized to overthrow the present communist re-gime," Pawley reported. Pedraza confirmed writing the memorandum offering his support. "He begged us to contact the different groups of organized opposi-tion in Miami . . . so they would start organizing their forces." Pawley asked the Dominicans if two or three training bases could be established in the Dominican Republic, along with "two strong radio stations," to support the invasion effort.[41]

The parties involved in the invasion plans began having second thoughts and mistrusting each other. Trujillo was hesitant to go ahead without U.S. approval, so Pawley was assigned the task of feeling out the official U.S. position. On December 15, he had dinner with Vice President Nixon to discuss the Dominican plan. What occurred during their talk is not on record, but the next day Pawley met with Allen Dulles at the CIA. The invasion was tentatively scheduled between December 26 and January 3 and would involve close to ten thousand men. The initial target would be the Isle of Pines. Pawley offered to have General Pedraza meet with U.S. officials to outline the invasion plans, but despite his pleas, the State Department instructed the Immigration Service to pick the general up if he entered the United States.[42] The Dominicans were disappointed, while others mistrusted Pawley.

One Cuban, Francisco Cajigas, who apparently knew Pawley from an earlier transaction in Cuba, feared and disliked him. He considered Pawley "a meddler" who does "more harm than good to the Cuban cause," and he worried that Pawley's support of Trujillo "might involve some future commitments." Jack Gillespie, who worked with Cuban exile groups, discussed Pawley with former assistant attorney general H. Graham Morrison, who "characterized [Pawley] as a great opportun-ist."[43] Freyre told Pawley that the FBI had interviewed him and that even J. Edgar Hoover "was mad with Pawley" for some unknown reason.[44]

Another Cuban exile Dr. Nuñez Portuondo, ambassador to the United Nations under Batista, accused Pawley of placing his brother's name on the list of Cubans who would form a junta when Castro was deposed with the hope that the brother would be killed. Portuondo also told fellow exiles that "Pawley was part of a group of Americans who had investments in Cuba" and that he "had offered Trujillo $3 million to invade Cuba" but "never gave him the three million." When Pawley learned of these "wild and dangerous statements" from a man who felt that "he alone could be selected as the next President of Cuba," he suggested Colonel King have a talk with the Cuban "and threaten him with expulsion from the United States if he does not stop his agitating tactics."[45]

Despite animosity from some Cuban exiles, Pawley continued supporting their efforts to overthrow "the bearded one," as he called Castro. Even the Cuban government knew about Pawley's participation. Mrs. Catherine Taaffe, who worked for Castro but passed information to the CIA, told her contact there was widespread belief in Cuba that the United States was sponsoring anti-Castro plots. Further, "one of those responsible for this belief appeared to be Edward P. Pawley [a handwritten note in the margin reads "probably Wm. D. Pawley"] who . . . encourages the belief that CIA is backing anti-Castro plotting and that he, Pawley, is working for CIA in this effort."[46]

Taaffe also reported Castro's minister of defense had authorized her to contact black market dealers to purchase twenty Hawker Hunter planes. An $11 million letter of credit drawn on a Swiss bank account in the names of Fidel, Raúl Castro, and Ernesto "Che" Guevara was to be used for the purchase. Fabio Freyre obtained a photostat copy of the letter of credit and gave it to Pawley, who in turn passed it to Colonel King at the White House.[47] Pawley passed every rumor, no matter how insignificant, to the White House, and some were far-fetched.

Although the British had stymied plans to use a Caribbean island for staging aircraft and infiltrating people into Cuba, the exiled Cubans still wanted to pursue them. Pawley reported the latest effort involved acquiring another island, but they encountered a problem. Howard Hughes held the lease on the island, and the Cubans were having difficulty finding the reclusive millionaire. In the meantime, a "paper" company was established to hold the lease once the Cubans finally made contact with Hughes.[48]

Pawley received word through Fabio Freyre that a Batista exile group was planning a large-scale invasion of Cuba with the help of Matthew M. Slepin, a Miami lawyer and Dade County chairman of the Republican State Committee.[49] Pawley sent Gen. Diaz Tamayo, a Cuban exile, to attend one of Slepin's meetings to learn everything he could and report back. According to Tamayo, Slepin told the twelve persons attending the meeting that he had "Vice President Nixon's support in an effort to organize a movement against the Castro government." According to Slepin, Nixon was making arrangements for $200 million to be given to a "responsible Cuban revolutionary group . . . to overthrow Fidel Castro."

Slepin asked the Cubans to raise $100,000, which would be his advance fee for brokering the deal. Pawley contacted the Florida State chairman of the Republican Committee and learned that Slepin "had direct entree to President Eisenhower and Vice President Nixon." Pawley characterized Slepin as a "lawyer with a bad reputation" and was concerned that news of this might leak out and "could have very far-reaching and damaging effects."[50] Wanting to inform Nixon immediately about the meeting, Pawley dictated a memo over the phone to Nixon's secretary Rose Mary Woods and asked her to pass it on to the vice president.[51] After Pawley repeated the information to J. C. King, nothing more was heard of Slepin's plan.

The State Department offered a wait-and-see policy toward Castro, "despite my own strong recommendation to the contrary," Nixon wrote, "one, incidentally, which was shared . . . by William Pawley . . . a widely acknowledged expert on Latin American affairs."[52] According to an interview Nixon gave, Pawley also had the confidence of Eisenhower: "I had several conferences with the President and finally he was convinced that the anti-Communist Cubans in Florida should be armed and given every assistance to overthrow the communist regime. Eisenhower wanted me to assume overall command of the operation, with veto power over the CIA, but Allen Dulles, joined by Christian Herter who was easily led, prevailed, and it became a CIA operation."[53]

Although it is doubtful that Eisenhower wanted him in charge, Pawley still took an active role in attempts to topple Castro. The president found it "profitable to talk with him" on Latin American issues and continued pressing to have Pawley appointed as undersecretary in Latin American affairs. "I told Secretary Herter that if I was to be put off on this matter again, I wanted to have some very convincing reason," Eisenhower wrote in his diary.[54]

While Eisenhower pushed for the appointment, Pawley was back-channel campaigning on his own. "He feels that the creation of this post now is essential," vice presidential aide James D. Hughes wrote in a memo to Nixon, "and would like to know if you thought that he should jog the President either verbally or in writing."[55] Pawley was even getting help from Senator George A. Smathers, who felt "Bill Pawley is the answer." Smathers discussed the matter with members of the Senate Foreign Relations Committee, concluding there would be "no difficulty in having the committee behind the appointment of Pawley to some post which would allow him to take a firm hand in our policy toward Latin America."[56]

Eisenhower felt creating the new position for Pawley would show "special concern for our Latin American neighbors" and wanted it accomplished soon.[57] Christian Herter told the president "that this matter was under reconsideration in the Department," but Eisenhower felt it was taking too long. Herter reported that

Eisenhower "felt very strongly on this score and said that, if we would agree to get legislation up which might be passed quickly, he would at once appoint William Pawley to the job."[58] When Undersecretary of State Douglas Dillon mentioned that getting Congress to create an additional undersecretary position might be difficult, Eisenhower suggested an alternative title, ambassador-at-large for Western Hemisphere affairs. Eisenhower still "liked Mr. Pawley very much" and wanted him for the post, but presidential advisers had misgivings. "The problem with Pawley," Dillon said, "is that he formerly had interests in the Dominican Republic and in Cuba, was known to have been close to Batista and Trujillo, and is considered a 'friend of dictators.'" Realizing these were "serious questions," Eisenhower began suggesting others for the job. "The big question is to get the right man," Eisenhower added. Pawley's name was never mentioned again.[59]

18
Invasion Plans

Nixon instructed his aide, James D. Hughes, to contact Brig. Gen. Robert E. Cushman, Jr., who was Nixon's assistant for National Security Council affairs, and have him keep Pawley "posted on Cuba."[1] In a follow-up letter, Nixon informed Pawley, "I have asked him [Cushman] to keep in touch with you regarding this matter of mutual interest" and to "keep our lines of communications open."[2] While the CIA busied itself with outlandish projects to oust or discredit Castro—such as developing exploding cigars, a food additive to make his hair fall out, or poisons— Pawley worked on other solutions. Although advocating assassination, Pawley became involved in a scheme to print counterfeit Cuban bonds, "presumably to jar the Castro economy." Cushman went to Florida in the summer of 1960 to discuss the plan, but the bond scheme was dropped.[3]

Pawley had other schemes. One of his contacts in Cuba was a lifelong friend of a helicopter pilot for Castro. The pilot was disenchanted with Castro, considered him a menace to Cuba, and felt that he should be "physically eliminated." Unable to bring himself to commit the act personally, the pilot was "ready and willing when chance arises to deliver Castro" to "any prearranged point copter can reach for whatever disposition of Castro *others* might wish to make of him." The difficulty in making advance arrangements was that Castro's flights were on a "highly irregular basis," and the pilot was never told the destination until Castro arrived at the hangar.[4] This proposal was not pursued as it was considered too risky.

Pawley's aggressive pursuit for a means to topple Castro was beginning to cause concern in Washington. The CIA was preparing scenarios to accomplish the task, but Pawley was eager to get the ball rolling. On June 10, 1960, Christian

Herter expressed his uneasiness during a conference with the president. Notes by Andrew Goodpaster, then White House staff secretary, stated that

> Mr. Herter next said that William Pawley has been working with a right-wing group of Cubans, including former Batista police. The CIA is working with former Castro people who have left him on the grounds that he has "betrayed the revolution." Their work will be spoiled, however, if this right-wing group can show U.S. support. The President asked Mr. Herter to call up Mr. Pawley and tell him to get out of this operation, or to have CIA call him up.[5]

Yet Pawley pressed on, utilizing his "back door" to the White House, Richard Nixon. "I'm in touch with Allen Dulles' people almost daily," Pawley wrote to Nixon two weeks after Eisenhower ordered Pawley out, "and things are shaping up reasonably well. The matter [killing Castro] is a very delicate problem and every care should be taken to handle it so as not to affect our Nation adversely, nor our political campaign."[6]

With Allen Dulles pressing him to take action, Eisenhower authorized a CIA plan to arm and train a paramilitary force of approximately thirty-five Cuban exiles. CIA director of plans Richard M. Bissell, Jr., conceived the plan, dubbed Operation Pluto, which called for setting up an underground resistance in Cuba and creating a political opposition to assume power once Castro was forced out. This plan resulted in setting up the Frente Revolucionario Democrático (FRD) to organize Cuban exile political factions. In August 1960, Eisenhower authorized $13 million in funds and approved the use of U.S. military instructors to train and equip Cuban exile teams, but he emphasized that "the members of the instructor cadre would never be committed to Cuban soil."[7]

Unexpected support for anti-Castro groups came from Florida Democratic senator George Smathers. He felt the time had come to "scrap the State Department-inspired policy of curtailing the activities of democratic anti-Castro Cuban exiles." The reaction in official circles to Smathers's suggestion was utter disbelief that a U.S. senator would publicly advocate violating the Neutrality Act.[8] Pawley felt the United States should take an even more drastic step and pull out of the Organization of American States.

On the eve of an OAS meeting in Costa Rica, Pawley complained the organization was ready to condemn Trujillo, a "true friend" of the United States, while letting Castro, a "Communist enemy," continue his anti-America policies. "It seems that the American government is sympathetic to dictators to the left [Castro] and is only too ready to condemn dictators to the right [Trujillo]," Pawley said, "even though in many cases dictators to the right practice greater human rights."[9] The State Department considered Pawley's proposal too radical, but he repeated his recommendation while testifying before a Senate subcommittee the following month.[10]

Nixon took an active role in Operation Pluto, seeing it as way of demonstrating to voters that the Republican Party was capable of nullifying a Communist threat ninety miles off the U.S. coast. Nixon's press secretary, Herbert Klein, said there were hopes that Castro would be out by October, giving them "a real trump card in the election."[11] But they encountered problems. The planners found the Cuban politicians increasingly unreliable and that creating the needed political opposition was taking too long.[12]

Nixon felt frustrated as the November election approached. "What in the world are they doing that takes months?" he asked the CIA staff supervising the operation. Directing Operation Pluto was CIA officer Jacob Esterline, and acting as the CIA's liaison with the Cuban exile leaders was Howard Hunt, who understood that Nixon was the "chief architect" of the project. Cushman told Hunt to call anytime he needed "high-level intervention" to get the job done.[13]

The unrealistic timetable, combined with Nixon's pressing for action, doomed the plan from the beginning. CIA overseer of the project, Richard Bissell, wryly commented, "Ike, Nixon, and Pawley don't know it, but we're the real revolutionaries."[14] With the U.S. presidential election going to the Democrats, it seemed prudent to let the matter rest on John F. Kennedy's shoulders, but the Eisenhower administration still had three months before leaving office.

By mid-November, the CIA discussed a "changing concept of the operation," because of "difficulty with air drops [to rebels in Cuba] . . . some change in approach was needed."[15] Pawley's approach was simple; he wanted to do whatever was necessary to get rid of Castro and as many of his lieutenants as possible. In this endeavor he requested an army technical manual on demolition from Colonel King to give to one of the Cuban exile groups.[16] Pawley also received a letter from Chairman José A. Benitez of the Democratic State Committee of Puerto Rico, asking Pawley to contact Capt. Eladio Del Valle, leader of a Cuban exile military group. "At the present time Captain Del Valle has 150 men. . . . They are well

equipped with arms. . . . His theory is that different battlefronts should be opened
. . . directed by people who know about military movements. . . . With your help,
Captain Del Valle can make bigger movement than the one he is ready to launch."[17]
Plots were coming from all directions.

The Mafia was also anxious to eliminate Castro, and evidence shows that the
CIA began conspiring in August 1960 with Sam Giancana and Santo Trafficante
to achieve that goal. Both men had extensive investments in Cuban casinos that
were still open, but restrictions imposed on their operations led them to believe
the end was near. Manuel Antonio "Tony" de Varona, a former Cuban minister,
whom Pawley described as "a 'big government' advocate who would not promote
private enterprise and who has 'socialist' ideas at times," claimed he could poison Castro through a Havana contact.[18] Socialist or not, Varona received financing
from Trafficante and Meyer Lansky, and the CIA supplied him with poison pills.
Varona's contact was a man working in a Havana restaurant Castro frequented, but
suddenly the bearded one stopped eating there.

Varona was in regular contact with Pawley and Howard Hunt, both of whom
kept Nixon apprised of Cuban exile activities. It is not difficult to conceive that
the vice president was aware of these assassination plots, but the link is hard to
connect. Nixon's personal secretary, Rose Mary Woods, typed a memo concerning
a cryptic telephone call from Pawley asking to see Nixon about the "problem we
are having south of Miami. . . . He was calling because he thinks the situation with
regard to Cuba becomes daily more desperate."[19] But Nixon was always cagey in
any response he made concerning the Cuban situation.

Training Cuban exiles for an invasion continued at supposedly secret
Guatemalan bases, but evidently the Castro government knew about it, as reported
in a November issue of the *Nation*.[20] Hunt said that after the election, "our natives there [in Guatemala] were getting very restless in their training camps," but
they could do nothing until President-elect Kennedy made a decision.[21] Contrary
to Hunt's opinion, however, evidence shows the Eisenhower administration wasn't
giving up just yet.

Meeting with Eisenhower at the White House on November 29 to discuss the
Guatemala group, Pawley felt "the effort in training of the people in Guatemala
was too slow and that at the present time we were really going backwards." The
five hundred men being trained were insufficient, and "the State Department had
begun to think along the same lines as Mr. Pawley, with respect to the number of

men needed and that State felt perhaps we should have two or three thousand." Pawley also mentioned that the committee on Cuba consisted of "very busy people" who didn't have the time needed for various projects and suggested that a strong executive head the group. Eisenhower warmed to the idea, but he "suspected Mr. Pawley himself would like this responsibility."

Instead, Eisenhower wanted Pawley to serve in a diplomatic capacity to enlist Latin American countries' assistance in helping solve the Cuban problem quickly because he did "not want to be in the position of turning over the government in the midst of a developing emergency."[22] The 5412 Group (a subcommittee of the National Security Council [NSC] responsible for coordinating government covert actions) was "of the opinion that it would be extremely useful to request Mr. Pawley as an immediate mission to call on [Argentinean] President [Arturo] Frondizi in a private capacity . . . to ascertain in detail the latter's attitude with respect to the present situation in Cuba and the extent to which he might be prepared to contribute to its solution."[23]

Arriving in Buenos Aires, Pawley unexpectedly ran into Roy Rubottom, who had recently been appointed ambassador to Argentina and was at the airport picking up his daughter. The surprised look on Rubottom's face told Pawley the ambassador had no advance knowledge of his mission. Rubottom asked if there was anything he could do during his visit. Pawley said no, but when Rubottom asked if he wanted to see President Frondizi, he quickly accepted the offer. The call came later that evening when Rubottom said that Frondizi would be sending his car to take Pawley to his residence. Arriving at Frondizi's home, Pawley was ushered into a room to meet privately with the president.

"Pawley," the president began, "this is the first time I have ever seen your government use what I consider good judgment in conveying a message to a Latin American Chief of State."

In his mind, Pawley must have thought of his unsuccessful visit with Batista when he felt limited in expressing the true reason for his mission.

"What usually happens," Frondizi continued, "is what occurred when Adlai Stevenson came down here a few weeks ago. He had a lot of assistants and interpreters and was accompanied by newsmen. All conversations were in the open. Both of us felt muzzled."

Frondizi then surprised Pawley by revealing that he knew the purpose of his visit. A group of exile Cubans had visited Frondizi ten days earlier and told him of

Pawley's part in plans to oust Castro. Unlike during the Stevenson visit, Frondizi felt at ease with Pawley. "I'm not going to be quoted," he told Pawley, "you're not going to give it to any newspaper, we don't need an interpreter, and this is really the way to do this."

Frondizi then said he found it inconceivable that the U.S. policymakers didn't know Castro was a Communist. Furthermore, he thought it incomprehensible that once they were aware he *was* a Communist, they didn't send in the Marines to overthrow him. Frondizi reminded Pawley that this action would have been justified under the provisions of the Rio Treaty, which gave the United States authority to rid Latin America of any outside power trying to gain a foothold in the hemisphere.

"I know that you are assisting the Cubans and that you have a large group in Guatemala and are getting ready to overthrow Castro," Frondizi stated. Again, Pawley was caught off guard by an unexpected disclosure, but Frondizi wasn't finished.

"Do not," the president told him in a serious and grave tone, "under any circumstances, put these men ashore unless you are willing to back them up with whatever it takes. A failure would be catastrophic. It would be a loss from which you might never recover."

Without being specific, Frondizi promised to help, emphasizing that U.S. fears of adverse Latin American reactions were groundless, and he offered to send his ambassador as a direct contact to Pawley in Washington. Frondizi had a request: "You haven't broken relations [with Cuba] and neither have we, but I want to know a day or two before you break relations so that I can do it simultaneously."[24]

Armed with the assurance of Argentinean support, Pawley flew to Lima to meet with President Manuel Prado y Ugarteche, who had already decided to break off relations with Cuba. The Communists were beginning to make inroads in Peru, having been fostered by huge sums of money that Castro was using to bribe military officers and politicians. Prado was only too happy to offer support for Castro's downfall. Prado's only request was that he also receive advance notice from the United States before any action took place to allow Peru to prepare.[25]

Pawley reported directly to Eisenhower on December 28 and outlined the positions of Peru and Argentina. Eisenhower was "impressed by what Pawley reported," but he also was concerned that both governments might "be overthrown by their people if they took a public stand, since Castroism has made great inroads,

particularly among the poorest classes of their people."[26] Acting on Pawley's information, he instructed Thomas C. Mann, assistant secretary of state for Latin
American affairs, to notify Frondizi two or three days before Washington severed
diplomatic relations with Cuba. Pawley then met with Secretary of State–designate
Dean Rusk, who was receiving regular briefings during the transition period.[27]

But Castro acted first. On January 2, 1961, he ordered half of the staff members of the U.S. Embassy in Havana to withdraw. The following day, the United
States severed all diplomatic relations with Cuba.[28] Pawley was in Miami when
he received a phone call from Frondizi, who was irate because he hadn't received
advance notification and demanded an explanation. Pawley couldn't believe what
he was hearing and told Frondizi he would check it out and get back to him. "When
I reached Tom Mann," Pawley recalled, "he blandly informed me that the matter slipped his mind." Forced to report this "feeble excuse" to Frondizi, Pawley
was relieved when the Argentine president calmly offered to send his emissary,
Congressman Enrique Bulit-Goñi, to see Pawley in Miami.

After a four-day session with Bulit in Miami, during which Pawley and five
Cuban exile leaders were briefed on the current situation, Pawley convinced Bulit
to meet in Washington with State Department officials. Sending advance notification to Dean Rusk that Bulit would be arriving and that he "is being sent to this
country by President Frondizi to confirm the Argentine Government's willingness
to cooperate fully in whatever needs to be done," Pawley waited to hear the out-
come of the meeting.[29] Pawley also informed Thomas Mann of Bulit's arrival, offering Mann the opportunity to atone for his earlier mistake.

"To my mortification and outrage," Pawley wrote, "Bulit was allowed to cool
his heels for three days in his hotel, fearful of leaving lest he miss a call, without
a single call from State." Furious that a foreign representative was treated in such
a manner, Pawley called Whiting Willauer, former Ambassador to Honduras and
China Defense Supplies corporate secretary, who in turn was "hot under the col-
lar" over such a flagrant discourtesy. Willauer, who was the only State Department
official who contacted Bulit during his visit to Washington, agreed to file a report
of Frondizi's cooperation on the Cuban matter.[30] Roy Rubottom later suggested
"providing [Frondizi] up-to-date summary Castro situation . . . to keep him satisfied U.S. carrying out effective consultation," but the affront was not forgotten.[31]

Even though he was not privy to the incoming president's intentions, Pawley
continued working on the plan to overthrow Castro. He kept Eisenhower ap-

prised with up-to-date information from his sources, but the outgoing president felt that "in these waning days of the Administration, about all I could do was to send it along to the two Agencies most concerned."[32] Aside from the actual operation, Pawley was most concerned about the provisional government to be put in place once Castro was defeated. Howard Hunt felt Pawley was pushing too hard to get conservative Cubans on the list, including Dr. Antonio Rubio Padilla, Fabio Freyre's uncle. "Pawley . . . had the ear of Vice President Nixon, and both [Frank] Bender [CIA agent whose real name was Gerard Droller] and Colonel King were obliged to spend long hours talking with Cubans who were 'dead but did not know it.'"[33]

Pawley made lists of prominent Cuban exiles who he felt "could be persuaded to function as one in the interest of the overthrow of Castro and the rebuilding of Cuba."[34] His choices, culled from the Cuban exile community, were educated professionals and industrialists, but most had previous ties with Batista, which made them unacceptable to the State Department. "These guys don't understand their Cuba is part of the past," Bender told Hunt after interviewing Dr. Rubio. "Now I suppose Rubio will tell Pawley he didn't get anywhere with me, and Pawley will beef to Nixon or Jake or King. Then I'll have to do it all over again."[35]

During the election campaign, Kennedy gave a speech in Milwaukee, proclaiming, "I have never advocated and I do not advocate intervention in Cuba in violation of our treaty obligations," but that position soon changed.[36] The CIA invasion plan, which the Joint Chiefs of Staff reviewed before passing it on to President Kennedy, called for an amphibious landing at the city of Trinidad. It was an ideal spot for several reasons. It was far from Havana, the residents were strongly anti-Castro, it had an airfield, and, most important, it was situated at the foot of the Escambray Mountains, making an ideal escape route if the operation failed. Kennedy's advisers were against the location because it would be readily apparent that the United States backed the operation. Kennedy ordered the CIA to find a less conspicuous spot for the landing.[37]

"It seems incredible that any military man would have approved the plans to invade Cuba through the Bahía de Cochinos, or Bay of Pigs," remarked Ruby Hart Phillips, a reporter who had spent years writing about Cuba.[38] Surrounded by swamps, the bay only had three roads leading inland. Its single advantage was no concentrations of Castro troops were in the vicinity, and if they did mount a counterattack, air support could quickly cut off military vehicles heading toward the area. In addition, the airfield at nearby Girón was more suitable for B-26 planes being used in the operation. The disadvantage, a formidable one, was the invaders would have no avenue for retreat except the open sea.

Nevertheless, on April 17, 1961, the Bay of Pigs invasion, dubbed Operation Zapata, commenced. The operation was a textbook example of Murphy's Law: everything went wrong. Outboard motors on landing craft wouldn't start due to seawater corrosion, the approach was not a sandy beach but treacherous coral, local militia began shooting at the invaders who were wading ashore, and by morning, Castro's regular army troops had arrived, supported by his small air force, which had not been nullified because the U.S. military force had canceled its air strikes.[39] "At first it sounded like it was a success," a radio operator stationed at the Guatemala training camp said, "then after a while Castro came on, announcing how he wiped us out."[40]

Battle reports sent chills through the CIA, the State Department, and the Kennedy administration. Allen Dulles went to Nixon's home in Washington on the evening of April 19. "Everything is lost," he told Nixon. "The Cuban invasion is a total failure."[41] He first blamed Kennedy's aides, who had advised canceling the air strikes, but later revised his opinion. In an unpublished account of the operation, Dulles blamed himself for not ensuring everyone knew "that air cover for the landing was an 'absolute' prerequisite."[42] Richard Bissell added, "The President was never told that the brigade's [Brigade 2506] air arm was potentially inadequate for its task."[43] Dulles briefed Eisenhower on April 21, but the former president heard the reasons directly from JFK the following day. "The chief apparent causes of failure were gaps in our intelligence," Kennedy told Eisenhower, "plus what may have been some errors in shiploading, timing, and tactics."[44] Pawley had a different opinion. The invasion "would have succeeded," he wrote, "had the Administration not made the terrible mistake of judgment in canceling the bomber strike on the Havana airport. . . ."[45]

On June 5, Eisenhower heard another version from Pawley. Handing Eisenhower a rough sketch of the invasion area that a member of the attack force had made, Pawley briefed him on what he had learned:

The man accompanied the attacking expedition from a port of embarkation in Central America. . . . The invasion force was escorted by a carrier and a couple of destroyers, and was carried in three or four small ships secured from the United Fruit Company. . . . The attack was to be supported by an air strike at first light the following morning. . . . These support strikes were not made and as a result the hostile air was permitted to operate freely and succeeded in sinking our principal supply ship. . . . In spite of these handicaps the man said that the force attacked efficiently and effectively and were finally forced to surrender by lack of support and when their ammunition was completely exhausted.

Mr. Pawley went on to say that the airplanes based on the carrier were over the attacking ships at the proper time but were recalled by the Admiral on what were said to be "orders from the White House."

Pawley told Ike he had heard a story about a White House meeting in which Adlai Stevenson "made strong representation against any participation by American forces in the attack." As a result, Kennedy called off the air strikes. Parodying JFK's book *Profiles in Courage*, Eisenhower wrote in his diary, "If true, this story could be called a 'Profile in Timidity and Indecision.'"[46]

Through Eisenhower, Pawley was given an appointment to see Kennedy at the White House on May 6, 1961. Attempting to disarm his visitor, Kennedy began by saying, "Now before we start, Pawley, I'd like you to know that I take full responsibility for the mistake at the Bay of Pigs." Pawley resisted mentioning Stevenson's intervention. He wouldn't be well received if he began with an argument. After reciting his background experience on Cuba, Pawley gave his opinion in straightforward, unequivocal terms.

"I think we have to drop ten thousand Marines in the environs of Havana," he told Kennedy. "There is a sugar plantation on the outskirts of the city that would be an excellent assembly area. The Marines should go into the city, take the Palace, release the Bay of Pigs prisoners and the other political prisoners, and we should establish a provisional government. I have brought with me a list of outstanding Cubans who would, in my opinion, command confidence in such a government."

Kennedy listened, but he made no comment. Pawley wasn't the first to recommend military action. Nixon had been invited to the Oval Office on April 20. When Kennedy asked what he would do now, Nixon had replied, "I would find a proper legal cover and I would go in."[47]

"When you have done that," Pawley continued, "I think you should have the provisional government remain in office for eighteen months. No reprisals of any sort should be allowed. . . . The main task of the provisional government would be to hold fair and free elections. . . . If you do this, sir, Cuba will be stabilized. . . . I'd have the Navy place a large number of warships seaward of Havana harbor, perhaps two or three miles offshore, as a display of force."

"Pawley," the president replied in a firm tone, "I don't intend to spill one drop of American blood in connection with this matter. I don't intend to put any Marines in Cuba."

Knowing it was unlikely he ever would have another opportunity to see Kennedy and discuss Cuba, Pawley asked what the alternatives were. Sidestepping the Cuban issue, Kennedy felt the real problem was stopping the spread of Communism in the Western Hemisphere. Kennedy said he was going to propose a $10 billion Alliance for Progress program. "We've got to get into Latin America with resources and lift these people out of the misery and poverty they've been living in for such a long time," he added.

Pawley told the president about his visit to Frondizi and his warning about failing. "If you offer money, right on top of a humiliating defeat, they will take it, but they will take it with contempt. . . . What counts with Latins is results. That, not our money, is what they respect."[48]

Kennedy disagreed. He pointed out that for years American businessmen (perhaps he had Pawley in mind) had exploited Cuba, and no other country in the Western Hemisphere had so much poverty, hunger, and misery.

"Mr. President," Pawley replied, "I have no idea who is informing you on this subject, but you are completely mistaken. Cuba before Castro was one of the most *prosperous* countries in the Western Hemisphere! It stood fourth in per capita income and ranked close to the top in education, literacy, social services and medical care."

Kennedy just shook his head. "Pawley, you're just *completely* misinformed." The president's patience was wearing thin, and Pawley knew his visit was coming to an end.

"I'm sorry, sir, but it has to be *you* who has been misinformed."

"Thank you for coming in," Kennedy said coolly.

Leaving the Oval Office, as he reached the door, Pawley paused and turned to offer one last plea before leaving. "Mr. President, for God's sake look into the real facts before you take action based on glaring misinformation. And I repeat, as emphatically as I can, please don't offer them money. Every dollar you sink in your Alliance for Progress, unless the Castro regime is rooted out first, will result in three dollars of foreign and Latin capital being scared away—'flight' capital."

"Thanks for coming in," Kennedy repeated, more coldly.[49]

After having given his best salesman's pitch to the President, Pawley turned his attention to the more pressing matter of how to get the prisoners taken in the Bay of Pigs invasion released.

On the evening of May 20, 1961, FRD representatives and Pawley gathered at the home of Dr. José Miró Cardona, president of the Cuban Revolutionary Council. They discussed Castro's offer to release the 1,214 prisoners. Confined to bed with a lung ailment, Miró listened to details of the proposal. When the subject of funding arose, Pawley stepped forward and offered to start the campaign by donating $25,000.[50]

Castro had visited the prisoners earlier that day and told them to choose ten representatives who would be flown to the United States to negotiate the remaining prisoners' release in exchange for tractors. He told them that feeding and housing the prisoners, plus the eight hundred guards, was a "heavy economic burden he wished to shed." Castro didn't mention another problem. Apparently he had been forced to rotate the guards continually because the prisoners were able to convert many to their way of thinking. Castro needed the tractors and wanted to rid himself of the troublesome prisoners in the bargain.

As they emerged from a Pan Am airliner at Miami Airport on May 22, 1961, the ten prisoners were greeted with cheers from a crowd of four hundred Cuban supporters.[51] U.S. Immigration Service agents met the prisoners on the tarmac, put them in Border Patrol cars, and took them to the DuPont Plaza Hotel for a press conference. Because of the massive crowd awaiting them, the press conference was canceled.

As they were being checked in, the hotel manager noticed one of the men was black. Citing hotel policy, he requested that the man be removed from the premises. Before the situation got out of hand, Pawley stepped forward and arranged for the entire group to stay at the Fontainebleau Hotel. After being introduced to representatives of the Cuban Revolutionary Council, they were escorted to Dr. Miró's home for a meeting.[52]

Castro's proposal called for releasing a "proportionate number" of prisoners as the tractors were delivered, repeating the process until the trade had been completed. He would hold those prisoners who he felt had higher barter value until the last shipment of tractors arrived "to prevent double-dealing." Listening to the plan at Dr. Miró's home, Pawley suggested that "this process might be streamlined and speeded" up if they brought in neutral supervisors from the Canadian government. One of the released prisoners said Castro had personally selected him to ensure that the tractors met specifications and that Castro wanted a five-year supply of spare parts included in the deal.[53]

President Kennedy acted quickly on the tractors-for-prisoners exchange offer, but he was concerned that the United States could not deal directly with Castro since it had not given his government official recognition. He called Dr. Milton Eisenhower and asked him to serve on a committee of private citizens that would raise the money for the exchange. Donations would be tax-deductible, but their efforts would have to be a private matter. Eleanor Roosevelt, who would chair the group, and United Automobile Workers (UAW) union president Walter Reuther agreed to serve on the committee. Eisenhower was worried they would be violating the Logan Act, which prevented private citizens from negotiating with foreign nations. He received White House assurance that the State Department would sanction the committee as long as Kennedy's name was not mentioned. "We make this proposal not as a response to a demand for political ransom," a telegram from the committee to Castro read in part, "but out of common humanity."[54]

In a speech he gave to farmers, Castro said he was willing to trade the prisoners for five hundred bulldozers, not small agricultural tractors, and equated the deal to one in which Spain had traded Napoleon's soldiers they had held captive for pigs.[55] The Tractors for Freedom Committee soon learned that dealing with Castro was not an easy matter. He rejected the offer of five hundred agricultural tractors; instead, Castro now wanted $28 million in tractors or cash. The committee disbanded June 23, but there remained the problem of what to do with the contributions it had received. A new group appointed by the ten-man prisoners' team and calling itself the Cuban Families Committee for the Liberation of Prisoners of War wanted the money.[56]

A tough-minded negotiator was needed to deal with Castro, and U.S. attorney general Robert Kennedy suggested James B. Donovan. A Harvard Law graduate, general counsel of the OSS in World War II, and assistant to Supreme Court justice Robert H. Jackson at the Nuremberg war crimes trials, Donovan was perfect for the job. The Cuban Families Committee, as it was called, began soliciting sponsors.[57] Among them were First Lady Jackie Kennedy's sister, Princess Lee Bouvier Radziwill; Cardinal Richard Cushing; Gen. Lucius D. Clay; Dame Margot Fonteyn; and William Pawley.[58]

Making an appearance on the Jack Paar TV show, Pawley talked about the tractors-for-prisoners exchange.[59] He was enthusiastic about the committee and tried encouraging prominent people to subscribe their names to the list. "I would be deeply grateful if you would permit us to have your name appear," he wrote former president Hoover, adding that no duties would be asked of him.[60] Hoover declined, citing that whenever his name appeared on any cause he received mail and requests for interviews. "I am just too old to take on anything more," Hoover replied. "When you get to be 88 years you will understand."[61]

The *New York Times* called it an "impressive" list of prominent people, but Castro was difficult to deal with and negotiations dragged on. In the meantime, Castro put the prisoners on trial. Hoping to achieve a propaganda coup by having them denounce the United States, Castro was met with hostility when the prisoners opted to die with honor before firing squads. Visiting the prisoners on April 8, Castro told them they had been found guilty, but their lives would be spared. He would still allow them to be ransomed, but now he had upped the payment to $62 million. He made another offer—a prisoner exchange for an equal number of political prisoners in various countries.[62] "The Americans offered me five hundred ridiculous toy tractors worth a little over three million dollars," Castro told members of the committee who came to Havana on April 10, 1962, to negotiate. "As a result, eleven months have gone by."[63]

Among those languishing at the Isle of Pines prison was Fabio Freyre, and Pawley was determined to get him released. Using U.S. ambassador to Canada Livingston Merchant as a conduit to the Cuban government, Pawley learned that Freyre's release could be "purchased" for $100,000. Jorge Govín Throckmorton, a prisoner whose family was wealthy, could be had for $50,000. Pawley added a third man to the list—Nestor Fitzgerald Williams, a black Cuban who had no wealthy family to rescue him. "I bought one colored fellow—$25,000—I did it so the Commies could not say that no one cares about the poor ones," Pawley said in a phone conversation with Nixon's secretary, Rose Mary Woods.[64]

"We would have to put $175,000 to the account of the Cuban Government in the Royal Bank of Canada," Pawley recalled, "and then wait for Cuba's next move. There would be no promises."[65]

Fifteen months after their capture, the three men arrived in Miami. They had physically deteriorated—Freyre lost seventy pounds—but were grateful for their freedom.

19

Operation Red Cross

After the Bay of Pigs, Cuban exiles continued pressuring the Kennedy administration to invade Cuba, but their pleas fell on deaf ears. Acting as their leader, José Miró met with President Kennedy on April 10, 1962, to seek his support. National Security Adviser McGeorge Bundy had already told Dr. Miró "this would mean open war against Cuba" and that the United States did not deem it "advisable in the present international situation." Further, Kennedy had agreed.[1] Pawley felt Kennedy was a weak president, and he waited for the right opportunity to show Americans that he was not the leader needed to make tough decisions. That moment came, as he saw it, after the Cuban Missile Crisis in November 1962.

Pawley felt Kennedy completely mishandled the missile crisis and viewed it similarly to how he thought the president had wavered during the Bay of Pigs operation. Evidence of missile installations being prepared in Cuba led Pawley to "draw the conclusion that Kennedy did in fact know about the Soviet missiles and was waiting for a politically opportune moment to announce his discovery." He may have been correct in his assumption because nineteen months before the president made the announcement, José Bosch, Carlos Prío's former finance minister, wrote in a paid advertisement published in the *New York Times*: "Just recently I have received confidential information that in the western part of the island of Cuba, specifically in the vicinity of the town of Soros, Province of Pinar del Río, an installation is being finished that has required hundreds of tons of portland cement, and has led observers to conclude that a rocket-launching pad is being prepared for use by the Soviet Union."[2] This ad was not the earliest warning of missile installations in Cuba. U.S. representative Dante Fascell of Florida told a reporter in February 1960 there had been speculation that Soviet officials were conferring with the Cubans to construct such a base.[3]

On October 10, 1962, Senator Keating, speaking from the floor of the U.S. Senate, announced he had received information that Cuba had begun construction on several launching sites for intermediate-range ballistic missiles. His allegations touched off a flurry of activity in the intelligence community because Kennedy felt he purposely had not been informed and was convinced that someone in the Defense Department was Keating's source of the leak.[4] Keating never revealed his source, insisting that "all my information . . . was either furnished or confirmed by Government sources."[5]

Clare Boothe Luce, the former ambassador to Italy under Eisenhower and wife of Henry Luce, publisher of *Time* and *Life* magazines, later confided to CIA director William Colby that "it was me who fed the missile stuff to Keating."[6] But she contradicted herself at a dinner party at her Watergate apartment in 1975. "The information [the Cubans] came out with was remarkably accurate—that the Russians were building missile sites in Cuba. I was told that the information was eventually fed to Sen. Ken Keating and was passed on to the White House."[7]

Reporters Rowland Evans and Robert Novak suggested another source in 1963. They claimed Keating "pruned published sources, checked through normal government channels of communication, snared minor tidbits of information from refugee leaders." They also said he used an article Hal Hendrix had published in the *Miami News* on October 7, 1962.[8] "Construction has begun in Communist Cuba on at least a half dozen launching sites for intermediate range tactical missiles, United States intelligence authorities have advised the White House," Hendrix wrote. The article said, "The ground-to-ground missiles can be operational from island Cuba within six months" and have the capability to "penetrate deeply into the United States in one direction and reach the Panama Canal Zone in the opposite direction."[9] Keating insisted that other members of Congress "were being offered the same Cuban intelligence he was utilizing."[10] It is also likely he received reports from Cuban exiles, many of whom were in regular contact with Pawley.

On October 22, 1962, Kennedy addressed the nation concerning the presence of missiles in Cuba. "The timing was just two weeks before the Congressional elections," Pawley noted.[11] Pawley felt the presence of offensive missiles in Cuba offered the United States a perfect opportunity to invade, but the opposite happened.

Defusing the crisis, Kennedy averted military action by pledging never to invade Cuba or to support any covert operation to overthrow Castro.

Kennedy's pledge infuriated anti-Castro groups. Removing the missiles was a "pseudo-victory unless the regime that made possible the installation is dismantled," voiced Tony Varona, head of the anti-Castro organization Rescate Democratico Revolucionario (RDR). Alpha 66, a group conducting raids on Cuba, said it would wait to see if Kennedy kept his promise. "Then, if it appears the U.S. is not going to take military action," a spokesman declared, "we will start shooting again."[12]

For his part, Pawley fired off a telegram to Kennedy urging nullification of the pact with the Soviets. The agreement, he wrote, would be "a devastating blow to the prestige of the U.S. and set us back in the cold war." The lengthy message continued, "We cannot make a deal with [Nikita] Khrushchev regarding Cuba without abandoning the Monroe Doctrine and the Rio Treaty and accepting the Khrushchev Doctrine in violation of the various treaties entered into between American states."

Pawley felt it was time for the United States to get even tougher with Cuba. Washington should be working with other Latin American countries to overthrow Castro. Further, he wrote,

> If this is not done, America will have lost the magnificent opportunity which was so well prepared by your administration last week. The entire hemisphere was solidly behind you and it is the first time in many years that we have had such support from Latin America.
>
> I pray you will not dissipate this partial victory and will go forward in carrying out your promise that a communist state will not be permitted to remain in this hemisphere.[13]

Kennedy never responded to Pawley's telegram.

Pawley elaborated on why he sent the telegram. "We've waited too long," he told reporters at his home in Miami. "We've temporarily lost the initiative, but it could be regained." Asked if the International Red Cross was capable of supervising the dismantling of the Cuban missile bases, as it had proposed, Pawley said the United States should handle it. "We're running great risks," he added. "We're backing away from a victory. Millions of Americans today do not believe we are following the right policy."[14]

With the missile crisis over, the matter of the remaining Bay of Pigs prisoners held in Cuba still needed to be resolved. Negotiations dragged on, with Castro refusing or modifying offers. An exchange of prisoners for food and medical supplies was finally agreed upon, and four planeloads of prisoners arrived December 23 in Florida. Castro did not release the last prisoners until he received a guarantee of the money that was promised for the sixty wounded prisoners released in April. On Christmas Eve, the last of the captives came home.[15] "I was always ashamed that we had to bargain for those men," Pawley said in an interview, "rather than go there and secure their release by force, as we easily could have done."[16]

Kennedy wanted to meet with the released prisoners and went against the advice of his aides, who felt it would be considered a defiant and belligerent gesture. On the contrary, Robert Kennedy said it was not only proper but fitting. President Kennedy attended a rally in Miami's Orange Bowl, and Jackie accompanied him and gave a speech in Spanish. Surviving members of Brigade 2506 presented him with their banner. Kennedy vowed, "This flag will be returned to this brigade in free Havana," and the crowd cheered.[17] "That's the best way for people to lose hope," Pawley commented, "make a beautiful phrase and a beautiful promise and then not follow through."[18]

Pawley turned again to his Cuban exile friends to figure out a way to retake Cuba. One group was Directorio Revolucionario Estudiantil (Revolutionary Student Directorate [DRE]), a student group organized in Cuba against Batista. When Castro took over, the group organized military operations to overthrow him. The CIA paid the DRE leaders a monthly retainer and supplied the group with weapons and ammunition. In November 1960, one DRE team landed in Cuba to organize anti-Castro students and carry out harassment operations. By April 1961, a four-hundred-man guerrilla force was operating in the Sierra Maestra mountains, but seventy-four were captured just prior to the Bay of Pigs invasion.

Their capture was a setback to the organization, but other DRE groups continued planning attacks, including the August 24, 1962, bombing of the Blanquita Theater in Havana by a group operating out of South Florida. Their target was the Hotel Icar, a waterfront resort housing Russian, Czech, Polish, and Chinese advisers and technicians. The DRE had received word that the advisers met every Friday night at the nearby empty Blanquita Theater and that Castro often joined them. Approaching the coastline in two small motorboats, when they were in range the DRE raiders opened fire.[19] Although the attack caused no serious injuries and the

rebels made it back to their Florida base, publicity from the raid gave them credibility, which they leveraged to raise private funds. Among those people providing
financing were Pawley and Clare Boothe Luce.[20]

Shortly after the Bay of Pigs fiasco, Luce received a call from her "great
friend" Pawley who told her he was organizing a small fleet of speedboats—ostensibly waterborne Flying Tigers—that would clandestinely land Cuban exiles for
intelligence-gathering missions in Cuba, and he wanted Luce to sponsor one of the
boats.[21] He said he had already signed up a few of his wealthy friends, including
Justin H. McCarthy, vice president of St. Regis Paper. Luce was enthusiastic about
the project, calling the three-man crew she adopted "my young Cubans."[22]

José Antonio Lanusa, press and public relations officer for the DRE, doubted
whether Luce or Pawley ever paid for the motorboats because, he said, "he knew
how all of the boats were acquired."[23] But Luce claimed that shortly after Kennedy
made the deal with Khrushchev to end the nuclear showdown, she received a call
from CIA director Allen Dulles. "He said get out of that boat business—he was
well aware of it, by the way—because the neutrality act has now been reasserted
and it was against the law to aid or abet the Cubans in any attempts to free their
country."[24] Pawley was also informed that the administration was invoking the
Neutrality Act and would not tolerate any more of the exiles' missions into Cuba.[25]

The South Florida Cuban exile community remained a hotbed of plotters and
gossipers. Rumors and conspiracies were commonplace, but in the spring of 1963,
word spread that despite the Kennedy-Khrushchev agreement, Soviet missiles were
still in Cuba. If true, the revelation could destroy Kennedy's credibility.[26] Having
been rebuked by the president following the Bay of Pigs disaster, Pawley would
gladly welcome the opportunity to embarrass Kennedy. In a long letter to Nixon
concerning Cuba, Pawley wrote, "All of the Cubans and most Americans in this
part of the country believe that to remove Castro you must first remove Kennedy,
and that is not going to be easy."[27]

Pawley may have been subconsciously encouraged by Nixon, who kept in
touch with his friend and supporter. In a letter to Pawley dated May 8, 1963, Nixon
wrote, "History will record that you were one of the very few Latin American experts who had Castro's number from the beginning. And, both the Eisenhower and
Kennedy Administrations must accept responsibility for what has happened—the
Eisenhower Administration for not acting sooner and the Kennedy Administration
for not acting decisively."[28]

Determined to act decisively, Pawley began assembling a team to carry out his plan. The cast of characters who participated in what became known as Operation Red Cross included mob figures, Cuban exile leaders, CIA operatives, and mercenary soldiers, some of whom would become well known names during the Watergate investigation a decade later.

Eduardo Pérez Gonzalez, also known as Col. "Eddie" Alberto Bayo, a Cuban who was a naturalized American, was a veteran of the rebel force that fought Batista. Fighting alongside Castro's brother Raúl, he was awarded the Frank Pais Medal—Cuba's equivalent of the Medal of Honor—for outstanding bravery. Bayo switched sides when Castro came into power, joining guerrilla groups raiding Cuba, including Alpha 66.[29] "Bayo was known as a 'rowboat man'—tough, cocky and ready to work on any operation."[30]

In the spring of 1963, Bayo circulated a letter in the Cuban exile community that he claimed was from guerrillas operating in Cuba. The letter stated that guerrillas were hiding two Soviet missile officers who had defected and wanted political asylum in the United States. If smuggled out of Cuba, they would offer proof that Castro still had missiles in Cuba in direct violation of the Kennedy-Khrushchev agreement.[31]

Bayo used the letter to bait Kennedy's wealthy political enemies in Florida. He wanted them to fund an operation with weapons, a boat, and men to extricate the two Soviets and bring them to the United States. "I want no part of the CIA," he declared, a reaction from previous experiences in mounting raids against Castro. Bayo was elated when Howard K. Davis, an American soldier of fortune and pilot who had flown for anti-Batista rebels and later for anti-Castro groups, read a copy of the letter and offered to seek funds through Theodore Racoosin, a wealthy New York financier with high contacts in the Kennedy administration. "We discussed Bayo's plan with Racoosin," Davis recalled, "and he came down to Miami. . . . He met with Bayo and at that time was satisfied that there were indeed such technicians who had defected."

Racoosin tried checking out Bayo's story, but no one in Washington could verify it. When he suggested that an intelligence officer should accompany Bayo's mission and meet the Russians, Bayo balked, saying the Russians didn't trust the CIA. He alone would have to go to Cuba, he insisted. Racoosin couldn't sell the plan to anyone in the Kennedy administration, so he steered Davis and Bayo to meet with several Cuban exile leaders in Miami. Attended by Racoosin, Davis, and Bayo, the meetings were held in offices at the *Miami News*. Gathered around a conference table, they met with several DRE leaders and other action groups to discuss a possible plan.

Among those at the meeting were John Martino and Gerry Patrick Hemming, shadowy characters who surfaced during the Kennedy assassination investigation. A low-level gangster and electronics expert who specialized in gaming machines, Martino became involved with anti-Castro groups after being released from a Cuban prison in October 1962. Hemming, a former Marine, went to Cuba in 1959 and offered his services to Castro in overthrowing Batista. He claimed to have met Lee Harvey Oswald earlier that year in Los Angeles. In 1961, Hemming switched sides and began training anti-Castro groups in Florida that were funded by the CIA. After the government cracked down on the Florida training groups, Hemming moved his training group, Interpen, to New Orleans.

A second meeting was held in the office of Jack W. Gore, publisher of the *Fort Lauderdale News*. This time Frank Fiorini (later known as Frank Sturgis during the Watergate era) attended. After the meeting, several of the men gathered to discuss Bayo's letter from the Russian defector. After listening to Bayo's story, Martino contacted Nathaniel Weyl, the right-wing author of *Red Star over Cuba* who was assisting Martino with a book titled *I Was Castro's Prisoner*, an account of Martino's prison stay. Weyl also worked as a ghostwriter on Pawley's never published memoir. Martino and Weyl contacted the Miami regional editor for *Life* magazine to support the operation. On April 16, 1963, Pawley received a call from Jay Sourwine, who served as the senior counsel of the Senate Internal Security Committee headed by Senator James O. Eastland. It was the same committee Pawley had testified before in September 1960.

Senator Eastland recently had met Martino, who told him the story of the two Soviet missile officers, and the senator wanted Pawley to help the operation to get them out of Cuba. Pawley told Eastland the "chances of success were slim," but he agreed to talk to Martino in Miami before making a decision. Martino repeated the story to Pawley, adding that ten Cuban exiles from Baracoa, a coastal town on the northeast tip of Cuba where the two Soviets were hiding, were in Miami and willing to bring the men out. Pawley asked to meet the Cubans. He wanted to grill them on the Baracoa area, which he knew well from his boyhood, "so they couldn't fool me on that score."[32]

On April 18, Pawley contacted Ted Shackley, chief of the CIA station in Miami. Dubbed JMWAVE, the Miami station became the largest CIA facility at the time, employing a staff of 450 agents and support personnel (normal overseas stations had no more than 30), in addition to financing two thousand Cuban exiles. The operation was housed in seven buildings and several other structures at Richmond Field, a World War II–era U.S. Navy blimp base (and today the site of the Miami Zoo). Formerly controlled by the University of Miami, which leased it to the CIA, it had a radio station capable of reaching most of Latin America and had a direct land link to CIA headquarters in Langley, Virginia.[33] Having been granted permission to work with JMWAVE, now Pawley sought advice from the station chief.[34]

Shackley had been an intelligence spook his entire adult life. In October 1945, eighteen-year-old Shackley joined the U.S. Army. Fluent in Polish, he was assigned to the army's Counterintelligence Corps to work with the occupation forces in Germany. He was still in the army when he enrolled at the University of Maryland after the war. Upon graduation he was sent back to Germany to recruit Polish agents. Joining the CIA in 1953, he was stationed at the Berlin office. Nicknamed the "Blond Ghost" because he avoided being photographed, he rose in the CIA ranks and was appointed deputy chief of JMWAVE in 1962. Among his assignments, Shackley provided supplies to Mafioso Johnny Rosselli that were to be used in plots to assassinate Castro.

When Pawley repeated his conversation with Sourwine to Shackley, he asked if the operation was feasible. Shackley saw a great opportunity and said the operation could not be accomplished legally without the CIA's participation. The Soviet defectors were a prize, and Shackley wanted the agency to have first crack at their debriefing. In Shackley's presence, Pawley called Sourwine and received permission to bring the CIA on board. Pawley also told Shackley that John Martino was to play a role in the operation. Although Shackley knew Martino as a shady character, he saw no reason not to include him.[35] Pawley then agreed to pay each Soviet defector $2,500, and the CIA would reimburse him "if they were legit."[36]

Needing all the help he could get, Pawley contacted CIA deputy director Lt. Gen. Pat Carter. Pawley wanted to use his own sixty-five-foot yacht, the *Flying Tiger II*, and he wanted Carter to "arrange for me to bring my boat back into my dock at Sunset Island without having to go through customs or immigration should we be successful in bringing out the defectors." Carter said the CIA could not be directly involved in the operation, but he would find "three good men . . . an armaments expert, a good navigator and a good radio operator."[37]

The plan called for the *Flying Tiger II* to tow a small speedboat to Hogsty reef, a deserted atoll eighty miles off the coast of Cuba. Pawley and the Cuban exile insertion team would leave later in a Catalina PBY-6A flying boat chartered from a company that regularly supplied aircraft to the CIA and rendezvous with the yacht at the atoll. The *Flying Tiger II* would tow the team within sight of the Cuban coastline, release the speedboat with the team aboard, and return to the atoll. The yacht would wait for radio contact from Bayo that the Soviets were on board and heading out to sea. The *Flying Tiger II* then would head to the agreed reference point, pick up the team, and return to Miami. Pawley even made plans to have the Russians taken to Eisenhower's Gettysburg farm for the debriefing.[38]

From the onset, the operation had problems and modifications that upset Pawley. First, Bayo had selected an eighteen-foot speedboat, or "a piece of junk," as Pawley described it. Out of his own pocket, Pawley purchased a twenty-two-foot boat with 100-horsepower inboard and outboard engines capable of reaching forty miles per hour. He also bought two ten-man rubber rafts for unexpected emergencies.[39]

The next surprise came the day before the *Flying Tiger II* was scheduled to depart for the atoll. Martino and Bayo told Pawley "they had accepted $15,000 from *Life* magazine with which they had bought the military equipment they needed for the voyage and that *Life* was to send along a reporter and a photographer." For a top secret mission, it seemed everyone had been invited to the party, but most of the guest list was being kept secret from the host. "As far as I was concerned," Pawley said, "that blew the deal. I couldn't conceive of the U.S. government letting me go ahead under those circumstances."

Pawley said Richard K. Billings, Miami bureau chief for *Life*, asked him to reconsider.[40] Still refusing, Pawley agreed to meet with *Life* managing editor George P. Hunt, who flew down from New York. Hunt gave Pawley a letter stating that if he allowed a reporter and photographer to tag along, all of the latter's film would be turned over to Pawley and no story would be published without his permission. Still not satisfied, Pawley called Senator Eastland and told him of the written promise from *Life*. Based on the letter, Eastland felt the operation could proceed as planned.[41] When the story of Operation Red Cross broke in 1976, Pawley said he had spent $22,000 of his own money on the operation. While confirming most of the details, Billings denied that *Life* had contributed any funds to finance the mission.[42]

On June 5, 1963, Pawley's yacht left Miami with Billings on board, along with the three men Carter had promised the CIA would provide: William "Rip" Robertson (one of the few Americans who went ashore during the Bay of Pigs invasion), Mickey Kappes, and a third man named Ken. Capt. Luis Paez Guerra, a Cuban national and longtime employee of Pawley's, commanded the *Flying Tiger II*.[43] Weapons on board included M3 submachine guns, FN FAL assault rifles, M2 carbines, Browning automatic rifles, and a Finnish-made 20mm Lahti antitank gun, a weapon capable of penetrating 2½ inches of armor. They also had excellent communication equipment—U.S. Army PRC-10 and PRC-6 radios, both unavailable at the time to civilians.[44]

Three days later, the flying boat Pawley had chartered, flown by a navy pilot, took off from Miami International Airport at 6 a.m. to rendezvous with the *Flying Tiger II* at the deserted atoll. On board were Pawley, Bayo and his team, and Terence Spencer, a British freelance photographer hired by *Life*. "I frisked every one of those guys as they got on board," Pawley said. "At this point, I had no assurances of any kind of what type of men I was dealing with . . . whether they were anti-Castro or pro-Castro."[45] Spencer recalled the raiding party was kept locked in a center compartment until the plane arrived at the atoll. JMWAVE radio transmissions recorded during the mission describe the confusion when the *Flying Tiger II* became lost on the way.[46]

Ironically, Pawley's brother Wallace was a member of the Coast Guard Reserve, and he happened to be on duty at the time. Flying a routine mission along coastal waters, he noticed the *Flying Tiger II* sitting in the water. Unaware of the secret operation, he radioed the vessel, asking if the men aboard needed help. Quickly grabbing the microphone, Pawley told his brother, "Get off the air!"[47]

Waiting at the atoll was the 174-foot *Rex*, a CIA raiding boat that flew a Nicaraguan flag for cover. Equipped with 40mm and 20mm cannons, it was also loaded with sophisticated electronics in case of emergencies. Establishing radio contact, the flying boat rendezvoused with the *Rex*. Using one of the boat's launches, the raiding party was shuttled to the small island to wait for their pickup.[48]

Seven hours behind schedule the *Flying Tiger II* arrived at the atoll. The CIA-hired navigator claimed the crewmen had lost their bearings during a tropical rainstorm. Pawley recalled what happened next:

We dropped anchor right close to the island and for the next three days took one of the exiles at a time up to the bow to teach him how to use the armaments and other equipment. At the end of three days they were in pretty good shape so I decided we should leave about 5 in the afternoon and we would get 10 miles off Baracoa by about 9 p.m.

We took off and headed for Baracoa, hoping to God we wouldn't run into a Cuban gunboat. Fortunately, we didn't.

As they approached the Cuban coastline they could see the city "lit up like a church." While one CIA operative manned a 20mm gun mounted on the foredeck of the yacht, Pawley unlocked the door of his stateroom. They removed the armaments and loaded them on the twenty-two-foot speedboat.

Watching the Cubans climb aboard the speedboat, Pawley saw the craft sink lower and lower into the water. He pleaded with Bayo to use only three men for the mission, saying it was absolutely foolish to take all ten in the small boat. Bayo refused. Pawley then insisted they at least use the two ten-man rubber boats, "because on a 10-mile-trip you don't know what you are going to encounter with a boat that heavily loaded." Again, Bayo refused. Before stepping into the speedboat, Bayo turned to Pawley and asked for his wristwatch, saying, "I'll be back with it the day after tomorrow."[49]

While the speedboat headed toward shore, the *Flying Tiger II* headed back to the atoll to wait for the men to complete their mission. "We had gone about 10 minutes when 'The Tiger' was illuminated by a big floodlight," Pawley recalled. "We were desperately afraid that a Cuban gunboat had found us." They were relieved to see it was only a passing cruise liner. The next morning the yacht arrived at the atoll. Efforts to raise the insertion team by radio failed, so Pawley wired the flying boat to "circle the area every day until those boys came out and to direct them back to the island."

Over the next five days, the plane searched the area. "We wasted a week waiting for the party to return," Billings said.[50] Pawley's group received no word from the landing party, so the *Flying Tiger II* headed back to Miami. Pawley wanted to mount a rescue operation, but Hemming, Pawley's consultant on the raid, advised against it. That part of Cuba was "hot," and Hemming warned they would have to "shoot their way in and out" of the area.[51] "Although I tried for several years to find out what happened," Pawley recalled thirteen years later, "no one has ever had the slightest idea." His watch was never returned, and Pawley had "great misgivings as to whether there actually were any Russian defectors."[52]

Several versions of what might have occurred popped up in the intervening years. Three months after Operation Red Cross, John Martino contacted a CIA staff employee to report he had received a letter from a man in Cuba named Victor Garcia. Dated August 28, 1963, the letter stated that Eddie Bayo and his men had been caught in a firefight at Mayari in Oriente Province. Losing two men in the skirmish, Bayo and the others retreated to the Moa area of Oriente, where they hoped reinforcements would be brought to Cuba.

A CIA memo from the JMWAVE chief of station concluded that although information on the fate of the raiding party could not be verified,

> this review does reveal, however, that the circumstantial evidence does indicate that these infiltrees are still operating in Oriente in the Sagua de Tanamo area. This conclusion is based primarily on the fact that none of the infiltrees have returned to Miami and we have not received any information from any reporting sources which would indicate that the infiltrees have been captured, killed or imprisoned. As a result of this negative reporting, JMWAVE can only conclude that the analysis . . . was correct i.e. the individuals who participated in Operation RED CROSS did not have any Soviet contacts but they developed a story about notional Soviet contacts in order to develop an operational proposal which was designed to obtain for them transportation, arms and infiltration into Cuba via the good offices of Pawley.[53]

Ted Shackley conveniently covered the CIA's role in the operation by foisting the onus on Pawley.

In 1977, the House committee investigating the assassination of President Kennedy served a subpoena to Loren Eugene Hall, a former GI who had been working in the casino of Santo Trafficante's Havana Hotel Capri when Castro seized power. The committee's interest in Hall centered both on the five months he had spent in a Cuban prison with Trafficante and on a taped interview he gave to a Dutch journalist in which he claimed, at a summer of 1963 meeting in Dallas, he was offered $50,000 to kill President Kennedy. Appearing before the committee on June 7, 1977, Hall refused to answer questions. While awaiting another committee appearance, however, Hall agreed to an interview with Dick Russell of the *Village Voice*.

During the interview, Hall described his relationship with Trafficante and a plot funded by organized crime to assassinate Castro. After the Bay of Pigs, Hall led an anti-Castro group of exiled Cubans who were working with other groups (Bayo's group among them) to mount a second invasion. Hall claimed he attended an April 1963 meeting at a Miami Beach hotel, where John Martino introduced him and Bayo to mob figures Johnny Rosselli and Sam Giancana. "Out of the other room came Santo Trafficante," Hall said in the interview. "Giancana looked at me and said, 'Is this the one?' Santo said, 'Yes,' and walked out. The only reason he was there was to verify me."

Hall said the meetings continued until late May. They concocted and widely circulated a cover story that "two Soviet colonels were prepared to defect and testify that Russian missiles were still on Cuban soil." Pawley readily swallowed the story, according to Hall, and planning for the operation proceeded with Hall remaining on the sidelines but maintaining contact with Martino the entire time. As for *Life* magazine financing the operation, Hall agreed with Billings that the magazine "didn't put up a dime." Hall said, "The money came from Sam Giancana. I saw Giancana give $30,000 to John Martino to buy supplies and equipment."[54]

Hall's story had slight variations when he talked to William W. Turner and Warren Hinckle in 1976. Their published account of the Bayo-Pawley raid appeared in movie producer Francis Ford Coppola's short-lived weekly, *City of San Francisco*. Hall told them Giancana offered the $30,000 bounty on Castro, but Trafficante negotiated a $15,000 advance with the balance to be paid after the mission succeeded. Considering the mistrustful nature of Mafiosos, this version has a ring of truth to it. Hall said Martino, an electronics expert, was supposed to rig devices to detonate explosives from a safe distance. Bayo wanted to "blow all to hell" the Presidential Palace with Castro inside and the Ministry of Agriculture Building for good measure. Pawley was conned, Hall told the authors; Bayo's real mission was to kill Castro and collect the $15,000 balance due.

On March 21, 1978, Gerry Hemming gave sworn testimony before the House Select Committee on Assassinations (HSCA). During the questioning, Hemming was asked about the role he had played in the Bayo-Pawley raid. He said that after meeting with Bayo, his "people" and Martino, he told them he would participate, but that he was against the operation because, "I did not believe the defectors were there." HSCA staff counsel William K. Triplett, who was conducting the questioning, asked Hemming if he heard "anyone else express an opinion that this raid may have had some other purpose?"

Hemming said, "Well, Martino was quite frank with me at that point in time, that this was a pure out-and-out plan to assassinate Castro, that this whole operation was being sold to the participants as an extraction operation of defectors where, in fact, they were going to insert a hit team and they were going to try and catch Castro July the 26 at Las Mercedes." That date was the tenth anniversary of the armed attack on the Moncada Barracks by a small rebel group led by Castro, and was considered the beginning of the Cuban Revolution. Hemming said it was felt that Castro would make two appearances that day, one at the Moncada Barracks, and later at the Camilo Cienfuegos School in Las Mercedes to honor a hero of the revolution after whom the school was named. "I confronted Bayo with that," Hemming continued. "He did not think it was a bad idea."[55] Hall said Bayo's brother-in-law, Luis Castillo, received word from a source in Cuba that the mission had failed. When the speedboat reached shore, Cuban militia ambushed the team. Bayo and two others managed to escape and made their way to Havana, only to be captured and thrown into La Cabaña Prison. Hall said he and several Cuban exiles organized a rescue mission to break Bayo out of prison and kill Castro while they were there. The rescue and assassination operation came to an end in October 1963, when custom agents seized the group's munitions at their base on No Name Key.[56]

Hall's version of the true objective of Operation Red Cross may have merit. Bayo's ten-man raiding party was equipped with an inordinate amount of high-explosives—twenty one-pound explosives in Hercules powder containers and fifty feet of primacord—hardly the armament for a team whose purpose was to get ashore, find the Soviet defectors, and get them out quickly.[57] In addition, Bayo allegedly had participated in two previous assassination plots against Castro, so it is likely he was attempting a third.

In their *Soldier of Fortune* magazine article on Operation Red Cross, Miguel Acoca and Robert K. Brown raised the possibility that President Kennedy knew all along about the operation. Theodore Racoosin, who met with Bayo in Miami and then tried checking out the story of the Soviet defectors, may have alerted Kennedy. The writers offer several scenarios: (1) Kennedy knew about the plot and was closely monitoring it; (2) Kennedy decided not to pursue the plot and was unaware the CIA was going through with it anyway; (3) Kennedy knew nothing about the operation, and it was organized by "low-level CIA echelons" who effectively could support the plan without Kennedy or the CIA knowing; and (4) Kennedy knew everything, including that Bayo's letter was a fake, and laughed at the possibility that Luce and *Life* magazine were being caught in a sting that cost them $15,000.[58]

No matter which scenario was true, the fact remained that those men who went ashore in Cuba had left families behind. A year after the failed operation, CIA director John McCone learned about it when the missing men's families pleaded with the State Department to find out what had happened to them. The sons of Luis Cantin, one of the team members, approached Pawley for some form of compensation, but only Alfredo Mir's family received any indemnification, and it came from *Life* magazine.[59]

Yet another bizarre tale purportedly explains the disappearance of the raiding party. In 1976, Johnny Rosselli's body was found in an oil drum in Biscayne Bay. Syndicated columnist Jack Anderson reported he had interviewed Rosselli prior to his death. According to Rosselli, the last Mafia hit team sent to Cuba—possibly he meant the missing crew of Operation Red Cross—had been captured. Rosselli claims that instead of executing the men, Castro had turned them and sent them back to the United States as the team that killed President Kennedy and set up Oswald as the fall guy.[60]

Although the mission to bring back two Soviet defectors from Cuba may have been an elaborate hoax, Pawley steadfastly believed that Operation Red Cross had been worth the risk. It was a long shot, ". . . even if it were a 100 to 1 or a 1,000 to 1 chance," Pawley said thirteen years later, "the costs were comparatively small and something that I could afford to do. The risk was worth taking."[61] While the outlay of money may have been negligible, Pawley omitted the fact that ten Cuban exiles never returned from the failed mission.

Pawley never gave up the thought of ousting Castro, but his efforts apparently never again included clandestine operations. Instead, he continued to work hand in hand with the CIA Miami station and continually fed it information on anti-Castro group activities in the area. In May 1964, dubbed a "special contact in the Miami business community," Pawley received "Covert Security Approval" to work with JMWAVE.[62]

Shortly after the failed mission, the CIA began receiving reports that Cuban exiles were planning another invasion of Cuba, this time based in Nicaragua. Former president of Nicaragua Luis Somoza was promoting a plan to train Cuban exiles and overthrow the Cuban government in collaboration with several other Central American countries. "I myself am willing to lead the invasion of Cuba by going into the front lines with the volunteers," Somoza declared during a Miami press conference on September 7, 1963, with Pawley at his side.[63] Somoza even boasted his plan had the support of President Kennedy, whom he had met at the conference of Central American leaders in San José, Costa Rica, in 1962. When the FBI heard rumors of these Cuban exile activities, it held a meeting with CIA officials on September 25, 1963, to discuss the matter.

The CIA flatly denied giving assistance to the exiles, in the form of intelligence sharing or providing arms and equipment. The officials claimed the Kennedy administration reviewed the "Somoza Plan" and "disapproved it." Conducting an investigation, agents had discovered that Somoza was in regular contact with former Cuban president Carlos Prío Socorrás and Pawley. The CIA was quick to say the agents were not using Prío or Pawley "in any capacity," and they would be "extremely interested" in any information the FBI had on these men and their activities.[64]

Two years after Kennedy's assassination in November 1963, Pawley made remarks to Eisenhower, who sent a letter in reply: "I understand and concur in your uneasiness about the situation in the Caribbean. . . . I see no flaw in your argument that we should not be 'protecting' Castro from exiled Cubans who want to regain their country for freedom."[65]

In 1974, Republican senator Barry Goldwater of Arizona addressed the Senate to oppose other senators' efforts to "move us closer to a détente with Communist Cuba which could, in the long run, lead to our recognizing the Castro government."[66] To support his argument, Goldwater read into the *Congressional Record* a letter that Pawley had sent to the editor of the *Washington Star*:

I am greatly distressed over the efforts being made by Senators [James] Fulbright, [Jacob] Javits and [Claiborne] Pell to reestablish diplomatic relations with Cuba.

We have watched Castro convert Cuba into a Russian missile, submarine and bomber base. . . . He maintains guerrilla training camps and actively conducts clandestine Red guerrilla operations in Central and South American countries.

Castro has confiscated, without compensation, all private business in Cuba, whether owned by Cubans, United States citizens or other nationals.

He has cruelly enslaved the Cuban people of all economic levels, confiscating their property and driving over a million of them into exile. Castro is a sadistic assassin and continues to be outspokenly anti-U.S.[67]

Incensed that President Gerald Ford was considering Secretary of State Henry Kissinger's suggestion that the United States support a move in the OAS leading to lifting economic and diplomatic sanctions against Cuba, Pawley fired off a letter to the president. Lt. Gen. Brent Scowcroft, deputy assistant to the president for national security affairs, wrote a response, which was entered into the *Congressional Record*. It assured Pawley that

> the President has stated publicly on several occasions that the U.S. would be willing to consider changing its policy toward Cuba when Cuba changes its policies toward us and the other nations in this Hemisphere. . . . However, as the President has also noted, we have seen no real evidence of a change in the attitude of the Cuban government towards us and therefore see no basis for a change in our policy at this time.[6]

As concerned as he was with the government of Cuba during the Batista and Castro years, at the same time, Pawley was also taking a personal interest in another Caribbean nation, namely, the dictator Rafael Trujillo's Dominican Republic.

20

Trujillo

Generalissimo Rafael Leónidas Trujillo Molina's dictatorship of the Dominican Republic lasted thirty-one years (1930–1961), an extraordinary span of time for a Latin American country. In many respects, the Dominican Republic's political history mirrored that of Cuba: revolutions, short periods of democracy, and U.S. armed intervention followed by financial and military support of a totalitarian government that eventually fell out of favor. From the beginning, Pawley played a role in the Trujillo regime that not only included financial investments in the small Caribbean nation but also a close, personal relationship with Trujillo.

Trujillo's regime began when he became president in May 1930 with a vote count that exceeded the total number of franchised voters. As soon as he ascended to office, Trujillo established the tone of his leadership by maintaining power with intimidation, brutality, and the suppression of individual rights.[1] In 1934, he revamped the Dominican Republic's constitution to suit his power base. Under new provisions, judges could be removed from office at will and their salaries reduced at any time. Export taxes specifically prohibited under the old constitution were now allowed, enabling Trujillo to tax his country's products to ease the growing financial debt. Another provision allowed Trujillo to bless the naming of any province or town with that of his own or of his relatives.

He made further changes in 1942. He eliminated the office of vice president and made a concession to allow women equal political rights. Two other provisions were made to the constitution that would radically change the national economy. First, article 90 allowed that "private individuals may acquire, by means of concessions that the law authorizes, or by means of contracts that the national congress

269

approves," the irrevocable right to exemptions from or limitation of taxes in "certain works or enterprises of public utility, to which it is fitting to attract the investment of new capital for the development of the national economy, or for any other object of social interest."

This concession was further delineated by article 96, which dealt with mineral deposits. It stated that "mineral deposits belong to the State, and may be exploited by private individuals only by virtue of concessions or contracts granted under the conditions that the law determines.[2] These two changes opened the door to foreign investment capital. William Pawley knew when opportunity knocked, he should answer it.

In 1955, Pawley was invited to Ciudad Trujillo to address a group of American and Dominican businessmen. At the dinner he sat with Trujillo and U.S. ambassador William T. Pheiffer at the head table. "Trujillo and I fell into a conversation about my mining and oil ventures [in Mexico]," Pawley recalled, "which led into the subject of the need for the Dominican Republic to develop its abundant natural resources."[3] Trujillo invited Pawley to help draft legislation that would allow foreign investment capital to develop the Dominican Republic's mineral and oil resources.[4]

"Herbert Hoover, Jr. was Under Secretary of State, so I called him and consulted with him," Pawley said during an interview. "I wanted to rewrite the laws with competent people." Bringing along a Cuban lawyer and one from Mexico, Pawley had Trujillo assign him three of his most competent lawyers, and together with an attorney specializing in petroleum legislation on loan from Hoover, they all spent three weeks hammering out new laws. "And we wrote what are today, in my opinion, the two best laws," Pawley recalled, "one on petroleum and one on minerals—in the Western Hemisphere."[5]

Seeing a golden opportunity based on the new legislation, Pawley formed two companies based in Santo Domingo. Minera y Beneficiadora Dominicana, capitalized at $1 million, served as the corporate entity to develop mineral deposits, specifically nickel and uranium, on close to four million acres. Petrolera Dominicana, capitalized at $3 million, operated as an oil exploration and development concern.[6] An astute businessman who knew his limitations, Pawley invited other American investors to share his newly legislated bounty. Shamrock Oil Company in Texas was selected to head a group of geologists and refinery experts to establish a modern petroleum refinery with the capacity to produce high-octane aviation fuel for domestic use and export. But Pawley was concerned that other "entities or individuals in the petroleum industry of the United States" would want part of the action.

Expecting the Dominican government to receive a flood of applications from attorneys representing U.S. oil interests, Pawley hoped he would have first crack to develop the valuable resources. "I have the hope that commitments will not be concluded with other agents until it is determined that the goal of our program might not be realized," he wrote to Trujillo.[7] Alcoa was already developing bauxite deposits in the Dominican Republic, but when the company relinquished a section under exploration, Pawley quickly stepped in. He sent Trujillo a map with an area marked in red indicating where he wanted to "search for and exploit bauxite." Pawley added it would be "most advantageous" for Trujillo because "taxes and benefits" paid "as dividends to the Dominican shares" would result in a "considerable portion of the products from these minerals" remaining in the country.[8] Reading between the lines, Trujillo knew his friend would ensure that a portion of the profits would see their way into his pocket. Trujillo instructed his secretary of state to draft a resolution granting Pawley's company the rights for "exploration and exploitation of bauxite and related minerals" in an area of close to a million acres.[9]

As in China, Pawley brought in family members to oversee his Dominican operations. His brother Ed opened offices in Ciudad Trujillo to direct exploration fieldwork, and William Pawley, Jr., was made a stockholder in the company. News reports indicated groups from California, New York, and Canada were financing a "large-scale operation" and had received a "blanket contract" from Trujillo to explore and develop mineral holdings. But speaking for Pawley, who could not be reached for comment, Miami Transit vice president R. W. Cole denied there was any Dominican government contract involved in the operation.[10]

Pawley shared his Dominican mining and oil interests with prominent people, including Assistant Secretary of State Henry Holland, who helped negotiate a contract between Alcoa and the Dominican Republic.[11] Pawley also arranged an agreement with the Texas Oil Company for "exploration and drilling in the Dominican Republic" in an area known as Ciabo.[12] Both contracts pleased Trujillo, who referred to Pawley as "Honorary Technical Advisor" for the Dominican government, an arrangement that would raise the question of why Pawley hadn't registered as a representative of a foreign government as required by U.S. law.[13]

The mineral explorations became an astounding success when workers discovered the largest nickel deposit in the Western Hemisphere. "I couldn't handle it," Pawley recalled. "It was too big for me—so I turned it over to Falconbridge Nickel of Canada in exchange for an interest in the venture."[14] Aside from his involvement in mineral and oil explorations, Pawley also purchased the Hotel Hamaca, a resort in the town of Boca Chica near the newly constructed international airport outside of Ciudad Trujillo.[15] But Pawley's relations with Trujillo sometimes ran into difficulties.

"A few weeks ago a mutual friend informed me that it had been said to Generalissimo Trujillo that Alcoa had paid me a compensation as the result of the negotiations which were terminated in a new agreement between the Dominican Government and the Aluminum Company of America," Pawley wrote to the Dominican ambassador to the United States Manuel de Moya Alonzo. The four-page letter outlined Pawley's contribution to the negotiations, "which on the part of the Republic is the most lucrative of those contracts which exist throughout the world." Adding that he unconditionally had offered "absolute integrity" during the negotiations, Pawley detailed every financial arrangement he had with anyone connected with the contract.[16] Unaware that rumors were circulating concerning Pawley's integrity, Trujillo stated he was "in agreement with the intervention of Mr. Pawley in favor of the national interests" in the concession agreement with Alcoa, and the matter was dropped.[17]

Pawley's close relationship with Trujillo began with the hurricane relief effort Pawley had helped deliver to the Dominican Republic shortly after Trujillo assumed power, and it was further cemented when Pawley acted as a mediator between Trujillo and Batista. The two dictators had distrusted each other for years; relations between them were cordial but distant. Right before the 1956 Christmas holiday, Pawley was preparing to leave the Dominican Republic for Miami when he stopped in to see Trujillo. The dictator received Pawley but appeared to be preoccupied with a matter upsetting him. When questioned, Trujillo unburdened his concern.

"I've built the most beautiful cattle fairgrounds anywhere in the world," Trujillo told him. "Every year I have a cattle fair and the Cubans always come over with magnificent horses and cattle, and I always buy."

He woefully complained that many of the Cuban cattlemen were close friends, but this year, Batista would not permit them to attend. Because the Cubans stood to make $1 million during the event, it didn't make any sense why Batista wouldn't allow them to come.

"Would you mind if I go over to Cuba and talk to Batista?" Pawley offered.

"Don't go over there and talk in my name," Trujillo said firmly. "I'm not begging him to send them."

Pawley flew to Havana and received an immediate audience with Batista. Wasting little time, he got right to the point concerning his visit. "Why are you depriving the Cubans of going to the Dominican Republic where they are perfectly safe, they have a wonderful time, and they sell a lot of cattle and horses?"

"Because this guy is calling me every kind of a s.o.b. in the book every night on his radio, and I'm not going to let the Cubans go over there when I'm being attacked by the Dominican radio to the extent that I am."

When Pawley said he had never listened to any of the broadcasts, Batista had an aide bring in a transcript of a broadcast. Reading the typewritten sheets, which Batista had heavily red-penciled, Pawley was horrified. "It was filthy," Pawley recalled. "They were taking it right off the air and it was awful—I mean just vulgar, nasty, brutal attacks."

"Well, I don't blame you for being so mad," Pawley told the Cuban dictator, "but this doesn't have anything to do with the cattle show. This is a problem between the two of you—and you two fellows shouldn't be enemies anyway."

Batista was adamant about his indignation until Pawley reminded him that his own state-controlled radio station was constantly attacking Trujillo. "You have a couple of Dominicans over here that are poison." Batista remained firm, saying he wouldn't fire the broadcasters.

"I'll make you a proposition," Pawley said. "If I can get the broadcasts stopped, would you let them go?"

"Yes. I'll go further than that. If you can get the broadcasts stopped, I'll let the cattlemen go and I'll send the Secretary of Agriculture [Fidel Barreto Martínez] with them."

Pawley called Trujillo from Miami and gave him the details of his conversation with Batista. The cattlemen would be allowed to attend the fair, but the broadcasts had to stop.

"What broadcasts?" Trujillo asked, as if they were news to him.

"The broadcasts your brother puts on every night, attacking Batista."

"If that's the only problem," Trujillo said, "there won't be any more—ever."[18]

The following day, Pawley visited Batista and, during a one-hour interview, asked if he had heard a broadcast the previous evening. Batista said no and that he had advised his secretary of agriculture to attend the Dominican livestock fair. Batista added that "this should not be given publicity for political reasons."[19] The negotiations had gone well, but there were other sensitive egos that Pawley had to massage.

First, the secretary of agriculture said he didn't want to go. "Hell, I'd be murdered," he told Pawley. Reassuring him that he would be safe, Pawley agreed to travel to Havana with him. Then Batista said he wouldn't provide airplanes to fly the Cubans or the cattle to the Dominican Republic. "They'll have to make other arrangements," he told Pawley. Fortunately, Trujillo later agreed to supply the airplanes, and the Cubans attended the fair.[20]

The Cubans were treated royally, including being greeted with a twenty-one-gun salute—although they were entitled to only eighteen—and the entire Dominican cabinet was on hand to welcome them. Pawley was invited to sit in the presidential box at the opening ceremony, and after the national anthems were completed, Trujillo called him over.

"Cuba has a great friend here in Pawley," Trujillo told the visiting Cuban secretary of agriculture.

"Yes, Generalissimo," the Cuban secretary replied. "That's right, but you have a great friend too or I wouldn't be here."

As a result of the warm reception the Cubans received, Pawley was able to discuss with Batista the possibility of reestablishing diplomatic relations with Trujillo. After further talks, Batista agreed to receive the Dominican minister of foreign relations Porfirio Herrera Báez and the Dominican ambassador to the United States, Manuel de Moya. The diplomats stayed at Pawley's Miami home before going to Havana, but when they arrived at the Cuban capital, the Nacional Hotel was completely booked. Pawley contacted U.S. ambassador to Cuba Arthur Gardner and asked if he had any friends staying at the hotel who wouldn't mind giving up their suites and relocating to the U.S. Embassy. Gardner made the arrangements, and the Dominicans settled into their two-room suites at the hotel while Pawley stayed at the embassy.

The next day, Pawley and the Dominican diplomats met with the Cuban foreign minister and Batista and drank champagne at ten o'clock in the morning to toast the meeting. The Dominican foreign minister presented Batista with an album containing every postage stamp ever issued in the Dominican Republic. A CIA memo revealed the closely guarded secret that Pawley had the exclusive concession for "procurement and world-wide sale of all new issues of Dominican postage stamps." Pawley's brother, Edward, who had an office in the Ciudad Trujillo post office building, managed this concession.[21]

The entire affair, from the delicate negotiations with Batista to allow the Cubans to attend the Dominican livestock fair to the ministers' private meeting in Havana, was handled without fanfare or publicity. As a result, both countries reestablished diplomatic relations a few months later.[22] For more than five years, the United States and Latin American countries had tried unsuccessfully to bring the two countries together; it took a cattle fair to accomplish it. "It was because of that, purely," Pawley would later recall, "that Batista was able to go to the Dominican Republic when he abdicated."[23]

In 1956, as part of a group of foreign businessmen, Pawley joined a committee seeking funds from the "foreign colony" to erect a statue of Trujillo in Ciudad Trujillo's Independence Park.[24] His Dominican Republic activities hadn't gone unnoticed. Columnist Drew Pearson kept a close eye on Pawley, chronicling his activities in the Caribbean nation. Pearson continually reported on prominent Americans with close ties to the Trujillo regime, including Lt. Col. George Gordon Moore, Jr., brother-in-law of Eisenhower, and Robert Hinshaw, son-in-law of John Foster Dulles. Pearson revealed Henry Holland, former State Department official for Latin American affairs, was on Pawley's payroll as a "mining consultant"; thus Holland avoided having to register as a foreign agent.[25]

Pearson also questioned Pawley's not registering as a foreign agent. Under the Logan Act, U.S. citizens who interacted "with intent to influence the measures or conduct of any foreign government," without registering with the State Department, were subject to a fine or imprisonment.[26] Igor Cassini, *New York Journal-American* columnist and head of Martial and Company, a public relations firm listing Trujillo among its clients, was indicted under the Logan Act in 1963 for failing to register as a foreign agent. Pleading nolo contendere, Cassini was given six months' probation and fined $10,000.[27]

Others tainted with ties to the Dominican Republic included Franklin D. Roosevelt, Jr., and Charles Patrick Clark, who split a $60,000 fee as special counsel for the Dominican Republic in the first year of a two-year contract. When protests of his Trujillo connection threatened Roosevelt's political aspirations, the contract was canceled. Former FBI agent and Washington attorney for the CIA John J. Frank was indicted for accepting pay from Trujillo and not registering as a foreign agent.[28] After a jury trial, he was convicted in 1957 and given two years in prison.[29] Trujillo had hired Frank to wire the entire presidential palace so the dictator could record every conversation in every room.[30]

Larry Fernsworth, Pearson's investigator, began compiling an extensive file on Pawley, checking such minute sources as Commerce Department records of trade in the Dominican Republic, World Trade Information Service bulletins, the Dominican telephone directory (Pawley wasn't listed), and the Bureau of Foreign Commerce. None, however, mentioned Pawley. "All around a complete cover-up job," Fernsworth concluded. "Push the question of his being a foreign agent and not registering, and his violation of the Logan Act," he advised Pearson. "Insist on his being prosecuted, and if not why not. Your column could put the fellow in jail, where he belongs."[31] Pearson didn't follow up, and Pawley was never officially investigated for his close ties with Trujillo.

By 1960, Trujillo had received too much attention, which spotlighted his brutal manner in maintaining control. Pawley, as well as State Department and Eisenhower administration officials, felt it was time for Trujillo to transform the Dominican Republic from a dictatorship to a true democracy. "If the transition could be engineered from on top, involving a gradual and orderly introduction of democratic processes, I felt sure it would benefit the Dominican people," Pawley later wrote.[32] To add credence to his efforts, Pawley conferred with his good friend Senator George Smathers of Florida, who agreed to help. Considering the Caribbean part of his constituency, Chairman of the Senate Subcommittee on Latin American Trade Smathers was embarking on a tour of ten Latin American countries, including the Dominican Republic.

"But I want you to go back there first and talk further with Trujillo," Smathers told Pawley, "to be absolutely certain that he is receptive to the idea of free elections. As a Senator, I can hardly afford to get involved in a possible misfire."[33]

Pawley visited Trujillo to discuss holding free elections and received assurances he would. To counteract the media attacks on Trujillo, Pawley suggested the Dominican dictator write a series of articles on innovations and benefits he had fostered in his country. Trujillo agreed, and Pawley saw that they were published in the *Miami Herald* in a four-part series.[34] Conferring again with Smathers, who by then was convinced that Trujillo would honor his promise of allowing free elections, Pawley arranged a meeting in Ciudad Trujillo.

The meeting was held on February 9, 1960, with Smathers, Pawley, the U.S. chargé d'affaires Henry Dearborn, President of the Dominican Republic Hector Trujillo (Trujillo's brother), Vice President Joaquín Antonio Balaguer Ricardo, and Ambassador to the United States de Moya. Smathers expressed his appreciation for Trujillo's battle against Communism, to which Trujillo said he "would appreciate a little help now and then" in the fight. Heaping platitudes upon the Caribbean dictator, Smathers gave him credit for accomplishments already achieved in the country, ending by saying he "would like to see him rise to even greater eminence." Telling the generalissimo that "all men had to die sometime," Smathers expressed his fear that enemies of both countries would rush in to fill the political void, as had happened in Cuba.

"I do not believe my people are so stupid as to accept such government," Trujillo told Smathers. He added his government already had a president and vice president, and he wasn't even in the line of succession. Dearborn listened without comment but later wrote that Trujillo's remark "showed either complete self-hypnosis or unadulterated cynicism," considering that Trujillo had been running the country for thirty years.

Focusing on the subject at hand, Smathers urged Trujillo to hold free municipal elections as a step toward establishing a true democratic government. Without debating the issue, Trujillo agreed that once constitutional reforms were implemented to allow a two-party system, elections would be held within a year. Dearborn must have cringed because he later wrote the embassy "does not in least agree" when Pawley interjected that the "outside world did not understand government by parties was not possible here under circumstances because Dominicans desired one party." Trujillo added he had welcomed the formation of opposition parties, but the invitation hadn't been accepted. There was good reason. "Fear of economic and physical reprisals alone prevent formation of opposition parties," Dearborn observed.

Nevertheless, Smathers felt he had received the generalissimo's promise of holding free elections and asked if he might repeat the statement to the press. Trujillo assented. Then Pawley raised the next issue—the recent wave of arrests in the Dominican Republic and the attention they were receiving in the world press.[35]

In the previous month, 850 to 1,500 people had been arrested for conspiracy to overthrow the Trujillo regime. In a series of trials that were still being held as Smathers met with Trujillo, more than 100 had been sentenced to thirty-year terms of hard labor.[36] Pawley suggested that those arrested were "misguided youths," and the United States wouldn't understand them being treated as hardened criminals. Pawley remarked that the Dominican judicial system was "excellent," much like the American system, except there was no trial by jury. Smathers proposed that Florida attorney general Richard Irvin be permitted to observe the trials to convince the world that justice was being done. Trujillo welcomed the suggestion, but Pawley opposed it on the grounds that no other government would allow it. When Smathers reiterated his proposal as a way to convince the outside press that the defendants were being treated justly, Pawley backed off.[37] When informed of the invitation, Irvin said he was flattered that Smathers would consider him a qualified observer, but he declined because he felt it was more a State Department matter.[38]

Immediately after the meeting, Trujillo led Smathers to the chapel on the palace grounds to have their photograph taken. They showed the dictator being made godfather to dozens of babies; it was a common practice for Trujillo, whose vanity showed no bounds. His image and name were plastered throughout the country. A thirty-dollar plaque—issued on an "or-else" basis—adorned the front doors of practically every home in the country, and Trujillo reaped additional revenue.[39]

If the orchestrated photo-op session with Smathers was meant to demonstrate a "happy triumvirate" of Trujillo, the United States, and the Catholic Church, the congeniality was short lived. After Smathers left the Dominican Republic, Trujillo publicly accused Roman Catholic bishops of "insincerity" in their protests of the ongoing arrests and trials.[40]

"Vanity is the dictator's point," Smathers told reporters after leaving the Dominican Republic. "I believe I touched him where he can feel it."[41] He was convinced Trujillo would make the effort for an orderly transition to democracy, pointing out that the Caribbean dictator was the best defense against Communism in the small Latin American country.[42]

As for his part in Trujillo's promise, Pawley wouldn't take credit. "I talked to both the general and the senator about the idea of holding democratic elections. . . . But I did not have to convince either of them." Pressed about his connections with Trujillo's country, Pawley denied having any financial concerns. "I do not now have a nickel invested in the Dominican Republic. . . . I have sold my Dominican interests recently, within weeks."[43] Although he had sold his Dominican interests, he failed to mention he "retained the right to repurchase at least 50% of the interests disposed," and it was believed his interests had only been conveyed to his brother Ed.[44]

Pawley also had a holding company, Compañía Industrios Dominicanas (CID), which he often used as a conduit for business opportunities. The Dominican Republic national airline Compañía Dominicana de Aviación (CDA), also known as Dominicana, was constantly losing money. In January 1958, Pawley recommended closing down the operation, but Trujillo balked at the idea and asked Pawley to submit a plan to continue it under a subsidy. Pawley's plan was to establish a joint operation between CDA and Riddle Airlines; however, Riddle was in worse financial shape than CDA.

Arthur Vining Davis, who had made his fortune with the Aluminum Company of America (ALCOA), was acquiring land and businesses in the Miami area at the time. Riddle caught his attention, and beginning in April 1955, he purchased close to $7 million of its stock. Comer J. Kimball was a financial adviser to Davis and chairman of the board of the First National Bank of Miami. Both Pawley and Davis were directors on the board. During a meeting with Kimball and Davis in early 1958, Pawley was asked to take over the operation of Riddle Airlines. Pawley declined, but offered to set up an administrative group to reorganize Riddle and CDA to develop a joint operation.

Through CID, Pawley negotiated a $1.5 million loan for Riddle with the Bank of Nova Scotia, using real estate owned by Riddle and Davis's signature as collateral. Riddle paid CID $60,000 for brokering the loan, and Davis gave Pawley a $300,000 personal loan, which he invested in CID. Two months later, Pawley paid Davis $100,000 back on the loan. There is no record of Pawley repaying the balance of the loan to Davis. In March 1960, Pawley dissolved CID and received a parcel of land in the Dominican Republic valued at $123,000 as a rebate.[45]

Returning to the United States, Smathers learned that Trujillo's promise of holding free elections had received extensive press coverage in the United States but not a single word had been mentioned within the Dominican Republic. Feeling Trujillo may have used him, Smathers said he would be "quite disappointed if he doesn't carry through."[46] The Eisenhower administration, however, was not about to wait and see if Trujillo would live up to his promise. It had received word that

Trujillo's family was taking large sums of money out of the country, so it looked as though the dictatorship wouldn't last more than a few weeks.

Edwin N. Clark, friend to both Eisenhower and Trujillo, suggested he act as a go-between to induce Trujillo to establish a constitutional government, retire from power, and leave his accumulated assets to a foundation administered by independent trustees. Eisenhower approved the mission, but Clark was not to act under the authority of the president or even say he "has even seen the President lately." The other matter being considered was whether to offer Trujillo and his family asylum in the United States. Secretary of State Christian Herter advised Eisenhower against it.[47] Clark's mission failed, and the Dominican problem continued to distress Washington.

21

The End of Trujillo

Pawley felt Trujillo could be convinced to keep his pledge for free elections, but he needed the cooperation of State Department and White House officials. In March 1960, Senator Smathers and Pawley met with Assistant Secretary of State Roy Rubottom to discuss their plan. The following week, Smathers sent a letter to Trujillo requesting approval to bring a group of distinguished political scientists to the Dominican Republic to evaluate the situation and offer recommendations for an orderly transition to democracy.[1]

Receiving a favorable response from Trujillo, Pawley wrote to Vice President Nixon to seek his support. Reminding Nixon of the U.S. government's failure in Cuba, Pawley hoped to prevent Communists from gaining a second Caribbean foothold by seeking a "peaceful transition" in the Dominican Republic. "Your help in the matter would be of tremendous value," Pawley wrote, "as I am convinced that some of the junior members of the Department of State are anxious for the overthrow of Trujillo without regard to the consequences."[2]

The Smathers-Pawley plan never got off the ground. Otto Vega, Trujillo's personal interpreter, told Pawley that Lear B. Reed, a low-level U.S. diplomatic service officer stationed in Ciudad Trujillo, spoke unofficially with Trujillo. Reed said he wanted to "warn Trujillo against cooperating with Smathers and Pawley in guiding his country toward democracy." Reed sought another appointment with Trujillo on June 6, 1960, but he only met with Vega, who wrote a memo about the conversation. Reed told Vega that two or three official representatives of the United States would soon be calling on Trujillo with the "object of asking him to give up the reins of power." According to Vega's notes, Reed added that upon conclusion of the talks, the United States would make "a show of force" against Trujillo and send warships off the Dominican Republic coast.

Vega delivered the message to Trujillo, who told his interpreter to report to Reed that he had recently received a visit from two emissaries of Khrushchev's. When they asked him to "give up the reins of power and to transfer these either to Fidel Castro or to [Venezuelan president] Rómulo Betancourt," Trujillo had replied that "he would be willing to hand over power to Castro." Trujillo's threat was likely an attempt to frighten the U.S. State Department, but the end results were the political scientists canceled their visit and Trujillo strengthened his resolve to remain in power. Reed later claimed he had neither "warned Trujillo of U.S. pressure nor had tried to intimidate him."[3]

On May 13, 1960, Pawley and Smathers presented their views directly to Eisenhower. Pawley charged that the U.S. government "is trying to bring about a breaking of relations of Peru, Colombia, and Venezuela with Trujillo." They told Eisenhower about their plan to take the political scientists to the Dominican Republic, adding that Trujillo must be "left alone for a while" in order to fulfill his promise to hold free elections. Eisenhower agreed and said the State Department "should definitely not engage in trying to stir up other Governments against Trujillo."[4]

Three days later, Pawley and Smathers met with Acting Secretary of State Douglas Dillon to discuss the State Department's role in Dominican affairs. Dillon wanted to discuss discrepancies between Pawley and Smathers's views and information he had received from other sources. As for Trujillo holding elections, Dillon said the dictator recently had stated that "he planned to remain in control of the situation until the year 2000." As for any State Department attempt to break relations between Trujillo and other Latin American leaders, Dillon flatly denied it. He pointed out that both Colombia and Venezuela broke off relations with the Dominican Republic when it became apparent that Trujillo had aided in sending revolutionary groups through Colombia and into Venezuela because "he fostered the invasion of Venezuela." Peru's reasons for breaking off relations were "less clear," according to Dillon. Pawley admitted the Dominican Republic's situation was intensifying and that "Trujillo sees the handwriting on the wall," but he still felt Trujillo was "entitled to the opportunity" of holding the elections "as it should be done."[5]

The Eisenhower administration also saw the "handwriting on the wall," but its reading differed from Trujillo's. By June 1960, Eisenhower was agreeing with the State Department that some form of provisional government should replace Trujillo's dictatorship. When this goal was accomplished, "we should recognize it quickly," Eisenhower said. "We could then move in with troops on their request if need should arise."[6] The diplomatic situation was rapidly deteriorating.

Prior to a scheduled meeting of the Organization of American States, the Peace Committee of the OAS released a report placing blame directly on the Dominican Republic for the attempted assassination of Betancourt. The report specifically accused the Trujillo regime of providing arms, the electronic device, and explosives used in the attempt.[7] As the ministers gathered for the conference in Costa Rica, discussions centered on what sanctions the OAS should levy on the Dominican Republic.

Venezuela, not surprisingly, demanded strict diplomatic and economic sanctions applied against Trujillo's regime, but U.S. secretary of state Christian Herter opted for a milder approach. He suggested an observation committee be sent to ensure free elections in the Dominican Republic, with sanctions applied if elections were not held.[8] After heated debate, the U.S. proposal was dismissed in favor of more stringent sanctions.

On August 20, 1960, the OAS agreed to "energetically condemn" the Dominican Republic by breaking off all diplomatic relations. It also embargoed arms shipments from any OAS member nation to Trujillo.[9] Just before the vote was taken, the Dominican delegates walked out of the conference in protest.[10] The United States abided by the OAS resolution to break off diplomatic relations but left a skeleton staff to man the embassy in Ciudad Trujillo.[11] Pawley noted that among those remaining staffers were intelligence personnel. Their presence may have led Trujillo to suspect that "an assassination plot was being hatched, and that we were implicated."[12]

Thomas Mann, assistant secretary of state for Inter-American affairs, was concerned that OAS sanctions were not enough to force Trujillo to abdicate. Corresponding with Henry Dearborn, U.S. consul general in the Dominican Republic, Mann suggested an intermediary be sent to induce Trujillo to leave. Vice President of Pan Am Wilbur Morrison was suggested, as well as the papal nuncio, but Mann was open to any other choices Dearborn might have.[13]

Dearborn, in the thick of the situation in Ciudad Trujillo, agreed that free elections would end up being a sham. He felt that as long as Trujillo remained, he would continue to dominate "whether he is President or dogcatcher." The pragmatic solution was to convince Trujillo to leave, but who should be assigned the task? "I do not believe he can be persuaded to leave under present circumstances by any U.S. citizen," Dearborn replied to Mann. Furthermore, Dearborn felt that using any intermediary to encourage him to leave would backfire because Trujillo most likely would complain to the United Nations that he was being coerced.

However, if the State Department felt an attempt should be made, Dearborn was emphatic on whom the intermediary should *not* be: "I do not think Bill Pawley should be considered." Dearborn also felt "the Papal Nuncio is out of the question" because of the Vatican's strained relations with Trujillo. Wilbur Morrison was also a bad choice because if Trujillo publicized the approach, Pan Am's reputation in Latin America might suffer. The only feasible option, Dearborn suggested, was for the United States to make the attempt "in concert with other countries." The OAS itself—or the United States with Argentina or Brazil or Chile or Mexico or even Canada—would have the best chance to convince Trujillo "the jig is up."

From a practical point of view, Dearborn had another thought that he felt he "should probably not even make." If Trujillo were to leave the Dominican Republic, he would still have millions and probably would devote his life to preventing any form of stable government to exist while he was in exile. Dearborn added that if he were a Dominican, "I would favor destroying Trujillo as being the first necessary step in the salvation of my country and would regard this, in fact, as my Christian duty. If you recall Dracula, you will remember it was necessary to drive a stake through his heart to prevent a continuation of his crimes."[14] Realpolitik measures were being suggested. It seemed a matter of time before Trujillo would be considered expendable, but until then, the diplomatic approach was still being sought.

Called upon in 1959 to ask Batista to step down, Pawley was again summoned to the White House to discuss Trujillo. In early November 1960, Pawley sat in the Oval Office as the president asked for his assistance. "I know of no one who might come closer to success," Eisenhower told him. "See if you can persuade Trujillo to leave the country, accompanied by his entire family, and move to the United States." The president's somber tone told Pawley that the offer was sincere, but he had reservations regarding the success of the mission.

"Mr. President," Pawley replied, "substantially the same proposal was put to Trujillo during the visit which I arranged for Senator Smathers. The Generalissimo was most receptive. I'm willing to have another try, but it's only prudent to warn you that this time it may not be as easy. He probably doesn't know any more *whom* to trust."

"Tell him that we're living in completely different times and that the movement toward democratic forms of government cannot be resisted," Eisenhower said. "It is possible, in fact, that in a completely fair and supervised democratic test, he might be overwhelmingly returned to office."

Pawley may have felt that after thirty years of Trujillo's iron rule, Dominicans would not vote for the dictator if they had a free choice. But Eisenhower was the president and his friend, so Pawley said he would try.

"I want you to impress upon him, also," Eisenhower added, "that I personally hold no ill feelings toward him, but that I am absolutely convinced that there is no alternative to the suggestions I am making. I am asking you to go to Trujillo because I feel sincerely that he will accept this message through you, whereas it could not possibly be effectively conveyed through official channels."[15]

Unlike the Batista mission, when State Department officials prevented Pawley from saying he was acting as Eisenhower's emissary, this time he could speak freely. But other factors still could hamper Pawley's objective. Eisenhower was now a lame-duck president, and Trujillo might not welcome the suggestion of stepping down. Instead, he might prefer to wait until Kennedy assumed office and hope a change in administration might bring about a change in the U.S. policy. Although Pawley was a staunch Republican, he had an ally in Democratic senator Smathers, who urged the president-elect "to take the position that he should not go along with the Department of State and have the dictator step down."[16]

Another factor giving Pawley pause came from former Dominican ambassador to the United States Manuel de Moya, who met with Pawley in Miami. "The situation has really changed, Bill," he said. "In my opinion, you'd be running a very serious personal risk." Moya offered no explanation for his ominous warning, but since Pawley knew that the former ambassador was a close friend of Trujillo's, the message remained in the back of his mind when he called Trujillo and asked for an appointment.

Arriving at the airport in Ciudad Trujillo the evening of November 16, 1960, Pawley drove to his suite at the Hotel Embajador, showered, and waited for Trujillo to summon him. As he was about to telephone his brother Ed, who lived in the city, Pawley was surprised when Trujillo drove up to the front entrance in a small car alone. As Pawley later remarked, "This was utterly out of character and, in view of the plots against his life, a glaring breach of security." They shook hands, and Trujillo asked if they could go up to Pawley's suite on the sixth floor. Once they were settled, Pawley offered his guest a brandy, but Trujillo shook his head.

"What do you want to discuss?" Trujillo asked abruptly.

As delicately and diplomatically as he could, Pawley outlined the proposal he had discussed with Eisenhower. "He could come to the United States and live," Pawley recalled telling the dictator, "and have his boat and have his beautiful cattle and horses that he so much loved, and he could travel to Europe and live a peaceful life and let the Dominican Republic, where he had done quite a wonderful job, come into a democratic process."[17]

For an hour, Pawley tried convincing Trujillo, who listened with an "icy detachment." Pawley was surprised when Trujillo "became tremendously infuriated—the only time he got really mad with me." Trujillo's mood suddenly changed to a more somber one as tears welled up in his eyes. He wiped them with his handkerchief and pointed his finger at Pawley as he spoke in a voice of "controlled fury": "You can come in here with the Marines, and you can come in here with the Army, and you can come in here with the Navy or even the atomic bomb, but I'll never go out of here unless I go out on a stretcher."

"Generalissimo, the President of the United States is interested in only one thing. He wants to see this country, which you've developed so beautifully, maintain a democratic form of government, and it can't be done as long as you remain the Generalissimo. Now, if you want your name on the ballot, there will be no reason not to put it there. That will demonstrate to the world that the people really like you, but you would have to agree not to serve."

Trujillo remained entrenched in his position and changed the conversation to discuss other topics, including repurchasing Pawley's Falconbridge shares. The meeting lasted for an hour and a half, leaving Pawley with the same feeling he had experienced after talking to Batista—that is, that he had failed in his mission. As they left Pawley's suite, walking down the corridor to the elevator, three chambermaids emerged from a room and immediately recognized the distinguished visitor. "Generalissimo Trujillo!" they exclaimed.

"Do you see, Pawley?" he said. "Everyone in this country loves me."

Reaching the hotel lobby, Trujillo saw one of his ministers and told him to take Pawley up to the eighth floor, where the minister of finance was holding a reception for a group of British businessmen. Meeting with the minister, Pawley was invited to visit him the following morning at his office.

Overnight his standing with the Dominican government had changed, and Pawley knew it. "I sensed the breach that must have been caused by my unwelcome message from Ike and decided to leave the next day." It was the right decision because within two days, the Trujillo-controlled Dominican press and radio attacked Pawley in strongly worded comments that made him virtually unwelcome in the country. Pawley reported to Eisenhower on the failure of his mission and never saw Trujillo again.[18]

Pawley continued to be a staunch supporter of Trujillo's after Kennedy took office. No longer a regular White House guest, Pawley used Senator Smathers as a conduit to persuade the new administration to act in favor of the Caribbean dictator's regime. Kennedy was considering "legislation to knock the Dominican Republic out of the quota allocation," and Smathers was urging the president to reconsider but couldn't convince him. This was the sugar quota provided in the 1948 Sugar Act by which countries were limited by the amount of sugar they could export to the U.S. When Castro took over, Eisenhower reallocated the Cuban quota to other sugar-producing nations. The DR would benefit from this "windfall allocation" but Eisenhower, and later Kennedy, felt that Trujillo should not receive it. Kennedy was proposing the legislation, but Trujillo had powerful friends in Congress. It would have been difficult for JFK to get it passed. One problem the Florida senator had was his close connection to Pawley. He had been criticized in the Florida newspapers "for having Pawley among his friends since Pawley is a 'great Republican.'"[19] Pawley had been directing criticism against the Kennedy administration, especially toward Assistant Secretary of State Mann, who he felt was a personal friend of Venezuelan president Betancourt. "Tom is brilliant," Pawley told a reporter. "Couldn't be a nicer fellow." But Pawley felt he was "influenced by Betancourt's feelings."[20]

Unknown to Pawley, arrangements already had begun under Eisenhower for the CIA to assist in assassinating Trujillo. The concern was that with Trujillo gone, how was the United States going to prevent a Castro-type government from replacing him? "You have approved a plan designed specifically to avoid this," Douglas Dillon reminded Eisenhower. "The [State] Department, CIA, and the Department of Defense are maintaining the closest liaison in order that all thinking and planning to this end are coordinated."[21]

Despite the fact that several Dominican military leaders were involved in the assassination plot, Trujillo had imposed tight controls on weapons at military bases that made it impossible to obtain the necessary guns in the country without raising suspicion. The CIA's role was limited to smuggling in the weapons, which it accomplished by breaking down the gun parts and importing them in food cans shipped to a supermarket in Ciudad Trujillo.[22] The operation was to occur while Cuba was being invaded, but when the Bay of Pigs landing in April ended in a fiasco, the assassination attempt was called off. The weapons had already been distributed to the plotters, however, and they had no intention of waiting. Despite the pleadings of U.S. officials, six weeks later the Dominican conspirators authorized the operation.

On the evening of May 30, 1961, Trujillo sat in the backseat of his chauffeur-driven 1959 Chevrolet Bel Air. Unescorted, the car headed for La Fundación, Trujillo's prize cattle farm in San Cristóbal, where he was to meet with his twenty-year-old mistress, Mona Sanchez. The plotters knew Trujillo customarily visited his ninety-four-year-old mother before heading out to San Cristóbal. Senator Modesto Diaz, brother of one of the assassins, lived in the neighborhood and signaled the plotters when Trujillo left his mother's home.

Considering the numerous previous attempts and threats on his life, it may have been foolhardy that Trujillo was traveling without an armed escort. But the proud, defiant dictator felt he could handle any situation that he encountered. On the seat beside him were two carbines and a pistol, along with a brown leather briefcase with $110,000 in U.S. dollars and Dominican pesos. "If money couldn't solve a problem," Trujillo often said, "guns could."[23]

On a stretch of highway between Trujillo's farm and the capital, three cars intercepted Trujillo's car, and gunmen opened fire with automatic weapons. One bullet wounded the dictator under the left arm as his car came to a halt. Opening the rear door, Trujillo stepped out, pistol in hand to meet his assassins face-to-face. Almost immediately, one of the attackers shot Trujillo point-blank. A fusillade followed, resulting in his body being riddled with twenty-seven bullets. Although Trujillo was dead, the assassins beat his body, "smashing his left arm into a pulp." They dumped his body into the trunk of one of the cars, and the killers sped off into the night.[24]

Trujillo's death did not bring about a democratic government. Instead, his son, Ramfis, headed a Provisional Council comprising Trujillo supporters. Washington adopted a wait-and-see policy toward the new governing body. Kennedy was informed at a June 7 White House meeting that Pawley had talked to Trujillo's daughter and learned that Ramfis "wanted to move toward a more moderate form of government." Attorney General Robert Kennedy suggested that "it was worth our while to wait out the situation." The president seemed to go along with his brother's suggestion, adding that he wanted "a Democratic regime in the Dominican Republic. Failing that we would prefer a friendly dictatorship, and the last thing we wanted was a Castro type regime."

At the conclusion of the meeting the White House decided that all contacts with anyone associated with the new government would be informal, and that "we would have no contacts through Pawley—that if he carried out his plans to go to the Dominican Republic we would be glad to hear his reports but he was in no way to involve State, CIA, the White House, etc., i.e. not to indicate that we approved what he said or authorized his visit. Secretary Rusk was detailed to communicate this to Pawley."[25] As a Republican who had sharply criticized the president, especially after the Bay of Pigs, Pawley was to be kept useful as a source of information but not as a confidant.

Pawley returned to the Dominican Republic on June 11, 1961, accompanied by his brother Ed. During his three-day visit, he managed to see several high-level Dominican officials, hear their views on the current state of affairs, and report back to White House CIA chief J. C. King and Secretary of State Dean Rusk. Pawley's immediate impression was that Ramfis Trujillo "had acted with statesmanship, courage and ability," by backing President Balaguer and declaring that "he had no political ambitions of any kind."[26]

At his brother's home close to the Country Club, Pawley met with Flor Trujillo, daughter of the slain dictator. Not always in her father's good graces, Flor had married seven times, including a trip to the altar with international playboy Porfirio Rubirosa.[27] "All the Trujillos have to go," she told Pawley. She considered her relatives, legitimate and illegitimate, "extremely mediocre and unattractive," and they would "contribute nothing to the stabilization of the country." When asked about her brother, Flor said she was proud of Ramfis: "He had left the Dominican Republic as a spoiled boy and had returned . . . as a man capable of assuming some responsibility." She told Pawley that at a family meeting, including the dictator's illegitimate children, Ramfis said they would all be recognized as legitimate heirs, and he wanted them to remain close. During the conversation, Flor said she had made arrangements for Pawley to visit her brother, Ramfis, the following morning at the airbase.

Although he wanted to speak to Ramfis in private, when Pawley and Ed arrived at the air base, two Trujillo relatives were present in the room when they talked. Pawley praised the young man, along with President Balaguer, for his efforts to stabilize the situation and rid the Dominican Republic of political and economic abuses. They had deactivated the dreaded secret police organization (SIM), converted the torture chambers where prisoners had been kept into a school, and canceled all the monopolies—cacao, plantains, coffee, meat, and milk, for a combined annual income of $18 million—that Trujillo and his friends previously held.

Ramfis assured Pawley that all exiles would be allowed to return and freedom of the press and speech would be restored. "It is obvious that there will be much criticism," he told Pawley, "but it will be better that way." When told that political parties would be allowed to organize as quickly as possible in order to be listed in upcoming elections, Pawley commented that maybe it was too soon since the elections were only eleven months away. "The President [Balaguer] insisted that they be held per schedule," Ramfis said, "that any change in that would be very disappointing to the people in general."[28]

Following their half-hour interview, Pawley and his brother drove to Ed's office in Ciudad Trujillo to meet with Dr. Temistocles Messina. Formerly in charge of UN affairs for the Dominican Republic, and Pawley's company lawyer for five years, Messina had been a prominent Trujillo oppositionist for years. A few days after Pawley tried convincing Trujillo to step down, Messina had been relieved of his government post, as had his son, Milton, who had been president of the Banco de Reservas. During their meeting, Messina told Pawley he felt the present arrangement, with Balaguer as president, Ramfis Trujillo as head of the armed forces, and Hector Trujillo (Ramfis's uncle) lending his support, "is the reason that the stability of the country has been maintained and a bloodbath did not occur." Other Trujillo family members might try some "power play," Messina speculated, but he was convinced that Ramfis was fully supporting Balaguer and would arrest any family member who interfered.

Pawley sent a telegram to Balaguer requesting an interview and received a reply by phone that he could come to the palace at five o'clock that afternoon. "I had prepared myself for a conversation which might have been taped," he recalled. To Pawley's surprise, when Balaguer came out to the waiting room, he sat next to him, and the entire conversation was carried out almost in a whisper. "I wondered if he, himself, thought that maybe the room was tapped and therefore wanted this private discussion to be secure."

Balaguer told Pawley that he knew Pawley was a friend to the Dominican Republic and was trustworthy. "He desperately needed someone to whom he could confide and someone whom he could seek advice from insofar as it dealt with U.S. matters." Pawley advised the president he was in the country as a private citizen with no official status, but he would gladly convey any message to friends in the United States. Balaguer said it was a miracle that Trujillo could be assassinated without a revolutionary upheaval. He was pleased that Ramfis and Hector Trujillo had been so helpful in maintaining order and stability, but he felt the Trujillos had to go. The OAS would be pleased with recent developments, but Balaguer was realistic and knew that peace could be maintained only if the United States offered its support. He hoped Kennedy would send a representative of ambassadorial rank, "a man of sufficient stature that it would be a counterbalance to the influence of the Trujillo family and their supporters." Above all, Balaguer told Pawley, it would be necessary for the United States to prevent a bloodbath "which might result in a Castro-type communist take-over."

Turning to financial matters, Pawley asked if the Dominican government had sufficient funds to carry on or if it would need U.S. assistance. Balaguer said that "by economizing and utilizing every dollar of government income to meet their immediate need, they could get by."

"You understand," Balaguer added, "I cannot continue to maintain a military establishment of 30,000 people. This I am going to have to reduce and, again, when this is started, I need the support of the type of man that I hope will be representing your country."

Although Pawley might have felt he would be the right man for the job, he had no delusions as to his standing with Kennedy. His name would never appear on a list of those candidates considered suitable for the position. Pawley mentioned that John Hill had recently arrived in the Dominican Republic to replace Henry Dearborn. Pawley expressed his opinion that Hill was "an extremely capable man," but Balaguer wanted "an older man of higher government position."

Their meeting was cut short by a scheduled press conference Balaguer was to hold, but before leaving, he told Pawley he would appreciate if he could make himself available for further talks. Pawley agreed and asked if he could pass on the details of their conversation to U.S. government officials. Balaguer had no objections and added that when Pawley wanted to see him in the future, Pawley should contact his brother Ed, who in turn would communicate with Balaguer by telephone or messenger.

Returning to his hotel, Pawley met with an old friend, Dr. Juan Arce Medina, Trujillo's private lawyer and the Dominican Government's director of mining. Again, Pawley heard concerns for the need to "maintain the status quo" until normal conditions returned. Pawley also conducted a man-in-the-street survey, talking with everyone from clerks and secretaries in his brother's office to the driver who had worked for the Pawleys for the past five years. "Without exception," he wrote, "they were all surprised that order had been maintained and they all felt that this condition should not be disturbed now."

During a two-hour interview at the U.S. Embassy in Ciudad Trujillo with Chargé d'Affaires *ad interim* John Calvin Hill, Pawley repeated his conversations with the Trujillo family and President Balaguer. Returning to Miami, Pawley sent off an eight-page memorandum to Secretary of State Dean Rusk and a copy to Allen Dulles at the CIA. He also called CIA White House chief J. C. King and reported everything he had learned during his three-day visit in the Dominican Republic.[29]

Ramfis didn't last long. In November 1961, he and his entire family fled to exile in France. Former president Joaquín Balaguer assumed control until February 1963. Following democratic elections, Juan Bosch took office. In September that year he was overthrown and replaced by military rule. When a civil war broke out in April 1965, U.S. president Lyndon Johnson sent in troops to prevent any possibility of a Communist takeover. The troops remained until 1966, when Joaquín Balaguer once again became president, this time democratically elected.

With the death of Trujillo, and having sold his Dominican holdings, Pawley turned his attention to his U.S. business investments. Always an astute political observer, Pawley also maintained a close watch on developments within the Republican Party during the next decade.

PART VI
Twilight in Miami

22

Talisman Sugar

The southern Florida sugar industry was in its infancy in 1960, but when the United States cut off imports from Cuba, investors began looking for land to grow cane and they built processing mills. Cuban businessmen were already building sugar mills in the Belle Glade section of Palm Beach County, the center of cane plantations. Sugar mills saved shipping costs, and their presence added impetus to the housing industry because of the jobs they created. The residue left from refining was used to produce blackstrap cattle feed, a benefit to area cattle raisers.[1]

By 1963, the Florida sugar industry was booming, attracting major producers who wanted a stake in the growing area. Because of worldwide shortages, sugar quotas in the United States were being eased as the price of sugar rose. North American Sugar Industries, once owner of Cuban sugar acreage, now turned to Belle Glade for construction of a liquid sugar refinery. Used in soft drinks, liquid sugar is also purchased by ice cream manufacturers, bakeries, fruit preserve and jelly makers, and fruit drink producers.[2] Already having a working knowledge of the sugar industry during the Batista regime in Cuba, William Pawley looked for an opportunity to invest in his own backyard.

Talisman Sugar Company in Belle Glade owned an 18,000-acre sugarcane plantation and processing mill, but unlike other Florida sugar producers, it had fallen on hard times. When freezing weather in December 1962 nearly destroyed its crops, Talisman went into receivership. Relying on $850,000 in loans, the company hoped to recover after the next year's harvest; instead, it lapsed into bankruptcy.[3] After negotiations with the bankruptcy court and Talisman's creditors, Pawley purchased the firm in 1964. To satisfy the company's $8 million debt, Pawley planned to pump in $4 million of his own money and acquire an additional $7 million with a long-term mortgage.[4] He also bought an additional 7,000 acres of land to plant more sugarcane. Unfortunately, the government froze sugarcane acreage usage a month later, and the land sat idle. "If it wasn't for my business background," Pawley said, "I would have already lost my shirt."[5]

One of the first changes Pawley made at Talisman was an attempt to employ field hands using the local labor market. Other plantation owners told him he would have to use offshore workers, but Pawley was convinced that an American labor force, partly made up of Cuban immigrants, would suffice. Pawley wrote, "I therefore chartered 60-passenger air-conditioned buses and arranged to have them park early in the morning at the Orange Bowl parking lot (where parking is available free during the day) and we advertised extensively for labor for the harvesting of our sugarcane crop. Not knowing how many would show up in one day, I provided enough transportation for 230 or 240 men."[6]

The advertised offer was $11.50 minimum per day wage and possibly reaching $15, but on the first morning only nine people showed up. After explaining the work required, only one accepted. "We sent a 60-passenger bus out to the mill with the one passenger," Pawley recalled. "This man worked one day and did not return."

Florida and Louisiana are major sugarcane producers, but their harvesting requires different methods. Louisiana cane stalks grow straight, allowing them to be cut by machine; field workers are employed to gather cut stalks and place them on a conveyance. Florida cane bends, forming clusters that are difficult to harvest. Workers must lie on their sides and cut each stalk with a machete while others gather the cuttings and load them on trucks. Accustomed to labor-intensive harvesting, workers from Jamaica, Trinidad, and Barbados readily accepted work in Florida sugarcane fields, but American laborers were not up to the task.

Pawley continued advertising for workers and kept buses on hand, but after several days when no one appeared, he gave up. Turning to the Jamaican labor market, he discovered that since his company was the last to file an application for temporary foreign labor, the available manpower was severely limited.[7] He finally secured the needed Jamaican labor in time to harvest the crop, but from then on he avoided employing American workers.

Sugar marketing quotas established by the Sugar Act of 1948 were another concern for Pawley's operations. The legislation was a delicate balancing of factors to provide consumers with reasonably priced sugar, to protect the domestic sugar industry, and to promote export trade of the product. Quotas were assigned for foreign sugar-producing areas and subdivided into major domestic sugar-producing areas. From 1963 to 1968, domestic output of sugar consistently fell below authorized quotas, allowing the Department of Agriculture to allocate the deficit to foreign producers as provided by the Sugar Act. But domestic deficits were a result of lower output from Puerto Rico and the Virgin Islands, not Florida and Louisiana.[8]

Pawley solicited help from Senator Barry Goldwater to enact legislation "that deficits in the domestic sugar quota be reallocated to other U.S. areas instead of to foreign countries." The General Accounting Office supported Pawley's suggestion, and Goldwater promised his support when legislation was proposed.[9] Shifting quotas and allowance of usable acreage would continue to be Pawley's most difficult problems in the sugar business.

In a telephone message to Nixon, Pawley expressed a thought on another use of the sugar camp. "It struck me that sometime in the immediate future I would like to turn this camp into a Negro Boys Club summer camp." He envisioned digging out a rock pit to put in a swimming area, complete with a beach. "I could put two or three canoes on it that would be fun." Along with academic studies of "reading, writing and arithmetic," he proposed offering instruction in the use of agricultural equipment. He wanted Nixon's opinion on "whether these boys should be made to do anything—there are things like weeding . . . the older ones might be able to be employed three hours a day toward contributing to their meals."[10] Nixon's response is unknown.

In 1968, Pawley attempted to sell Talisman Sugar to Holly Sugar Corporation, a major beet sugar manufacturer in the western United States. But Pawley wasn't sole owner; Lukens Steel Company held 20 percent. During negotiations, Pawley entertained Holly officers aboard his yacht in Miami, but they said no agreement had been reached. Pawley claimed otherwise. Not only was there a contract, Pawley said, but he also had been acting as an agent for Holly while negotiating with Lukens for their shares.

One lawsuit after another began flooding the courts. Lukens sued Pawley and Holly for reneging on an agreement to purchase its 20 percent for $1.2 million. Pawley filed against Holly, maintaining a contract existed and that Holly was backing out of the deal for both his shares and those of Lukens. The lawsuits became personal as individuals began suing each other. Holly sued Charles L. Huston, president of Lukens, and six other company officers; Pawley sued Holly officials and its president John B. Bunker, son of Ambassador to South Vietnam Ellsworth Bunker. Although Pawley claimed his share of the sale amounted to $7.2 million, and Lukens was looking for $1.2 million, the lawsuits totaled more than $40 million.

Charges of fraud, bad-faith dealing, and contract breaches peppered the court documents. Holly claimed Pawley shortened Talisman's fiscal year by omitting non-harvest months and showing a $1.2 million profit instead of a $26,000 loss. Pawley countered that Holly, who had the opportunity to inspect company records, spending $1 million in the process. Holly accused Lukens of "trying to sell a dead horse," saying that Pawley "made at least 60 efforts to unload this Talisman stock and he couldn't find a buyer." Holly also charged that Lukens and Pawley violated Securities and Exchange Commission rules by not disclosing full financial information in stock transactions.

During ten days of pretrial motions in a Miami federal court, the combatants geared for a trial expected to last seven days, but on September 10, 1971, all parties settled their claims in court. The agreement called for Holly to buy Lukens's 20 percent share for $750,000. Lukens agreed to retire a $450,000 note held on a loan to Pawley's sugar mill that was already in default and owed $75,000 in interest. Talisman would issue new notes—one to Lukens for $275,000 and two for $250,000 total to pay Pawley's lawyers. Pawley agreed to buy the 20 percent Holly was buying from Lukens, but instead of cash, he gave Holly a $750,000 note secured by the stock shares and he retained voting rights on the shares. When the dust settled, Pawley owned the entire company without having to reach into his pocket for a dime.[11]

He owned the company, but labor problems soon hampered operations. On January 9, 1972, Nicolas Raymond, a truck driver at Talisman for four years, led a group of truck drivers and heavy equipment operators to seek union representation from the International Association of Machinist and Aerospace Workers. The union already represented some Talisman workers, but the contract between Talisman and the workers specifically excluded "agricultural employees, agricultural truck drivers who haul cane from loading stations to the mill and those who perform jobs incidental to the agricultural operations."[12] Citing contract provisions, Talisman refused to recognize the union as a bargaining agent and fired the drivers the following day.

Determined to be heard, Raymond set up a picket line at the entrance to the Talisman plantation, but the protest had little effect. The machinists' union quietly dropped their support, leaving Raymond and his group alone in their fight. Pawley claimed an unsolicited statement signed by 325 of his 500 workers pledged to support him. "I'm absolutely determined to do what the majority of the men working for my company want," Pawley said, "and they have said they don't want a union."[13] A week later, Florida Migrant Ministry members stopped to talk with the striking workers. "We want a union because our rights are not paid attention to," Raymond told them. "We just want a union—a legal organization that can represent us."[14]

The Florida Migrant Ministry put the strikers in contact with the United Farm Workers Organizing Committee (UFWOC). Victorious in uniting California grape workers, César Chávez had been focusing the might of the UFWOC on the Florida agricultural industry. On January 21, the black eagle on a red flag insignia of the Chávez union appeared for the first time in a Florida labor dispute. On U.S. Highway 27, just outside the Talisman mill, 75 to 100 workers and organizers joined the picket line.

Chávez sent Pawley a telegram seeking an immediate meeting to establish his union as the collective bargaining agent for the Talisman workers, including the cane cutters, who had not been involved in the strike. Chávez also appointed his cousin Manuel to spearhead the attack on Pawley's company.[15] Protesters waved signs at cane truck drivers and shouted "*Huelga* (strike)!" at anyone attempting to cross the picket line.

Belle Glade plantation workers consisted of two groups—a thousand Jamaican laborers who cut cane and a small number of truck drivers and field equipment operators who were hired from the domestic labor force. The Jamaican workers stayed on the plantation except for a trip into town every other Saturday on company-provided transportation. A description of the camp appears in a 1973 court case:

The camp consisted of housing for 1050 in the form of concrete block buildings. It had kitchen facilities, a mess hall, recreation facilities, a chapel, an infirmary, a laundry, and a store. Twice a week, the company brought in a minister to conduct religious services. In the store, it carried a general line of merchandise, including food and sundry items such as clothing. Traditionally municipal functions such as fire protection, sewage disposal, and garbage collection were handled by Talisman. There was a post office in the camp, but there was no public telephone of any kind.[16]

Moreover, the camp was eight miles from the nearest highway and twenty-five miles from the nearest town, virtually isolating it from the outside world.

During the second week of the strike, tragedy struck. Nan Freeman was an eighteen-year-old freshman at New College in Sarasota who had joined the picket line. Called Morning Glory by her friends, Nan had worked with learning-disabled children while attending high school in Wakefield, Massachusetts. A National Merit Scholar, she volunteered to work at a day care center for black children in Sarasota and spent time on a self-help housing project for farm workers. In late 1971, after working at a halfway house in North Carolina, Nan became one of the first students to join the striking Talisman workers.

Talisman hired replacement drivers for the double trailers loaded with 70,000 pounds of sugarcane. According to one report, Nan, along with Kacie Crisp, another student from New College, was assigned to work alongside José Romero, a union man who handed leaflets to drivers as they stopped at Talisman's front gates before heading onto the highway. At 3:15 a.m., the two coeds were standing thirty feet from the highway when a truck pulled up and stopped. Romero jumped on the running board to talk to the driver while Nan and Kacie stood to one side. Police assigned to keep order told strikers not to block the front gate, so when Romero noticed a second truck approaching, he stepped down and waved the driver on. "Suddenly they realized that the first truck was not going to clear the guard rail," union attorney Judy Peterson said. "Romeo threw one girl clear but as he turned to get Nan she was caught by the truck and thrown under the wheels."[17]

Palm Beach County Sheriff's deputies who were keeping an eye on the picketing workers rushed to her side. Covering her with a blanket, they called for an ambulance, which arrived twenty-five minutes later. Nan was rushed to a local hospital and pronounced dead at 4:19 a.m. Chávez said from UFW headquarters, "There are no words to thank her for what she has done. . . . We must work together to build a farm workers' union that is worthy of her love and her sacrifice."[18]

Two weeks after the fatal accident, Pawley finally made a statement. "This girl was not run over by a Talisman truck and we feel confident that no Talisman truck struck her, that she was a victim of Route 27," he said. "We believe she may have been hit on (Highway) 27 by an automobile, and not run over," he added. "We feel she may have been hit elsewhere and pulled there (to the gate of the sugar mill)."[19]

To support his claim, Pawley referred to a sheriff's report in which a striker identified the Talisman truck involved in the accident by its number. According to a report in the *Miami Herald*, the Florida Highway Patrol (FHP) would neither confirm nor deny Pawley's statements. Capt. J. W. Hagans, supervisor of the FHP in Palm Beach County, said the investigation was incomplete because the FHP was unable to locate a missing witness to the accident, another girl from Sarasota.[20] The sheriff found the truck identified hadn't been out of the garage for a week. Another truck number given by a picketer was proven not to have been at the gate when the accident occurred. Another New College coed Pamela Albright, who said she was a witness to the accident, denied Pawley's version. "There definitely was a truck and it wasn't on the public highway either," she said. "It was after it turned off."[21]

Florida Highway Patrol took over the investigation, but it was hampered by the number of confusing statements. Two sheriff's deputies stationed at the Talisman front gate now said they hadn't seen Nan hit, although one said he called for the ambulance.[22] Pamela Albright was subpoenaed to give a sworn statement, but her testimony only added to the confusion. "After talking to [Miss Albright] it has been determined that she cannot identify the vehicle as being a cane truck," Florida Highway trooper D. L. Pursell said.[23] Nan Freeman became the first person killed during a United Farm Workers' strike, and no one has ever been charged for her death.

When the strike drew national attention, a picket line went up in front of Talisman's downtown Miami offices. Shirley Chisholm, a Brooklyn Democrat and presidential candidate, joined protesters carrying signs reading "Talisman Unfair to Farm Workers."[24] Presidential hopeful Senator George McGovern also joined the picket line for a photo opportunity.[25] Local groups added their support, including the United Puerto Ricans of Miami, who joined the picket line, and church ministers of several faiths criticized Talisman in their sermons.[26]

As the picketing continued, reports of company strong-arm tactics and retaliation by strikers began surfacing. Workers sympathetic to the strikers said armed Talisman employees threatened them on several occasions, but Pawley denied the charges. "No one employed by Talisman Sugar Corporation is permitted to have or carry arms except the labor camp manager, who is a deputy sheriff," Pawley said.[27]

A truck that Talisman rented to haul sugarcane was found damaged in a parking lot. The windshield was smashed, and gas had been poured on one tire and set afire.[28]

On February 17, Pawley's brother Edward became involved in a confrontation at Talisman headquarters in Miami. Manuel Chávez, who was giving a press conference in front of the building, spotted Edward on the street. "I'm Manuel Chávez of the United—," Chávez said before Pawley cut him off. "I'm not with you," Edward said, pulling away, knocking over a television camera, and stepping over it as it crashed to the pavement. Wearing a yachting cap, Edward turned and ended up face-to-face with a photographer, who backed away for a better shot. As Edward continued toward the building's entrance, the photographer refused to retreat, and Edward ended up nose to lens with the camera. "You see?" Chávez shouted. "You see how violent the Pawleys are?" Miami police investigated and determined the television camera incident was an accident.[29]

Meanwhile, another confrontation was brewing outside the Talisman plantation entrance. UFWOC attorney Judith Peterson and two ministers appeared at the front gate and asked permission to talk with the Jamaican workers. When they were asked to leave, they got in their car and drove through the gate, heading toward the mill. The gate guard radioed ahead to guards at an inner gate, telling them not to let the car pass. When a deputy sheriff summoned by the gate guard arrived, he told Peterson and the others, "Get in your car and get out." He added, "If you come back I'll arrest you for trespassing." Undaunted, they chose to submit to arrest in protest.[30]

When the case came to trial, the judge dismissed the trespassing charges on the grounds that "to prevent their entry might lead to a condition where employees are subjected to a form of involuntary servitude, wherein the masters decide who may communicate with the servants."[31]

Peterson filed a class action suit in federal court on February 7, 1972, seeking permission to enter the camp before March 1 when the Jamaican workers were scheduled to return home.[32]

Acting on a complaint filed by the UFW, the Florida State Division of Labor sent an investigator to determine if the Jamaican workers were doing work other than cutting cane. Talisman's contract with the British West Indies government specifically stated the Jamaicans were only to cut cane. When an investigator arrived at the gate, however, he wasn't allowed in.[33] "Talisman is holding these canecutters prisoners in the camp," Manuel Chávez charged, and asked Florida governor Reubin Askew to intervene.[34] "We want to see that these workers have the right to talk to anyone they want to," Chávez said, "just like any other human being."[35] Chávez was looking for ways to force Talisman's hand. He vowed to visit Washington to bring his complaint to Jamaican officials, "and if they don't do something about it we will consider picketing Jamaican airline offices and the tourist board." He said UFW officials were contacting House and Senate agricultural committee members to investigate the "Talisman situation."[36] The UFW began flexing its muscles, getting a tremendous boost from the American Federation of Labor–Congress of Industrial Organizations (AFL-CIO), which announced that the Chávez union would be recognized. "They will now be constituted as a national union affiliated with the AFL-CIO," President George Meany said.[37]

Agricultural workers were exempt from the National Labor Relations Act, so Chávez threatened a secondary boycott. He took aim at another company with exclusive rights to purchase all of Talisman's sugar output, namely, Borden. "Nobody likes to boycott," Chávez said, "but they leave us no alternative if they do not negotiate with us." UFW officials met with Borden officials, but according to UFW director of organization Jim Drake, they were told, "You can't come here and kick Elsie the Borden Cow around."[38] A Borden spokesman said, "We want to avoid antagonizing either side." Attempts were made to have Talisman negotiate with the union, but Pawley refused.

A source of contention was using the secret ballot to determine union representation. The UFW resisted it in California. "The reason we stay away from the secret ballot is that growers don't do it in good faith," Chávez claimed. "There's intimidation of the workers and we can't have a real secret ballot." However, when it came to Pawley's company, Chávez advocated the secret ballot, saying he challenged Talisman to hold one. "No secret ballot election has ever been suggested by him [Chavez]," said Pawley, who felt his workers were being pressured. "A man should no more be forced to join a union than he should be forced to join a social club."[39]

The argument between Pawley and the UFW centered on the Jamaican workers. The union wanted them included in negotiations, but Pawley wouldn't agree. He maintained, "The Jamaicans are here as part of a contract between our company and the U.S. and Jamaican governments and couldn't possibly be represented by the union."[40] The union, however, contended the Jamaicans were nothing more than strikebreakers being "forced to perform jobs that do not come within the province of their contract." The UFW charged that workers were being held in "bond-age," a serious accusation Pawley emphatically denied.[41]

"I don't want the citizens of Miami thinking I'm running a slave camp out there," Pawley said. He said the Jamaicans were well fed, well housed, paid a fair wage, worked reasonable hours, provided with adequate medical treatment, and not forced to remain on the plantation. In an interview with a *Miami Herald* staff writer, Pawley went into specific detail on each point.

Each worker was given three hot meals a day, Pawley said. "They're getting better than 5,000 calories a day." Jamaican government officials monitor the treatment of the workers, Pawley said, "and in all the years I've been here, we have had no complaints." Jamaican officials had even told him the workers "live better [on the Talisman plantation] than they do at home." If a worker wanted food or supplies other than those supplied by Talisman, they could purchase them in the company commissary. "That's strictly a service operation," Pawley claimed, "not a profit making one." He added that commissary prices were 25 to 30 percent below retail levels.

The contract called for workers to receive $1.80 an hour. "But, we tell the workers when they arrive that we want them to make more than this." They have the option of working at the hourly rate, he said, or by piece work, receiving $14 for each row of cane cut. "He can make $28 to $42 a day if he's strong enough." No matter how much the worker cuts, Pawley added, he is at least paid the minimum hourly wage. Pawley also initiated an incentive program. At the end of the season, the worker cutting the most cane is presented a silver-plated machete and a $300 prize. As to the UFW's charges that the Jamaicans labored long hours in the fields, Pawley said, "I doubt that many of them work more than six hours a day."

The UFW claimed the Jamaicans were not allowed to leave the plantation, preventing the union from having contact with them. Pawley said that assertion was not true. After payday every week, company trucks transported the workers to nearby Belle Glade. "If [the UFW] want to talk to them, let them see them in Belle Glade," Pawley said. Union organizers were refused access to the plantation "because that's private property and we don't just allow anybody to go wandering over it, making trouble."

"There are no better facilities for the working man anywhere," Pawley concluded. To prove his point he said, "85 percent of the men who work here, return the following year."[42] As to charges he was waging a one-man war against the union, Pawley stated he wasn't acting on his own beliefs. "I'm absolutely determined to do what the majority of the men working for my company want," he said. "And they have said they don't want a union." Although the UFW disagreed, Pawley added, "My record proves I've not been anti-union. But I'm opposed to some type of union abuses. They're too powerful."[43]

A major UFW victory in Florida came when the union signed an agreement with Minute Maid to represent twelve hundred migrant workers employed by the Coca-Cola subsidiary. It was the first UFW labor contract in Florida, and César Chávez called it a breakthrough.[44] Bolstered by the foothold, Chávez stepped up pressure on Talisman. When matters began getting out of hand, Circuit Court judge Hugh MacMillan issued a "mutually restraining" order against both sides not to threaten, attack, or harass each other.[45] A week later, the suit brought by the union in federal court to seek access to the Talisman property was finally decided.

U.S. District Court judge Charles B. Fulton disallowed the union the right to enter the sugar plantation property to meet with the Jamaican workers. Fulton called the suit "nothing more or less than a labor dispute," and the union wanted access to the property, not to "improve the economic and social position of the agricultural workers," but to "man these Jamaican-held positions with their own union workers."[46]

The U.S. Court of Appeals for the Fifth Circuit heard the appeal. In May 1973, in a 2–1 decision, the judges reversed the lower court ruling, citing the balancing between the property rights of the owner against the free speech rights of the union. "There are no effective alternatives open to the plaintiffs for communicating with the Jamaican workers other than access to the living area of the labor camp," the judges determined. "The biweekly trip into Belle Glade is insufficiently frequent and otherwise inadequate to afford a reasonable opportunity for discussions between the [union] and the workers."[47]

Chávez also claimed the Jamaicans endured poor conditions at Talisman and petitioned the federal court to allow the union to inspect the camp, but the suit was denied. "There is no evidence to the contrary," Judge Fulton wrote in his decision. The UFW also called upon the Rural Manpower Service to investigate violations of medical care, working hours, and availability of water at the camp. The resulting investigation found all charges untrue.[48]

The UFW continued the fight by asking the federal court to issue an injunction stopping the importation of Jamaican workers. In October 1972, Judge Peter T. Fay denied the injunction. "It is my opinion," he wrote, "that even while the Jamaicans are coming here, what greater protection is there to domestic workers than to know that they are qualified and if they apply for work they must be given the job."[49] Following the ruling, Chávez called for congressional hearings to investigate the Florida sugar industry "right here and see what the conditions are," labeling them "exploitive, discriminatory and arbitrary."[50]

In poor health and facing high interest payments on notes for improvements and crop loans, Pawley looked for a way out of the company. "Never sell a majority position in a company," Pawley always preached to his son, but now he asked Edward Ball, who handled the Dupont holdings, to buy a controlling interest in Talisman. When Ball purchased 62 percent from Pawley, he refused to have the company pay off the $4 million in bank loans Pawley had signed for personally.

"It was killing Dad," Bill Pawley, Jr., recalled. "He thought he was going to go broke." He told his father he had a Cuban friend in Miami who had people in Latin America interested in buying the remaining 38 percent of the company. "You're wasting your time," Pawley told his son. "Nobody who knows anything about business is going to buy a minority position in this company." Nevertheless, Bill felt the possibility might exist. "What difference is it to you if I waste my time?" he asked his father.

Bill learned a major insurance company had conducted an appraisal on Talisman Sugar two years before when it was considering purchasing the company as an investment. "The appraisal was thick, maybe four or five inches," Bill remembered, "and it appraised the company at $94 million." Armed with this information, Bill and his Cuban friend sought out a buyer. When they found someone, Bill went to his father and asked for a letter of commission to close the deal. "After a long time of refusing, he finally gave me a letter of commission, but he gave me only sixty days to sell the stock," Bill recalled.

"What do you want for your 38 percent of the stock in the company?" Bill asked his father.

"Six and a half million."

"Dad, the stock is worth $38 million," Bill said. "I happen to know that it was appraised two years ago at $94 million, and since then you have put in $6 million worth of new boilers and rolling equipment, and you bought some more land. The company is worth over $100 million."

Pawley said that assessment was ridiculous, telling his son he was crazy. Undaunted, Bill talked to his Cuban friend, and they agreed to split the commission upon a successful sale. The prospective buyer, representing a Venezuelan group, flew to Miami to discuss the deal. Because Pawley remained at home, never visiting the office, they went to the house to see him. The buyer was willing to make a $500,000 deposit while examining the company's books but was concerned if the deposit was refundable. "Absolutely," Pawley said.

While the buyer headed back to Venezuela to get approval from his board, Bill's Cuban partner had lunch with a stockbroker who represented another sugar company in Palm Beach County. The pending deal came up in their conversation, after which the broker immediately contacted the sugar company he represented. They made a counteroffer through the Talisman office in Miami. When the new offer was accepted, it was discovered the letter of commission held by Bill and his Cuban partner was still in force.

Pawley's attorney drew up a letter of release for Bill and the Cuban to sign, offering the Cuban $100,000 and Bill $50,000 to sign off on the deal. "You're being cheated," Bill told his partner. "Normally, I would not sue my father, but if you want to sue, I'll join the suit." The Cuban decided against the lawsuit and split the commission with Bill. Pocketing $6.5 million from the sale of his Talisman stock, for the first time in almost fifty years William Pawley no longer had any business investments.

23

Nixon and Home in Florida

On January 15, 1960, Richard Nixon arrived in Miami on a campaign swing through Florida as he gathered support to become the Republican nominee for president. Close to a thousand people were at the airport to greet the candidate, and among the official welcoming party was William Pawley.[1] Nelson Rockefeller had already visited Florida in December, hoping to garner support for his candidacy, but when the slate of twenty-six Florida delegates to the Republican convention was announced at the end of February, all were pledged to Nixon. Pawley was among those delegates representing the Fourth Congressional District (Dade and Monroe Counties).[2]

Nixon sent a note to Pawley congratulating him on being selected as a delegate, and said he was "looking forward to participating" with him in the convention meetings.[3] Ironically, Pawley had also received a letter from the (Lyndon) Johnson for President Committee, which mistakenly asked him as a delegate to the Democratic Convention to bear in mind the candidacy of Senator Johnson.[4]

Although Pawley once said he had supported Eisenhower, not because Ike was a Republican, but because he "liked the man," by 1960, Pawley was espousing a different reason for backing Ike. "I changed parties in 1951 because I could see what was happening in China," he said at the Republican National Convention in Chicago, "and the Democratic administration refused to pay any attention to my warnings." As for endorsing Nixon, he said, "He is the best qualified, best trained, and I think by far the greatest citizen in American politics today to lead the nation."[5] After Nixon received the nomination, five Florida delegates threw their support behind Barry Goldwater for the running mate spot. Pawley didn't join them, feeling that "all delegates should line up solidly behind the team which Nixon feels will have strongest public support."[6]

After Henry Cabot Lodge was chosen as the vice presidential nominee, Pawley headed to Florida to help get the ticket elected. In the 1952 and 1956 national elections, Pawley had worked on the Florida Citizens for Eisenhower organization. This time, Floridians for Nixon-Lodge set its sights on garnering Florida Democrats' and independents' votes. Pawley was chosen to head the southeast Florida area—including Dade, Broward, Palm Beach, and Monroe Counties—and began the campaign by taking out half-page ads in local newspapers for contributions and volunteers.[7]

While concentrating his efforts on Florida, Pawley still offered comments on the national campaign, especially on the televised Kennedy-Nixon debates. Pawley was dead set against them because Nixon was "in an official capacity every time he answers a question. Therefore, Senator Kennedy always has the advantage of being on the attack." If the debates were to continue, Pawley added, he had a few suggestions:

1. In the question of the debates, I personally believe that the Vice President should not allow the press to conduct the debate. I feel that Kennedy had notes, which makes me wonder whether he knew the questions in advance. I would like to see a real debate, in which the candidates would ask questions of each other. In this way, we could be sure that the candidates did not know the questions in advance.

2. In my opinion, Governor [Allan] Shivers is the greatest speaker in America since Roosevelt, and he was able to win Texas for Eisenhower when everyone in Texas thought it could not be done. He (Gov. Shivers) should be used to a maximum degree in the South on National TV—He is the most powerful speaker with the exception of the man I am going to mention next.

3. My friends and I are hopeful that the President would consider appearing on National TV once or twice and pointing out the Vice President's experience and qualifications. The President's statement of "give me a week and I might think of an example," has been widely quoted to the Vice President's detriment.

4.   The Cuban situation has been mentioned frequently in the cam-
     paign, but I do not believe that we have used the maximum oppor-
     tunity to point out the loss of many other countries (e.g., China)
     during Democrat Administrations. We should point up the fact that
     Eisenhower was elected on a ticket to stop the war in Korea, which
     we did.[8]

After Nixon lost the election, Pawley urged him to continue leading the
Republican Party. "It would be lamentable if a man who has been so magnificently
trained to serve this great nation and the world were to temporarily drop out of
politics." He begged Nixon to "hold yourself in readiness to be our candidate four
years from now, as I am sure that the lessons we have learned from this campaign
will lead us to victory."[9]

Pawley kept in contact with Nixon, maintaining a friendship that had begun
during Nixon's first term as vice president. "Hardly a day passes, Dick, that I do
not recognize the tragedy to this country of our failure to be able to elect you
President of the United States," Pawley wrote. He extended an invitation for Nixon
and his family to visit him in Florida before Nixon settled in his law practice.[10]
"Nothing would be more welcome than the opportunity to spend a week with you
and Edna on Miami Beach," Nixon replied. While demands on his political and
personal life prevented him from taking a vacation, he invited Pawley to "feel free
to write me any comments or suggestions you have as to what approach I might
take in my public statements."[11]

Pawley needed little encouragement to offer his views. The main topic Pawley
always wanted to discuss with Nixon was Cuba, but they never wrote their concerns
in the letters that passed between them. Pawley wrote about the "many problems
. . . particularly those having to do with the Cuban difficulties," and he received
a handwritten postscript back from Nixon: "I hope before too long we can have a
good talk about Cuba and other problems."[12] Shortly before Nixon's run for governor of California, Pawley paid the expenses for a speaker on the Cuban problem to
give speeches on the West Coast during the campaign. "There is so much going on
about Cuba that is extremely bad that I would appreciate your calling me by telephone at your earliest convenience," Pawley wrote in a letter. A handwritten note
in the margin of the letter indicates Nixon did call.[13] Pawley's letter was dated five
days before President Kennedy addressed the nation concerning the missile crisis.

During Nixon's gubernatorial campaign in 1962, Pawley and Edna had been
on a world tour and stopped in San Francisco for four days before heading home.
While there, they visited friends of Edna's nephew Sam Coil, engaging in a lively
discussion of the upcoming election. Writing to Nixon about their evening, Pawley
offered suggestions on how to organize a grassroots voters drive, recalling the
work he did in 1952 in Virginia for Eisenhower. "I would rather see you win this
Governor's race than any campaign now before the American people," Pawley
wrote. "I hope that those responsible for your organizational work will not over-
look recruiting every person in the state who is willing to put in a few hours a week
on behalf of your campaign." Pawley also enclosed a $1,000 contribution.[14]

On the eve of the election, Pawley sent a letter supporting Nixon to be published in eight leading newspapers in California. Claiming Nixon would become
"one of California's great governors," Pawley focused on the Cuban issue:

> Richard Nixon would not have made the tremendous error of judgment of
> the Bay of Pigs, nor this second blunder of stopping short of removing the
> communist controlled government of Fidel Castro from Cuba.
>
>   The Castro "cancer" remains, and Americans will pay the price of
> this disastrous error of judgment.
>
>   Every disturbed American who places his Nation above partisan poli-
> tics can, in good conscience, vote for this great American.[15]

When Nixon lost the election and gave his famous quote to the press—"You
won't have Nixon to kick around any more"—Pawley called Rose Mary Woods to
leave a message. "I think Dick made an error of judgment in his statement before
the press and television people," Pawley said. "Rosemary, I want him to recover
from this because I think . . . he has hurt himself deeply. Also we feel that this will
continue to dog him for a long time." He ended the call by asking her to "tell my
friend, Dick, that I think he has let himself down more than anyone else."[16]

In a follow-up letter, Pawley told his friend, "Do not bow out, Dick." Telling
Nixon that his "contribution to the nation's welfare must be always available,"
Pawley also reminded him, "You are a young man and it is hard to say at this time
where the future may take you."[17] Nixon waited six months before replying to
Pawley's letter, blaming the "heavy backlog of correspondence" since the election.
"I can assure you that nothing is more heartwarming after losing a hard-fought

election than to receive a note of encouragement such as yours," Nixon wrote. As for the future, he was considering several offers in the private sector "to provide for my family," adding that he would still find time to participate in public affairs.[18]

Acknowledging Nixon's letter, Pawley expressed disappointment that his friend hadn't contacted him during a Florida visit. "Actually, Dick, I thought you might have picked up the telephone on your way through to the Keys," Pawley wrote. Personal comments aside, Pawley went on to voice his opinion on the present administration's handling of foreign policy. "I have become quite pessimistic and depressed," he wrote. Focusing again on Cuba, Pawley recounted the disastrous decisions that both the Eisenhower and the Kennedy administrations had made. There was only one way out of the mess, according to Pawley: "All of the Cubans and most Americans in this part of the country believe that to remove Castro you must first remove Kennedy, and that is not going to be easy."[19]

Remaining a supporter of Republican candidates, Pawley readily endorsed conservative Barry Goldwater in the 1964 campaign. As state chairman of Florida Citizens for Goldwater-Miller, Pawley was also honorary chairman of the Florida delegation to the Republican National Convention.[20] When Nixon barnstormed around the country for Goldwater, Pawley greeted his old friend during a stop in Miami.[21] To express appreciation for his support, in 1971 Goldwater honored Pawley at a $150-a-plate dinner at the Miami Beach Eden Roc Hotel. Reading from a letter sent by President Nixon, Goldwater added his praise of Pawley as "a tireless fighter for the cause of freedom" and a man who "courageously expressed his views."[22]

Pawley liked Nixon from the first time they met during the Eisenhower era, and their friendship never wavered. "Through the years," Nixon wrote in 1975, "Pat and I have often remarked that we have never had a more loyal friend, whether we were up or down, than Bill Pawley."[23] But their relationship was sometimes strained. In a 1964 phone conversation with Rose Mary Woods, Pawley complained that Nixon had visited Florida numerous times without contacting him. "I decided what Dick feels is that I am only a political friend—not as a real friend," he told Nixon's secretary. "None of this has changed my feeling for RN—I like him— I am his friend but he needs to watch treating his friends this way."[24]

Nevertheless, when Nixon sought the 1968 nomination, Pawley was a staunch supporter. Along with a $500 check for the campaign, Pawley offered Maurice Stans, chairman of the election finance committee, some advice. "Dick made a tremendous mistake in going to see Nelson [Rockefeller] during his first campaign," he wrote. "I don't know how we can persuade the liberals to satisfy themselves with a moderate like Dick," he added, hoping that Eisenhower might be persuaded to unite leading Republicans to support "whoever the convention decides upon."[25] Writing directly to Nixon, Pawley asked, "what part Ike will play in the coming campaign. Would it be possible to persuade him to interest himself in your candidacy?"[26]

Although Pawley continued making contributions to Nixon's campaign, he declined to undertake the responsibility of heading a fund-raising committee in South Florida. His decision was based "not for lack of interest," but he had various other commitments, including running Talisman Sugar.[27] This did not preclude his offering advice. In one of his many calls to Rose Mary Woods, Pawley asked her to pass along a message to Nixon. "When RN ran for President in 1960, I read in the paper one morning that RN was going to debate," he told her. "I called you and he was right there and you put him on. I said I think it is a big mistake to debate." Pawley was now calling to prevent Nixon from making another mistake.

"He made a statement about getting the war over with," he said. "That frightened me a little bit because this is a tough one." Pawley felt the war should continue until victory was achieved but not with American troops. How did Pawley propose it could be done? "The answer to that is very simple," he told Rose Mary Woods. "If we are elected he is going to substitute the millions of Asiatics who want to fight against communists and we will supply them the materials, the training, etc.—but let the Asiatics fight this for themselves."[28] Nixon would later adopt this policy but using only South Vietnamese troops.

Speaking at a Pensacola Chamber of Commerce luncheon in March 1968, Pawley left no doubt about whom he supported and why. President Johnson had to "pull a miracle" in Vietnam to be reelected, Pawley said, or Nixon "could be the next President." With Governor George Romney of Michigan and Governor Rockefeller both out of the race, Pawley felt it was time for Republicans to rally around Nixon: "He has done more for the Republican Party than any one person in recent history. He has more contact with world leaders than anyone in America today. He has the most experience in these difficult times . . . he's the only Republican the Republicans want." Pawley also suggested Republicans shouldn't spend millions on "beating each other's brains out in the primary." Instead, he said, "we need to save these resources for the battle."[29]

When a group of former ambassadors formed the Ambassadors for Nixon Committee, Pawley was only too eager to join. "Based on our experience as former ambassadors of the United States," a spokesperson said, "we are convinced that Richard Nixon is by far the best prepared by intensive training and successful experience to provide the leadership so urgently needed by this nation." Seventeen former ambassadors, most having served under Eisenhower, joined the group.[30]

After Nixon secured the top spot on the ticket, Pawley turned his concerns to whom Nixon would choose as a running mate. Never one to hold back his opinion, Pawley sent Nixon a list of those nominees being proposed, along with his recommendations:

Rockefeller in the second spot would under no circumstances be acceptable.

The views expressed before the Platform Committee by Mayor [John] Lindsay [of New York City] make him extremely vulnerable and I believe we would lose a large part of the South to protest votes that would go for [Governor George] Wallace [of Alabama].

[U.S. Senator Charles Harting] Percy [of Illinois] looked pretty good until he shifted to Rockefeller. This was unfortunate and would appear to eliminate him and he, too, would contribute to the loss of a substantial Southern vote.

[Senator] John Tower [of Texas] appears to be the one most acceptable and one that all with whom I consulted felt would do the greatest harm to the Wallace movement and pick up the greatest support in the South; thereby greatly strengthening your ticket.

Of course, [Governor Ronald] Reagan [of California] and you together would sweep the country. I have been disappointed over feeling that there was very little chance that this could be brought about; however, this would be the number one choice.[31]

There is no record of Pawley's feelings on Governor Spiro Agnew of Maryland getting the second spot on the ticket. Being an avid Nixon supporter, however, he almost certainly applauded the choice.

With his friend successfully in the White House, Pawley continued to support the president. When the media continued applying pressure to the Nixon administration, Pawley became involved with a conservative group that decided to take action.

Miami's Channel 10 television station, under the call letters WPST, was originally licensed to Public Service Television, Inc., a National Airlines subsidiary. In 1961, after a long court battle with the Federal Communications Commission (FCC), the company lost its license, which was awarded to L. B. Wilson, Inc. The new owners operated the American Broadcasting Company affiliate under the call letters WLBW and pumped in more than $1 million for a new studio and office building. In 1969, Wilson sold the station for $20 million to Post-Newsweek Stations, Inc., the corporate company of the *Washington Post*, which already owned WTXT in Jacksonville.[32] Katharine Graham, president of the parent company, changed the station's call letters to WPLG in honor of her late husband, Phillip L. Graham.

With its license up for renewal the following year, Post-Newsweek filed an application for continuation of its operating authority. Before the deadline, Greater Miami Telecasters (GMT) filed a license application asking the FCC to reject the Post-Newsweek's license renewal. In the two-inch-thick application, GMT argued the present owners were "incapable of giving Miami the public service programs which members of the community could provide."[33] FCC regulations allowed any station's license to be challenged, and if a majority of the seven-member commission felt another group's qualifications were superior, the license could be transferred.

The *Washington Post* had come under attack by Vice President Agnew, who accused the newspaper of waging a deliberate campaign against the Nixon administration. Agnew contended the *Post*'s conglomerate of newspaper, magazine, and television and radio stations were "all grinding out the same editorial line."[34] Larry Israel, chairman of the board of Post-Newsweek, said, "There will be a lot of things read into" the GMT application, but he felt the challenge wasn't politically motivated.[35] "I think it's simply the contagion of our times," he added. "There are a lot of broadcasters whose licenses are being challenged by new groups."[36] But a close look at the people behind the GMT challenge poses the possibility that a request for change of licensee might have had more incentive than simply pursuing a business opportunity.

W. Sloan McCrea, wholesale food dealer, banker, and real estate investor, was president of GMT. Along with GMT's treasurer, Hoke T. Maroon, the two were principal owners of Fisher Island, a man-made island off the Miami shore slated for luxury residential development. Charles "Bebe" Rebozo, a friend and confidant of Nixon's, also had a financial stake. Nixon had owned stock in the Fisher Island development group valued at $400,000, but he sold it prior to the 1968 election. Other GMT stockholders included former U.S. senator George Smathers's brother, Frank; H. Earl Smalley, part owner of the Miami Dolphins; and William Pawley.[37] As a whole, the group was capable of applying enormous political pressure to get the license. "One or two votes on the [FCC] commission would make a difference," an assistant to a commissioner said, "and if it seems that these might be politically influenced, that's a form of pressure on the station's editorial policies."[38]

GMT's application to the FCC offered no legal arguments as to why Post-Newsweek should relinquish its license. GMT offered to build a new station "or make changes in the existing station," adding that it had been offered a nearby site to build a transmitter and tower if a new facility became necessary.[39] Its application was filled with charts and graphs from community surveys, along with financial data and suggestions of programming changes GMT hoped to implement to better serve Miami viewers.[40] GMT had the money and political clout, but Post-Newsweek was well prepared to wage a battle. "I would say that influential politicians and bureaucrats in the nation's capital read The Post more than any other paper," commented columnist Jack Roberts, but added that "two members of the FCC weren't happy with Post-Newsweek acquiring the station in the first place." The fight for the license might last a year or more, "depending on the spirit the Miami group shows in pursuing its case," FCC director of broadcasting facilities Mark Levy predicted.[41]

The GMT challenge posed a formidable obstacle to Post-Newsweek because the Miami group met the standard of being local community leaders. Furthermore, a source close to FCC commissioner Nicholas Johnson said GMT "have no other media interests and on balance are more related to the community than *The Washington Post* which is sort of a national holding company." No matter what Post-Newsweek did to improve programming to benefit the local community, its record presented before FCC committee hearings would be based solely on the two months it held the license prior to the renewal challenge.[42]

Although the GMT challenge was eventually dropped, tapes made public during the Watergate investigation (1972–1974) suggested there was a link between the Nixon administration and the FCC's fight for control of the Miami station.

During a September 15, 1972, meeting in the Oval Office with Nixon, John Dean, and H. R. Haldeman, the license renewal was discussed. Nixon said, "The main, the main thing is the Post is going to have damnable, damnable problems out of this one."[43]

Congressman Torbert Macdonald of Massachusetts, who served as chairman of the House Subcommittee on Communications, said Nixon's remarks were indicative of "the desire of Government to control the news." He added it was no surprise, "because I was convinced more than a year ago that there was a casual connection between the two challenges to the Post-Newsweek station in Jacksonville and Miami and the paranoia in the White House."[44] The second challenge that Macdonald referred to was against the *Post*'s Jacksonville station WJXT and led by Florida financier Edward Ball. Post-Newsweek still owns both television stations.

The one issue troubling Pawley the most, meanwhile, was the Watergate scandal. He supported Nixon in both terms, and although he did not "approve of the actions of those involved in Watergate," Pawley felt compelled to rally around his president by publishing, as a paid advertisement, a 1973 *National Review* article titled "The White House Witch Hunt." The article condemned the media's "presumptions of guilt" and denounced Nixon for "not telling, immediately, everything about everybody." The reprint accused the *New York Times, Washington Post, Newsweek*, and *Time* of transforming "deserters, rioters, subverters, turncoats, draft-dodgers, and America-haters into innocent victims and folk heroes."[45]

Jack Kofoed, in his *Miami Herald* column, took Pawley to task for attacking the press. Kofoed wrote that Pawley failed to mention those who were conducting the investigation. "They are senators, Mr. Pawley, yet you attack only the press," he noted. "You did not, once even," Kofoed wrote, "mention those who have admitted they were guilty of burglary, perjury and other crimes. Does that mean you favor covering up such acts?"[46] Jack Kassewitz in his *Miami News* column was more to the point: "Mr. Pawley should be thankful he lives in a democracy that still has a free press. He has the right to complain and we have the privilege to respond. We think he's wrong."[47]

Active in supporting political candidates, Pawley also served his community and was a member of several social organizations in southern Florida. Founded in 1926, the Bath Club was an exclusive ($1,000 membership fee) social gathering spot for winter visitors. Originally limited to members who did not live permanently within a fifty-mile radius, the restriction was lifted in 1949. Pawley became a member and was installed as its president in 1960.[48] He also joined the Indian Creek and La Gorse Country Clubs, as well as private clubs in Washington and New York City. A member of Alianza Interamericana, a social organization promoting friendship among the Americas, Pawley was chosen as its Man of the Year in 1959.[49]

In 1961, Pawley headed a committee of Miami business leaders to review operations of the area's United Fund.[50] In 1966, he was elected to the national board of directors of the Boys Clubs of America.[51] He was a member of the Eisenhower Presidential Library Committee and served on the advisory board for the George C. Marshall Library at the Virginia Military Institute.[52] When the Marshall Library ran into financial difficulties finishing the building, Pawley donated $60,000 toward its completion.[53]

Pawley's conservatism and patriotic feelings were sorely tested during the social unrest of the sixties and the demonstrations against the Vietnam War. When violence erupted at the 1968 Democratic National Convention in Chicago, Pawley found the news coverage disturbing. "I felt two of the networks—CBS [Columbia Broadcasting System] and NBC [National Broadcasting Company]—were extremely unfair on their coverage of the convention as it had to do with rioting." He was indignant that Chicago police were portrayed as villains. "To put all the blame on the police seemed extremely unfair," he said. Although he didn't hold the police blameless—"I think that in any case where force has to be used there are going to be excesses, and in Chicago there unquestionably were excesses"—Pawley felt some of the blame should go to the "trained organizers who helped to provoke the police."

Showing support for police forces, Pawley established an annual award of $1,000 to the outstanding police officer in both Miami and Miami Beach. "We've only the police forces of our cities and towns to defend the American public," he said. "I don't believe they should be so unjustly criticized, and for that reason, I as a private citizen wanted to show some interest in the terrible and unfair criticism of what I think to be in this country a magnificent police organization."[54]

Pawley never feared voicing his opinion, which he often did with paid advertisements in Miami newspapers or essays in conservative publications. With the United States embroiled in Vietnam, he offered "A Way Out of Vietnam," published in the *Washington Report*, the newsletter of the American Security Council (ASC). A rightist organization, the ASC was founded in 1955 by former FBI agents who supported Joseph McCarthy's campaign to rid the government of allegedly disloyal workers. Originally called the Mid-American Research Library, the ASC amassed "the largest private collection on revolutionary activities in America." Dues-paying ASC members could access the collection of dossiers on individuals and organizations deemed subversive. The foundation's members represented a cross-section of corporations—for example, General Electric, Kraft Foods, Lockheed, U.S. Steel, and Honeywell—and powerful individuals. Generals Nathan Twining and Curtis LeMay, along with Clare Booth Luce and Dr. Edward Teller, were among the members of the National Strategy Committee, the policy-advising board of the ASC.[55]

Pawley's article was published in 1969, after the Nixon administration announced its intention of gradually withdrawing U.S. ground troops from Vietnam with the hope of resolving the war solely by supplying South Vietnam with arms. But Pawley had an alternative plan. "The solution lies in making use of an enormous resource which we have cultivated and financed for two decades," he wrote. "I refer to the armed forces of the Chinese Nationalists on Taiwan." Pawley proposed that "each time 25,000 American troops are removed from Vietnam, 25,000 Chinese Nationalists take their places." With the Seventh Fleet offshore to protect the troops and to supply the Chinese Nationalists with weapons and military stores "for a quarter of what American soldiers cost us in that Asian theater," Pawley felt the war was "winnable."

"Why should we not allow Asians to fight Asians in the cause of freedom?" he asked. Citing the "ignominious draw" the United States had settled for in the Korean War, Pawley argued his strategy would place the Communists "on notice that their long run of easy pickings is at an end." He felt there were no moral, legal, or ethical barriers to his plan. "Asians would fight Asians for Asian objectives," he proclaimed, and "the propaganda onus of Americans fighting Orientals will vanish."[56]

Critics denounced the controversial plan as being racist, but Chiang Kai-shek supported the idea: "Over the past twenty years, it has been my conviction that the responsibility for the security of Asia should be borne by the Asians themselves. Furthermore, I have never ceased in my belief that, in recovering the Chinese mainland, we shall need the participation of no American combat troops whatsoever, but only moral and logistic support from the United States and other friendly nations."[57]

U.S. policymakers would never consider his radical plans, but it didn't stop Pawley from voicing his opinion on the Vietnam War and other topics. Pawley paid for another advertisement in 1973, this time a reprint of an article by Gen. Ira C. Eaker, USAF (Ret.), titled "Why We Lost the War in Vietnam." Believing "news coverage does not include many vital subjects," Pawley felt compelled to reprint the article to offer "information essential to our national welfare." The Eaker essay blamed Congress for losing the war when it voted to stop bombing targets in Cambodia. According to Eaker, this action denied Nixon the power to continue with the "Vietnamization" plan to wind down the war.[58]

In 1974, concerned that the United States had fallen behind in the arms race owing to Secretary of Defense Robert McNamara's policies, Pawley supported funding outlays of $20 billion for the B-1 bombers and Trident submarines. Reprinting another article written by Eaker, Pawley urged citizens to write their senators and congressmen, "if you feel as I do." Calling national security "our number one priority," Eaker emphasized the importance of research programs to develop military hardware because the United States was "in grave danger of becoming dangerously inferior." Among his suggestions, Eaker proposed improving the country's navigation satellites, which "could revolutionize world navigation and weapon delivery."[59]

When a particular topic annoyed him enough, Pawley still would fire off a letter to the editor of the local newspaper. One of his letters touched on the issues of unemployment and the recession, which he blamed on environmentalists. "They have increased the cost of automobiles by at least $500 by unnecessary regulations and restrictions on the automobile industry," he wrote. He accused antipollutionists for the supersonic air transport program's cancellation, which he maintained would "cost the country at least $5 billion annually in future aircraft sales." Pawley also denounced them for delaying construction of the Alaska pipeline for three years "in favor of a few reindeer." He condemned "overzealous environmentalists" for quashing "efforts to produce new sources of energy," even suggesting these groups were "responsible for advocating unnecessary deficit spending and reducing our defense appropriations."[60]

For more than a year Pawley had been suffering from a painful rash called shingles. Caused by the chickenpox virus, it attacks nerve endings on the skin, forming blisters. In most cases the disease runs its course in six to eight weeks, leaving small, white scars behind, but for Pawley, the blisters broke out near his eyes, resulting in unbearable pain. Even contact with sunlight became too painful, forcing him to sit in a darkened room most of the time. He sought relief with opiates and other painkillers as prescribed by the Ochsner Clinic in New Orleans, but the relief was only temporary. "He was in considerable pain," said his niece, Anita. "The pain was excruciating. He didn't see any end to it."[61]

A little after one o'clock on the afternoon of January 7, 1977, Pawley ate a bowl of cereal and put on a pair of light blue pajamas. He talked a while to Edna, and as she left the room, she heard a loud noise. "Edna," she heard her husband say, "I've just shot myself." Returning to the bedroom, Edna saw a semiautomatic pistol lying on her husband's wounded chest. Edna took the gun, laid it on the nightstand, and called Pawley's Biscayne Boulevard office. Miami Beach detective Sgt. Ray Duncan arrived at the Sunset Island home at 1:30 p.m., followed shortly by a fire rescue squad. "We talked to her for a few minutes," Duncan said. "She was pretty upset, really broken up. Then some relatives came in and once she saw them, she just went to pieces."[62] The gun, a .38 caliber Colt, had seven bullets left in its eight-round magazine.

The fire rescue squad rushed Pawley, still alive but unconscious, to the Mt. Sinai Hospital emergency room, where doctors made an incision in his chest in an effort to save him. The bullet had traversed the aorta, passed through the left lung, and exited through the back. The doctors pronounced William Douglas Pawley dead at 2:18 p.m.[63] He was eighty years old.

After the police left, a maid found a note scribbled in pencil on a scrap of paper: "Edna, please forgive me. I can't get well. Have Ed help you." Less than two weeks prior to his death, Pawley had talked about his illness on the phone with Bill Miller, general manager of the Sugar Cane Growers Cooperative of Florida. "He said the only relief were opiates. Apparently he'd just quit taking them. I asked him why and he said 'I wasn't going to do that to my body.'"[64]

Memorial services were held at the Miami Beach Community Church, after which the body was cremated.[65] During the services, Miami Beach police formed an honor guard amid numerous floral arrangements, including a red, white, and blue one from the Nixon family.[66] Among the four hundred mourners gathered in the church were representatives from the Brazilian and Peruvian consulates.[67] Pawley was survived by his ex-wife, Annie-Hahr; his second wife, Edna; three children; and two brothers.[68]

Both the *New York Times* and *Time* magazine carried his obituary, noting his long and varied career both as a businessman and as an envoy for several presidents. "A man with a flair for supersalesmanship and high adventure," wrote the *New York Times*, "William Douglas Pawley led a life that could have been the substance of several old-time dime novels."[69]

An editorial in the *Miami Herald* called him "opinionated" with "his own concept of patriotism." It also revealed: "A side of Bill Pawley few persons knew because in humbleness he didn't want it emphasized was his compassion for people in trouble and his generosity to charities and cultural enterprises. When a civic activity appeared to be running out of steam or cash, Bill Pawley was there to rescue it with his enthusiasm and his fortune, which he doled out liberally. There is, we think, no better way to be remembered."[70]

William Pawley had traveled the world to seek his fortune and to serve his country in a manner he thought best. But in the passing of time, as his world narrowed to the community surrounding him, he continued to address the ills of society as he saw them and attempted to correct them. The stage on which he played had shrunk, but the man never did.

NOTES

Chapter 1. An Adventurous Early Life

1. Eisenhower to Doolittle, July 26, 1954, DDE Papers, Ann Whitman File, Administration File, Allen Dulles Folder, Eisenhower Library.
2. David Cannon, "More Ruthless Than the Enemy," File 009766, House Select Committee on Assassinations, National Archives.
3. Special Study Group Report (Doolittle), September 30, 1954, CDROM Id: 1978040100023, *Declassified Documents*, PSmedia.
4. "'A Creditable Job' Is Verdict on C.I.A.,'" *New York Times*, October 20, 1954.
5. Special Study Group Report (Doolittle).
6. "William D. Pawley Kills Himself," *Miami Herald*, January 8, 1977.
7. Vera Glaser, "Panel Asks Pawley's Testimony on JFK," *Miami Herald*, December 14, 1975.
8. Charlotte Kaminski Prevost and Effie Leland Wilder, *Pawley's Island: A Living Legend* (Columbia, SC: The State Printing Company, 1972), 3.
9. George C. Rogers, Jr., *The History of Georgetown County, South Carolina* (Columbia: University of South Carolina Press, 1970), 57–58.
10. Prevost and Wilder, *Pawley's Island*, 3.
11. Ibid., 8.
12. *Roberts & Hoge* v. *Pawley*, 50 S.C. 491; 27 S.E. 913 (September 30, 1897).
13. Robert Walden Coggeshall, *Ancestors and Kin* (Spartanburg, SC: Reprint Company, 1988), 161.
14. William Douglas Pawley (WDP) family history notes, October 7, 1968; courtesy of Annie-Hahr McKay.
15. The United States was obligated to pay an annual rent of $4,085. Only one check has been cashed since Castro came into power. See Theodore K. Mason, *Across the Cactus Curtain: The Story of Guantánamo Bay* (New York: Dodd, Mead, 1984), 148.
16. Memorandum on Pawley license, July 9, 1910, National Archives, General Records of Department of State, Group 59, Decimal File 811.34537/21.
17. Marion E. Murphy, *The History of Guantánamo Bay* (Guantánamo Bay, Cuba: U.S. Navy, 1953), 12.
18. Mary Ellene Chenevey McCoy, "Guantánamo Bay: The United States Naval Base and Its Relationship with Cuba" (PhD diss., University of Akron, OH, 1995), 82.

19. Acting secretary of state (Francis Mairs Huntington Wilson) to American minister in Cuba (John B. Jackson), August 18, 1910, National Archives, General Records of Department of State, Group 59, Decimal File 811.34537/24.

20. American minister in Cuba (Jackson) to secretary of state, August 27, 1910, U.S. Department of State, *Foreign Relations of the United States*, vol. 1 (Washington, DC: Government Printing Office, 1911), 113. (Hereafter cited as FRUS, followed by year: volume, page.)

21. "History Around Us," *Miami Herald*, June 11, 1989.

22. William Douglas Pawley, "Why the Communists Are Winning," 8, manuscript privately printed for the Pawley family by Dudley A. Whitman, edited by Richard R. Tryon.

23. William Douglas Pawley, Jr., Annie-Hahr McKay, and Irene Baldwin, in an interview with the author at the home of Irene and Jack Baldwin, March 2003.

24. Confidential FBI report, 3, 23, January 5, 1954, Pre-presidential Paper Series, 320.103.66B.2, Nixon Library, Yorba Linda, CA. (Hereafter confidential FBI report.)

25. Unpublished manuscript, author unknown, Historical Museum of Southern Florida, Pawley file.

26. "China Swashbuckler," *Time* 40 (September 7, 1942): 98.

27. "Venezuela Pearl Beds Have Been Worked 2000 Years," *Houston Chronicle*, June 19, 1957.

28. Compagnie biographique, *Blue Book of Hayti* (New York: Klebold Press, 1919), 139–40.

29. Nixon Smiley, "The Private Wars of William Pawley," *Miami Herald*, August 22, 1971.

30. Introduction for WDP manuscript by Bruce K. Holloway, June 21, 1975, private collection of Dudley Whitman.

31. Interview with Pawley's daughter, Irene Baldwin, March 2003.

32. *National Cyclopedia of American Biography* (New York: James T. White, 1981), 60:215–6.

33. "Miss Annie Dobbs to Be Married Next Friday," *Hearst's Sunday American*, July 20, 1919; and Coggeshall, *Ancestors and Kin*, 161.

34. Letter from WDP to Annie-Hahr, August 1, 1920, private collection of Irene Baldwin.

35. Smiley, "The Private Wars."

36. Interview with Pawley's daughter, Annie-Hahr McKay, March 2003.

37. Interview with Pawley family, March 2003.

38. Confidential report on "The American Aircraft Industry in China," April 10, 1939, 3, James Marshall McHugh, Papers, #2770, Box 2, Folder 14, Department of Manuscripts and University Archives, Cornell University Libraries. (Hereafter McHugh Papers, Cornell.)

39. Handwritten notes, April 2, 1939, Box 4, Folder 4, McHugh Papers, Cornell; and confidential FBI report, 3, 23.

40. Confidential FBI report, 3–4.

41. Chief Special Agent Thomas Freeman Fitch to Edward Stettinius, December 19, 1944, Vertical File, Pawley, William D., FDR Library.

42. Advertisement (Edward E. Dammers), *Miami Herald*, September 13, 1925.

43. WDP to Annie-Hahr, January 9, 1925, private collection of Irene Baldwin.

44. Ibid., January 15, 1925.

45. Smiley, "The Private Wars."

46. Advertisement (H. Clifton Dobbs), *Miami Herald*, September 21, 1925.

47. Advertisement (Boca Del Faro), *Miami Herald*, September 18, 1925.

48. WDP to Annie-Hahr, September 11, 1925, private collection of Irene Baldwin.

49. Smiley, "The Private Wars."

50. WDP to Annie-Hahr, November 1, 1927, private collection of Irene Baldwin.
51. "'Air Taxi' Network Planned by Curtiss," *New York Times*, September 7, 1928.
52. "Many Notables in Aero Club Member List," *Miami Daily News*, February 16, 1930.
53. Grace Wing Bohne, "International Adventurer," *Village Post*, April 1968, 24; "Sky Circus Opens Airport at Miami," *New York Times*, January 8, 1929; and "Miami Turns Eyes to Indies Flights," *New York Times*, January 9, 1929.
54. "350 Planes to Compete at Miami," *New York Times*, January 12, 1930.
55. "Planes Assembled for National Meet," *New York Times*, January 7, 1931; and "Crash Kills Three at Miami Air Meet," *New York Times*, January 10, 1931.
56. "Diplomats at Miami Are Honored at Ball," *New York Times*, January 13, 1935.
57. Page Shamburger and Joe Christy, *The Curtiss Hawks* (Kalamazoo, MI: Wolverine Press, 1972), 144fn.
58. "Cuba Selects 3 from 18 Air Bids," *New York Times*, October 25, 1929; and "Starts Cuban Air Taxi Service," *New York Times*, November 4, 1929.
59. "China Swashbuckler."
60. Bohne, "International Adventurer," 24.
61. "2 Cuban Accidents Cost Dozen Lives," *Miami Daily News*, February 25, 1930.
62. "2 Cuban Fliers Killed at Airport Dedication," *New York Times*, February 25, 1930.
63. Bohne, "International Adventurer," 24.
64. Annie-Hahr to WDP, July 25, 1929, private collection of Irene Baldwin.
65. "2 Armored Planes Are Sold to Cuba," *Miami Daily News*, January 30, 1930.
66. "New City-Cuba Aviation Line to Open Dec. 15," *Miami Daily News*, July 30, 1930.
67. "Hurricane Toll Now 1,200," *New York Times*, September 6, 1930; and "Santo Domingo Toll Reaches 4,000 Dead," *New York Times*, September 7, 1930.
68. R. Michael Malek, "Rafael Leónidas Trujillo Molina: The Rise of a Caribbean Dictator" (PhD diss., University of California, Santa Barbara, 1971), 193–94.
69. "Fly with Supplies to Santo Domingo," *New York Times*, September 6, 1930.
70. "Hurricane Strikes Dominican Capital; Disaster Is Feared," *New York Times*, September 4, 1930; "Santo Domingo Lies in Noted Gale Area," *New York Times*, September 4, 1930; and "Santo Domingo Wrecked by Hurricane," *New York Times*, September 5, 1930.
71. "Fly with Supplies to Santo Domingo."
72. William D. Pawley, Jr., telephone interview with author, April 17, 2003.
73. "More Relief Going to Santo Domingo," *New York Times*, September 8, 1930.
74. Transcript, William Douglas Pawley oral history interview, April 4, 1967, 30–31, Hoover Library.
75. "President of Cuban Airline Visits Miami," *Miami Herald*, December 8, 1930.
76. "New City-Cuba Aviation"; and "Mail Volume to Be Boosted by Cuba Line,"*Miami Daily News*, October 30, 1930.
77. "Pan American Gets Cuban Air Service," *New York Times*, April 13, 1932.
78. Tom R. to James McHugh, May 27, 1939, Box 1, Folder 3, McHugh Papers, Cornell.

Chapter 2. China

1. H. E. Talbott to Senator Claude Pepper, January 6, 1945, Box 39, Folder: Confidential Report about People: William D. Pawley, Morgenthau Collection, FDR Library. (Hereafter folder is noted as Confidential Report about People.)
2. Telegram from WDP to Annie-Hahr, January 10, 1933, private collection of Irene Baldwin.
3. "Heads Aviation Company," *New York Times*, August 19, 1933.
4. Robert Daley, *An American Saga: Juan Trippe and His Pan Am Empire* (New York: Random House, 1980), 117–18.
5. Undersecretary of the treasury (John Wesley Hanes, Sr.) to Henry Morgenthau, October

20, 1939, in Henry Morgenthau, Jr., *The Morgenthau Diaries*, Robert E. Lester, project coordinator, microfilm (Bethesda, MD: University Publications of America, 1995–1997), 218:209 (hereafter cited as *Morgenthau Diaries*).

6. William D. Pawley, Jr., telephone interview with author, July 14, 2004.
7. Marylin Bender and Selig Altschul, *The Chosen Instrument: Pan Am, Juan Trippe* (New York: Simon & Schuster, 1982), 206.
8. William D. Pawley, *Wings over Asia: A Brief History of China National Aviation Corporation* (New York: China National Aviation Association Foundation, 1941), 7–9.
9. Harrison Forman, "China Spreads Her Wings," *Aviation*, June 1936, 24.
10. Wilbur Burton, "Mandate from Heaven," *Asia*, August 1935, 464; and Forman, "China Spreads Her Wings," 25.
11. William D. Pawley, "Russia Is Winning" (unpublished manuscript, George Marshall Library, Lexington, VA), 16.
12. Ibid., 25–26.
13. William M. Leary, Jr., *The Dragon's Wings: The China National Aviation Corporation and the Development of Commercial Aviation in China* (Athens: University of Georgia Press, 1976), 73.
14. WDP to Annie-Hahr, March 11, 1933, private collection of Irene Baldwin.
15. "American Airline Adds Link in China," *New York Times*, April 1, 1933.
16. Leary, *The Dragon's Wings*, 73.
17. Harrison Forman, "Aircraft Manufacturing in China," *Aviation*, June 1934, 174.
18. Henry Lewis Stimson, telegram to minister in China (John Van Antwerp MacMurray), April 27, 1929, FRUS 1929: 2, 530.
19. William M. Leary, Jr., "Wings for China: The Jouett Mission, 1932–1935," *Pacific Historical Review* 38, no. 4 (November 1969): 449.
20. Edward R. Hooton, "Air War over China," *Air Enthusiast*, September–December 1987, 8; and "Sees Gain by China in Army Air Fleet," *New York Times*, April 29, 1934.
21. "China Completing Big New Air Base," *New York Times*, December 24, 1934; and "China Begins Work on Great Air Base," *New York Times*, February 11, 1935.
22. Minister in China (Nelson Trusler Johnson), telegram to secretary of state, March 28, 1932, FRUS 1932: 3, 636–37. See also minister in China (Johnson), telegram to secretary of state, April 9, 1932, FRUS 1932: 3, 680.
23. Acting secretary of state (William Richard Castle, Jr.), telegram to consul general at Shanghai (Edwin S. Cunningham), March 29, 1932, FRUS 1932: 3, 643.
24. Acting secretary of state (Castle), telegram to consul general at Shanghai (Cunningham), April 19, 1932, FRUS 1932: 3, 702.
25. John H. Jouett, "War Planes over China," *Asia*, December 1937, 827; and "China Buys New Planes," *New York Times*, January 14, 1934.
26. Leary, "Wings for China," 452–53.
27. Burton, "Mandate from Heaven," 461.
28. Jouett, "War Planes over China," 827–28.
29. Military attaché in China (Walter Scott Drysdale) to U.S. Army chief of staff (Douglas MacArthur), November 21, 1934, FRUS 1934: 3, 315–17.
30. Consul general at Shanghai (Clarence Edward Gauss), memorandum to James Marshall McHugh, April 13, 1939, Box 1, Folder 3, McHugh Papers, Cornell.
31. Gordon K. Pickler, "United States Aid to the Chinese Nationalist Air Force: 1931–1949" (PhD diss., Florida State University, Tallahassee, 1971), 15.
32. Consul general at Shanghai (Cunningham), telegram to secretary of state, April 22, 1933, FRUS 1933: 3, 285. See also consul general at Shanghai (Cunningham), telegram to secretary of state, May 1, 1933, FRUS 1933: 3, 301.
33. Military attaché in China (Drysdale) to U.S. Army chief of staff (MacArthur), November 21, 1934, FRUS 1934: 3, 316.

34. Pickler, "United States Aid to the Chinese Nationalist Air Force," 9.
35. Military attaché in China (Drysdale) to U.S. Army chief of staff (MacArthur), November 21, 1934, FRUS 1934: 3, 316–17.
36. "Chinese Fliers: Jouett, American, Training Air Force," *Newsweek*, May 20, 1933, 19.
37. Statement by the Department of State, June 30, 1933, FRUS 1933: 3, 563.
38. Consul at Hong Kong (Louis Hill Gourley) to secretary of state, October 24, 1934, FRUS 1934: 3, 517.
39. Minister in China (Johnson), telegram to secretary of state, April 13, 1934, FRUS 1934: 3, 490.
40. Minister in China (Johnson), telegram to secretary of state, April 28, 1934, FRUS, 1934: 3, 491.
41. Pickler, "United States Aid to the Chinese Nationalist Air Force," 10.
42. Irving Brinton Holley, Jr., *Buying Aircraft: Matériel Procurement for the Army Air Forces* (Washington, DC: Office of the Chief of Military History, 1964), 19, 196.
43. Pickler, "United States Aid to the Chinese Nationalist Air Force," 11.
44. Holley, *Buying Aircraft*, 197, 200.
45. Consul general at Shanghai (Gauss), memorandum to McHugh, April 13, 1939, Box 1, Folder 3, McHugh Papers, Cornell.
46. WDP to Annie-Hahr, April 14, 1933, private collection of Irene Baldwin.
47. Ibid., April 17, 1933.
48. Ibid., May 5, 1933.
49. Report No. 1-39, April 10, 1939, "The American Aircraft Industry in China," 3, Box 2, Folder 14, McHugh Papers, Cornell.
50. WDP to Annie-Hahr, May 8, 1933, private collection of Irene Baldwin.
51. Ibid., May 15, 1933.
52. Ibid., June 24, 1933.
53. Ray Wagner, "The Chinese Air Force, 1931–1940," *American Aviation Historical Society Journal*, Fall 1974, 163.
54. Thomas A. Morgan to undersecretary of the treasury (Hanes), U.S. Congress, Senate, Committee on the Judiciary, *Morgenthau Diary: China*, 89th Cong., 1st sess. (Washington, DC: Government Printing Office, 1965). See also FRUS 1938: 4, 234–35.
55. Consul general at Hankow (Paul Reitler Josselyn) to secretary of state, January 14, 1938, FRUS 1938: 4, 234–35; and Hallett Abend, "Firm Here to Build Airplanes in China," *New York Times*, December 8, 1933.
56. Burton, "Mandate from Heaven," 463.
57. Report No. 1-39.
58. Morris McLemore, "Flying Tigers and Bill Pawley," *Miami News*, April 11, 1969.
59. Morgan to Hanes, October 27, 1939, *Morgenthau Diary: China*.
60. Consul general at Shanghai (Gauss), memorandum to McHugh, April 13, 1939, Box 1, Folder 3, McHugh Papers, Cornell.
61. Irene Baldwin, interview with author, March 2003.
62. Pickler, "United States Aid to the Chinese Nationalist Air Force," 12.
63. Daniel Ford, *Flying Tigers: Claire Chennault and the American Volunteer Group* (Washington, DC: Smithsonian Institution Press, 1991), 22.
64. Wagner, "Chinese Air Force," 166.
65. Undated notes by William Pawley, Jr.
66. Randall Gould, *China in the Sun* (Garden City, NY: Doubleday, 1946), 214.

Chapter 3. Pawley and Chennault
1. WDP to Annie-Hahr, October 11, 1934, private collection of Irene Baldwin.
2. Ibid., May 1, 1935.
3. Ibid., July 19, 1935.

4. Ibid.

5. "Society News," *Miami Daily News*, September 22, 1935.

6. Annie-Hahr, cablegram (and handwritten note) to WDP, May 13, 1936, private collection of Irene Baldwin.

7. Boyd Heber Bauer, "General Claire Lee Chennault and China: 1937–1958" (PhD diss., American University, Washington, DC, 1973), 63.

8. Chargé d'affaires in China (Gauss), telegram to secretary of state Hull, January 25, 1935, FRUS 1935: 3, 18.

9. Hull, telegram to chargé d'affaires in China (Gauss), January 26, 1935, FRUS 1935: 3, 21.

10. Consul general at Shanghai (Cunningham) to secretary of state, June 10, 1935, FRUS 1935: 3, 225. See also memorandum by Raymond C. Mackay, Division of Far Eastern Affairs, August 24, 1935, FRUS 1935: 3, 339.

11. Charles R. Bond, Jr., and Terry Anderson, *A Flying Tiger's Diary* (College Station: Texas A & M University Press, 1984), 8; and Sterling Seagrave, *The Soong Dynasty* (New York: Harper & Row, 1985), 360.

12. Pickler, "United States Aid to the Chinese Nationalist Air Force," 14–15.

13. Claire Lee Chennault, *Way of a Fighter: The Memoirs of Claire Lee Chennault* (New York: G. P. Putnam's Sons, 1949), 38.

14. Counselor of embassy in China (Willys Ruggles Peck), telegram to secretary of state, February 6, 1936, FRUS 1936: 4, 555.

15. Memorandum by Raymond C. Mackay, Division of Far Eastern Affairs, August 24, 1935, FRUS 1935: 3, 339.

16. Robert Moody Smith and Philip D. Smith, *With Chennault in China: A Flying Tiger's Diary* (Blue Ridge Summit, PA: Tab Books, 1984), 4.

17. Bond, *Flying Tiger's Diary*, 7.

18. Chennault, *Way of a Fighter*, 11–12.

19. Ford, *Flying Tigers*, 15.

20. Martha Byrd, *Chennault: Giving Wings to the Tiger* (Tuscaloosa: University of Alabama Press, 1987), 60.

21. William M. Smith, Jr., "Claire Lee Chennault: The Early Years" (Master's thesis, Northeast Louisiana University, Monroe, 1989), 166; "See Them at the Air Races," *Miami Herald*, December 10, 1935; and "Program Given for Maneuvers," *Miami Herald*, December 12, 1935. In *Way of a Fighter*, 29, Chennault erroneously recalls the January 1936 Pan-American Air Show in Miami as their final performance. See also, Maurer Maurer, *Aviation in the U.S. Army, 1919–1939* (Washington, DC: Office of Air Force History, 1987), 421.

22. *Air Corps News Letter* 19, no. 2 (Washington, DC: Information Division, Air Corps), January 15, 1936.

23. Reginald Cleveland, "Army Air Armada Opens Miami Meet," *New York Times*, January 11, 1935; and Sterling Seagrave, *Soldiers of Fortune* (Alexandria, VA: Time-Life Books, 1981), 75–76. Byrd (*Chennault*, 60) and Ford (*Flying Tigers*, 17) place the meeting with Mao at the December 1935 show; however, there is no record of Mao being in Miami at that time.

24. "Reception Is Arranged for Chinese Officials," *Miami Herald*, January 6, 1935; photo caption of Pawley with Chinese delegation, *Miami Herald*, January 10, 1935; "Chinese Minister of Aviation Will Be Honored at Smart Afternoon Fete," *Miami Daily News*, January 6, 1935; and "Chinese Air Chief Finds Things 'Just Lovely' in Miami Area," *Miami Daily News*, January 9, 1935.

25. Malcolm Rosholt, *Claire L. Chennault: A Tribute* (Rosholt, WI: Flying Tigers of the 14th Air Force Association, 1983), 5; and Ford, *Flying Tigers*, 17.

26. "Roney Plaza Hotel Plans Two Events," *Miami Daily News*, January 9, 1935; "Important

Figures in World of Events Attend Reception," *Miami Daily News*, January 10, 1935; "Amused Smiles Greet Mention of Chop Suey," *Miami Daily News*, January 18, 1935; and "Brilliant Reception Honors General Mow," *Miami Herald*, January 11, 1935.

27. "Chinese Village in Coral Gables Setting for Tea," *Miami Daily News*, January 13, 1935; and "Scenes at Chinese Village Tea," *Miami Daily News*, January 14, 1935.

28. "Ball for Aviators Will Be Colorful," *Miami Herald*, January 12, 1935; and "Widely Known Guests Attend Dance," *Miami Herald*, January 14, 1935.

29. *Air Corps News Letter* (Washington, DC: Information Division, Air Corps), February 1, 1935.

30. *Air Corps News Letter* 19, no. 16 (Washington, DC: Information Division, Air Corps), August 15, 1936.

31. Jerome A. Ennels, "Those Daring Young Men: The Role of Aero Demonstration Teams in the Evolution of Pre–World War II Pursuit Tactics, 1932–1937" (Research paper, Office of History, Air University, Maxwell Air Force Base, AL, 1994), 26.

32. Pickler, "United States Aid to the Chinese Nationalist Air Force," 18–19; and Smith, "Claire Lee Chennault," 182.

33. Byrd, *Chennault*, 60; and Smith, "Claire Lee Chennault," 198.

34. Consul at Shanghai (Gauss), telegram to secretary of state, August 15, 1937, FRUS 1937: 4, 520.

35. Secretary of state, telegram to consul at Shanghai (Gauss), August 17, 1937, FRUS 1937: 4, 521.

36. Secretary of state, telegram to consul at Hong Kong (Howard Donovan), August 21, 1937, FRUS 1937: 4, 522. See also chief of the Division of Far Eastern Affairs (Maxwell McGaughey Hamilton), memorandum of conversation, FRUS 1938: 3, 28.

37. Ambassador in China (Johnson), telegram to secretary of state, September 1, 1937, FRUS 1937: 4, 523.

38. Secretary of State, telegram to Ambassador in China (Johnson), September 7, 1937, FRUS 1937: 4, 525.

39. Byrd, *Chennault*, 61.

40. Michael Schaller, *The U.S. Crusade in China, 1938–1945* (New York: Columbia University Press, 1979), 69.

41. "MacArthur, Bride Visiting Here," *San Francisco Examiner*, May 9, 1937.

42. William C. McDonald, Jr., "The Chennault I Remember," *Air Power Historian* 6 (April 1959): 89; Bauer, "General Claire Lee Chennault and China," 65; and Seagrave, *Soldiers of Fortune*, 81.

43. Chennault, *Way of a Fighter*, 32–33.

44. Rosholt, *Claire L. Chennault*, 5.

45. Seagrave, *Soong Dynasty*, 360.

46. Chennault, *Way of a Fighter*, 38; and Wagner, "Chinese Air Force," 167.

47. Ford, *Flying Tigers*, 21.

48. Annie-Hahr to Pawley, September 3, 1936, private collection of Irene Baldwin.

49. Annie-Hahr McKay, interview with author, March 2003.

50. Pawley, cablegram to Annie-Hahr, May 7, 1937, with additional handwritten notes by Annie-Hahr, private collection of Irene Baldwin.

51. Photo caption, "Southern Sunshine," *Miami Tribune*, May 14, 1937.

52. Pawley family, interview by author, March 2003; and "Edward P. Pawley Dies after Illness," *Miami Herald*, July 3, 1937.

53. "Leaves for Duke," *Miami Herald*, September 22, 1937.

54. Bond, *Flying Tiger's Diary*, 8.

55. Ford, *Flying Tigers*, 21.

56. Chennault, *Way of a Fighter*, 39; Seagrave, *Soldiers of Fortune*, 82–83; and Bond, *Flying Tiger's Diary*, 9.

57. Robert Lee Scott, Jr., *Flying Tiger: Chennault of China* (Garden City, NY: Doubleday, 1959), 83–84.
58. Philip N. Brown, "Claire Lee Chennault: Military Genius" (Research paper, Air War College, Maxwell Air Force Base, AL, 1995), 13–14.
59. Ford, *Flying Tigers*, 22.
60. Gould, *China in the Sun*, 215.
61. "Chinese Air Bombs Kill 600 in Shanghai," *New York Times*, August 15, 1937.
62. Martin Caidin, *The Ragged, Rugged Warriors* (New York: E. P. Dutton, 1966), 55; and William M. Smith, Jr., "Mercenary Eagles: American Pilots Serving in Foreign Air Forces Prior to United States Entry into the Second World War, 1936–1941" (PhD diss., University of Arkansas, Fayetteville, 1999), 114.
63. Ford, *Flying Tigers*, 23–24.
64. Wanda Cornelius and Thayne Short, *Ding Hao: America's Air War in China, 1937–1945* (Gretna, LA: Pelican Publishing, 1980), 89.
65. Bauer, "General Claire Lee Chennault and China," 72.
66. Wagner, "Chinese Air Force," 166.
67. Byrd, *Chennault*, 87–88.
68. Bauer, "General Claire Lee Chennault and China," 71.
69. Chennault, *Way of a Fighter*, 70.
70. Caidin, *Ragged, Rugged Warriors*, 72.
71. Bernard C. Nalty, *Tigers over Asia* (New York: Elsevier-Dutton, 1978), 26; and Seagrave, *Soong Dynasty*, 361.
72. Consul at Hong Kong (Southard), dispatch to secretary of state, December 2, 1937, National Archives, 893.113/1665.
73. Consul at Hong Kong (Southard), dispatch to secretary of state, December 22, 1937, FRUS 1937: 4, 547.
74. Charles Barton, "Wings for the Dragon," *Air & Space*, April–May 1988, 85.
75. Byrd, *Chennault*, 94–95.
76. Report No. 1-39.
77. Handwritten notes, undated, Box 4, Folder 4, McHugh Papers, Cornell.
78. Letter from WDP to Annie-Hahr, November 29, 1937, private collection of Irene Baldwin.
79. Sp. agent to secretary of the treasury, June 9, 1941, *Morgenthau Diaries*, 406:233.
80. Office of Coordinator of Information Report, November 27, 1941, *Morgenthau Diaries*, 468:359.

Chapter 4. Competition and War Clouds

1. Pickler, "United States Aid to the Chinese Nationalist Air Force," 12.
2. Minutes of meeting, February 11, 1938, Box 1, Folder 2; Box 2, Folder 14, McHugh Papers, Cornell.
3. Shamburger, *Curtiss Hawks*, 246; and Ford, *Flying Tigers*, 28–29.
4. Chennault, *Way of a Fighter*, 71.
5. Ibid., 70; and Jack Samson, *Chennault* (New York: Doubleday, 1987), 28.
6. Byrd, *Chennault*, 85.
7. Duane Schultz, *The Maverick War: Chennault and the Flying Tigers* (New York: St. Martin's Press, 1987), 73.
8. Elwyn Gibbon, "Commuting to War," *Collier's,* November 12, 1938, 72.
9. Chennault, *Way of a Fighter*, 70; and Caidin, *Ragged, Rugged Warriors*, 73.
10. Smith, "Claire Lee Chennault," 241; and Pickler, "United States Aid to the Chinese Nationalist Air Force," 23.
11. Samson, *Chennault*, 28–29.

12. Edward L. Leiser, "Memoirs of Pilot Elwyn H. Gibbon, the Mad Irishman," *American Aviation Historical Society Journal*, Spring 1978, 4.
13. Ford, *Flying Tigers*, 29.
14. Gibbon, "Commuting to War," 71.
15. Byrd, *Chennault*, 85.
16. Chennault, *Way of a Fighter*, 71.
17. Cornelius, *Ding Hao*, 91.
18. Nalty, *Tigers over China*, 26–27; Samson, *Chennault*, 29; and Schultz, *Maverick War*, 73.
19. Chennault, *Way of a Fighter*, 71.
20. Smith, "Mercenary Eagles," 123.
21. "Foreign Legion of Air Disbanded by China," *New York Times*, March 24, 1938.
22. Report No. 1-39.
23. Handwritten notes, April 2, 1939, Box 4, Folder 4, McHugh Papers, Cornell.
24. McHugh to naval attaché (Harvey Edward Overesch) at American Embassy in Peiping, February 16, 1938, Box 1, Folder 2; and McHugh to Skipper, October 2, 1938, Box 1, Folder 3, McHugh Papers, Cornell.
25. Morgan to Hanes, October 27, 1939, *Morgenthau Diary: China*.
26. Smiley, "The Private Wars."
27. Ford, *Flying Tigers*, 36.
28. Robert B. Hotz, *With General Chennault: The Story of the Flying Tigers* (Washington, DC: Zenger, 1943), 198; and Pickler, "United States Aid to the Chinese Nationalist Air Force," 58.
29. Olga S. Greenlaw, *The Lady and the Tigers* (New York: E. P. Dutton, 1943), 246.
30. "New Route, New Factory," *Time* 34 (November 13, 1939): 24–25; and William C. Johnstone, *The United States and Japan's New Order* (New York: Oxford University Press, 1941), 192.
31. Edgar Snow, *The Battle for Asia* (New York: World Publishing, 1942), 181.
32. "China Swashbuckler."
33. Byrd, *Chennault*, 97.
34. Sebie Biggs Smith, "Reminiscences of Sebie Biggs Smith: Oral History, 1981," 99–100 (Columbia University Oral History Research Office Collection, Columbia University, NY). (Hereafter CUOHROC.)
35. Ibid., 127–28.
36. Chennault to Commission of Aeronautical Affairs, December 13, 1938, Box 1, Folder 3, McHugh Papers, Cornell.
37. Chennault to Burdette S. Wright, December 13, 1938, Box 2, Folder 14, McHugh Papers, Cornell.
38. Samson, *Chennault*, 123.
39. Pawley to Chennault, January 31, 1939, Box 1, Folder 3, McHugh Papers, Cornell.
40. Memorandum of conversation between Paul Meyer and Chennault, February 27, 1939, Box 4, Folder 4, McHugh Papers, Cornell.
41. Handwritten notes, undated, Box 4, Folder 4, McHugh Papers, Cornell.
42. Arthur N. Young, *China and the Helping Hand, 1937–1945* (Cambridge, MA: Harvard University Press, 1963), 139.
43. Ford, *Flying Tigers*, 36.
44. Shamburger, *Curtiss Hawks*, 104, 246.
45. Michael Schaller, *The United States and China in the Twentieth Century* (New York: Oxford University Press, 1990), 57.
46. Young, *China and the Helping Hand*, 139.
47. Byrd, *Chennault*, 98.
48. Acting secretary of state (Benjamin Sumner Welles), telegram to chargé d'affaires in China (Peck), March 21, 1939, FRUS 1939: 3, 744–45.

49. Chargé d'affaires in China (Peck), telegram to secretary of state, March 28, 1939, FRUS 1939: e, 745; and summary of contract detailed in *Morgenthau Diaries*, 187: 352–53.
50. Addendum to Report No. 1-38 (April 10, 1939), July 27, 1939, 2, 8, Box 4, Folder 4, McHugh Papers, Cornell.
51. Letter addressed to Tom, July 18, 1939, Box 1, Folder 4, McHugh Papers, Cornell.
52. Memorandum Re: Purchase by Chinese Government of Airplanes and Airplane Parts, *Morgenthau Diaries*, 187:351.
53. McHugh to Paul Meyer, July 26, 1939, Box 1, Folder 4, McHugh Papers, Cornell.
54. Addendum to Report No. 1-38.
55. Letter addressed to Tom.
56. Handwritten notes, undated.
57. McHugh to Paul Meyer, July 26, 1939, Box 1, Folder 4, McHugh Papers, Cornell.
58. Handwritten notes, August 10, 1939, Box 4, Folder 4, McHugh Papers, Cornell.
59. Chennault to McHugh, August 4, 1939, Box 4, Folder 4, McHugh Papers, Cornell.
60. McHugh to Paul Meyer, July 26, 1939, Box 1, Folder 4, McHugh Papers, Cornell.
61. McHugh, memorandum to the American ambassador, August 18, 1939, Box 4, Folder 4, McHugh Papers, Cornell.
62. Byrd, *Chennault*, 99.
63. Ford, *Flying Tigers*, 37.
64. American consul at Rangoon (Austin C. Brady) to secretary of state, January 10, 1940; and U.S. consul at Rangoon, telegram to secretary of state, February 8, 1940, *Morgenthau Diaries*, 234:136, 240:227.
65. Dr. Louis L. Williams, Jr., to Dr. Thomas Parran, Jr., Surgeon General of the United States, January 8, 1940, *Morgenthau Diaries*, 242:6–8.
66. Memorandum by chief of the Division of Far Eastern Affairs (Hamilton), January 3, 1940, FRUS 1939: 3, 773–74.
67. Leiser, "Memoirs of Pilot Elwyn H. Gibbon," 14.
68. William D. Pawley, *Americans Valiant and Glorious* (New York: Caleb Printing, 1945), 5–6.
69. Leighton's meeting with the chief of naval operations is detailed in a sixty-nine-page memorandum prepared by John King Fairbank in 1942 at the request of Roosevelt adviser Lauchlin Currie (Fairbank memorandum), 3. I am indebted to Dr. William M. Leary, Coulter Professor of History, University of Georgia, who provided me with a copy.
70. Byrd, *Chennault*, 120; and Ford, *Flying Tigers*, 38.

Chapter 5. Money and Men for a Volunteer Group
1. Young, *China and the Helping Hand*, 131.
2. Samson, *Chennault*, 62.
3. "China Essay Contest On," *New York Times*, April 7, 1940.
4. Pawley, "Russia Is Winning," 31–32.
5. Transcript, William Douglas Pawley oral history interview, April 4, 1967, 9, Hoover Library.
6. Young, *China and the Helping Hand*, 133.
7. Ford, *Flying Tigers*, 39.
8. Young, *China and the Helping Hand*, 133.
9. Summary of telephone conversation, July 23, 1940, *Morgenthau Diaries*, 285:295.
10. Minutes of meeting, September 25, 1940, *Morgenthau Diary*, 308:156–57, and 305:211–15.
11. Charles F. Romanus and Riley Sunderland, *Stilwell's Mission to China* (Washington, DC: Office of the Chief of Military History, Department of the Army, 1953), 8.
12. Young, *China and the Helping Hand*, 135.

13. Memorandum by the chief of the Division of Far Eastern Affairs (Hamilton), January 3, 1940, FRUS 1939: 3, 773–74; and Young, *China and the Helping Hand*, 148–49.
14. Pawley, "Russia Is Winning," 2.
15. Secretary of the navy (William Franklin Knox) to secretary of state, October 19, 1940, FRUS 1940: 4, 671.
16. State Department, memorandum to Navy Department, October 23, 1940, FRUS 1940: 4, 677.
17. Johnstone, *The United States and Japan's New Order*, 92.
18. Byrd, *Chennault*, 106.
19. Edward R. Stettinius, Jr., *Lend-Lease: Weapon for Victory* (New York: Macmillan, 1944), 116; Smith, *With Chennault in China*, 4–5; Bond, *Flying Tiger's Diary*, 10; and "Chiang Aide in America to Obtain Further Help," *Japan Times and Advertiser*, November 7, 1940.
20. Ambassador in China (Johnson), telegram to secretary of state, October 20, 1940, FRUS 1940: IV, 673.
21. Romanus, *United States Army in World War II*, 9.
22. American consul at Rangoon (Brady), memorandum to secretary of state, March 9, 1940, *Morgenthau Diaries*, 246:165.
23. American vice consul at Rangoon (W. Leonard Parker), telegram to secretary of state, July 20, 1940, *Morgenthau Diaries*, 284:314.
24. American vice consul at Rangoon (Parker), dispatch to secretary of state, August 12, 1940, National Archives, 600.45C9/12. See also *Morgenthau Diaries*, 324:143.
25. Fairbank memorandum, 3.
26. U.S. consul in Rangoon (Brady) to secretary of state, October 22, 1940, *Morgenthau Diaries*, 324:143.
27. Ford, *Flying Tigers*, 42. A report filed by Ed Pawley with American ambassador to China Nelson T. Johnson indicated that thirty-six Japanese bombers took part in the raid. (Dispatch No. 704, Johnson to secretary of state, November 19, 1940, *Morgenthau Diaries*, 331:157.)
28. U.S. consul in Rangoon (Brady) to secretary of state, January 8, 1941, FRUS 1941: V, 598–99.
29. Dispatch No. 704.
30. U.S. consul in Rangoon (Brady), telegram to secretary of state, November 4, 1940, FRUS 1940: 4, 907.
31. Memo by vice consul at Kunming (Stephen C. Brown), November 20, 1940, *Morgenthau Diaries*, 331:162.
32. "Mekong Bridge Destruction Is Fatal," *Japan Times and Mail*, November 2, 1940; and "Japanese Air Raids Make Road Useless," *Japan Times and Advertiser*, November 12, 1940.
33. Memo by chief of the Division of Controls (Joseph Coy Green), October 31, 1940, FRUS 1940: 4, 683. Roosevelt created the Liaison Committee on December 6, 1939. Its purpose was to establish contacts with foreign governments that wanted to purchase war materials from the United States. The committee provided clearance for contracts signed for war materials, ensuring that goods were being shipped only to friendly nations.
34. Fairbank memorandum, 4.
35. Young, *China and the Helping Hand*, 141.
36. Romanus, *United States Army in World War II*, 10–11; and Smith, *With Chennault in China*, 5.
37. Stettinius, *Lend-Lease*, 116.
38. Byrd, *Chennault*, 109.

39. G. E. Forbush, memorandum to Morgenthau, November 28, 1940, *Morgenthau Diaries*, 332:340.
40. Samuel Klaus, interoffice communication to Morgenthau, November 28, 1940, *Morgenthau Diaries*, 332:286.
41. Memorandum of conversation, December 10, 1940, *Morgenthau Diaries*, 342-A:10.
42. Map from Soong, *Morgenthau Diaries*, 342-A:13; and meeting with Roosevelt, December 20, 1940, *Morgenthau Diaries*, 342-A:18.
43. Transcript of meeting, December 20, 1940, *Morgenthau Diaries*, 342-A:18.
44. Young, *China and the Helping Hand*, 142.
45. Romanus, *United States Army in World War II*, 11–12.
46. Undersecretary of state (Welles), memorandum of conversation, December 14, 1940, FRUS 1940: 4, 711.
47. Pawley to army historian Charles F. Romanus, July 6, 1950, National Archives, His 330.14 CBI 1950.
48. U.S. ambassador in China (Johnson), telegram to secretary of state, November 5, 1940, FRUS 1940: 4, 685.
49. Secretary of state (Hull), memorandum of conversation, November 26, 1940, FRUS 1940: 4, 697.
50. Transcript of meeting, November 30, 1940, *Morgenthau Diaries*, 333:251–58.
51. Ford, *Flying Tigers*, 39.
52. Schultz, *Maverick War*, 8.
53. Monica Lynne Niznik, "Thomas G. Corcoran: The Public Service of Franklin Roosevelt's 'Tommy the Cork'" (PhD diss., University of Notre Dame, IN, 1981), 536–37, 565–66.
54. Samson, *Chennault*, 63; Byrd, *Chennault*, 113, 120; Schultz, *Maverick War*, 8; and Niznik, "Thomas G. Corcoran," 542.
55. Memorandum by chief of the Division of Controls (Green), November 5, 1940, FRUS 1940: 4, 685.
56. Memorandum by advisor on political relations (Stanley K. Hornbeck), November 6, 1940, FRUS 1940: 4, 686.
57. Memorandum by chief of the Division of Controls (Green), November 7, 1940, FRUS 1940: 4, 686.
58. Philip Young, memorandum to Morgenthau, November 30, 1940, *Morgenthau Diaries*, 333:291.
59. Transcript of meeting at Morgenthau's home, *Morgenthau Diaries*, 334:4–20.
60. Jesse Jones to Roosevelt, December 2, 1940, *Morgenthau Diaries*, 334:27.
61. Press release by the president, November 30, 1940, *Morgenthau Diaries*, 334:28.
62. Ibid.; and Young, *China and the Helping Hand*, 136.
63. Department of State, oral statement to Chinese Embassy, December 4, 1940, FRUS 1940: 4, 705–708; Young, *China and the Helping Hand*, 142; and Romanus, *United States Army in World War II*, 11.
64. "The History and Status of the First American Volunteer Group," 9-10, Box 4, Folder 5, McHugh Papers, Cornell. For the complete memorandum, see *Morgenthau Diaries*, 342-A:4–7. See also Byrd, *Chennault*, 109.
65. Notes of meeting, December 3, 1940, *Morgenthau Diaries*, 342-A:2.
66. Translation of telegram from Chiang to Roosevelt, December 12, 1940, *Morgenthau Diaries*, 342-A:15.
67. Memorandum of conversation, December 18, 1940, *Morgenthau Diaries*, 342-A:12.
68. Notes on conference at Morgenthau's home, December 21, 1940, *Morgenthau Diaries*, 342-A:24–25.
69. Memo of meeting at Stimson's home with Morgenthau, Knox, and Marshall, December 22, 1940, *Morgenthau Diaries*, 342-A:27.

70. Notes on conference in office of secretary of state, December 23, 1940, *Morgenthau Diaries*, 342:47–49.
71. Notes on conference, January 1, 1941, *Morgenthau Diaries*, 344:12.
72. Byrd, *Chennault*, 112.
73. Transcript of meeting, January 2, 1941, *Morgenthau Diaries*, 344:35–37; transcript of meeting, January 3, 1941, *Morgenthau Diaries*, 344:253, 259; and transcript of meeting, November 18, 1941, *Morgenthau Diaries*, 463:17–19.
74. Morgenthau to Hull, January 10, 1941, *Morgenthau Diaries*, 346:383-A, 342:51. Apparently Curtiss-Wright had already assumed the AVG would get the planes because its records show billing to China began January 6, 1941. See, Shamburger, *Curtiss Hawks*, 144.
75. Minutes of group meeting at Treasury Department, December 23, 1940, *Morgenthau Diaries*, 342:77–82.
76. Young to Morgenthau, January 10, 1941, *Morgenthau Diaries*, 346:382.
77. Young to Morgenthau, January 13, 1941, *Morgenthau Diaries*, 347:83.
78. British Embassy, aide-mémoire to U.S. Department of State, January 7, 1941, FRUS 1941: 5, 597–98.
79. Ford, *Flying Tigers*, 52.
80. American consul at Rangoon (Brady) to secretary of state, January 8, 1941, *Morgenthau Diaries*, 346:112; and consul at Rangoon (Brady) to secretary of state, January 8, 1941, FRUS 1941: 5, 598–99.
81. Chadbourne, Wallace, Park & Whiteside to Senator Claude Pepper, January 3, 1945, Box 39, Folder: Confidential Report about People: William D. Pawley, Morgenthau Collection, FDR Library.
82. Young to Morgenthau, January 27, 1941, *Morgenthau Diaries*, 351:300.
83. Pawley to Young, February 3, 1941, *Morgenthau Diaries*, 370:67.
84. Group meeting minutes, Treasury Department, January 30, 1941, *Morgenthau Diaries*, 353:20–21.
85. Confidential FBI report, 25.
86. Ron Heiferman, *Flying Tigers: Chennault in China* (New York: Ballantine, 1971), 18; Fairbank memorandum, 8; and Stettinius, *Lend-Lease*, 117.
87. Chennault, *Way of a Fighter*, 100–101.
88. Notes on meetings, *Morgenthau Diaries*, 342-A:24; 344:2.
89. Telephone transcript, Morgenthau with Senator Claude Denson Pepper, January 3, 1945, Confidential Report about People.

Chapter 6. Those Willing to Take the Risk

1. Forrest C. Pogue, *George C. Marshall: Ordeal and Hope* (New York: Viking, 1966), 353; and Romanus, *United States Army in World War II*, 17–18.
2. Paul R. Scott to Senator Claude Pepper, December 21, 1944, Confidential Report about People.
3. Young, *China and the Helping Hand*, 149.
4. Nalty, *Tigers over Asia*, 33; and Byrd, *Chennault*, 116.
5. Attachment to Pawley letter to army historian Charles F. Romanus, July 6, 1950, National Archives, His 330.14 CBI 1950. (This is a copy of a letter dated February 18, 1941, from Pawley in Washington, DC, to Octavio Cuevas at Intercontinent offices in New York, instructing Cuevas to "send the following cable to Eddie." [Edward Pawley].)
6. Joseph Alsop and Robert Kintner, "Lauchlin Currie's Report on China," *Washington Post*, March 25, 1941.
7. Phone conversation between Corcoran and Morgenthau, February 21, 1941, *Morgenthau Diaries*, 374:163–65.

8. Alfred Edward Housman, "Epitaph on an Army of Mercenaries," *Last Poems* (New York: Henry Holt, 1965), 144.
9. Peter Dale Scott, *The War Conspiracy: The Secret Road to the Second Indochina War* (Indianapolis: Bobbs-Merrill, 1972), 7. The Fairbank memorandum says Roosevelt gave "verbal assent" to the releasing of American servicemen for duty in China (p. 18). See also, Byrd, *Chennault*, 116–17.
10. Smith, "Mercenary Eagles," 215.
11. Fairbank memorandum, 18.
12. Ibid., 18–19.
13. Larry M. Pistole, *The Pictorial History of the Flying Tigers* (Orange, VA: Moss Publications, 1981), 41.
14. Malcolm Rosholt, *Days of the Ching Poa: A Photographic Record of the Flying Tigers–14th Air Force in China in World War II* (Amherst, WI: Palmer Publications, 1978), 24.
15. Russell Whelan, *The Flying Tigers: The Story of the American Volunteer Group* (New York: Viking, 1942), 33.
16. Pawley, *Americans Valiant and Glorious*, 6.
17. Chennault, *Way of a Fighter*, 102–3.
18. Fairbank memorandum, 19–20. In 1932, Royal Canadian Air Force fliers offered their services to China. They were even willing to renounce their citizenship to fight in the undeclared war. "Canadian Flyers Waive Citizenship," *San Antonio Express*, March 2, 1932.
19. George Bookman, "U.S. Releases Pilots to Fight for China," *Washington Post*, June 1, 1941; and Fairbank memorandum, 20.
20. Byrd, *Chennault*, 117–18.
21. Samson, *Chennault*, 67.
22. Pawley, "Russia Is Winning," 59C.
23. McLemore, "Flying Tigers and Bill Pawley."
24. Walter W. Pentecost and James J. Sloan, "Advance of the Flying Tigers," *American Aviation Historical Society Journal*, Summer 1970, 137–38. Since learning to fly at the age of sixteen, Pentecost remained in aviation and became a project engineer on a portion of the Manned Orbiting Laboratory (MOL).
25. Smith, *With Chennault*, 16.
26. Ford, *Flying Tigers*, 5, 60 ff.
27. Byrd, *Chennault*, 117.
28. Fairbank memorandum, 20.
29. "The History and Status of the First American Volunteer Group," October 19, 1941, 5, Box 4, Folder 5, McHugh Papers, Cornell.
30. Fairbank memorandum, 20.
31. Copy of original agreement signed by George T. Burgard, August 27, 1941, http://www.members.tripod.com/Flying-tiger-ace/id39.htm (accessed August 9, 2010).
32. James H. Howard, *Roar of the Tiger* (New York: Orion, 1991), 62–63.
33. Romanus, *United States Army in World War II*, 18.
34. Nalty, *Tigers over China*, 46.
35. Byrd, *Chennault*, 120.
36. Chennault, *Way of a Fighter*, 107.
37. Cornelius, *Ding Hao*, 108.
38. Ford, *Flying Tigers*, 69.
39. Chennault, *Way of a Fighter*, 109.
40. Smith, *With Chennault*, 21.
41. Howard, *Roar of the Tiger*, 77.
42. Pentecost, "Advance of the Flying Tigers," 138.

43. Chennault, *Way of a Fighter*, 106.
44. Scott, *Flying Tiger*, 59.
45. Pentecost, "Advance of the Flying Tigers," 138–39.
46. Ibid., 139.
47. Byron A. Glover, "Assembling and Testing P-40's in Burma," *Aviation*, December 1942, 97–98.
48. Walter Pentecost, "Here Come the Flying Tigers!," *Liberty*, July 25, 1942, 42.
49. Pentecost, "Advance of the Flying Tigers," 139, 143.
50. Howard, *Roar of the Tiger*, 78.
51. Smith, *With Chennault*, 21; and Chennault, *Way of a Fighter*, 100.
52. Chennault, *Way of a Fighter*, 110.
53. Young, *China and the Helping Hand*, 151–52.
54. Cornelius, *Ding Hao*, 109.
55. "Reminiscenses of Paul W. Frillmann: Oral History, 1962," 108, CUOHROC.
56. Paul Frillmann and Graham Peck, *China: The Remembered Life* (Boston: Houghton Mifflin, 1968), 56.
57. Ford, *Flying Tigers*, 64, 71.
58. Frillmann, *Remembered Life*, 65.
59. Heiferman, *Flying Tigers*, 25.
60. Smith, *With Chennault*, 19.
61. "'Convoys' to China," *Time* 32 (June 23, 1941): 34.
62. Erik Shilling, *Destiny: A Flying Tiger's Rendezvous with Fate* (private printing, 1993), 73.
63. Fairbank memorandum, 23.
64. Schaller, *U.S. Crusade in China,* 77; and Romanus, *United States Army in World War II*, 18. The *Northampton* sank during the war, and the *Salt Lake City* was used in the Bikini atoll bomb test after the war.
65. Smith, *With Chennault*, 17, 19; and Howard, *Roar of the Tiger*, 70.
66. Schultz, *Maverick War*, 109.
67. Gregory Boyington, *Baa Baa Black Sheep* (New York: G. P. Putnam's Sons, 1958), 15.
68. Schultz, *Maverick War*, 109.
69. O'Dowd Gallagher, *Retreat in the East* (London: George G. Harrap, 1942), 86.
70. *Fei Hu: The Story of the Flying Tigers*, video transcript, transcript by Frank Boring, directed by Frank Christopher (Santa Barbara, CA: Fei Hu Films, 1993), 11, http://www.flyingtigersvideo.com (accessed August 15, 2010).
71. Boyington, *Baa Baa Black Sheep*, 16.
72. Pentecost, "Here Come the Flying Tigers!," 42.
73. Chennault, *Way of a Fighter*, 103.
74. Fairbank memorandum, 23.
75. Consul at Rangoon (Brady), dispatch to secretary of state, July 14, 1941, FRUS 1941: 5, 675.
76. Marshall to Currie, June 16, 1941, *Morgenthau Diaries*, 421:366.
77. Byrd, *Chennault*, 125.
78. Pentecost, "Advance of the Flying Tigers," 143.
79. Robert E. Sherwood, *Roosevelt and Hopkins: An Intimate History* (New York: Harper & Brothers, 1948), 403.
80. William L. Langer and S. Everett Gleason, *The Undeclared War, 1940–1941* (New York: Harper & Brothers, 1953), 711.
81. Sherwood, *Roosevelt and Hopkins*, 405.
82. Pentecost, "Advance of the Flying Tigers," 143.
83. Rosholt, *Claire L. Chennault*, 11.
84. Shilling, *Destiny*, 87.

85. Caidin, *Ragged, Rugged Warriors*, 213; and Scott, *Flying Tiger*, 61, 69.
86. Howard, *Roar of the Tiger*, 64.
87. Stettinius, *Lend-Lease*, 117; and Malcolm Rosholt, *Flight in the China Air Space: 1910–1950* (Rosholt, WI: Rosholt House, 1984), 110.
88. Langer, *Undeclared War*, 711–12.
89. Russ Johnston, "Japs Are Their Specialty," *Flying* 31, no. 2 (August 1942): 24.
90. Ford, *Flying Tigers*, 76.
91. Pawley to Chennault, September 8, 1941, Chennault Papers, Hoover Institution. I am indebted to Ray Wagner for providing me a copy.

Chapter 7. The Tiger Roars
1. Greenlaw, *Lady and the Tigers*, 43–44; and Ford, *Flying Tigers*, 79.
2. Boyington, *Baa Baa Black Sheep*, 42; Stanley Weintraub, *Long Day's Journey into War: December 7, 1941* (New York: Truman Talley Books-Dutton, 1991), 383; and Seagrave, *Soldiers of Fortune*, 86.
3. Byrd, *Chennault*, 127.
4. Seagrave, *Soldiers of Fortune*, 86; and Byrd, *Chennault*, 129.
5. Chennault, *Way of a Fighter*, 135; and Howard, *Roar of the Tiger*, 104.
6. Walter Pentecost, "Date with Destiny," *Liberty*, August 1, 1942, 24.
7. Johnston, "Japs Are Their Specialty," 24.
8. Disney Studios also designed the Fighting Eagle logo for the American Eagle Squadron fighting in England. See Smith, "Mercenary Eagles," 165. According to Willauer, Chennault insisted that the tiger symbol was based on the Louisiana State University mascot. See Niznik, "Thomas G. Corcoran," 543n; and Byrd, *Chennault*, 136.
9. Shilling, *Destiny*, 288; and Ford, *Flying Tigers*, 119–20.
10. Soong to coordinator of information (Donovan), August 16, 1941, FRUS 1941: 5, 705–8.
11. Sherwood, *Roosevelt and Hopkins*, 408–9.
12. Stettinius, *Lend-Lease*, 118.
13. Currie, telegram to Hornbeck, November 1, 1941, FRUS 1941: 5, 737.
14. T. V. Soong, memorandum to Morgenthau, November 8, 1941, *Morgenthau Diaries*, 459:237.
15. O.C.I. Report, November 27, 1941, *Morgenthau Diaries*, 468:359.
16. Ford, *Flying Tigers*, 85.
17. Romanus, *United States Army in World War II*, 24.
18. Schultz, *Maverick War*, 124.
19. Chennault, *Way of a Fighter*, 118.
20. Pawley, *Americans Valiant and Glorious*, 6–7.
21. Chennault, *Way of a Fighter*, 118.
22. Fairbank memorandum, 58.
23. "Flying Tigers," *Miami Herald*, January 3, 1971.
24. Schultz, *Maverick War*, 125.
25. Chennault, *Way of a Fighter*, 132.
26. Bond, *Flying Tiger's Diary*, 40.
27. Byrd, *Chennault*, 129–31.
28. Young, *China and the Helping Hand*, 153; and Stettinius, *Lend-Lease*, 118.
29. Byrd, *Chennault*, 133.
30. Johnston, "Japs Are Their Specialty," 86.
31. Howard, *Roar of the Tiger*, 94.
32. Weintraub, *Long Day's Journey into War*, 383; and Boyington, *Baa Baa Black Sheep*, 44.
33. "Flying Tigers," *Miami Herald*.
34. Byrd, *Chennault*, 134–35.

35. Shamburger, *Curtiss Hawks*, 145.
36. Pentecost, "Advance of the Flying Tigers," 144.
37. Ford, *Flying Tigers*, 95.
38. Pawley, *Wings over Asia*, 13.
39. Byrd, *Chennault*, 135.
40. Smith, *With Chennault*, 32.
41. Shamburger, *Curtiss Hawks*, 145–46; and Byrd, *Chennault*, 135.
42. Gallagher, *Retreat in the East*, 83; and Byrd, *Chennault*, 135.
43. Ford, *Flying Tigers*, 125–32. Henry Gilbert was one of the pilots killed. Ford wrote, "Gilbert was two months past his twenty-second birthday. As the story was told, he had married just before embarking on *Klipfontein*, and his wife, who was pregnant, did not even have a photograph to remember him by."
44. Gallagher, *Retreat in the East*, 84; Nalty, *Tigers over Asia*, 65; and Johnston, "Japs Are Their Specialty," 86.
45. Byrd, *Chennault*, 135.
46. Frillmann, *Remembered Life*, 97; and Shamburger, *Curtiss Hawks*, 147.
47. "Flying Tigers," *Miami Herald*; Pawley, *Americans Valiant and Glorious*, 7; and Nalty, *Tigers over Asia*, 69.
48. Chennault, *Way of a Fighter*, 134.
49. Holz, *With General Chennault*, 46–47; Seagrave, *Soldiers of Fortune*, 91; Frillmann, *Remembered Life*, 98; Nalty, *Tigers over Asia*, 69; Samson, *Chennault*, 100; and Ford, *Flying Tigers*, 143, 149.
50. Ford, *Flying Tigers*, 149, 154.
51. Schultz, *Maverick War*, 161.
52. Chennault, *Way of a Fighter*, 131–32.
53. Samson, *Chennault*, 122.
54. Nalty, *Tigers over Asia*, 65; and Chennault, *Way of a Fighter*, 132.
55. Schultz, *Maverick War*, 161–62.
56. Letter from Pawley to Chennault, January 11, 1942, in Schultz, *Maverick War*, 162.
57. Ibid.
58. McHugh to Currie, January 13, 1942, Box 1, Folder 9, McHugh Papers, Cornell.
59. Confidential FBI report, 26.
60. Seagrave, *Soldiers of Fortune*, 94.
61. J. Helsdon Thomas, *Wings over Burma* (Braunton, Devon, England: Merlin Books, 1984), 30.
62. Shamburger, *Curtiss Hawks*, 150–51.
63. "Flying Tigers," *Newsweek* 19 (April 6, 1942): 20.
64. Shamburger, *Curtiss Hawks*, 151.
65. Ibid., 151; and Smith, *With Chennault*, 112.
66. Gallagher, *Retreat in the East*, 88–89.
67. "China Swashbuckler," *Time*.
68. Melvin D. Hildreth, letter to the editor, *New York Times*, April 16, 1944.
69. Randy Roberts and James S. Olson, *John Wayne: American* (New York: Free Press, 1995), 218–19; Johnston, "Japs Are Their Specialty," 22–23; and Ford, *Flying Tigers*, 361.
70. Closing credits, written by Kenneth Gamet and Barry Trivers, *Flying Tigers*, VHS, directed by David Miller (Hollywood, CA: Republic Pictures Corporation, 1942).
71. "Lectures Scheduled," *Washington Post*, October 7, 1945.
72. *Art News*, August 1–31, 1945, 24.
73. "Tribute to the Tigers," *Art Digest*, August 1, 1945, 17.
74. Notice of exhibition, Smithsonian Institution Archives, Record Unit 311, Box 41, Folder 16.

75. Invitation lists from Intercontinent Corporation, Smithsonian Institution Archives, Record Unit 311, Box 41, Folder 16.
76. "Flying Tiger Art Exhibit Opens," *Museum of Aviation News* (Warner Robins, GA) 1 (Fall 1998): 1.
77. Pawley, *Americans Valiant and Glorious*, 11; and Romanus, *United States Army in World War II*, 17–18.
78. Samson, *Chennault*, 254.
79. Chennault, *Way of a Fighter*, 133.

Chapter 8. Divorce and Remarriage
1. "Factory in India Overhauls 600 Aircraft in One Year," *American Aviation*, September 15, 1945, 93.
2. "China Swashbuckler"; and Samson, *Chennault*, 122.
3. "Factory in India."
4. "India Plans Factory," *American Aviation*, July 1, 1941, 42.
5. Shamburger, *Curtiss Hawks*, 106.
6. "Plane Factory Steel Unloaded in Miami Today," *Miami Daily News*, November 5, 1940.
7. "Largest War Industry in Florida Is Purchased by Vultee Aircraft," *New York Times*, July 18, 1942; "Vultee Purchases Intercontinent Aircraft Corp.," *American Aviation*, August 1, 1942, 35; and "Intercontinent Incorporated in Miami," *American Aviation*, February 1, 1941, 47.
8. "American Makes Planes in India," *Life* 14 (March 22, 1943): 30.
9. Pawley to Cox, August 27, 1942, Oscar Cox Collection, Box 26, Pawley file, FDR Library.
10. Wesley Frank Craven and James Lea Cate, eds., *The Army Air Forces in World War II*, vol. 5, *The Pacific: Matterhorn to Nagasaki* (Washington, DC: Government Printing Office, 1983), 182–83.
11. Pawley, "Russia Is Winning," 41A.
12. Jonathan Daniels, *White House Witness: 1942–1945* (Garden City, NY: Doubleday, 1975), 226–27.
13. William D. Pawley, "Pawley Sees Vast Trade if Britain, U.S. Co-Operate," *Miami Daily News*, February 11, 1945.
14. Pawley, "Russia Is Winning," 42–43.
15. Personal notes, Irene Pawley Baldwin, September 24, 2004.
16. Greenlaw, *Lady and the Tigers*, 80.
17. Annie-Hahr, telegram to Intercontinent, November 4, 1939, private collection of Irene Baldwin.
18. Annie-Hahr, cable to WDP, May 23, 1940, private collection of Irene Baldwin.
19. "China Swashbuckler."
20. Confidential FBI report, 18.
21. Unsigned memorandum to Stettinius, December 16, 1944, Franklin D. Roosevelt Papers as President, Official File, Pawley Folder, FDR Library.
22. *Pawley v. Pawley*, 46 So.2d 464 (April 6, 1950).
23. "Pawley's Ex-Wife Asks $5,000 Extra Alimony," *Miami Herald*, September 8, 1946.
24. Annie-Hahr McKay, interview with author, March 2003.
25. *Snafu*, George Army Air Field newspaper, Lawrenceville, IL, March 27, 1943.
26. Notes courtesy of William Pawley, Jr.
27. Pawley family, interview with author, March 2003.
28. Confidential FBI report, 2.
29. Unsigned memorandum to Stettinius.
30. "Envoy Pawley Sued by Wife for Support," *Miami Daily News*, September 7, 1946.

31. "Pawley's Ex-Wife."
32. "Pawley Says Income Far Below Claim," *Miami Herald*, October 23, 1946.
33. Unsigned memorandum to Stettinius.
34. *Pawley v. Pawley.*
35. "Pawley's Divorce in Cuba Upheld," *Miami Daily News*, June 2, 1948.
36. C. G. Berning, "Pawley's Cuban Divorce Is Upheld as Former Wife Loses Florida Suit," *Miami Herald*, June 2, 1948.
37. *Pawley v. Pawley.*
38. *Pawley v. Pawley*, 340 U.S. 866 (October 23, 1950).
39. Cover letter from William D. Hassett (secretary to the president) to acting secretary of state Joseph H. Grew, April 27, 1945, White House Central Files: Official File (WHCF: OF) 534, Truman Papers, Truman Library.
40. Letter to MIS, September 23, 1942, CIA File F81-0351-D0367, CIA Pawley File 78435, National Archives.
41. Dispatch 127, CMI CRA, January 15, 1945, CIA File F81-0351-D0367, CIA Pawley File 78435, National Archives.
42. Mary Jane Sertel to Annie-Hahr, November 24, 1944, private collection of Annie-Hahr McKay.
43. Irene Baldwin, interview with author, March 2003.
44. Hannegan to Truman, April 17, 1945, WHCF:OF 534, Truman Papers, Truman Library.
45. "Pawley Named Envoy to Peru," *Miami Daily News*, May 31, 1945.
46. Pawley, "Russia Is Winning," 50–51.
47. Telephone transcript between Morgenthau and Stettinius, December 18, 1944, Confidential Report about People.
48. Currie, memorandum to FDR, December 21, 1944; and FDR, memorandum to Morgenthau, December 22, 1944, Franklin D. Roosevelt Papers as President, Official File, Pawley Folder, FDR Library.
49. Currie to Morgenthau, December 23, 1944, Confidential Report about People.
50. FDR, memorandum to Morgenthau, December 23, 1944, Franklin D. Roosevelt Papers as President, Official File, Pawley Folder, FDR Library.
51. Chief Special Agent Fitch to Edward Stettinius, December 19, 1944, Vertical File, Pawley, William D., FDR Library.
52. Telephone transcript between Morgenthau and Stettinius, December 30, 1944, Confidential Report about People.
53. Telephone transcript between Morgenthau and Pepper, January 3, 1945, Confidential Report about People.
54. Telephone transcript between Hannegan and Morgenthau, March 13, 1945, *Morgenthau Diaries*, 827:145–51.
55. Elmer Lincoln Irey, memorandum to Morgenthau, February 15, 1945, Confidential Report about People.
56. Minutes of group meeting at the Treasury Department, March 24, 1945, *Morgenthau Diaries*, 832:23–34.
57. Confidential FBI report, 22–23.
58. Morgenthau, memorandum to FDR, March 24, 1945, Franklin D. Roosevelt Papers as President, Official File, Pawley Folder, FDR Library.
59. Pawley, "Russia Is Winning," 51.
60. Drew Pearson, "Foreign Policy Storm Due Soon," *Washington Post*, December 31, 1944.
61. Pawley, "Russia Is Winning," 75–77.
62. Williamson Murray and Allan R. Millett, *A War to Be Won: Fighting the Second World War* (Cambridge, MA: Belknap Press of Harvard University Press, 2000), 482.
63. Pawley, "Russia Is Winning," 55–56.

Chapter 9. Peru and Brazil

1. Pawley, "Russia Is Winning," 57.
2. Minerals attaché in Peru (William O. Vanderburg), memorandum to ambassador in Peru (White), February 1, 1945, FRUS 1945: IX, 1333–35.
3. Editorial, "Ambassador 'Bill' Pawley," *Miami Herald*, June 1, 1945; and Editorial, "Ambassador Bill," *Miami Daily News*, June 1, 1945.
4. "Pawley Takes Oath as New Envoy to Peru," *Miami Herald*, June 17, 1945.
5. Pawley, "Russia Is Winning," 58.
6. Ibid., 59C–60, 64–65.
7. Ibid., 67.
8. Cecil B. Lyon to Anita Pawley, May 20, 1948, with attachment of Department of State Office Memorandum dated May 17, 1948; and Cecil B. Lyon to Pawley, May 10, 1948, Cecil Lyon Papers, Box 1, Folder 55, Georgetown University Library.
9. Evelyn Peyton Gordon, "Evie Figures Bess Should Ease Up on Social Security," *Washington Daily News*, October 17, 1945.
10. "Peru Names President," *New York Times*, July 23, 1945.
11. "New Head of Peru Outlines Policies," *New York Times*, June 27, 1945.
12. *Encyclopaedia Britannica 2011*, s.v. "Víctor Raúl Haya de la Torre," http://www.britannica.com/EBchecked/topic/257669/Victor-Raul-Haya-de-la-Torre.
13. Pawley, "Russia Is Winning," 68–72.
14. Smiley, "The Private Wars," 11.
15. "Peruvian Minister Tells of New Goals," *New York Times*, December 6, 1945.
16. Memorandum from Pawley to State Department, "Report of Our Accomplishments in Peru," undated, WHCF: President's Secretary's Files (PSF), Truman Papers, Truman Library.
17. "Apra Enters," *Time* 47 (February 4, 1946): 47.
18. Pawley, telegram to secretary of state (Dean Acheson), February 2, 1946, FRUS 1946: 11, 1251.
19. Pawley, telegram to Acheson, January 30, 1946, FRUS 1946: 11, 1265.
20. Pawley, telegram to Acheson, February 9, 1946, FRUS 1946: 11, 1266.
21. Pawley, telegram to Acheson, February 23, 1946, FRUS 1946: 11, 1266–67.
22. Pawley, telegram to Acheson, April 10, 1946, FRUS 1946: 11, 1267–68.
23. Memorandum by acting assistant chief of the Division of North and West Coast Affairs (Hall), July 25, 1946, FRUS 1946: 11, 1268–69.
24. Medal for Merit Board to Truman, February 23, 1946, WHCF: OF 357-C, Truman Papers, Truman Library.
25. Ibid.; and "Truman Decorates Pawley," *New York Times*, May 14, 1946.
26. Memorandum by chief of the Division of North and West Coast Affairs (Flack), October 18, 1945, FRUS 1945: 9, 1323.
27. Pawley to secretary of state, April 3, 1946, FRUS 1946: 11, 1210–13.
28. Memorandum by assistant chief of the Division of North and West Coast Affairs (Wells), May 6, 1946, FRUS 1946: 11, 1214–15.
29. Memorandum by assistant chief of the Division of North and West Coast Affairs (Wells), May 17, 1946, FRUS 1946: 11, 1215.
30. Secretary of state (Byrnes), telegram to chargé d'affaires in Peru (Donnelly), May 31, 1946, FRUS 1946: 11, 1216.
31. Pawley to Truman, letter of resignation, May 14, 1946, WHCF: OF 534, Truman Papers, Truman Library; and chargé d'affaires in Peru (Donnelly), telegram to secretary of state (Byrnes), June 6, 1946, FRUS 1946: 11, 1216–17.
32. Pawley, "Russia Is Winning," 83–85.
33. Pawley, telegram to secretary of state (Byrnes), June 8, 1946, FRUS 1946: 11, 1217–

18; and chargé d'affaires in Peru (Donnelly), telegram to secretary of state (Byrnes), June 28, 1946, FRUS 1946: 11, 1218–19.

34. Cooper, telegram to secretary of state, October 26, 1946, FRUS 1946: 11, 1225–27.
35. "Brazil Accepts Pawley," *New York Times*, April 5, 1946; and "Named to Argentina," *New York Times*, April 10, 1946.
36. "Messersmith Seen in Argentine Post," *New York Times*, April 3, 1946.
37. Pawley, "Russia Is Winning," 87, 90.
38. Ibid., 87.
39. Letters and memos between Pawley and secretary of treasury (Snyder), October and November 1947, Snyder Papers, Truman Library; and Pawley, "Russia Is Winning," 142–43.
40. "Vargas Says Berle Aided in Downfall," *New York Times*, December 5, 1946.
41. Pawley, "Russia Is Winning," 108–11.
42. Ibid., 88–92.
43. Margaret Acer, "Life's Calmer Now," *Miami Daily News*, April 15, 1959.
44. Jerry Hannifin, "Pawley Style Diplomacy," June 27, 1947, dispatches from *Time* magazine correspondents, 1942–1955, Houghton Library, Harvard University, Folder 409.
45. Years later, as CIA deputy director, Walters testified before the Senate Watergate Committee. He had been labeled a "good friend" of the White House who was placed in the CIA to "have some influence over the agency" and get the CIA to "shoulder the blame" for the Watergate break-in. See Marjorie Hunter, "Dean Says White House Put a 'Friend' in C.I.A.," *New York Times*, June 26, 1973.
46. Pawley to Truman, August 12, 1946, WHCF: CF, Truman Papers, Truman Library.
47. Pawley, "Russia Is Winning," 111–12.
48. Translation of address by president of the Constituent Assembly of Brazil (Fernando de Melo Viana), WHCF: CF, Truman Papers, Truman Library.
49. Eisenhower to Pawley, August 10, 1946, in Dwight David Eisenhower, *Papers of Dwight David Eisenhower: The Chief of Staff*, ed. Louis Galambos (Baltimore: John Hopkins University Press, 1978), 1232.
50. Pawley, "Russia Is Winning," 141–42.
51. Pawley to Braddock, June 15, 1946, FRUS 1946: 11, 138–40.
52. Acheson, telegram to Pawley, June 15, 1946, FRUS 1946: 11, 140–41.
53. Messersmith, telegram to secretary of state, June 21, 1946, FRUS 1946: 11, 141.
54. Pawley to Clayton, July 23, 1946, FRUS 1946: 11, 144–45.
55. Acheson, telegram to Messersmith, September 5, 1946, FRUS 1946: 11, 149–50.
56. Pawley, airgram to secretary of state, January 22, 1947, FRUS 1947: 8, 467–68.
57. "Pawley Dispels Rumors," *New York Times*, April 5, 1947; and Richard F. O'Toole, memorandum to chief of the Division of Brazilian Affairs (Dawson), March 3, 1947, FRUS 1947: 8, 468–69.
58. Leo I. Highby of the International Resources Division, memorandum to Dawson, April 23, 1947, FRUS 1947: 8, 469–70.
59. Pawley, telegram to secretary of state, August 30, 1947, FRUS 1947: 8, 473.
60. Marshall, telegram to Pawley, September 12, 1947, FRUS 1947: 8, 474.
61. Pawley, "Russia Is Winning," 113–14.
62. Assistant secretary of state for political affairs (Armour), memorandum to undersecretary of state (Lovett), October 4, 1947, FRUS 1947: 8, 476–79.
63. Pawley testimony, Senate subcommittee hearing, "Communist Threat to the United States through the Caribbean," 743, September 2 and 8, 1960 (Washington, DC: Government Printing Office, 1960). (Hereafter cited as Pawley testimony, "Communist Threat.")
64. Lovett, telegram to Pawley, October 17, 1947, FRUS 1947: 8, 479–80.
65. Pawley, "Russia Is Winning," 115.

66. Lovett, telegram to Pawley.
67. Pawley, "Russia Is Winning," 116.
68. "Ambassador Pawley's Grave Revelation," as quoted in the *Congressional Record–Senate*, 87th Cong., 1st sess., April 18, 1961, A2581.
69. Hannifin, "Pawley Style Diplomacy."
70. "Pawley's Testament," *Time* 51 (April 26, 1948): 35.

Chapter 10. Latin American Diplomacy
1. Pawley to Tom C. Clark, July 19, 1946, Clark Papers, Truman Library.
2. Pawley to Hoover, August 29, 1946, in Pawley, "Russia Is Winning," 122.
3. Clark to Pawley, August 16, 1946, Clark Papers, Truman Library.
4. Pawley, "Russia Is Winning," 122–23.
5. Military Intelligence memorandum, March 5, 1947, Pawley testimony, "Communist Threat," 716–21.
6. Pawley, "Russia Is Winning," 95.
7. Von der Becke to Pawley, March 13, 1961, National Archives, Pawley CIA file.
8. Military Intelligence memorandum, March 5, 1947, Pawley testimony, "Communist Threat," 720.
9. Pawley, "Russia Is Winning," 96.
10. Pawley testimony, "Communist Threat," 721–22; and Pawley, "Russia Is Winning," 97–100.
11. Pawley testimony, "Communist Threat," 717.
12. Pawley, telegram to secretary of state, February 25, 1946, FRUS 1946: 11, 222.
13. Anthony Leviero, "Byrnes Reaffirms U.S. View on Peron," *New York Times*, October 23, 1946.
14. Spruille Braden, *Diplomats and Demagogues: The Memoirs of Spruille Braden* (New Rochelle, NY: Arlington House, 1971), 364.
15. Leviero, "Byrnes Reaffirms."
16. Bertram D. Hulen, "Braden Supported by Byrnes, Truman," *New York Times*, November 1, 1946.
17. Frank Kluckhohn, "Halsey By-passes Argentina on Tour," *New York Times*, July 25, 1946.
18. Braden, *Diplomats and Demagogues*, 379.
19. "Denies Braden Is Quitting," *New York Times*, January 29, 1946.
20. Drew Pearson, "Why Braden Resigned," *Washington Post*, June 17, 1946.
21. "Braden Showdown on Argentina Seen," *New York Times*, October 22, 1946.
22. Drew Pearson, "Miami's Ambassador Bill Pawley Denies He's after Braden's Job," *Miami Herald*, October 20, 1946.
23. "The Braden-Pawley Feud," *Newsweek,* November 18, 1946, 27.
24. Braden, *Diplomats and Demagogues*, 379–80.
25. Pawley, "Russia Is Winning," 118.
26. Augusto Bernardino Leguía y Salcedo (1863–1932) was a Peruvian politician who twice occupied the presidency of Peru, from 1908 to 1912 and from 1919 to 1930. Pearson, "Why Braden Resigned."
27. Pawley, "Russia Is Winning," 119–20.
28. Memorandum by Braden, July 16, 1946, FRUS 1946: 11, 22–23.
29. Pawley, telegram to Byrnes, August 2, 1946, FRUS 1946: 11, 23–24; and Messersmith, telegram to Byrnes, August 24, 1946, FRUS 1946: 11, 25.
30. Pawley, telegram to Byrnes, December 20, 1946, FRUS 1946: 11, 26–27.
31. Byrnes, telegram to Pawley, December 21, 1946, FRUS 1946: 11, 27.
32. Eisenhower, *Papers of Dwight David Eisenhower,* 1469fn.

33. Eisenhower to Pawley, January 31, 1947, William D. Pawley Papers, Box 1, Folder 3, George C. Marshall Library. (Hereafter cited as Pawley Papers.)
34. Pawley to Clark, June 13, 1947, Clark Papers, Truman Library.
35. Pawley to Truman, May 31, 1947, Clark Papers, Truman Library.
36. Pawley to Clark, June 2, 1947, Clark Papers, Truman Library.
37. Pawley to Clark, June 13, 1947, Clark Papers, Truman Library.
38. Clark to Pawley, June 25, 1947, Clark Papers, Truman Library.
39. Pawley to Clark, June 13, 1947, Clark Papers, Truman Library.
40. Truman's appointment book for March 25, April 4, April 9, and April 24, 1947, WHCF: SF, Truman Papers, Truman Library.
41. "Pawley Sees Truman," *New York Times*, July 19, 1947; and memorandum of telephone conversation between Pawley, Clark Clifford, and Walter Donnelly, August 5, 1947, WHCF: SF, Truman Papers, Truman Library.
42. Marshall, memorandum to Truman, July 31, 1947, WHCF: OF, Truman Papers, Truman Library; and Bertram Hulen, "Marshall to Head Delegation at Rio," *New York Times*, August 2, 1947.
43. Pawley to Truman, July 31, 1947; and Truman to Pawley, August 12, 1947, WHCF: OF, Truman Papers, Truman Library.
44. Vernon A. Walters, *Silent Missions* (Garden City, NY: Doubleday, 1978), 144.
45. Forrest C. Pogue, *George C. Marshall: Statesman* (New York: Viking Press, 1987), 382.
46. Senate Committee on Foreign Relations, *A Decade of American Foreign Policy* (Washington, DC: Government Printing Office, 1950), 421–26.
47. Walter Donnelly, memorandum of telephone conversation with Pawley, August 2, 1947, FRUS 1947: supplement, 127.
48. "Marshall Misses Dance," *New York Times*, August 20, 1947.
49. Pawley, telegram to Connelly, August 21, 1947, WHCF, Truman Papers, Truman Library; Margaret Truman, *Harry S. Truman* (New York: William Morrow, 1973), 375; and "*Salve!*," *Time* 50 (September 15, 1947): 21–22.
50. "Truman Dislikes 'Missouri Waltz,'" *Houston Chronicle*, December 29, 1960.
51. Diary entry, September 3, 1947, Diaries of William D. Leahy (Library of Congress microfilm edition, University of Texas at Arlington), 72.
52. Pawley, "Russia Is Winning," 144–46.
53. "*Salve!*"
54. Diary entry, September 3, 1947, Diaries of William D. Leahy (Library of Congress microfilm edition, University of Texas at Arlington), 73.
55. C. P. Trussell, "Truman Safe as Auto Skids on Brazilian Mountain Road," *New York Times*, September 7, 1947; and "*Salve!*"
56. C. P. Trussell, "President Sailing Directly for Home aboard Battleship," *New York Times*, September 8, 1947.
57. "*Carioca* Climax," *Time* 50 (September 15, 1947): 34.
58. Joe Alex Morris, ed., *The Private Papers of Senator Vandenberg* (Westport, CT: Greenwood Press, 1952), 371.
59. "Pawley Leaves Today for U.S.," *New York Times*, September 28, 1946.
60. Pawley, "Russia Is Winning," 128.
61. "Pawley to Take Sick Leave," *New York Times*, October 26, 1946; and "Ambassador Pawley in Hospital," *New York Times*, November 2, 1946.

Chapter 11. El Bogotazo

1. "Pawley Returning to U.S.," *New York Times*, September 20, 1947.
2. Pawley to Marshall, December 26, 1947, Pawley Papers.
3. "Ambassador Pawley to Assist in Preparatory Work for Inter-American Conference at Bogotá." *Department of State Bulletin* 18, no. 448 (February 1, 1948): 149.

Notes

4. David Green, "The Cold War Comes to Latin America," in *Politics and Policies of the Truman Administration*, ed. Barton J. Bernstein (Chicago: Quadrangle Books, 1970), 175–76.
5. Pawley to Marshall, December 26, 1947, Pawley Papers.
6. "Customers' Man," *Time* 51 (February 16, 1948): 51.
7. Memorandum of conversation, State Department, January 19, 1948, Clayton-Thorp Papers, Truman Library.
8. Pawley to Truman, February 12, 1948, WHCF: CF, Truman Papers, Truman Library.
9. Pawley, memorandum to Truman, February 12, 1948, WHCF: CF, Truman Papers, Truman Library.
10. Diary entry, January 23, 1948, Diaries of William D. Leahy (Library of Congress microfilm edition, University of Texas at Arlington), 7–8.
11. Martin to Pawley, February 11, 1949, WHCF: SF, Truman Papers, Truman Library.
12. Pawley to Truman, February 17, 1948, WHCF: SF, Truman Papers, Truman Library.
13. "No Bogota Applause for U.S. Half Billion," *New York Times*, April 9, 1948.
14. Pawley to Marshall, March 8, 1948, Pawley Papers.
15. "Diplomats Resign Posts," *New York Times*, March 17, 1948; "William D. Pawley," *New York Times*, March 27, 1948; and Pawley to Truman, February 5, 1948, WHCF: OF, Truman Papers, Truman Library.
16. Truman to Pawley, February 19, 1948, WHCF: OF, Truman Papers, Truman Library.
17. "Pawley's Testament."
18. Motley to Truman, March 30, 1948, and Truman to Motley, April 7, 1948, WHCF: PSF, Truman Papers, Truman Library.
19. Milton Bracker, "Bogota News Curb Called Complete," *New York Times*, April 13, 1948.
20. Pawley, "Russia Is Winning," 151, 158–61, 163–64.
21. Undated letter by Edna Pawley, Pawley Papers; and Bertram D. Hulen, "Marshall Visits Colombian Center," *New York Times*, April 5, 1948.
22. Willard L. Beaulac, *Career Ambassador* (New York: Macmillan, 1951), 235.
23. Ibid., 236; and Mario Lazo, *Dagger in the Heart: American Policy Failures in Cuba* (New York: Funk & Wagnalls, 1968), 129.
24. William D. Pawley, "The Bogotá Uprising" (unpublished monograph, George Marshall Library, Lexington, VA), 4.
25. Lazo, *Dagger*, 129–30.
26. Fidel Castro, interview transcript, published in *El Siglo* (Bogotá), Latin American Network Information Center (Austin: University of Texas, April 11, 1982), http://lanic.utexas.edu/project/castro/db/1982/19820411.html (accessed August 13, 2010).
27. Georgie Anne Geyer, *Guerrilla Prince: The Untold Story of Fidel Castro* (Boston: Little, Brown, 1991), 79–81.
28. William S. White, "Marshall Scoffed at Early Warnings on Reds in Bogota," *New York Times*, April 16, 1948.
29. Lazo, *Dagger*, 130; Geyer, *Guerrilla Prince*, 82; and "Focus on Bogota," *New York Times*, April 11, 1948.
30. Nathaniel Weyl, *Red Star over Cuba: The Russian Assault on the Western Hemisphere* (New York: Devin-Adair, 1960), 10–12.
31. Scotland Yard Report by Sir Norman Smith, 15, July 8, 1948, British Public Record Office, Ref. F0371168217.
32. Beaulac, *Career Ambassador*, 242.
33. Fidel Castro, interview transcript.
34. Pawley, "The Bogotá Uprising," 23, 32.

35. "Bogota Uprising Is Quelled, Coalition Regime Formed; Parley's Fate Left to U.S.," *New York Times*, April 11, 1948.

36. "Colombia Battles Leftist Mobs Burning and Looting the Capital; Inter-American Parley Is Halted," *New York Times*, April 10, 1948; and Milton Bracker, "Bogota Talks to Continue; Martial Law in Colombia; Red Role in Uprising Seen," *New York Times*, April 12, 1948.

37. Edna Pawley to Celeste, April 17, 1948, Pawley Papers.

38. Beaulac, *Career Ambassador*, 242.

39. Pawley testimony, "Communist Threat," 725.

40. Pawley, "Russia Is Winning," 186.

41. Beaulac, telegram to secretary of state, April 24, 1948, State Department Files, 821.00/4-2348, National Archives.

42. Fidel Castro, interview transcript.

43. Beaulac, *Career Ambassador*, 245.

44. Edna Pawley to Celeste.

45. Pawley, "The Bogotá Uprising," 38.

46. W. O. Galbraith, *Colombia: A General Survey* (New York: Royal Institute of International Affairs, 1953), 131.

47. Beaulac, *Career Ambassador*, 247.

48. Walters, *Silent Missions*, 164–65; and Bracker, "Bogota Talks to Continue."

49. Bertram D. Hulen, "Pan-America Talks Resume in Bogota," *New York Times*, April 15, 1948; and Pawley, "The Bogotá Uprising," 50–52.

50. Milton Bracker, "Marshall Leaves Bogota as Parley Nears Conclusion," *New York Times*, April 24, 1948.

51. Pawley to Truman, April 20, 1948, WHCF: PSF, Truman Papers, Truman Library.

52. Pawley, "The Bogotá Uprising," 47–48.

53. Beaulac, *Career Ambassador*, 256.

54. Bertram Hulen, "U.S. Aide Commends Results of Bogota," *New York Times*, April 30, 1948.

55. Milton Bracken, "Success in Bogota Held Exaggerated," *New York Times*, May 3, 1948.

56. Ruby Hart Phillips, *The Cuban Dilemma* (New York: Ivan Obolensky, 1962), 17–18.

57. Drew Pearson, "Del Pino—Once a Castro Man—Now Hates Him," *Miami Herald*, April 16, 1959.

58. Green, "The Cold War Comes to Latin America," 177.

59. Edna Pawley to Celeste.

Chapter 12. Spain, a Movie Star, and India

1. "Pawley's Son to Wed on June 17," *New York Times*, June 1, 1948.

2. Memorandum by Miss Barrows, July 6, 1948, WHCF: GF, Truman Papers, Truman Library.

3. "C. D. Pawleys United in Church on Anniversary of First Date," *Miami Herald*, June 18, 1948; Personally Speaking column, *Miami Herald*, June 19, 1948; and "Miss DePass, Mr. Pawley Marry in Beach Church," *Miami Daily News*, June 18, 1948.

4. Oral history interview, Matthew J. Connelly, November 30, 1967, 285, Truman Library.

5. Anthony Leviero, "Something New Is Added at the White House," *New York Times*, August 1, 1948.

6. Oral history interview, Oscar L. Chapman, August 18, 1972, Truman Library.

7. Oral history interview, Matthew J. Connelly, 290.

8. Oral history interview, Tom. C. Clark, October 17, 1972, 174, Truman Library.

9.   Johnson, telegram to Pawley, October 16, 1948, WHCF: OF, Truman Papers, Truman Library.
10. Johnson to Connelly, October 16, 1948, WHCF: OF, Truman Papers, Truman Library.
11. Pawley, telegram to Johnson, undated, WHCF: OF, Truman Papers, Truman Library.
12. Pawley to Marshall, October 19, 1948, Pawley Papers.
13. Anita Pawley to Cecil B. Lyon, August 25, 1948, Cecil Lyon Papers, Box 1, Folder 55, Georgetown University Library.
14. Arthur P. Whitaker, *Spain and Defense of the West: Ally and Liability* (New York: Harper & Brothers, 1961), 36.
15. Pawley, "Russia Is Winning," 225–26.
16. Whitaker, *Spain and Defense of the West*, 17.
17. Pawley to Franco, February 1, 1963, Pawley Papers.
18. Pawley, "Russia Is Winning," 229–33.
19. Ibid., 233–34.
20. Long, telegram to Truman, November 3, 1948, WHCF: OF, Truman Papers, Truman Library.
21. C. L. Sulzberger, "U.S. Diplomats Abroad Deplore Private Envoys," *New York Times*, November 8, 1948.
22. Pawley, "Russia Is Winning," 229.
23. Pawley to Marshall, May 9, 1949, Pawley Papers.
24. Pawley, "Russia Is Winning," 235–37.
25. Pawley to Marshall, May 9, 1949.
26. Truman, telegram to Pawley, April 23, 1949; WHCF: President's Personal File (PPF), Truman Papers, Truman Library.
27. Clark, handwritten note to Pawley, April 22, 1949, Clark Papers, Truman Library.
28. Brenda Maddox, *Who's Afraid of Elizabeth Taylor?* (New York: M. Evans, 1977), 66; Dick Sheppard, *Elizabeth: The Life and Career of Elizabeth Taylor* (Garden City, NY: Doubleday, 1974), 64; and Fred Tasker, "The Man Who Would Marry Liz," *Miami Herald*, February 27, 1997.
29. William D. Pawley, Jr., "Elizabeth Taylor's First White Diamond" (unpublished manuscript), 24.
30. William Pawley, Jr., interview with author, April 17, 2003.
31. Elizabeth Taylor, *Elizabeth Taylor: An Informal Memoir* (New York: Harper & Row, 1964), 27.
32. "Elizabeth Taylor to Wed Pawley's Son Next Year," *Miami Daily News*, June 7, 1949.
33. Sheppard, *Elizabeth*, 67.
34. "Elizabeth Taylor and Fiance, William D. Pawley Jr.," *New York Herald Tribune*, June 8, 1949.
35. Grace Wing, "High School May Delay Pawley-Taylor Nuptials," *Miami Daily News*, June 8, 1949; and "Elizabeth Taylor and Pawley Set February for Wedding," *Miami Herald*, June 8, 1949.
36. Tasker, "The Man Who Would Marry Liz."
37. C. David Heymann, *Liz: An Intimate Biography of Elizabeth Taylor* (New York: Birch Lane Press, 1995), 75–76.
38. "Pawley Engagement Off," *New York Times*, September 20, 1949.
39. Tasker, "The Man Who Would Marry Liz."
40. "Barkley Derides Foes' Talk of 'Statism,' Sees Victories," *New York Times*, December 3, 1949.
41. Pawley to Acheson, November 29, 1949, Acheson Papers, Truman Library.
42. Boyle to Donald S. Dawson, January 11, 1951, WHCF: OF, Truman Papers, Truman Library.

43. Eisenhower to Pawley, February 16, 1951, in Eisenhower, *Papers of Dwight David Eisenhower*, 59; and Pawley, "Russia Is Winning," 239.

44. "Appointment of Officers—William Pawley," *Department of State Bulletin* 24, no. 611 (March 19, 1951): 477; "Pawley, Former Envoy, Made Aide to Acheson," *New York Times*, February 20, 1951; and "Pawley Is Aide to Acheson," *Miami Daily News*, February 19, 1951.

45. Jack Thale, "Diplomatic Job Handed to Pawley," *Miami Herald*, February 20, 1951.

46. Editorial, "Pawley at Peak of Career," *Miami Daily News*, February 20, 1951.

47. "Annie Hahr Pawley, Mr. McKay Wed in Quiet Ceremony Sunday," *Miami Herald*, February 5, 1951.

48. Pawley testimony, "Communist Threat," 728–29.

49. "Pawley on Mission for Acheson," *New York Times*, June 2, 1951.

50. "Hoffman and Pawley in Madrid," *New York Times*, June 14, 1951; and "U.S. Reassures India," *New York Times*, June 23, 1951.

51. Pawley to Franco, February 1, 1963, Pawley Papers.

52. Paul Preston, *Franco: A Biography* (New York: Basic Books, 1994), 611.

53. Pawley, "Russia Is Winning," 241–43.

54. Ibid., 243.

55. Bruce K. Holloway, introduction to unpublished Pawley manuscript, June 21, 1975, private collection of Dudley Whitman.

56. Pawley, "Russia Is Winning," 257–58.

57. *United States Relations with China with Special Reference to the Period 1944–1949* (Washington, DC: Department of State, 1949), xvi.

58. Pawley, "Russia Is Winning," 261.

59. Appendix to "China—Statement of Hon. John F. Kennedy, of Massachusetts," *Congressional Record–House*, 81st Cong., 1st sess., February 21, 1949, A993.

60. Pawley, memorandum to Acheson, November 7, 1949, WHCF: OF, Truman Papers, Truman Library.

61. Michael Schaller, *Douglas MacArthur: The Far Eastern General* (New York: Oxford University Press, 1989), 170.

62. Webb to Pawley, December 15, 1949, Pawley testimony, "Communist Threat," 730.

63. Dean Acheson, *Present at the Creation: My Years in the State Department* (New York: W. W. Norton, 1969), 344.

64. Pawley to Gen. Marshall S. Carter, December 15, 1969, Pawley Papers.

65. Pawley, "Russia Is Winning," 278–79.

66. Anthony Kubek, *How the Far East Was Lost: American Policy and the Creation of Communist China, 1941–1949* (Chicago: Henry Regnery, 1963), 427.

67. Jonathan E. Helmreich, *Gathering Rare Ores: The Diplomacy of Uranium Acquisition, 1943–1954* (Princeton, NJ: Princeton University Press, 1986), 51–52.

68. Pawley, "Russia Is Winning," 299–302.

69. Editorial, "Aid to India," *New York Times*, May 4, 1951.

70. Pawley, "Russia Is Winning," 303.

71. "U.S. Aides in India See Prestige Loss," *New York Times*, May 13, 1951.

72. Pawley, "Russia Is Winning," 305.

73. Deputy undersecretary of state (Matthews), memorandum to executive secretary of the National Security Council (Lay), November 13, 1951, FRUS 1951: VI, 1695–98.

74. "Ambassador Pawley and the India Grain Bill," *Congressional Record–House*, 82nd Cong., 1st sess., June 26, 1951, A3898.

75. Pawley, "Russia Is Winning," 305–7.

76. Deputy undersecretary of state (Matthews), memorandum.

Chapter 13. Troubleshooting

1. Pawley, "Russia Is Winning," 307.
2. Pawley to Rankin, August 8, 1951, Karl Rankin Papers, Box 5, Folder 4, Seely G. Mudd Manuscript Library, Princeton University.
3. Pawley to Rankin, September 12, 1951, Karl Rankin Papers.
4. Constantine Brown, "MacArthur Seeking Use of Nationalists," *Miami Daily News*, February 17, 1951.
5. "Clifton Pawley Dies in Mexico; Rites Pending," *Miami Daily News*, September 27, 1951.
6. Personal notes, Irene Pawley Baldwin, September 24, 2004.
7. "Clifton Pawley Dead," *New York Times*, September 27, 1951.
8. "Pawley's Son Dies of Polio in Mexico City," *Miami Herald*, September 27, 1951.
9. Pawley, "Russia Is Winning," 307.
10. Truman, telegram to Pawley, September 28, 1951, and Pawley to Truman, October 8, 1951, WHCF: PPF&PSF, Truman Papers, Truman Library.
11. Lovett to Pawley, September 26, 1951, Pawley Papers.
12. Eisenhower to Pawley, November 24, 1951, in Eisenhower, *The Papers of Dwight David Eisenhower*, 733.
13. Eisenhower to Pawley, October 18, 1948, in ibid., 252–53.
14. Eisenhower to Pawley, February 16, 1951, in ibid., 59.
15. Eisenhower to Pawley, November 24, 1951, in ibid., 733.
16. Pawley to Acheson, November 20, 1951, and Acheson to Pawley, November 30, 1951, Acheson Papers, Truman Library.
17. Radford Mobley, "Let's Call in Bill Pawley," *Miami Herald*, January 13, 1952.
18. "Ex-Envoy to Help Lovett Speed Arms," *New York Times*, December 11, 1951.
19. Pawley, "Russia Is Winning," 310.
20. Lovett to Pawley, January 10, 1952, Pawley Papers.
21. Pawley, "Russia Is Winning," 311.
22. "Pawley Flying to Paris," *New York Times*, April 15, 1952.
23. Lovett, memorandum to Pawley, April 11, 1952, Pawley Papers.
24. Pawley, "Russia Is Winning," 312–14.
25. Eisenhower, cable to Joint Chiefs of Staff, February 11, 1952, in Eisenhower, *The Papers of Dwight David Eisenhower*, 968–69.
26. Doris M. Condit, *History of the Office of the Secretary of Defense*, vol. 2, *The Test of War, 1950–1953* (Washington, DC: Historical Office of the Secretary of Defense, 1988), 409.
27. Eisenhower, cable to Joint Chiefs of Staff.
28. Pawley, "Russia Is Winning," 314–15.
29. Lovett, memorandum to Pawley, September 16, 1952, Pawley Papers.
30. Pawley, "Russia Is Winning," 318–19.
31. Notes of meeting at India House, October 18, 1952, Pawley Papers.
32. Notes of meeting at India House, October 20, 1952, Pawley Papers.
33. Pawley, "Russia Is Winning," 320.
34. Pawley to Truman, October 1, 1950, WHCF: PPF, Truman Papers, Truman Library.
35. Personal notes, Irene Pawley Baldwin.
36. Pawley, "Russia Is Winning," 246–48.
37. Pawley to Eisenhower, November 16, 1951, in Eisenhower, *The Papers of Dwight David Eisenhower*, 734.
38. Pawley to Eisenhower, January 12, 1960, Pawley, William Douglas file, General Correspondence (Series 320), Pre-presidential Papers of Richard M. Nixon, National Archives, Pacific Region (Laguna Niguel). (Hereafter cited as Nixon Pre-presidential Papers.)

39. Pawley to Nixon, March 15, 1960, and letter from Nixon to Pawley, March 25, 1960, Nixon Pre-presidential Papers.

Chapter 14. Ike and Guatemala

1. Pawley, "Russia Is Winning," 322–25.
2. "Pawley Counts Himself in Camp of Ike," *Miami Herald*, September 3, 1952.
3. John B. McDermott, "Why Ex-Demo Envoy's in GOP," *Miami Herald*, July 28, 1960.
4. Smalley to Matt Connelly, September 3, 1952, WHCF: OF, Truman Papers, Truman Library.
5. Pogue, *George C. Marshall*, 499.
6. Pawley to Dulles, December 4, 1952, John Foster Dulles Papers, Box 63, Seeley G. Mudd Manuscript Library, Princeton University.
7. Pawley to Messersmith, January 13, 1953; and Pawley, "Russia Is Winning," 327.
8. Pawley, "Russia Is Winning," 328–29.
9. Handwritten postscript, Eisenhower to Lovett, January 28, 1952, in Eisenhower, *The Papers of Dwight David Eisenhower*, 926.
10. Eisenhower to Pawley, August 3, 1953, in ibid., 454.
11. Eisenhower to Pawley, April 9, 1955, in ibid., 1667–68. The discussion concerned Pawley's wanting the public to know that Eisenhower had not wanted to allow the Russians to enter the Pacific war in 1945. "We must remember that the Far Eastern subject was really none of our [SHAEF] business," Ike added in his letter.
12. Eisenhower to Pawley, November 15, 1955, in ibid., 1893–94. See also footnotes.
13. Stephen Schlesinger and Stephen Kinzer, *Bitter Fruit: The Untold Story of the American Coup in Guatemala* (Garden City, NY: Doubleday, 1982), 50.
14. George Black, *The Good Neighbor* (New York: Pantheon Books, 1988), 97.
15. Max Gordon, "A Case History of U.S. Subversion: Guatemala, 1954," *Science & Society* 35, no. 2 (Summer 1971): 131.
16. Carlos Castillo Armas, "How Guatemala Got Rid of the Communists," *American Mercury*, January 1955, 137–42.
17. Ronald M. Schneider, *Communism in Guatemala: 1944–1954* (New York: Frederick A. Praeger, 1959), 192–95.
18. Richard H. Immerman, *The CIA in Guatemala: The Foreign Policy of Intervention* (Austin: University of Texas Press, 1982), 108–9.
19. Piero Gleijeses, *Shattered Hope: The Guatemalan Revolution and the United States, 1944–1954* (Princeton, NJ: Princeton University Press, 1991), 229.
20. Gerald K. Haines, CIA History Staff Analysis, "CIA and Guatemala Assassination Proposals, 1952–1954," 2, June 1995, Record Group 263, National Archives.
21. Immerman, *CIA in Guatemala*, 121; and Gleijeses, *Shattered Hope*, 230.
22. Immerman, *CIA in Guatemala*, 134.
23. John Moors Cabot, *First Line of Defense: Forty Years' Experiences of a Career Diplomat* (Washington, DC: School of Foreign Service Georgetown University, 1979), 87.
24. Gleijeses, *Shattered Hope*, 255.
25. Black, *Good Neighbor*, 99.
26. Haines, "CIA and Guatemala Assassination Proposals."
27. Dulles, memorandum of conversation with the president, May 19, 1954, CDROM Id: 1981070100215, *Declassified Documents*, PSmedia.
28. Pawley, "Russia Is Winning," 330.
29. Ibid., 332–33.
30. Black, *Good Neighbor*, 100; and Haines, "CIA and Guatemala Assassination Proposals," 4.

31. Interview with Howard Hunt, episode 18, "Backyard Cold War Interviews," February 21, 1999, National Security Archives, http://www.gwu.edu/~nsarchiv/coldwar/inter-views/ (accessed August 13, 2010).
32. Philip C. Roettinger, "The Company, Then and Now," *The Progressive*, July 1986, 50.
33. Haines, "CIA and Guatemala Assassination Proposals," 4.
34. Gleijeses, *Shattered Hope*, 288–89.
35. Pawley, "Russia Is Winning," 344–45.
36. Gordon, "A Case History of U.S. Subversion," 144.
37. Pawley, "Russia Is Winning," 335A.
38. Sharon I. Meers, "The British Connection: How the United States Covered Its Tracks in the 1954 Coup in Guatemala," *Diplomatic History*, Summer 1992, 409–28.
39. Walter A. Payne, "The Guatemalan Revolution, 1944–1954: An Interpretation," *Pacific Historian*, Spring 1973, 22.
40. Meers, "The British Connection," 415.
41. Schlesinger and Kinzer, *Bitter Fruit*, 147–51.
42. Immerman, *CIA in Guatemala*, 168.
43. Pawley, "Russia Is Winning," 339.
44. Ibid., 340; and Immerman, *CIA in Guatemala,* 168.
45. Gleijeses, *Shattered Hope*, 375.
46. W. Marks Frederick, III, "The CIA and Castillo Armas in Guatemala, 1954: New Clues to an Old Puzzle," *Diplomatic History*, Winter 1990, 73.
47. Pawley, "Russia Is Winning," 341.
48. Sevilla-Sacasa to Pawley, June 19, 1954, in ibid., 343.
49. Black, *Good Neighbor*, 101.
50. David Graham, "Castillo's Guatemala," *The Nation*, May 21, 1955, 440.
51. Cullather, Nicholas, "Operation PBSUCCESS: The United States and Guatemala, 1952–1954," 90–91, CIA History Staff Report, National Archives, Guatemala Files.
52. Gordon, "A Case History of U.S. Subversion," 148–52.
53. Dulles to Pawley, July 7, 1954, John Foster Dulles Papers, Box 85, Seeley G. Mudd Manuscript Library, Princeton University.
54. Dulles, memorandum of conversation with the president, July 11, 1954, CDROM Id: 1985100102564, *Declassified Documents*, PSmedia.
55. "Pawley Back on Job for Government," *Miami Herald*, June 28, 1954.

Chapter 15. Buses and Trolleys

1.   Bryan Donaldson, "Beach Buses Show Profit While Miami Line Runs in Red," *Miami Herald*, August 21, 1955.
2.   Miami-Dade, "Transit History: 1873–1969," http://www.miamidade.gov/transit/about_history_1930.asp (accessed August 13, 2010).
3.   Pawley to Marshall, October 19, 1948, Pawley Papers.
4.   Editorial, "New Hope for Bus Improvements," *Miami Daily News*, June 12, 1948.
5.   Luther Voltz, "City Rejects Pawley Offer to Sell Two Bus Lines, Suggests Increase in Fares," *Miami Herald*, January 26, 1952.
6.   Al Neuharth, "Buses Run by Port Authority Urged for County by C of C," *Miami Herald*, May 19, 1955.
7.   Al Neuharth, "Dade Bus Plan Called a Scheme to Unload Line," *Miami Herald*, May 20, 1955.
8.   Jane Wood, "Where You Will Sit in Miami Bus Fight," *Miami Daily News*, June 22, 1955; and Jane Wood, "Has Bus System Taken Mr. Pawley For a Ride?" *Miami Daily News*, June 23, 1955.
9.   "City Studies Buying Miami Transit Line," *Miami Daily News*, August 24, 1955; and "Pawley Writes Out Terms on Bus Sale," *Miami Herald*, September 14, 1955.

10. Jack W. Roberts, "Drivers Hit City-Owned Busses Plan," *Miami Daily News*, August 24, 1955.
11. "Beach Bus Union Wins Pay Raises," *Miami Herald*, August 10, 1955.
12. "Committee Sends Bus Tangle Back to City Transit Firm," *Miami Daily News*, August 25, 1955.
13. "Issue of Busline Franchise Depends on Result of Survey," *Miami Daily News*, August 27, 1955; and "City Calls on Expert to Air Bus Franchise at a $100-a-Day Fee," *Miami Herald*, August 27, 1955.
14. "Pawley Urges 'Joint Audit' of Bus Books," *Miami Daily News*, August 28, 1955; and "Transit Firm Offers to Pay for Bus Study," *Miami Herald*, August 28, 1955.
15. Jack Oswald, "Mayor's Tentative OK Given to Bus Expert Study Panel," *Miami Daily News*, August 28, 1955.
16. Henry Cavendish, "New Bus Plan to Be Offered by Aronovitz," *Miami Daily News*, August 29, 1955.
17. "Pawley Not Needed, Bus Official Claims," *Miami Daily News*, August 30, 1955.
18. Jack W. Roberts, "New Truce Plan Lessens Threat of Bus Strike," *Miami Daily News*, August 31, 1955.
19. David J. Kraslow, "He's an Expert among Experts," *Miami Herald*, September 4, 1955; and David J. Kraslow, "Inside City Hall," *Miami Herald*, September 5, 1955.
20. David J. Kraslow, "Pawley Rejects Expert's Proposal," *Miami Herald*, September 2, 1955; and Jack W. Roberts, "Pawley Rejects Profit Plan, Dampens Hope of Bus Truce," *Miami Daily News*, September 2, 1955.
21. John L. Boyles, "Pawley Interests Purchase South Miami's Coach Service," *Miami Herald*, August 31, 1956.
22. "Adams Bus Line Sold to Pawley," *Miami Herald*, September 12, 1956.
23. Fred Porter, "Bus Shut Down Delayed 15 Days," *Miami Herald*, July 29, 1960; and Bob Reno, "Bus Fare Boost Expected Soon?," *Miami Herald,* August 13, 1960.
24. Stan Johnson, "How to Make $300,000 a Year with No Taxes," *Miami Herald*, May 17, 1959.
25. Leo Adde, "'I'd Grab at Bus Lines Myself,' Campbell Says," *Miami Herald*, July 28, 1959.
26. Verne O. Williams, "Transit Board 'Named,'" *Miami News*, March 9, 1960; and John McDermott, "Transit Unit Sets Talks on Miami Buses," *Miami Herald*, September 15, 1960.
27. "Metro Nearing Price for All 4 Bus Lines," *Miami News*, October 25, 1960.
28. Paul Einstein, "25 Drivers Return Metro's Bus Forms," *Miami News*, January 22, 1962.
29. Dick Nellius, "Metro Gets Court OK to Buy Buses," *Miami News*, January 28, 1962; and Denis Sneigr, "Union Forcing Takeover, Dade Told," *Miami News*, January 30, 1962.
30. R. Hart Phillips, "Dade Vote Backs County's Merger," *New York Times*, May 13, 1962.
31. George Lardner, "Bus System Interest to Total $4 Million," *Miami Herald*, November 6, 1962.
32. "William D. Pawley Kills Himself."
33. Pawley, "Russia Is Winning," 348.
34. "Pawley Reveals Havana Transport Deal," *Miami Daily News*, March 3, 1950.
35. Jack Thale, "Cuba OKs Pawley's Plan for Modern Bus System," *Miami Herald*, March 10, 1950.
36. "Army Runs Havana Trolleys," *Miami Herald*, March 8, 1950.
37. Confidential FBI report, 5.
38. "Pawley to Move to Cuba to Run New Bus Lines," *Miami Sunday News*, March 12, 1950.

39. "Pawley Reveals Havana Transport Deal."
40. "Wizard at Work," *Time* 55 (March 20, 1950): 36.
41. "Pawley to Buy British Busses," *Miami Daily News*, March 6, 1950.
42. "Wizard at Work."
43. "Pawley Reveals Havana Transport Deal."
44. "Wizard at Work."
45. Smiley, "The Private Wars."
46. "Pawley Firm Gets Cuban Interventor," *Miami Sunday News*, November 19, 1950.
47. "Havana Seizes Bus Line," *New York Times*, November 19, 1950.
48. CIA file 78435 CSA/IB/3, William Pawley, January 12, 1960, National Archives file F-81-0351 D0367; and "Cuban Labor Chief Held for Murder," *New York Times*, June 29, 1952.
49. Smiley, "The Private Wars."

Chapter 16. Batista
1. Pawley to Wood, October 11, 1954, Robert E. Wood Papers, Box 12, Hoover Library.
2. J. M. Richardson to Wood, September 20, 1954, Robert E. Wood Papers, Box 12, Hoover Library.
3. Pawley to Wood, October 11, 1954.
4. Pawley to Wood, November 30, 1954, Robert E. Wood Papers, Box 12, Hoover Library.
5. John Frank Rys, "Tensions and Conflicts in Cuba, Haiti, and the Dominican Republic between 1945 and 1959" (PhD diss., American University, Washington, DC, 1966), 127–29, 149–50.
6. Hugh Thomas, "The U.S. and Castro, 1959–1962," *American Heritage*, October–November 1978, 30.
7. Pawley, "Russia Is Winning," 351.
8. Dulles, memorandum of conversation with the president, December 20, 1956, CDROM Id: 198501000363, *Declassified Documents*, PSmedia.
9. Pawley testimony, "Communist Threat," 737–38.
10. Earl E. T. Smith testimony, Senate subcommittee hearing, "Communist Threat to the United States Through the Caribbean," 24, August 30, 1960 (Washington, DC: Government Printing Office, 1960). (Hereafter cited as Smith testimony, "Communist Threat.")
11. "How U.S. Helped Castro," *U.S. News & World Report*, October 8, 1962, 47–48.
12. Pawley testimony, "Communist Threat," 740–41.
13. Weyl, *Red Star over Cuba*, 159.
14. Fulgencio Batista, *Cuba Betrayed* (New York: Vantage Press, 1962), 71–72.
15. Lazo, *Dagger in the Heart*, 159–60.
16. Thomas, "The U S. and Castro," 29.
17. Lester D. Langley, *The Cuban Policy of the United States: A Brief History* (New York: John Wiley and Sons, 1968), 172.
18. Pawley, "Russia Is Winning," 353–54.
19. There is inconsistency in Pawley's feelings that Castro was a Communist. Jules du Bois, Latin American expert for the *Chicago Tribune*, said, "When I saw [Pawley] at Miami Airport in January 1958 on his way to the Dominican Republic, he said he didn't think Castro was going to be good for Cuba, but said then he didn't think he was a communist." John T. O'Rourke, "Our Man in Havana, William D. Pawley," *Washington Daily News*, February 20, 1961.
20. Gerard Colby and Charlotte Dennett, *Thy Will Be Done: The Conquest of the Amazon: Nelson Rockefeller and Evangelism in the Age of Oil* (New York: HarperCollins, 1995), 313.

21. Thomas G. Paterson, *Contesting Castro: The United States and the Triumph of the Cuban Revolution* (New York: Oxford University Press, 1994), 207.
22. Pawley testimony, "Communist Threat," 739.
23. Pawley, "Russia Is Winning," 359.
24. John Dorschner and Roberto Fabricio, *The Winds of December* (New York: Coward, McCann & Geoghegan, 1980), 153.
25. Lazo, *Dagger in the Heart*, 162; and Pawley, "Russia Is Winning," 359–60.
26. O'Rourke, "Our Man in Havana"; and Paterson, *Contesting Castro*, 209.
27. Pawley, "Russia Is Winning," 360.
28. Ibid., 360–62.
29. Dorschner and Fabricio, *Winds of December*, 154.
30. Lazo, *Dagger in the Heart*, 157–58.
31. Earl E. T. Smith, *The Fourth Floor: An Account of the Castro Communist Revolution* (New York: Random House, 1962), 165–69.
32. Anthony Summers, *The Arrogance of Power: The Secret World of Richard Nixon* (New York: Viking, 2000), 178–79.
33. Michael R. Beschloss, *The Crisis Years: Kennedy and Khrushchev, 1960–1963* (New York: HarperCollins, 1991), 94.
34. Paterson, *Contesting Castro*, 209.
35. Pawley, "Russia Is Winning," 362. Dorschner, in *Winds of December*, 158, interviewed Güell who said that Pawley ignored his State Department instructions, implying clearly that the message was coming directly from Eisenhower. Years later, Batista's reaction in an interview would contradict this assertion.
36. Dorschner and Fabricio, *Winds of December*, 159.
37. John B. McDermott, "Batista Breaks His Silence: U.S. Goofed," *Miami Herald*, March 9, 1961 (letter from Batista to *Miami Herald* managing editor George Beebe).
38. Pawley, "Russia Is Winning," 364.
39. Pawley testimony, "Communist Threat," 739.
40. McDermott, "Batista Breaks His Silence."
41. Pawley, "Russia Is Winning," 364–65.
42. Robert E. Quirk, *Fidel Castro* (New York: W. W. Norton, 1993), 203.
43. McDermott, "Batista Breaks His Silence."
44. Smith, *Fourth Floor*, 170–75.
45. Ruby Hart Phillips, *Cuba: Island of Paradox* (New York: McDowell, Obolensky, 1959), 388.
46. Leslie Bethell, ed., *Cuba: A Short History* (London: Cambridge University Press, 1993), 93.
47. Ramón L. Bonachea and Marta San Martín, *The Cuban Insurrection: 1952–1959* (New Brunswick, NJ: Transaction, 1974), 305–7; and Rolando E. Bonachea, "United States Policy Toward Cuba: 1959–1961" (PhD diss., Georgetown University, Washington, DC, 1975), 45.
48. Smith, *Fourth Floor*, 184–85.
49. Batista, *Cuba Betrayed*, 137.
50. Smith, *Fourth Floor*, 186.
51. Batista, *Cuba Betrayed*, 139.
52. Beschloss, *Crisis Years*, footnote, 94–95.
53. Department of State Staff Summary Supplement, July 30, 1959, CDROM Id: 1985010100133 *Declassified Documents*, PSmedia.
54. "Ex-Cuban Dictator, Batista Dies at 72," *Corpus Christi Caller*, August 7, 1973.
55. Goodpaster, memorandum of conference with Eisenhower, May 16, 1960, DDE Papers, Ann Whitman File, Box 50, Staff Notes, May 1960, Eisenhower Library.

Chapter 17. Castro

1. Oland D. Russell, "Pawley Also Warned on China," *Washington Daily News*, February 20, 1961; "1958 Move to Bar Castro Disclosed," *New York Times*, February 12, 1961; Robert S. Allen and Paul Scott, "How Miami's Pawley Tried to 'Save' Cuba," *Miami News*, February 9, 1961; and Dom Bonafede, "Pawley Tells of Plan to Block Fidel," *Miami Herald*, February 11, 1961.
2. Rose Mary Woods, conversation with Pawley, January 1, 1961, Nixon Pre-presidential Papers.
3. "Batista Rejected Caretaker Regime," *Palm Beach Post*, February 17, 1961.
4. Pawley testimony, "Communist Threat," 746.
5. Arthur Gardner testimony, Senate subcommittee hearing, "Communist Threat to the United States Through the Caribbean," 10, August 27, 1960 (Washington, DC: Government Printing Office, 1960).
6. Smith testimony, "Communist Threat," 20, 32–33.
7. Richard Eder, "U.S. Cuban Expert Restored to Duty," *New York Times*, July 19, 1965.
8. Pawley testimony, "Communist Threat," 713–15.
9. John A. Goldsmith, "Pawley Charges Cuba Bungling," *Washington Post*, February 20, 1961.
10. "Ex-Envoy Scores Spruille Braden," *New York Times*, February 20, 1961.
11. Editorial, "Backbiting," *Washington Post*, February 23, 1961; and editorial, "Villainy," *Washington Post*, February 27, 1961.
12. Editorial, "The Red Herring's Return," *Chicago Daily Tribune*, February 20, 1961.
13. Willard Edwards, "Urges Probe of Red Plot in State Dept.," *Chicago Daily Tribune*, February 20, 1961.
14. Roscoe Drummond, "Senate Probe Blurs Cuban Issue," *Washington Post*, February 26, 1961.
15. Marquis Childs, "Changes Conceal Cuban Realities," *Washington Post*, February 22, 1961.
16. Editor's Notebook, "Pawley vs. Braden," *Miami Herald*, February 26, 1961.
17. "Pawley Replies to the Notebook," *Miami Herald*, March 8, 1961.
18. "U.S. Bungled Plan in Cuba, Batista Says," *Houston Chronicle*, March 12, 1961.
19. Batista, *Cuba Betrayed*, footnotes, pages 20, 72, 138.
20. McDermott, "Batista Breaks His Silence."
21. Pawley, "Russia Is Winning," 367–68.
22. George E. Sokolsky, "Batista's Letter to Herald Opens New Policy Question," *Miami Herald*, March 17, 1961.
23. Memorandum of first meeting of Cuba Study Group, April 22, 1961, FRUS 1961–1963: 10, 6.
24. Thomas, "The U.S. and Castro," 30, 35.
25. "William D. Pawley Kills Himself."
26. "Cuba Booting Lansky's Kin," *Miami Herald*, May 8, 1959.
27. Summers, *Arrogance of Power*, 180.
28. Charles Rappleye and Ed Becker, *All American Mafioso: The Johnny Rosselli Story* (New York: Doubleday, 1991), 218–19.
29. Fawn M. Brodie, *Richard Nixon: The Shaping of His Character* (New York: W. W. Norton, 1981), 395.
30. Summers, *Arrogance of Power*, 182–83.
31. Memorandum of conversation with Reichhardt, October 8, 1959, Pawley CIA File, National Archives. The CIA already knew about the offer for use of the island. The British government verified Colonel Hill's offer, which it considered "off base," and would "not entertain such a notion." Memorandum from Martha Thorpe, October 13, 1959, Pawley CIA file, National Archives.

32. Report of contact with Pawley, September 25, 1959, Pawley File, National Archives.
33. J. C. King, memorandum to Joseph Langdon, October 7, 1959, Pawley CIA file, National Archives; and Acting Chief, Support Branch, memorandum to chief, SB/1, October 6, 1959, Pawley CIA File, National Archives.
34. Memorandum for chief, Investigative Division, November 9, 1959, CIA file D-00820, Pawley CIA File, National Archives; and chief, WH Division, memorandum to deputy director of security, November 17, 1959, CIA file D-00819, Pawley File, National Archives.
35. King memo to Langdon.
36. Reichhardt, memorandum to chief, WH Division, October 2, 1959, CIA file 201-77378, Pawley file, National Archives.
37. Director of security (Edwards), memorandum to director of Central Intelligence, December 29, 1959, CIA File D00812, Pawley CIA File, National Archives.
38. Martha Thorpe, memorandum of conversation between Pawley and unidentified Cuban, October 20, 1959, CIA file 201-77378, Pawley file, National Archives.
39. Memorandum by Martha Thorpe, November 25, 1959, Pawley CIA File, National Archives.
40. Memorandum by Martha Thorpe, November 27, 1959, Pawley CIA File, National Archives.
41. Memorandum of meeting at Pawley's office, December 9, 1959, Pawley CIA file, National Archives.
42. Person known as Thompson, memorandum of meeting with Fabio Freyre and Pawley, December 16, 1959, Pawley CIA file, National Archives.
43. (Jacob) Esterline, memorandum to chief, White House Division CIA, February 12, 1960, Pawley CIA file, National Archives.
44. Rudolph E. Gomez, CIA deputy chief, Western Hemisphere Division, memorandum of phone conversation with Pawley, February 18, 1960, Pawley CIA file, National Archives.
45. Rudolph E. Gomez, memorandum of phone conversation with Pawley, December 31, 1959; and Pawley, memorandum of conversation with Dr. Nuñez Portuondo, January 13, 1960, CIA File 201-77378, Pawley CIA file, National Archives.
46. Memorandum to chief, Confidential Informant Staff, from chief, CIA Contact Division, January 20, 1960, CIA file 12848, Pawley CIA file, National Archives.
47. Thompson memo of meeting with Freyre and Pawley; and letter written from Pawley to King, December 22, 1959, CIA Pawley file, National Archives.
48. Miami WHD representative, dispatch to chief, WHD, January 23, 1960, Pawley CIA file, National Archives.
49. Rudolph E. Gomez, CIA deputy chief, Western Hemisphere Division, memorandum of phone conversation with Pawley, February 18, 1960, Pawley CIA file, National Archives.
50. Letter written from Pawley to Col. J. C. King, February 19, 1960; and Gomez, memorandum of phone conversation with Pawley, February 23, 1960, Pawley CIA file, National Archives.
51. Memo from Pawley phone conversation dictated to Rose Mary Woods, February 26, 1960, Nixon Pre-presidential Papers.
52. Richard M. Nixon, *Six Crises* (Garden City, NY: Doubleday, 1962), 352.
53. Warren Hinckle and William W. Turner, *Deadly Secrets: The CIA-Mafia War against Castro and the Assassination of J.F.K.* (New York: Thunder's Mouth Press, 1982), 44.
54. Diary entry, April 25, 1960, DDE Papers, Ann Whitman File, Box 11, ACW Diary 4/60 (1), Eisenhower Library.
55. Hughes, memorandum to Nixon, May 11, 1960, Nixon Pre-presidential Papers.
56. Hughes, memorandum to Nixon, May 27, 1960, Nixon Pre-presidential Papers.

57. Goodpaster, memorandum of conference with the president, April 26, 1960, DDE Papers, Ann Whitman File, Box 49, Staff Notes, April 1960, Eisenhower Library.
58. Herter, memorandum for Douglas Dillon, April 25, 1960, Herter Papers, Box 21, Meetings with the President, July 30, 1957, to January 20, 1961, Eisenhower Library.
59. Andrew Jackson Goodpaster, memorandum of conference with the president, May 7, 1960, DDE Papers, Ann Whitman File, Box 32, Staff Notes, May 1960, Eisenhower Library.

Chapter 18. Invasion Plans
1. Hughes, memorandum to Nixon, June 27, 1960, Nixon Pre-presidential Papers.
2. Nixon to Pawley, July 8, 1960, Nixon pre-Presidential Papers.
3. Peter Wyden, *Bay of Pigs: The Untold Story* (New York: Simon & Schuster, 1979), 29–30; and Brodie, *Richard Nixon*, 406.
4. Cable message to CIA director, July 14, 1960, CIA file 201-77378, Pawley CIA file, National Archives.
5. Goodpaster, memorandum of conference with the president, July 5, 1960, CDROM Id: 1998030101089, *Declassified Documents*, PSmedia.
6. Pawley to Nixon, July 18, 1960, Nixon Pre-presidential Papers.
7. Memorandum of first meeting of Cuba Study Group, April 22, 1961, FRUS Cuba 1961–1962: 10, 3–4.
8. David J. Kraslow, "Aid Castro Foes, Smathers Urges," *Miami Herald*, August 11, 1960.
9. John McDermott, "U.S. Is Urged to Quit OAS by Ex-Ambassador Pawley," *Miami Herald*, August 16, 1960.
10. Dom Bonafede, "Good Will of Latins Not for Sale—Pawley," *Miami Herald*, February 20, 1961.
11. Brodie, *Richard Nixon*, 406.
12. Memorandum of first meeting of Cuba Study Group, 4.
13. Summers, *Arrogance of Power*, 185.
14. E. Howard Hunt, *Give Us This Day* (New Rochelle, NY: Arlington House, 1973), 83.
15. Memorandum of first meeting of Cuba Study Group, 6.
16. Pawley to King, July 22, 1960, Pawley CIA file, National Archives.
17. Benitez to Pawley, October 18, 1960, CIA file D0740, Pawley CIA file, National Archives.
18. Unsigned memorandum of meeting with Pawley, March 14, 1960, CIA file 201-77378, Pawley CIA file, National Archives.
19. Memo of Pawley phone conversation to Nixon from Rose Mary Woods, January 4, 1960, Nixon Pre-presidential Papers.
20. Carleton Beals, "Cuba's Invasion Jitters," *Nation*, November 12, 1960, 360.
21. Interview with Howard Hunt, "Backyard Cold War Interviews."
22. Gordon Gray, special assistant to the president, memorandum of meeting with the president, December 5, 1960, DDE Papers, Special Assistant Series, Presidential Subseries, Box 5, Folder: "1960 Meetings with the President," Eisenhower Library.
23. Dillon, memorandum for the president, December 2, 1960, DDE Papers, Dulles-Herter Series, Box 11, Herter, December 1960, Eisenhower Library.
24. Transcript, William Douglas Pawley oral history interview, April 4, 1967, 17–18, Hoover Library.
25. Pawley, "Russia Is Winning," 415–20.
26. Goodpaster, memorandum of conference with the president, January 6, 1961, DDE Papers, Box 55, Staff notes December 1960, Eisenhower Library.
27. Pawley, "Russia Is Winning," 420.

28. John Prados, *Presidents' Secret Wars: CIA and Pentagon Covert Operations Since World War II* (New York: Morrow, 1986), 189.
29. Pawley to Rusk, Miami, January 30, 1961, Pawley, "Russia Is Winning," 422.
30. Ibid., 422–23.
31. Cable to director CIA, March 13, 1961, Pawley CIA file, National Archives.
32. Eisenhower to Pawley, January 11, 1961, in Eisenhower, *The Papers of Dwight David Eisenhower*, 2244.
33. Hunt, *Give Us This Day*, 28–29.
34. Pawley to Thomas Mann, March 3, 1961, Pawley CIA file, National Archives.
35. Hunt, *Give Us This Day*, 43.
36. Editorial, "Cuba and Guatemala," *The Nation*, November 5, 1960, 337.
37. Mario Lazo, "Decision for Disaster," *Reader's Digest*, September 1964, 244–46.
38. Phillips, *Cuban Dilemma*, 338.
39. Immerman, *CIA in Guatemala*, 188–89.
40. Terry Southern, "How I Signed Up at $250 a Month for the Big Parade through Havana Bla-Bla-Bla and Wound Up in Guatemala with the CIA," *Esquire*, June 1963, 140.
41. Richard Nixon, "Cuba, Castro and John F. Kennedy," *Reader's Digest*, November 1964, 289.
42. Lucien S. Vandenbroucke, "The 'Confessions' of Allen Dulles: New Evidence on the Bay of Pigs," *Diplomatic History*, Fall 1984, 368.
43. Richard M. Bissell, Jr., "Response to Lucien S. Vandenbroucke, "The 'Confessions' of Allen Dulles: New Evidence on the Bay of Pigs," *Diplomatic History*, Fall 1984, 380.
44. Prados, *Presidents' Secret Wars*, 207.
45. Pawley letter to editor, "The Cuban Story," *Esquire*, August 1963, 12.
46. Diary entry, June 5, 1961, DDE Papers, Box 10, Cuba, Post-Presidential, Eisenhower Library.
47. Nixon, "Cuba, Castro and John F. Kennedy," 291.
48. Pawley, "Russia Is Winning," 431–36. Pawley would reiterate his opinion the following year in a speech before the Miami Rotary Club: "Goodwill is not for sale . . . we are talking about a 20-billion-dollar program. This is a tremendous amount of American taxpayers' money. And yet, it won't solve the problem." Charles Whited, "We Should Quit OAS, Pawley Claims," *Miami Herald*, January 26, 1962.
49. Pawley, "Russia Is Winning," 431–36.
50. Sam Pope Brewer, "Exile Leader Hopeful," *New York Times*, May 21, 1961; and Milt Sosin, "Captives Come to Trade for Lives," *Miami News*, May 21, 1961.
51. Sosin, "Captives Come to Trade for Lives."
52. Lt. Frank Chapel to Sheriff Thomas J. Kelly, May 22, 1961, Dade County OCB file #153, Cuban Information Archives, http://www.cuban-exile.com/doc_026-050/doc0031.html (accessed August 13, 2010).
53. JMWAVE cable, May 21, 1961, Pawley CIA file, National Archives.
54. Milton S. Eisenhower, *The Wine Is Bitter: The United States and Latin America* (Garden City, NY: Doubleday, 1963), 274–75.
55. Phillips, *Cuban Dilemma*, 340.
56. Peter Kihss, "Prisoners Renew Tractor Effort," *New York Times*, July 6, 1961.
57. Haynes Johnson, *The Bay of Pigs: The Leaders' Story of Brigade 2506* (New York: W. W. Norton, 1964), 305–6.
58. Richard J. H. Johnson, "Group Is Organized to Raise Ransom for Cuban Prisoners," *New York Times*, June 27, 1962.
59. Pawley family, interview with author, March 2003.
60. Pawley to Hoover, June 27, 1962, Post-Presidential Papers, Box 175, Hoover Library.

61. Hoover to Pawley, June 28, 1962, Post-Presidential Papers, Box 175, Hoover Library.
62. Eisenhower, *Wine Is Bitter*, 278.
63. Lazo, *Dagger in the Heart*, 312.
64. Rose Mary Woods, memorandum to Nixon, August 7, 1962, Pre-presidential Papers Series, Box 238, Folder 1379, Richard Nixon Library, Yorba Linda.
65. Pawley, "Russia Is Winning," 442–43.

Chapter 19. Operation Red Cross
1. Philip Zelikow, "American Policy and Cuba, 1961–1963," *Diplomatic History*, Spring 2000, 321.
2. Paid letter by José Bosch to editor, *New York Times*, March 24, 1961.
3. "Soviet Base for Cuba?," *Miami News*, February 15, 1960; and "Reds Eye Cuba for Missiles?," *Miami Herald*, February 16, 1960.
4. Max Holland, "A Luce Connection: Senator Keating, William Pawley, and the Cuban Missile Crisis," *Journal of Cold War Studies* 1, no. 3 (Fall 1999): 140–41.
5. Thomas G. Paterson, "The Historian as Detective: Senator Keating, the Missiles in Cuba, and His Mysterious Sources," *Diplomatic History*, Winter 1987, 68.
6. Holland, "A Luce Connection," 140.
7. Betty Beale, "Clare Boothe Luce Weaves a Fascinating Tale," *Washington Star*, November 16, 1975.
8. Rowland Evans and Robert Novak, "Inside Report: The Cuba Expert," *New York Herald Tribune*, July 12, 1963.
9. Hal Hendrix, "Soviets Build 6 Cuban Missile Bases," *Miami News*, October 7, 1962.
10. Warren Weaver, Jr., "Capital Guesses at Keating's Aims," *New York Times*, February 21, 1963.
11. Pawley, "Russia Is Winning," 445.
12. Dom Bonafede, "Miami's Cuban Exile Groups Uniting," *Miami Herald*, November 4, 1962.
13. "'Overthrow Castro'—Pawley," *Miami Herald*, November 4, 1962.
14. "Pawley Calls Pact 'Devastating Blow,'" *Oakland Tribune*, November 4, 1962.
15. Lazo, *Dagger in the Heart*, 314–19.
16. Robert K. Brown and Miguel Acoca, "The Bayo-Pawley Affair," *Soldier of Fortune*, February 1976, 19.
17. Black, *Good Neighbor*, 110.
18. Transcript, William Douglas Pawley oral history interview, April 4, 1967, 29, Hoover Library.
19. Hinckle and Turner, *Deadly Secrets*, 146.
20. Appendix to Hearings, 81–83, House Select Committee on Assassinations, vol. 10, March 1979 (Washington, DC: Government Printing Office, 1979).
21. Beale, "Clare Boothe Luce Weaves a Fascinating Tale"; and Gaeton Fonzi, *The Last Investigation* (New York: Thunder's Mouth Press, 1993), 53.
22. Hinckle and Turner, *Deadly Secrets*, 148.
23. Appendix to Hearings, 86.
24. Earl Golz, "Cuban Rebels Told Ex-Envoy of Oswald Trip," *Dallas Morning News*, May 10, 1979.
25. Fonzi, *Last Investigation*, 54.
26. Anthony Summers, *Conspiracy* (New York: McGraw-Hill, 1980), 449.
27. Pawley to Nixon, April 15, 1963, Nixon Pre-presidential Papers.
28. Nixon to Pawley, May 8, 1963, Nixon Pre-presidential Papers.
29. Hinckle and Turner, *Deadly Secrets*, 189.
30. Patricia Orr, telephone interview of William Turner, November 10, 1977, CIA File

89-3, Box 89, File # 003225, 004234, House Select Committee on Assassinations, National Archives.

31. Brown and Acoca, "The Bayo-Pawley Affair," 17.
32. Don Bohning, "Miamian Pawley Tells of '63 Cuba Operation, Loss of 10 Exiles," *Miami Herald*, January 8, 1976.
33. Grayston L. Lynch, *Decision for Disaster: Betrayal at the Bay of Pigs* (Washington, DC: Brassey's, Inc., 1998), 170.
34. R. K. Davis, cable to JMWAVE, May 23, 1961, CIA file 201-77378, National Archives.
35. David Corn, *Blond Ghost: Ted Shackley and the CIA's Crusade* (New York: Simon & Schuster, 1994), 100.
36. Notes on Bayo-Pawley Raid, October 30, 1977, CIA files, Box 19, Folder 12, Items 3 and 4, National Archives.
37. Bohning, "Miamian Pawley Tells."
38. Warren Hinckle and William Turner, "The CIA and the Flying Tiger Caper," *City of San Francisco*, January 13, 1976, 16.
39. Hinckle and Turner, *Deadly Secrets*, 192; and Bohning, "Miamian Pawley Tells."
40. After the Kennedy assassination, Billings was a member of the *Life* magazine group that negotiated the purchase of the film that observer Abraham Zapruder took as the president was shot. Subsequently, Billings worked on obtaining exclusive rights to Marina Oswald's story.
41. Bohning, "Miamian Pawley Tells."
42. "Ex-Envoy, Life Staffer in '63 Cuba Raid," *Washington Star*, January 8, 1976.
43. Notes on Bayo-Pawley Raid.
44. Brown and Acoca, "The Bayo-Pawley Affair," 20.
45. Bohning, "Miamian Pawley Tells." The ten men were Tomas Vaquero, Luis Jimenez, Denis Rigal, Rene Lamoru, Rolando Rodriguez, Francisco Hernandez, Luis Cantin, Alfredo Mir, Ernesto Duenas, and Eduardo "Eddie Bayo" Perez.
46. Notes on Bayo-Pawley Raid.
47. Pawley family, interview with author, March 2003.
48. Hinckle and Turner, "The CIA and the Flying Tiger Caper," 16.
49. Bohning, "Miamian Pawley Tells."
50. "Former Envoy Confirms 1963 Cuba Raiding Party," *Washington Post*, January 9, 1976.
51. Hinckle and Turner, "The CIA and the Flying Tiger Caper," 17.
52. Bohning, "Miamian Pawley Tells."
53. Information obtained by Alan Jules Weberman through the Freedom of Information Act (FOIA) request, http://www.ajweberman.com/coupt5.htm. (Nodule 13). See also http://www.maryferrell.org/mffweb/archive/viewer/showDoc.do?docId=105573&relPageId=223.
54. Dick Russell, "Loran Hall and the Politics of Assassination," *Village Voice*, October 3, 1977, 23.
55. Gerald Patrick Hemming, transcript of testimony, March 21, 1978, Record # 180-10086-10250, File # 006790, House Select Committee on Assassinations, National Archives.
56. Hinckle and Turner, *Deadly Secrets*, footnote, 431–32.
57. Notes on Bayo-Pawley Raid.
58. Brown and Acoca, "The Bayo-Pawley Affair," 20.
59. Hinckle and Turner, *Deadly Secrets,* 194.
60. Russell, "Loran Hall," 23.
61. Bohning, "Miamian Pawley Tells."
62. Deputy director of security (White), memorandum to chief, CIA White House Division, May 19, 1964, CIA File D00839, National Archives.

63. Carlos Martinez, "Castro Will Fall if Exiles Armed, Willing—Somoza," *Miami Herald*, September 8, 1963.
64. D. J. Brennan, Jr., memorandum to W. C. Sullivan, September 27, 1963, FBI file CR-62-79985-NR; and FBI director, memorandum to SAC (special agent in charge), NY, October 4, 1963, FBI file CR-109-584-3752, JFK Assassination files, National Archives.
65. Eisenhower to Pawley, May 26, 1965, Pawley, "Russia Is Winning," 447.
66. "Cuba," *Congressional Record–Senate*, 93rd Cong., 2nd sess., November 26, 1974, 37466.
67. Pawley letter to editor, "Stay Tough on Cuba," *Washington Star-News*, October 11, 1974.
68. Scowcroft to Pawley, November 16, 1974, *Congressional Record–Senate*, 93rd Cong., 2nd sess., December 19, 1974, 41083.

Chapter 20. Trujillo
1. Raymond H. Pulley, "The United States and the Trujillo Dictatorship, 1933–1940: The High Price of Caribbean Stability," *Caribbean Studies*, October 1965, 22.
2. Jesús de Suarez Galíndez, *The Era of Trujillo: Dominican Dictator* (Tucson: University of Arizona Press, 1973), 86–89.
3. Pawley, "Russia Is Winning," 366.
4. Robert D. Crassweller, *Trujillo: The Life and Times of a Caribbean Dictator* (New York: Macmillan, 1966), 278.
5. Transcript, William Douglas Pawley oral history interview, April 4, 1967, 31, Hoover Library.
6. Milton Bracker, "Mysteries Strain U.S.-Dominican Tie," *New York Times*, September 2, 1957; and *National Cyclopedia of American Biography*, s.v. "William Douglas Pawley," 215–16.
7. Pawley to Trujillo, May 26, 1956, attachment to FBI File 97-4587-579, translation in file 62-79985, National Archives. (Hereafter cited as attachment to FBI file.)
8. Pawley to Trujillo, August 23, 1956, attachment to FBI file.
9. Joaquín Balaguar, secretary of state, Dominican Republic, to Pawley, September 17, 1956, attachment to FBI file.
10. Al Neuharth, "Pawley to Hunt Uranium," *Miami Herald*, December 6, 1955.
11. Memorandum by Luis R. Mercado, Dominican secretary of state for agriculture, December 28, 1956, attachment to FBI file.
12. Pawley, telegram to Trujillo, January 21, 1957, attachment to FBI file.
13. Trujillo, cablegram to Pawley, January 22, 1957, attachment to FBI file.
14. Transcript, William Douglas Pawley oral history interview, April 4, 1967, 32, Hoover Library.
15. CIA chief of station, Ciudad Trujillo, airgram to CIA chief, White House Division, June 12, 1958, CIA file 201-77378, Pawley CIA File, National Archives.
16. Pawley to Manuel de Moya, May 4, 1959, attachment to FBI file.
17. Trujillo to Manuel de Moya, May 16, 1959, attachment to FBI file 97-4587-579, translation in file 62-79985, National Archives.
18. Transcript, William Douglas Pawley oral history interview, April 4, 1967, 35–37, Hoover Library.
19. Secretary of state for agriculture (Luis R. Mercado), memorandum to Trujillo, December 19, 1956, FBI record 124-10201-10414, National Archives.
20. Secretary of state for agriculture (Mercado) memorandum to Trujillo, December 28, 1956, FBI record 124-10201-10414, National Archives.
21. CIA chief of station, Ciudad Trujillo, airgram to CIA chief.
22. CIA chief of station, [unknown—blacked out], airgram to CIA chief, White House Division, January 27, 1957, CIA File 201-77378, Pawley CIA File, National Archives.

23. Transcript, William Douglas Pawley oral history interview, April 4, 1967, 40, Hoover Library.
24. Germán E. Ornes, *Trujillo: Little Caesar of the Caribbean* (New York: Thomas Nelson & Sons, 1958), 19.
25. Drew Pearson, "Kin of Officials Close to Trujillo," *Washington Post*, June 5, 1957.
26. Private correspondence with foreign governments, *U.S. Code* 18 (1948) USCS § 953.
27. Peter Maas, "Boswell of the Jet Set," *Saturday Evening Post*, January 19, 1963, 28; and Igor Cassini, "Personal Lives: When the Sweet Life Turns Sour; a Farewell to Scandal," *Esquire*, April 1964, 94.
28. Fletcher Knebel, "How Trujillo Spends a Million in the U.S.A.," *Look*, August 20, 1957, 61–63.
29. "Ex-FBI Agent Is Sentenced," *Corpus Christi Caller*, December 20, 1957.
30. Drew Pearson, "Morse Preparing Weekly Ike Blasts; Dominican-Go-Around," *Washington Post*, June 4, 1957.
31. Notes, Fernsworth to Pearson, February 23, 1961 and June 7, 1961, Personal Papers of Drew Pearson, Box G240, Lyndon Baines Johnson Library.
32. Pawley, "Russia Is Winning," 373.
33. Ibid., 374.
34. Ibid., 375.
35. Chargé d'affaires in the Dominican Republic (Henry Dearborn), telegrams to State Department, February 9, 11, 1960, FRUS 1958–1960: 5 (microfiche supplement).
36. Edward Burks, "More Are Convicted by Trujillo Regime," *New York Times*, February 12, 1960.
37. Chargé d'affaires (Dearborn), telegrams to State Department.
38. Leo Adde, "Trujillo Sincere—Smathers," *Miami Herald*, February 11, 1960.
39. Germán E. Ornes and John McCarten, "Trujillo: Little Caesar on Our Own Front Porch," *Harper's Magazine*, December 1956, 68.
40. Adde, "Trujillo Sincere."
41. Ibid.
42. Leo Adde, "Must Play Ball with Dictators, Smathers Says," *Miami Herald*, February 12, 1960.
43. Leo Adde, "Miamian Pawley Had a Part in Trujillo's 'Free Vote' Vow," *Miami Herald*, February 13, 1960.
44. Dillon, memorandum to Eisenhower, May 12, 1960, DDE Papers: Ann Whitman Files, Dulles-Herter Series, Box 10, Herter Christian, May 1960 (3).
45. Hector Trujillo to Dominican secretary of state for agriculture and commerce (undated, but referring to memos dated March 18, 1960), attachment to FBI file; Pawley to Trujillo, January 10, 1958, attachment to FBI file; Pawley to de Moya, May 4, 1959, attachment to FBI file.
46. David Kraslow, "Smathers 'Used' by Trujillo?," *Miami Herald*, February 18, 1960.
47. Memorandum of conference with Eisenhower, March 1960, FRUS 1958–1960: 5 (microfiche supplement).

Chapter 21. The End of Trujillo

1. Department of State memorandum of conversation (Dillon, Smathers, Pawley), May 16, 1960, *Declassified Documents*, Id: 1984010101685; and Pawley, "Russia Is Winning," 381. The political scientists were former director Dr. Evron Kirkpatrick and Assistant Director Mark Ferber of the American Political Science Association; Chairman Dr. Howard Penniman of the Political Science Department, Georgetown University; and Richard Scammon, an expert on elections.
2. Pawley to Nixon, May 10, 1960, in Pawley, "Russia Is Winning," 382–83.
3. Memorandum of meeting (Vega and Reed), June 6, 1960, in ibid., 384–86.

4. A. J. Goodpaster memorandum of conference with Eisenhower, May 13, 1960, DDE Papers, Ann Whitman File, Box 50, Staff Notes—May 1960, Eisenhower Library.
5. Department of State memorandum of conversation (Dillon, Smathers, Pawley); A. J. Goodpaster memorandum of conference with Eisenhower, May 13, 1960, DDE Papers, Ann Whitman File, Box 50, Staff Notes—May 1960, Eisenhower Library.
6. A. J. Goodpaster memorandum of June 10 conference with Eisenhower, July 5, 1960, *Declassified Documents*, Id: 1998030101089.
7. Hal Hendrix, "Report Pins Assassination on Trujillo," *Miami News*, August 16, 1960.
8. Hal Hendrix, "U.S. Seeks Sanctions on Trujillo," *Miami News*, August 18, 1960, 4; and "A 'Quarantine' for Trujilloland?," *Miami News*, August 19, 1960.
9. "Trujillo Censured by OAS," *Miami News*, August 20, 1960.
10. "Walk Out of OAS Parley," *Miami News*, August 21, 1960.
11. "U.S. Breaks Off with Trujillo," *Miami News*, August 26, 1960.
12. Pawley, "Russia Is Winning," 389.
13. Mann to Dearborn, October 10, 1960, FRUS 1958–1960: 5 (microfiche supplement).
14. Dearborn to Mann, October 27, 1960, FRUS 1958–1960: 5 (microfiche supplement).
15. Pawley, "Russia Is Winning," 389–91.
16. Memorandum from CIA White House chief (Esterline), November 18, 1960, Pawley CIA file, National Archives.
17. Transcript, William Douglas Pawley oral history interview, April 4, 1967, 32, Hoover Library.
18. Pawley, "Russia Is Winning," 393–96; and transcript, William Douglas Pawley oral history interview, April 4, 1967, 33, Hoover Library.
19. Confidential FBI cable to Kennedy, February 19, 1961, *Declassified Documents*, Id: 1998110103461.
20. O'Rourke, "Our Man in Havana."
21. Dillon, memorandum to Eisenhower, May 12, 1960, DDE Papers: Ann Whitman Files, Dulles-Harter Series, Box 10, Herter Collection, May 1960 (3), Eisenhower Library.
22. Norman Gall, "How Trujillo Died," *New Republic*, April 13, 1963, 19–20.
23. Ibid., 20; and Bernard Diederich, *Trujillo: The Death of the Goat* (Boston: Little, Brown, 1978), 3–4.
24. "Trujillo Died with Gun in His Hand," *Houston Chronicle*, June 1, 1961; Pawley, "Russia Is Winning," 396; Gall, "How Trujillo Died," 19; and Diederich, *Trujillo*, 4–5.
25. Dick Goodwin, memorandum to McGeorge Bundy, June 8, 1961, CDROM Id: 1998030101064, *Declassified Documents*, PSmedia.
26. Pawley, memorandum to Rusk, June 15, 1961, CIA File 201-77378, Pawley CIA File, National Archives.
27. Ornes, "Trujillo: Little Caesar," 69.
28. Pawley, memorandum to Rusk, June 15, 1961, CIA File 201-77378, Pawley CIA File, National Archives; memorandum of telephone conversation between J. C. King and Pawley, June 14, 1961, CIA File D0424, Pawley CIA File 201-77378, National Archives. NOTE: From end of text covered by footnote 27 (Ornes, "Trujillo: Little Caesar," 69), page 336 to footnote 28, page 340, that entire section comes from an eight-page memorandum from Pawley to Rusk and the King memorandum - Pawley, memorandum to Rusk, June 15, 1961, CIA File 201-77378, Pawley CIA File, National Archives; memorandum of telephone conversation between J. C. King and Pawley, June 14, 1961, CIA File D0424, Pawley CIA File 201-77378, National Archives.
29. Pawley, memorandum to Rusk, June 15, 1961; and memorandum of telephone conversation between J. C. King and Pawley, June 14, 1961, CIA File D0424, Pawley CIA File 201-77378, National Archives.

Chapter 22. Talisman Sugar

1. Tom Smith, "Sugar 'Sweetens' Glades Economy," *Miami Herald*, February 1, 1961.
2. James Russell, "Everglades Sugar Boom Lures More Big Firms," *Miami Herald*, September 1, 1963.
3. Tom Smith, "Sugar Industry's Prospects Sweet," *Miami Herald*, September 2, 1963.
4. "Pawley Cash to Be Put into Sugar," *Miami Herald*, February 11, 1964.
5. Smiley, "The Private Wars."
6. Pawley to Senator Spessard L. Holland, March 4, 1965, *Congressional Record–Senate*, March 9, 1965, 4475.
7. Ibid.
8. Letter, secretary of agriculture (Clifford Morris Hardin) to U.S. comptroller general (Elmer Boyd Staats), June 27, 1969, folder "Ford Confirmation Hearings Campaign Finance File—Pawley, William D.," Box 251, Ford Vice Presidential Papers, Gerald R. Ford Library.
9. Letter, Goldwater to Pawley, August 5, 1970, folder "Ford Confirmation Hearings Campaign Finance File—Pawley, William D."
10. Pawley, phone message to Nixon, January 5, 1967, Unnumbered Series Correspondence, Series II, Box 42, Folder 17, Richard Nixon Library, Yorba Linda.
11. Margaret Carroll, "Pawley Sugar Mill Lawsuits Are Settled in Court," *Miami Herald*, September 18, 1971.
12. Georgia Martinez, "La Huelga Begins," *Miami Herald*, February 6, 1972.
13. "Chavez Blight Spreads East," *Nation's Business*, May 1972, 34.
14. Georgia Martinez, "Sugar Plant Hit by Chavez Pickets," *Miami Herald*, January 22, 1972; and "Co-ed's Death Embitters Sugar Mill–Union Struggle," *Miami News*, February 1, 1972.
15. "Strike Talk Proposed by Chavez," *Miami Herald*, January 23, 1972.
16. *Petersen et al. v. Talisman Sugar Corporation*, 478 F.2d 73 (5th cir., May 3, 1973).
17. "Truck Hits, Kills Coed Picketing Sugar Plant," *Miami Herald*, January 26, 1972.
18. Newsletter, Division for the Spanish Speaking, Department of Social Development, February 1972 (Lansing, Michigan).
19. Tom Smith, "Picket Hit by Another Vehicle?," *Miami Herald*, February 8, 1972.
20. Tom Smith, "Coed Hit by Someone Else," *Miami Herald*, February 8, 1972.
21. Ibid.
22. Georgia Martinez, "FHP Not Close to Solving Fatality near Sugar Plant," *Miami Herald*, February 10, 1972.
23. Georgia Martinez, "Accident Car Still Unidentified in Coed's Death at Sugar Mill," *Miami Herald*, February 12, 1972.
24. Photo caption, "Candidate Joins Pickets," *New York Times*, February 25, 1972.
25. "McGovern Joins Farm Picketing," *Miami Herald*, January 30, 1972.
26. Georgia Martinez, "Chavez Wires Support for Sugar Workers," *Miami Herald*, January 27, 1972.
27. "Sugar Boss: No Guns Used," *Miami News*, January 29, 1972.
28. "Arson Eyed in Talisman Truck Fire," *Miami Herald*, February 1, 1972.
29. James Buchanan, "TV Camera Is Victim of Pawley Brother Melee," *Miami Herald*, February 18, 1972.
30. Georgia Martinez, "Woman Lawyer, Clergy Charged in Sugar Row," *Miami Herald*, February 2, 1972.
31. *State v. Peterson et al.*, Case No. 72M-8209, Small Claims-Magistrate Court, Criminal Division, Palm Beach, Florida.
32. Georgia Martinez, "3 Sue Talisman to Enter Camp," *Miami Herald*, February 9, 1972.
33. Georgia Martinez, "Sugar Mill Bars State Investigator," *Miami Herald*, February 15, 1972.

34. "Cane Cutters Held Captive, Says Chavez," *Miami News*, February 17, 1972.
35. "Union: Armed Guards Isolate Workers," *Miami Herald*, February 17, 1972.
36. Buchanan, "TV Camera Is Victim."
37. Edna Buchanan, "AFL-CIO Gives Union Status to Chavez' Farming Group," *Miami Herald*, February 22, 1972.
38. Jay Maeder, "Borden Boycott Brews, Chavez Says," *Miami Herald*, February 12, 1972.
39. "Chavez Blight."
40. James Buchanan, "Pawley Denies Charges That Sugar Workers Carry Guns," *Miami Herald*, January 29, 1972.
41. Georgia Martinez, "Can't Enter Talisman Plant to Prove Charges, Union Says," *Miami Herald*, February 24, 1972.
42. Darrell Eiland, "Pawley: Sugar Worker Treated Well," *Miami Herald*, February 24, 1972.
43. "Chavez Blight."
44. Edna Buchanan, "Chavez, Coke Agree on Pact," *Miami Herald*, March 1, 1972.
45. Georgia Martinez, "Talisman, Union Told to Halt Fights, Threats," *Miami Herald*, March 8, 1972.
46. "Union Undecided on Talisman Suit Appeal," *Miami Herald*, March 14, 1972.
47. *Petersen et al.*, 478 F.2d 73.
48. "Chavez Blight."
49. "Clash Likely Between Sugar Industry and Farm Union," *New York Times*, October 10, 1972.
50. "Chavez Seeks Investigation of Florida's Sugar Industry," *New York Times*, November 20, 1972.

Chapter 23. Nixon and Home in Florida
1. Charles F. Hesser, "You'll Do Well in South, Nixon Told," *Miami News*, January 16, 1960.
2. Charles F. Hesser, "GOP Picks Slate Pledged to Nixon," *Miami News*, February 29, 1960.
3. Nixon to Pawley, July 11, 1960, Nixon Pre-presidential Papers.
4. James L. Fortuna, Jr., to Pawley, June 29, 1960, Nixon Pre-presidential Papers.
5. McDermott, "Why Ex-Demo Envoy's in GOP."
6. John B. McDermott, "Florida Split over Veep Spot," *Miami Herald*, July 28, 1960.
7. Charles F. Hesser, "GOP Opens Net to Catch Dade Demo Ditherers," *Miami News*, September 1, 1960.
8. Pawley, memorandum to James D. Hughes, October 18, 1960, Nixon Pre-presidential Papers.
9. Pawley to Nixon, November 10, 1960, Nixon Pre-presidential Papers.
10. Pawley to Nixon, March 14, 1961, Nixon Pre-presidential Papers.
11. Nixon to Pawley, April 28, 1961, Nixon Pre-presidential Papers.
12. Pawley to Nixon, July 22, 1961, and Nixon to Pawley, August 4, 1961, Nixon Pre-presidential Papers.
13. Pawley to Nixon, October 17, 1962, Nixon Pre-presidential Papers.
14. Pawley to Nixon, September 20, 1962, Nixon Pre-presidential Papers.
15. Pawley to editor, *Los Angeles Times*, October 30, 1962, Nixon Pre-presidential Papers.
16. Telephone transcript, Pawley to Woods, November 9, 1962, Nixon Pre-presidential Papers.
17. Pawley to Nixon, November 12, 1962, Nixon Pre-presidential Papers.
18. Nixon to Pawley, April 8, 1963, Nixon Pre-presidential Papers.

19. Pawley to Nixon, April 15, 1963, Nixon Pre-presidential Papers.
20. "Pawley Named Barry Leader," *Miami News*, August 18, 1964.
21. John McDermott, "Upheavals Aid Barry—Nixon," *Miami Herald*, October 18, 1964.
22. Colin Dangaard, "Goldwater Rips U.S. Critics, Honors Pawley," *Miami Herald*, October 3, 1971.
23. Nixon to Pawley, October 14, 1975, Post-presidential Correspondence, Richard Nixon Library, Yorba Linda.
24. Transcript of phone call from Pawley to Woods, June 30, 1964, Pre-presidential Papers, Box 238, Folder 1379, Richard Nixon Library, Yorba Linda.
25. Pawley to Stans, July 28, 1967, Unnumbered Series Correspondence, Series II, Box 42, Folder 17, Richard Nixon Library, Yorba Linda.
26. Pawley to Nixon, September 19, 1967, Unnumbered Series Correspondence.
27. Pawley to Stans, January 16, 1968, Unnumbered Series Correspondence.
28. Transcript of phone call from Pawley to Woods, March 14, 1968, Unnumbered Series Correspondence.
29. Bill Prime, "'Johnson Needs Miracle'—Pawley," *Pensacola Journal*, March 28, 1968.
30. "17 Ex-Ambassadors Form a Nixon Group," *New York Times*, May 27, 1968.
31. Pawley to Nixon, August 1, 1968, Unnumbered Series Correspondence.
32. Jack Anderson, "Ch. 10 Is Sold for $20 Million," *Miami Herald*, March 6, 1969.
33. Haines Colbert, "Local Group Asks Channel 10 Permit," *Miami News*, January 5, 1970.
34. "Post Script," *New Republic*, March 7, 1970, 9.
35. "Nixon Friends Seek TV License in Miami Held by News Group," *New York Times*, January 7, 1970.
36. "Florida Group Challenges Post-Newsweek Station License," *Washington Post*, January 7, 1970.
37. "Group Seeks Miami Station of Post Firm," *Washington Evening Star*, January 7, 1970; and "Channel 10, Challengers to Slug It Out before FCC," *Miami News*, January 6, 1970.
38. "Nixon Friends Seek TV License."
39. Jack Anderson, "Miami Businessmen Merge to Compete for Channel 10," *Miami Herald*, January 6, 1970.
40. "Nixon's Friends Seek License to a TV Unit of Firm Hit by Agnew," *Wall Street Journal*, January 7, 1970.
41. Jack Roberts, "Political Clout May Decide Ch. 10 Case," *Miami News*, January 7, 1970.
42. "Post Script."
43. "Challengers Withdrawing Bid to Take Channel 10 License," *Miami Herald*, November 27, 1974.
44. "F.C.C. Petitioned on Post Charge," *New York Times*, May 23, 1974.
45. Paid advertisement by Pawley, "The White House Witch Hunt," *Miami Herald*, July 12, 1973.
46. Jack Kofoed, "Does Mr. Pawley Favor a Coverup?" *Miami Herald*, July 14, 1973.
47. Jack Kassewitz, "Mr. Pawley's Wrong about Free Press in Democracy," *Miami Daily News*, July 17, 1973.
48. Helen Wells, "Pawley Named President of Bath Club," *Miami Herald*, February 16, 1960; and "They're Building a Road Through Bath Club," *Miami News*, December 18, 1960.
49. "Pawley: Man of the Year," *Miami News*, April 14, 1959; and "Alianza Will Honor Transit Chief Pawley," *Miami Herald*, April 12, 1959.
50. "Pawley to Head UF Study," *Miami Herald*, March 12, 1961.
51. *National Cyclopedia of American Biography* (New York: James T. White, 1981), 60:215–16.

52. *Who Was Who in America* (New Providence, NJ: Marquis Who's Who, 1977–1981), 7:440.
53. Pawley to Evelyn Mitchell, October 6, 1970, Pawley Papers.
54. Arnold Markowitz, "Former Diplomat Pledges Award for Police," *Miami Herald*, December 6, 1968.
55. William W. Turner, *Power on the Right* (Berkeley, CA: Ramparts Press, 1971), 199–200.
56. William D. Pawley, "A Way Out of Vietnam," *American Security Council Washington Report*, December 1, 1969.
57. Chiang Kai-shek to Pawley, December 24, 1969, Pawley Papers.
58. Paid advertisement by Pawley, "Why We Lost the War in Vietnam," *Miami Herald*, August 28, 1973.
59. Paid advertisement by Pawley, "Have You Ever Faced the Possibility That Your Country Could Cease to Exist?" *Miami Herald*, April 2, 1974.
60. The People Speak, letter from William Pawley, *Miami News*, January 23, 1975.
61. "William Pawley, Ex-Envoy to Brazil, Aviation Expert," *Washington Post*, January 9, 1977; and Bohning, "Miamian Pawley Tells."
62. "William D. Pawley Kills Himself."
63. Autopsy Report, Miami-Dade Office of the Medical Examiner, Case #77-62, January 8, 1977.
64. "William D. Pawley Kills Himself."
65. "Services Set for William Pawley," *Miami Herald*, January 9, 1977; and "William D. Pawley Memorial Services Scheduled Today," *Miami News*, January 10, 1977.
66. Edna Pawley to Nixon, January 25, 1977, Post-presidential Correspondence, Richard Nixon Library, Yorba Linda.
67. "400 Family, Friends Mourn Industrialist Pawley," *Miami Herald*, January 11, 1977.
68. Annie-Hahr Dobbs Pawley died April 30, 1986; Edna Pawley died August 28, 2004; Eugene Pawley died July 10, 1977; Edward Pawley died August 31, 1978; and Wallace Pawley died April 11, 1974.
69. "William D. Pawley, Financier, Dies at 80," *New York Times*, January 8, 1977; and "Died," *Time* 109 (January 17, 1977): 68.
70. Editorial, "William Pawley, Many-Sided Man," *Miami Herald*, January 9, 1977.

BIBLIOGRAPHY

Magazine Articles

Air & Space—April–May 1988, 79–89, Barton, Charles, "Wings for the Dragon."

Air Enthusiast—34 (September–December 1987): 7–24, Hooton, Edward R., "Air War over China."

Air Power Historian—6 (April 1959): 88–93, McDonald, William C., Jr., "The Chennault I Remember."

American Aviation

September 15, 1945, 93, Bramley, Eric, "Factory in India Overhauls 600 Aircraft in One Year."

August 1, 1942, 35, "Vultee Purchases Intercontinent Aircraft Corp."

July 1, 1941, 42, "India Plans Factory."

February 1, 1941, 47, "Intercontinent Incorporated in Miami."

American Aviation Historical Society Journals

Spring 1978, 2–18, Leiser, Edward L., "Memoirs of Pilot Elwyn H. Gibbon, the Mad Irishman."

Fall 1974, 162–71, Wagner, Ray, "The Chinese Air Force 1931–1940."

Summer 1970, 137–44, Pentecost, Walter E., and James J. Sloan, "Advance of the Flying Tigers."

American Heritage—October–November 1978, Thomas, Hugh, "The U.S. and Castro, 1959–1962."

American Mercury—January 1955, 137–42, Castillo Armas, Carlos, "How Guatemala Got Rid of the Communists."

Art Digest—August 1, 1945, 17, "Tribute to the Tigers."

Art News—August 1–31, 1945, 24.

Asia

December 1937, 826–30, Jouett, John H., "War Planes over China."

August 1935, 458–65, Burton, Wilbur, "Mandate from Heaven."

Aviation

December 1942, 96–101, Glover, Byron A., "Assembling and Testing P-40's in Burma."

June 1936, 24–26, Forman, Harrison, "China Spreads Her Wings."

June 1934, 172–75, Forman, Harrison, "Aircraft Manufacturing in China."

Caribbean Studies—5, no. 3 (October 1965): 22–31, Pulley, Raymond H., "The United States and the Trujillo Dictatorship, 1933–1940: The High Price of Caribbean Stability."

City of San Francisco—January 13, 1976, 16–17, Hinckle, Warren, and William Turner, "The CIA and the Flying Tiger Caper."

Collier's—November 12, 1938, 44, Gibbon, Elwyn, "Commuting to War."

Diplomatic History

    Spring 2000, 317–34, Zelikow, Philip, "American Policy and Cuba, 1961–1963."

    Summer 1992, 409–28, Meers, Sharon I., "The British Connection: How the United States Covered Its Tracks in the 1954 Coup in Guatemala."

    Winter 1990, 67–95, Marks, Frederick W., III, "The CIA and Castillo Armas in Guatemala, 1954: New Clues to an Old Puzzle."

    Winter 1987, 67–70, Paterson, Thomas G., "The Historian as Detective: Senator Kenneth Keating, the Missiles in Cuba, and His Mysterious Sources."

    Fall 1984, 368, Vandenbroucke, Lucien S., "The 'Confessions" of Allen Dulles: New Evidence on the Bay of Pigs."

    Fall 1984, 380, Bissell, Richard M., Jr., "Response to Lucien S. Vandenbroucke, 'The "Confessions" of Allen Dulles: New Evidence on the Bay of Pigs.'"

Esquire

    June 1963, 67, Southern, Terry, "How I Signed Up at $250 a Month for the Big Parade through Havana Bla-Bla-Bla and Wound Up in Guatemala with the CIA."

    August 1963, 12, Pawley's letter to the editor, "The Cuban Story."

    April 1964, 94, Cassini, Igor, "Personal Lives: When the Sweet Life Turns Sour; a Farewell to Scandal."

Flying—31, no. 2 (August 1942): 22–24, Johnston, Russ, "Japs Are Their Specialty."

Harper's Magazine—December 1956, 67–72, Ornes, Germán E., and John McCarten, "Trujillo: Little Caesar on Our Own Front Porch."

Journal of Cold War Studies—1, no. 3 (Fall 1999):139–67, Holland, Max, "A Luce Connection: Senator Keating, William Pawley, and the Cuban Missile Crisis."

Liberty

    July 25, 1942, 9–11, Pentecost, Walter, "Here Come the Flying Tigers!"

    August 1, 1942, 20–25, Pentecost, Walter, "Date with Destiny."

Life—March 22, 1943, 14:30+, "American Makes Planes in India."

Look—August 20, 1957, 61–63, Knebel, Fletcher, "How Trujillo Spends a Million in the U.S.A."

Museum of Aviation News—Warner Robins, GA, Fall 1998, 1:3, "Flying Tiger Art Exhibit Opens."

The Nation

    November 12, 1960, 360–62, Beals, Carleton, "Cuba's Invasion Jitters."

    November 5, 1960, 337, Editorial, "Cuba and Guatemala."

    May 21, 1955, 440–42, Graham, David, "Castillo's Guatemala."

Nation's Business—May 1972, 32–35, "Chavez Blight Spreads East."

New Republic

    March 7, 1970, 9–10, "Post Script."

    April 13, 1963, 19–20, Gall, Norman, "How Trujillo Died."

Newsweek

    November 18, 1946, 27, The Periscope, "The Braden-Pawley Feud."

    April 6, 1942, 19:20–21, "Flying Tigers."

    May 20, 1933, 19, "Chinese Fliers: Jouett, American, Training Air Force."

Pacific Historian—Spring 1973, 1–31, Payne, Walter A., "The Guatemalan Revolution, 1944–1954: An Interpretation."

Pacific Historical Review—38, no. 4 (November 1969): 447–62, Leary, William M., Jr., "Wings for China, the Jouett Mission, 1932–1935."

The Progressive—July 1986, 50, Roettinger, Philip C., "The Company, Then and Now."

Reader's Digest

    November 1964, 281, Nixon, Richard M., "Cuba, Castro and John F. Kennedy."

    September 1964, 241, Lazo, Mario, "Decision for Disaster."

Saturday Evening Post—January 19, 1963, 28+, Maas, Peter, "Boswell of the Jet Set."

Science & Society—35, no. 2 (Summer 1971): 129–55, Gordon, Max, "A Case History of U.S. Subversion: Guatemala, 1954."

Snafu—George Army Air Field Newspaper, Lawrenceville, IL, March 27, 1943, 1:3.

Soldier of Fortune—February 1976, 12–21+, Brown, Robert K., and Miguel Acoca, "The Bayo-Pawley Affair."

Time

    109 (January 17, 1977): 68, "Died."

    55 (March 20, 1950): 36, "Wizard at Work."

    51 (April 26, 1948): 35–36, "Pawley's Testament."

    51 (February 16, 1948): 39, "Customers' Man."

    50 (September 15, 1947): 34, "*Carioca* Climax."

    50 (September 15, 1947): 21–32, "*Salve!*"

    47 (February 4, 1946): 38, "Apra Enters."

    40 (September 7, 1942): 98–99, "China Swashbuckler."

    32 (June 23, 1941): 3, "'Convoys' to China."

    34 (November 13, 1939): 24–25, "New Route, New Factory."

U.S. News & World Report—October 8, 1962, 47–48, "How U.S. Helped Castro."

Village Post—April 1968, 24, Bohne, Grace Wing, "International Adventurer."

Village Voice—October 3, 1977, 23, Russell, Dick, "Loran Hall and the Politics of Assassination."

Newspaper Articles

Chicago Daily Tribune

    February 20, 1961, Edwards, Willard, "Urges Probe of Red Plot in State Dept."

    February 20, 1961, Editorial, "The Red Herring's Return."

Corpus Christi Caller

    August 7, 1973, "Ex-Cuban Dictator, Batista Dies at 72."

    December 20, 1957, "Ex-FBI Agent Is Sentenced."

Dallas Morning News—May 10, 1979, Golz, Earl, "Cuban Rebels Told Ex-Envoy of Oswald Trip."

Hearst's Sunday American—July 20, 1919, "Miss Annie Dobbs to Be Married Next Friday."

Houston Chronicle

    June 1, 1961, "Trujillo Died with Gun in His Hand."

    March 12, 1961, "U.S. Bungled Plan in Cuba, Batista Says."

    February 19, 1961, "Ex-Diplomat Accuses Ex-Leader of Red Aid."

    December 29, 1960, "Truman Dislikes 'Missouri Waltz.'"

    June 19, 1957, "Venezuela Pearl Beds Have Been Worked 2000 Years."

Japan Times and Advertiser

    November 12, 1940, "Japanese Air Raids Make Road Useless."

    November 7, 1940, "Chiang Aide in America to Obtain Further Help."

Japan Times and Mail—November 2, 1940, "Mekong Bridge Destruction Is Fatal."

Miami Daily News

    July 17, 1973, Kassewitz, Jack, "Mr. Pawley's Wrong about Free Press in Democracy."

April 15, 1959, Acer, Margaret, "Life's Calmer Now."

April 14, 1959, "Pawley: Man of the Year."

September 2, 1955, Roberts, Jack W., "Pawley Rejects Profit Plan, Dampens Hope of Bus Truce."

August 31, 1955, Roberts, Jack W., "New Truce Plan Lessens Threat of Bus Strike."

August 30, 1955, "Pawley Not Needed, Bus Official Claims."

August 29, 1955, Cavendish, Henry, "New Bus Plan to Be Offered by Aronovitz."

August 28, 1955, Oswald, Jack, "Mayor's Tentative OK Given to Bus Expert Study Panel."

August 28, 1955, "Pawley Urges 'Joint Audit' of Bus Books."

August 27, 1955, "Issue of Busline Franchise Depends on Result of Survey."

August 25, 1955, "Committee Sends Bus Tangle Back to City Transit Firm."

August 24, 1955, Roberts, Jack W., "Drivers Hit City-Owned Busses Plan."

August 24, 1955, "City Studies Buying Miami Transit Line."

June 22, 1955, Wood, Jane, "Where You Will Sit in Miami Bus Fight."

June 23, 1955, Wood, Jane, "Has Bus System Taken Mr. Pawley For a Ride?"

September 28, 1951, "Rites Tomorrow for C. D. Pawley."

September 27, 1951, "Clifton Pawley Dies in Mexico; Rites Pending."

February 20, 1951, Editorial, "Pawley at Peak of Career."

February 19, 1951, "Pawley Is Aide to Acheson."

February 17, 1951, Brown, Constantine, "MacArthur Seeking Use of Nationalists."

March 6, 1950, "Pawley to Buy British Busses."

March 3, 1950, "Pawley Reveals Havana Transport Deal."

June 8, 1949, Wing, Grace, "High School May Delay Pawley-Taylor Nuptials."

June 7, 1949, "Elizabeth Taylor to Wed Pawley's Son Next Year."

June 18, 1948, "Miss DePass, Mr. Pawley Marry in Beach Church."

June 12, 1948, Editorial, "New Hope for Bus Improvements."

June 2, 1948, "Pawley's Divorce in Cuba Upheld."

September 7, 1946, "Envoy Pawley Sued by Wife for Support."

June 1, 1945, Editorial, "Ambassador Bill."

May 31, 1945, "Pawley Named Envoy to Peru."

February 11, 1945, Pawley, William D., "Pawley Sees Vast Trade if Britain, U.S. Co-Operate."

November 5, 1940, "Plane Factory Steel Unloaded in Miami Today."

September 22, 1935, "Society News."

January 18, 1935, "Amused Smiles Greet Mention of Chop Suey."

January 14, 1935, "Scenes at Chinese Village Tea."

January 13, 1935, "Chinese Village in Coral Gables Setting for Tea."

January 10, 1935, "Important Figures in World of Events Attend Reception."

January 9, 1935, "Chinese Air Chief Finds Things 'Just Lovely' in Miami Area."

January 9, 1935, "Roney Plaza Hotel Plans Two Events."

January 6, 1935, "Chinese Minister of Aviation Will Be Honored at Smart Afternoon Fete."

October 30, 1930, "Mail Volume to Be Boosted by Cuba Line."

July 30, 1930, "New City-Cuba Aviation Line to Open Dec. 15."

February 25, 1930, "2 Cuban Accidents Cost Dozen Lives."

February 16, 1930, "Many Notables in Aero Club Member List."

January 30, 1930, "2 Armored Planes Are Sold to Cuba."

Miami Herald

February 27, 1997, Tasker, Fred, "The Man Who Would Marry Liz."

June 11, 1989, "History Around Us."

January 11, 1977, "400 Family, Friends Mourn Industrialist Pawley."

January 9, 1977, "Services Set for William Pawley."

January 9, 1977, Editorial, "William Pawley, Many-Sided Man."

January 8, 1977, "William D. Pawley Kills Himself."

January 8, 1976, Bohning, Don, "Miamian Pawley Tells of '63 Cuba Operation, Loss of 10 Exiles."

December 14, 1975, Glaser, Vera, "Panel Asks Pawley's Testimony on JFK."

November 27, 1974, "Challengers Withdrawing Bid to Take Channel 10 License."

August 28, 1973, Advertisement by Pawley, "Why We Lost the War in Vietnam."

July 14, 1973, Kofoed, Jack, "Does Mr. Pawley Favor a Coverup?"

July 12, 1973, Advertisement by Pawley, "The White House Witch Hunt."

April 2, 1974, Advertisement by Pawley, "Have You Ever Faced the Possibility That Your Country Could Cease to Exist?"

March 14, 1972, "Union Undecided on Talisman Suit Appeal."

March 8, 1972, Martinez, Georgia, "Talisman, Union Told to Halt Fights, Threats."

March 1, 1972, Buchanan, Edna, "Chavez, Coke Agree on Pact."

February 24, 1972, Martinez, Georgia, "Can't Enter Talisman Plant to Prove Charges, Union Says."

February 24, 1972, Eiland, Darrell, "Pawley: Sugar Worker Treated Well."

February 22, 1972, Buchanan, Edna, "AFL-CIO Gives Union Status to Chavez' Farming Group."

February 18, 1972, Buchanan, James, "TV Camera Is Victim of Pawley Brother Melee."

February 17, 1972, "Union: Armed Guards Isolate Workers."

February 15, 1972, Martinez, Georgia, "Sugar Mill Bars State Investigator."

February 12, 1972, Maeder, Jay, "Borden Boycott Brews, Chavez Says."

February 12, 1972, Martinez, Georgia, "Accident Car Still Unidentified in Coed's Death at Sugar Mill."

February 10, 1972, Martinez, Georgia, "FHP Not Close to Solving Fatality near Sugar Plant."

February 9, 1972, Martinez, Georgia, "3 Sue Talisman to Enter Camp."

February 8, 1972, Smith, Tom, "Picket Hit by Another Vehicle?"

February 8, 1972, Smith, Tom, "Coed Hit by Someone Else."

February 6, 1972, Martinez, Georgia, "La Huelga Begins."

February 2, 1972, Martinez, Georgia, "Woman Lawyer, Clergy Charged in Sugar Row."

February 1, 1972, "Arson Eyed in Talisman Truck Fire."

January 30, 1972, "McGovern Joins Farm Picketing."

January 29, 1972, Buchanan, James, "Pawley Denies Charges That Sugar Workers Carry Guns."

January 27, 1972, Martinez, Georgia, "Chavez Wires Support for Sugar Workers."

January 26, 1972, "Truck Hits, Kills Coed Picketing Sugar Plant."

January 23, 1972, "Strike Talk Proposed by Chavez."

January 22, 1972, Martinez, Georgia, "Sugar Plant Hit by Chavez Pickets."

January 3, 1971, "Flying Tigers."

October 3, 1971, Dangaard, Colin, "Goldwater Rips U.S. Critics, Honors Pawley."

September 18, 1971, Carroll, Margaret, "Pawley Sugar Mill Lawsuits Are Settled in Court."

January 6, 1970, Anderson, Jack, "Miami Businessmen Merge to Compete for Channel 10."

March 6, 1969, Anderson, Jack, "Ch. 10 Is Sold for $20 Million."

December 6, 1968, Markowitz, Arnold, "Former Diplomat Pledges Award for Police."

October 18, 1964, McDermott, John, "Upheavals Aid Barry—Nixon."

February 11, 1964, "Pawley Cash to Be Put into Sugar."

September 8, 1963, Martinez, Carlos, "Castro Will Fall if Exiles Armed, Willing—Somoza."

September 2, 1963, Smith, Tom, "Sugar Industry's Prospects Sweet."

September 1, 1963, Russell, James, "Everglades Sugar Boom Lures More Big Firms."

November 6, 1962, Lardner, George, "Bus System Interest to Total $4 Million."

November 4, 1962, "'Overthrow Castro'—Pawley."

November 4, 1962, Bonafede, Dom, "Miami's Cuban Exile Groups Uniting."

January 26, 1962, Whited, Charles, "We Should Quit OAS, Pawley Claims."

March 17, 1961, Sokolsky, George E., "Batista's Letter to Herald Opens New Policy Question."

March 12, 1961, "Pawley to Head UF Study."

March 9, 1961, McDermott, John B., "Batista Breaks His Silence: U.S. Goofed."

March 8, 1961, "Pawley Replies to the Notebook."

February 26, 1961, Editor's Notebook, "Pawley vs. Braden."

February 20, 1961, "Diplomat Fired Due to Red Ties—Pawley."

February 20, 1961, Bonafede, Dom, "Good Will of Latins Not for Sale—Pawley."

February 11, 1961, Bonafede, Dom, "Pawley Tells of Plan to Block Fidel."

February 1, 1961, Smith, Tom, "Sugar 'Sweetens' Glades Economy."

September 15, 1960, McDermott, John, "Transit Unit Sets Talks on Miami Buses."

August 16, 1960, McDermott, John, "U.S. Is Urged to Quit OAS by Ex-Ambassador Pawley."

August 13, 1960, Reno, Bob, "Bus Fare Boost Expected Soon?"

August 11, 1960, Kraslow, David J., "Aid Castro Foes, Smathers Urges."

July 29, 1960, Porter, Fred, "Bus Shut Down Delayed 15 Days."

July 28, 1960, McDermott, John B., "Why Ex-Demo Envoy's in GOP."

July 28, 1960, McDermott, John B., "Florida Split over Veep Spot."

February 18, 1960, Kraslow, David, "Smathers 'Used' by Trujillo?"

February 16, 1960, "Reds Eye Cuba for Missiles?"

February 16, 1960, Wells, Helen, "Pawley Named President of Bath Club."

February 13, 1960, Adde, Leo, "Miamian Pawley Had a Part in Trujillo's 'Free Vote' Vow."

February 12, 1960, Adde, Leo, "Must Play Ball with Dictators, Smathers Says."

February 11, 1960, Adde, Leo, "Trujillo Sincere—Smathers."

July 28, 1959, Adde, Leo, "'I'd Grab at Bus Lines Myself,' Campbell Says.'"

May 17, 1959, Johnson, Stan, "How to Make $300,000 a Year with No Taxes."

May 8, 1959, "Cuba Booting Lansky's Kin."

April 16, 1959, Pearson, Drew, "Del Pino—Once a Castro Man—Now Hates Him."

April 12, 1959, "Alianza Will Honor Transit Chief Pawley."

September 12, 1956, "Adams Bus Line Sold to Pawley."

August 31, 1956, Boyles, John L., "Pawley Interests Purchase South Miami's Coach Service."

December 6, 1955, Neuharth, Al, "Pawley to Hunt Uranium."

September 14, 1955, "Pawley Writes Out Terms on Bus Sale."

September 5, 1955, Kraslow, David J., "Inside City Hall."

September 4, 1955, Kraslow, David J., "He's an Expert among Experts."

September 2, 1955, Kraslow, David J., "Pawley Rejects Expert's Proposal."

August 28, 1955, "Transit Firm Offers to Pay for Bus Study."

August 27, 1955, "City Calls on Expert to Air Bus Franchise at a $100-a-Day Fee."

August 21, 1955, Donaldson, Bryan, "Beach Buses Show Profit While Miami Line Runs in Red."

August 10, 1955, "Beach Bus Union Wins Pay Raises."

May 20, 1955, Neuharth, Al, "Dade Bus Plan Called a Scheme to Unload Line."

May 19, 1955, Neuharth, Al, "Buses Run by Port Authority Urged for County by C of C."

June 28, 1954, "Pawley Back on Job for Government."

September 3, 1952, "Pawley Counts Himself in Camp of Ike."

January 26, 1952, Voltz, Luther, "City Rejects Pawley Offer to Sell Two Bus Lines, Suggests Increase in Fares."

January 13, 1952, Mobley, Radford, "'Let's Call in Bill Pawley.'"

September 29, 1951, "Pawley Rites Scheduled for Today."

September 27, 1951, "Pawley's Son Dies of Polio in Mexico City."

February 20, 1951, Thale, Jack, "Diplomatic Job Handed to Pawley."

February 5, 1951, "Annie Hahr Pawley, Mr. McKay Wed in Quiet Ceremony Sunday."

March 10, 1950, Thale, Jack, "Cuba OKs Pawley's Plan for Modern Bus System."

March 8, 1950, "Army Runs Havana Trolleys."

June 8, 1949, "Elizabeth Taylor and Pawley Set February for Wedding."

June 19, 1948, Personally Speaking column.

June 18, 1948, "C. D. Pawleys United in Church on Anniversary of First Date."

June 2, 1948, Berning, C. G., "Pawley's Cuban Divorce Is Upheld as Former Wife Loses Florida Suit."

October 31, 1946, Pearson, Drew, Merry-Go-Round column.

October 23, 1946, "Pawley Says Income Far Below Claim."

October 20, 1946, Pearson, Drew, "Miami's Ambassador Bill Pawley Denies He's after Braden's Job."

September 8, 1946, "Pawley's Ex-Wife Asks $5,000 Extra Alimony."

June 17, 1945, "Pawley Takes Oath as New Envoy to Peru."

June 1, 1945, Editorial, "Ambassador 'Bill' Pawley."

September 22, 1937, "Leaves for Duke."

July 3, 1937, "Edward P. Pawley Dies after Illness."

December 12, 1935, "Program Given for Maneuvers."

December 10, 1935, "See Them at the Air Races."

January 14, 1935, "Widely Known Guests Attend Dinner Dance."

January 12, 1935, "Ball for Aviators Will Be Colorful."

January 11, 1935, "Brilliant Reception Honors General Mow."

January 10, 1935, Photo caption, Pawley with Chinese Delegation.

January 6, 1935, "Reception Is Arranged for Chinese Officials."

December 8, 1930, "President of Cuban Air Line Visits Miami."

September 21, 1925, Advertisement, H. Clifton Dobbs.

September 18, 1925, Advertisement, Boca Del Faro.

September 13, 1925, Advertisement, Edward E. Dammers.

Miami News

January 10, 1977, "William D. Pawley Memorial Services Scheduled Today."

January 23, 1975, The People Speak, letter from William Pawley.

February 17, 1972, "Cane Cutters Held Captive, Says Chavez."

February 1, 1972, "Co-ed's Death Embitters Sugar Mill–Union Struggle."

January 29, 1972, "Sugar Boss: No Guns Used."

January 7, 1970, Roberts, Jack, "Political Clout May Decide Ch. 10 Case."

January 6, 1970, "Channel 10, Challengers to Slug It Out before FCC."

January 5, 1970, Colbert, Haines, "Local Group Asks Channel 10 Permit."

April 11, 1969, McLemore, Morris, "Flying Tigers and Bill Pawley."

August 18, 1964, "Pawley Named Barry Leader."

October 7, 1962, Hendrix, Hal, "Soviets Build 6 Cuban Missile Bases."

January 30, 1962, Sneigr, Denis, "Union Forcing Takeover, Dade Told."

January 28, 1962, Nellius, Dick, "Metro Gets Court OK to Buy Buses."

January 22, 1962, Einstein, Paul, "25 Drivers Return Metro's Bus Forms."

May 21, 1961, Sosin, Milt, "Captives Come to Trade for Lives."

February 20, 1961, "Braden Says Pawley Story Is Not True."

February 9, 1961, Allen, Robert S., and Paul Scott, "How Miami's Pawley Tried to 'Save' Cuba."

December 18, 1960, "They're Building a Road Through Bath Club."

October 25, 1960, "Metro Nearing Price for All 4 Bus Lines."

September 1, 1960, Hesser, Charles F., "GOP Opens Net to Catch Dade Demo Ditherers."

August 26, 1960, "U.S. Breaks Off with Trujillo."

August 21, 1960, "Walk Out of OAS Parley."

August 20, 1960, "Trujillo Censured by OAS."

August 19, 1960, "A 'Quarantine' for Trujilloland?"

August 18, 1960, Hendrix, Hal, "U.S. Seeks Sanctions on Trujillo."

August 16, 1960, Hendrix, Hal, "Report Pins Assassination on Trujillo."

March 9, 1960, Williams, Verne O., "Transit Board 'Named.'"

February 29, 1960, Hesser, Charles F., "GOP Picks Slate Pledged to Nixon."

February 15, 1960, "Soviet Base for Cuba?"

January 16, 1960, Hesser, Charles F., "You'll Do Well in South, Nixon Told."

Miami Sunday News

November 19, 1950, "Pawley Firm Gets Cuban Interventor."

March 12, 1950, "Pawley to Move to Cuba to Run New Bus Lines."

Miami Tribune—May 14, 1937, Photo caption, "Southern Sunshine."

New York Herald Tribune

July 12, 1963, Evans, Rowland, and Robert Novak, "Inside Report: The Cuba Expert."

June 8, 1949, "Elizabeth Taylor and Fiance, William D. Pawley Jr."

New York Times

January 8, 1977, "William D. Pawley, Financier, Dies at 80."

May 23, 1974, "F.C.C. Petitioned on Post Charge."

June 26, 1973, Hunter, Marjorie, "Dean Says White House Put a 'Friend' in C.I.A."

November 20, 1972, "Chavez Seeks Investigation of Florida's Sugar Industry."

October 10, 1972, "Clash Likely Between Sugar Industry and Farm Union."

February 25, 1972, Photo caption, "Candidate Joins Pickets."

January 7, 1970, "Nixon Friends Seek TV License in Miami Held by News Group."

May 27, 1968, "17 Ex-Ambassadors Form a Nixon Group."

July 19, 1965, Eder, Richard, "U.S. Cuban Expert Restored to Duty."

February 21, 1963, Weaver, Warren Jr., "Capital Guesses at Keating's Aims."

June 27, 1962, Johnson, Richard J.H., "Group Is Organized to Raise Ransom for Cuban Prisoners."

May 13, 1962, Phillips, R. Hart, "Dade Vote Backs County's Merger."

July 6, 1961, Kihss, Peter, "Prisoners Renew Tractor Effort."

May 21, 1961, Brewer, Sam Pope, "Exile Leader Hopeful."

March 24, 1961, Paid letter by José Bosch to editor.

February 20, 1961, "Ex-Envoy Scores Spruille Braden."

February 12, 1961, "1958 Move to Bar Castro Disclosed."

February 12, 1960, Burks, Edward, "More Are Convicted by Trujillo Regime."

September 2, 1957, Bracker, Milton, "Mysteries Strain U.S.-Dominican Tie."

October 20, 1954, "'A Creditable Job' Is Verdict on C.I.A."

June 29, 1952, "Cuban Labor Chief Held for Murder."

April 15, 1952, "Pawley Flying to Paris."

December 11, 1951, "Ex-Envoy to Help Lovett Speed Arms."

September 27, 1951, "Clifton Pawley Dead."

June 23, 1951, "U.S. Reassures India."

June 14, 1951, "Hoffman and Pawley in Madrid."

June 2, 1951, "Pawley on Mission for Acheson."

May 13, 1951, "U.S. Aides in India See Prestige Loss."

May 4, 1951, Editorial, "Aid to India."

February 20, 1951, "Pawley, Former Envoy, Made Aide to Acheson."

November 19, 1950, "Havana Seizes Bus Line."

December 3, 1949, "Barkley Derides Foes' Talk of 'Statism,' Sees Victories."

September 20, 1949, "Pawley Engagement Off."

November 8, 1948, Sulzberger, C. L., "U.S. Diplomats Abroad Deplore Private Envoys."

August 1, 1948, Leviero, Anthony, "Something New Is Added at the White House."

June 1, 1948, "Pawley's Son to Wed on June 17."

May 3, 1948, Bracker, Milton, "Success in Bogota Held Exaggerated."

April 30, 1948, Hulen, Bertram, "U.S. Aide Commends Results of Bogota."

April 24, 1948, Bracker, Milton, "Marshall Leaves Bogota as Parley Nears Conclusion."

April 16, 1948, White, William S., "Marshall Scoffed at Early Warnings on Reds in Bogota."

April 15, 1948, Hulen, Bertram D., "Pan-America Talks Resume in Bogota."

April 13, 1948, Bracker, Milton, "Bogota News Curb Called Complete."

April 12, 1948, Bracker, Milton, "Bogota Talks to Continue; Martial Law in Colombia; Red Role in Uprising Seen."

April 11, 1948, "Bogota Uprising Is Quelled, Coalition Regime Formed; Parley's Fate Left to U.S."

April 11, 1948, "Focus on Bogota."

April 10, 1948, "Colombia Battles Leftist Mobs Burning and Looting the Capital; Inter-American Parley Is Halted."

April 9, 1948, "No Bogota Applause for U.S. Half Billion."

April 5, 1948, Hulen, Bertram D., "Marshall Visits Colombian Center."

March 27, 1948, "William D. Pawley."

March 17, 1948, "Diplomats Resign Posts."

September 20, 1947, "Pawley Returning to U.S."

September 8, 1947, Trussell, C.P., "President Sailing Directly for Home Aboard Battleship."

September 7, 1947, Trussell, C.P., "Truman Safe as Auto Skids on Brazilian Mountain Road."

August 20, 1947, "Marshall Misses Dance."

August 2, 1947, Hulen, Bertram, "Marshall to Head Delegation at Rio."

July 19, 1947, "Pawley Sees Truman."

April 5, 1947, "Pawley Dispels Rumors."

December 5, 1946, "Vargas Says Berle Aided in Downfall."

November 2, 1946, "Ambassador Pawley in Hospital."

November 1, 1946, Hulen, Bertram D., "Braden Supported by Byrnes, Truman."

October 26, 1946, "Pawley to Take Sick Leave."

October 23, 1946, Leviero, Anthony, "Byrnes Reaffirms U.S. View on Peron."

October 22, 1946, "Braden Showdown on Argentina Seen."

September 28, 1946, "Pawley Leaves Today for U.S."

July 25, 1946, Kluckhohn, Frank, "Halsey By-passes Argentina on Tour."

May 14, 1946, "Truman Decorates Pawley."

April 10, 1946, "Named to Argentina."

April 5, 1946, "Brazil Accepts Pawley."

April 3, 1946, "Messersmith Seen in Argentine Post."

January 29, 1946, "Denies Braden Is Quitting."

December 6, 1945, "Peruvian Minister Tells of New Goals."

July 23, 1945, "Peru Names President."

June 27, 1945, "New Head of Peru Outlines Policies."

April 16, 1944, Melvin D. Hildreth, Letter to the editor.

July 18, 1942, "Largest War Industry in Florida Is Purchased by Vultee Aircraft."

April 7, 1940, "China Essay Contest On."

March 24, 1938, "Foreign Legion of Air Disbanded by China."

August 15, 1937, "Chinese Air Bombs Kill 600 in Shanghai."

February 11, 1935, "China Begins Work on Great Air Base."

January 13, 1935, "Diplomats at Miami Are Honored at Ball."

January 11, 1935, Cleveland, Reginald, "Army Air Armada Opens Miami Meet."

December 24, 1934, "China Completing Big New Air Base."

April 29, 1934, "Sees Gain by China in Army Air Fleet."

January 14, 1934, "China Buys New Planes."

December 8, 1933, Abend, Hallett, "Firm Here to Build Airplanes in China."

August 19, 1933, "Heads Aviation Company."

April 1, 1933, "American Airline Adds Link in China."

April 13, 1932, "Pan American Gets Cuban Air Service."

January 10, 1931, "Crash Kills Three at Miami Air Meet."

January 7, 1931, "Planes Assembled for National Meet."

September 8, 1930, "More Relief Going to Santo Domingo."

September 7, 1930, "Santo Domingo Toll Reaches 4,000 Dead."

September 6, 1930, "Hurricane Toll Now 1,200."

September 6, 1930, "Fly with Supplies to Santo Domingo."

September 5, 1930, "Santo Domingo Wrecked by Hurricane."

September 4, 1930, "Hurricane Strikes Dominican Capital; Disaster Is Feared."

September 4, 1930, "Santo Domingo Lies in Noted Gale Area."

February 25, 1930, "2 Cuban Fliers Killed at Airport Dedication."

January 12, 1930, "350 Planes to Compete at Miami."

November 4, 1929, "Starts Cuban Air Taxi Service."

October 25, 1929, "Cuba Selects 3 from 18 Air Bids."

January 9, 1929, "Miami Turns Eyes to Indies Flights."

January 8, 1929, "Sky Circus Opens Airport at Miami."

September 7, 1928, "'Air Taxi' Network Planned by Curtiss."

Oakland Tribune—November 4, 1962, "Pawley Calls Pact 'Devastating Blow.'"

Palm Beach Post—February 17, 1961, "Batista Rejected Caretaker Regime."

Pensacola Journal—March 28, 1968, Prime, Bill, "'Johnson Needs Miracle'—Pawley."

San Antonio Express—March 2, 1932, "Canadian Flyers Waive Citizenship."

San Francisco Examiner—May 9, 1937, "MacArthur, Bride Visiting Here."

Tropic, Miami Herald—August 22, 1971, Smiley, Nixon, "The Private Wars of William Pawley."

Wall Street Journal—January 7, 1970, "Nixon's Friends Seek License to a TV Unit of Firm Hit by Agnew."

Washington Daily News
  February 20, 1961, O'Rourke, John T., "Our Man in Havana, William D. Pawley."
  February 20, 1961, Russell, Oland D., "Pawley Also Warned on China."
  October 17, 1945, Gordon, Evelyn Peyton, "Evie Figures Bess Should Ease Up on Social Security."
Washington Evening Star—January 7, 1970, "Group Seeks Miami Station of Post Firm."
Washington Post
  January 9, 1977, "William Pawley, Ex-Envoy to Brazil, Aviation Expert."
  January 9, 1976, "Former Envoy Confirms 1963 Cuba Raiding Party."
  January 7, 1970, "Florida Group Challenges Post-Newsweek Station License."
  February 27, 1961, Editorial, "Villainy."
  February 26, 1961, Drummond, Roscoe, "Senate Probe Blurs Cuban Issue."
  February 23, 1961, Editorial, "Backbiting."
  February 22, 1961, Childs, Marquis, "Changes Conceal Cuban Realities."
  February 20, 1961, Goldsmith, John A., "Pawley Charges Cuba Bungling."
  June 5, 1957, Pearson, Drew, "Kin of Officials Close to Trujillo."
  June 4, 1957, Pearson, Drew, "Morse Preparing Weekly Ike Blasts; Dominican-Go-Around."
  June 17, 1946, Pearson, Drew, "Why Braden Resigned."
  October 7, 1945, "Lectures Scheduled."
  December 31, 1944, Pearson, Drew, "Foreign Policy Storm Due Soon."
  June 1, 1941, Bookman, George, "U.S. Releases Pilots to Fight for China."
  March 25, 1941, Alsop, Joseph, and R. Kintner, "Lauchlin Currie's Report on China."
Washington Star
  January 8, 1976, "Ex-Envoy, Life Staffer in '63 Cuba Raid."
  November 16, 1975, Beale, Betty, "Clare Boothe Luce Weaves a Fascinating Tale."
Washington Star-News, October 11, 1974, Pawley letter to editor, "Stay Tough on Cuba."

Court Cases
Roberts & Hoge v. Pawley, Supreme Court of South Carolina. 50 S.C. 491; 27 S.E. 913 (September 30, 1897).
Pawley v. Pawley. 46 So. 2d 464 (April 6, 1950).
Pawley v. Pawley. 340 U.S. 866; 71 S. Ct. 90, No. 325 (October 23, 1950).
Petersen et al. v. Talisman Sugar Corporation, US Court of Appeals, 5th Circuit. 478 F.2d 73, 72-2057 (May 3, 1973).

Books
Acheson, Dean. *Present at the Creation: My Years in the State Department*. New York: W. W. Norton, 1969.
Batista, Fulgencio. *Cuba Betrayed*. New York: Vantage, 1962.
Beaulac, Willard L. *Career Ambassador*. New York: Macmillan, 1951.
Bender, Marylin, and Selig Altschul. *The Chosen Instrument: Pan Am, Juan Trippe: The Rise and Fall of an American Entrepreneur*. New York: Simon & Schuster, 1982.
Bernstein, Barton J., ed. *Politics and Policies of the Truman Administration*. Chicago: Quadrangle Books, 1970.
Beschloss, Michael R. *The Crisis Years: Kennedy and Khrushchev, 1960–1963*. New York: HarperCollins, 1991.
Bethell, Leslie, ed. *Cuba: A Short History*. London: Cambridge University Press, 1993.
Black, George. *The Good Neighbor*. New York: Pantheon Books, 1988.
Bonachea, Ramón L., and Marta San Martín. *The Cuban Insurrection: 1952–1959*. New Brunswick, NJ: Transaction, 1974.

Bond, Charles R., Jr., and Terry Anderson. *A Flying Tiger's Diary*. College Station: Texas A & M University Press, 1984.

Boyington, Gregory. *Baa Baa Black Sheep*. New York: G. P. Putnam's Sons, 1958.

Braden, Spruille. *Diplomats and Demagogues: The Memoirs of Spruille Braden*. New Rochelle, NY: Arlington House, 1971.

Brodie, Fawn M. *Richard Nixon: The Shaping of His Character*. New York: W. W. Norton, 1981.

Byrd, Martha. *Chennault: Giving Wings to the Tiger*. Tuscaloosa: University of Alabama Press, 1987.

Cabot, John Moors. *First Line of Defense: Forty Years' Experiences of a Career Diplomat*. Washington, DC: School of Foreign Service, Georgetown University, 1979.

Caidin, Martin. *The Ragged, Rugged Warriors*. New York: E. P. Dutton, 1966.

Chennault, Claire Lee. *Way of a Fighter: The Memoirs of Claire Lee Chennault*. New York: G. P. Putnam's Sons, 1949.

Coggeshall, Robert Walden. *Ancestors and Kin*. Spartanburg, SC: Reprint Company, 1988.

Colby, Gerard, and Charlotte Dennett. *Thy Will Be Done: The Conquest of the Amazon: Nelson Rockefeller and Evangelism in the Age of Oil*. New York: HarperCollins, 1995.

Compagnie biographique. *Blue Book of Hayti*. New York: Klebold Press, 1919.

Condit, Doris M. *History of the Office of the Secretary of Defense*. Vol. 2, *The Test of War, 1950–1953*. Washington, DC: Historical Office of the Secretary of Defense, 1988.

Corn, David. *Blond Ghost: Ted Shackley and the CIA's Crusade*. New York: Simon & Schuster, 1994.

Cornelius, Wanda, and Thayne Short. *Ding Hao: America's Air War in China, 1937–1945*. Gretna, LA: Pelican, 1980.

Crassweller, Robert D. *Trujillo: The Life and Times of a Caribbean Dictator*. New York: Macmillan, 1966.

Craven, Wesley Frank, and James Lea Cate, eds. *The Army Air Forces in World War II*. Vol. 5, *The Pacific: Matterhorn to Nagasaki*. Washington, DC: Government Printing Office, 1983.

Daley, Robert. *An American Saga: Juan Trippe and His Pan Am Empire*. New York: Random House, 1980.

Daniels, Jonathan. *White House Witness, 1942–1945*. Garden City, NY: Doubleday, 1975.

Diederich, Bernard. *Trujillo: The Death of the Goat*. Boston: Little, Brown, 1978.

Dorschner, John, and Roberto Fabricio. *The Winds of December*. New York: Coward, McCann & Geoghegan, 1980.

Eisenhower, Dwight David. *The Papers of Dwight David Eisenhower: The Chief of Staff*. (Volume VIII), Edited by Louis Galambos. Baltimore: Johns Hopkins University Press, 1978.

———. *The Papers of Dwight David Eisenhower: Columbia University*. (Volume X), Edited by Louis Galambos. Baltimore: Johns Hopkins University Press, 1984.

———. *The Papers of Dwight David Eisenhower: Keeping the Peace*. (Volume XXI), Edited by Louis Galambos. Baltimore: Johns Hopkins University Press, 2001.

———. *The Papers of Dwight David Eisenhower: NATO and the Campaign of 1952*. (Volumes XII and XIII), Edited by Louis Galambos. Baltimore: Johns Hopkins University Press, 1989.

———. *The Papers of Dwight David Eisenhower: The Presidency: The Middle Way*. (Volumes XIV and XVI), Edited by Louis Galambos. Baltimore: Johns Hopkins University Press, 1996.

Eisenhower, Milton S. *The Wine Is Bitter: The United States and Latin America*. Garden City, NY: Doubleday, 1963.

Fonzi, Gaeton. *The Last Investigation*. New York: Thunder's Mouth Press, 1993.

Ford, Daniel. *Flying Tigers: Claire Chennault and the American Volunteer Group*. Washington, DC: Smithsonian Institution Press, 1991.

Frillmann, Paul, and Graham Peck. *China: The Remembered Life*. Boston: Houghton Mifflin, 1968.

Galbraith, W. O. *Colombia: A General Survey*. New York: Royal Institute of International Affairs, 1953.

Galíndez, Jesús de Suarez. *The Era of Trujillo: Dominican Dictator*. Tucson: University of Arizona Press, 1973.

Gallagher, O'Dowd. *Retreat in the East*. London: George G. Harrap. 1942.

Geyer, Georgie Anne. *Guerrilla Prince: The Untold Story of Fidel Castro*. Boston: Little, Brown, 1991.

Gleijeses, Piero. *Shattered Hope: The Guatemalan Revolution and the United States, 1944–1954*. Princeton, NJ: Princeton University Press, 1991.

Gould, Randall. *China in the Sun*. Garden City, NY: Doubleday, 1946.

Greenlaw, Olga S. *The Lady and the Tigers*. New York: E. P. Dutton, 1943.

Heiferman, Ron. *Flying Tigers: Chennault in China*. New York: Ballantine, 1971.

Helmreich, Jonathan E. *Gathering Rare Ores: The Diplomacy of Uranium Acquisition, 1943–1954*. Princeton, NJ: Princeton University Press, 1986.

Heymann, C. David. *Liz: An Intimate Biography of Elizabeth Taylor*. New York: Birch Lane, 1995.

Hinckle, Warren, and William W. Turner. *Deadly Secrets: The CIA-Mafia War against Castro and the Assassination of J.F.K*. New York: Thunder's Mouth Press, 1982.

Holley, Irving Brinton, Jr. *Buying Aircraft: Matériel Procurement for the Army Air Forces*. Washington, DC: Office of the Chief of Military History, 1964.

Hotz, Robert B. *With General Chennault: The Story of the Flying Tigers*. Washington, DC: Zenger, 1943.

Housman, Alfred Edward. *Last Poems*. New York: Henry Holt, 1965.

Howard, James H. *Roar of the Tiger*. New York: Orion, 1991.

Hunt, E. Howard. *Give Us This Day*. New Rochelle, NY: Arlington House, 1973.

Immerman, Richard H. *The CIA in Guatemala: The Foreign Policy of Intervention*. Austin: University of Texas Press, 1982.

Johnson, Haynes. *The Bay of Pigs: The Leaders' Story of Brigade 2506*. New York: W. W. Norton, 1964.

Johnstone, William C. *The United States and Japan's New Order*. New York: Oxford University Press, 1941.

Kubek, Anthony. *How the Far East Was Lost: American Policy and the Creation of Communist China, 1941–1949*. Chicago: Henry Regnery, 1963.

Langer, William L., and S. Everett Gleason. *The Undeclared War, 1940–1941*. New York: Harper & Brothers, 1953.

Langley, Lester D. *The Cuban Policy of the United States: A Brief History*. New York: John Wiley and Sons, 1968.

Lazo, Mario. *Dagger in the Heart: American Policy Failures in Cuba*. New York: Funk & Wagnalls, 1968.

Leary, William M., Jr. *The Dragon's Wings: The China National Aviation Corporation and the Development of Commercial Aviation in China*. Athens: University of Georgia Press, 1976.

Lynch, Grayston L. *Decision for Disaster: Betrayal at the Bay of Pigs*. Washington, DC: Brassey's, Inc., 1998.

Maddox, Brenda. *Who's Afraid of Elizabeth Taylor?* New York: M. Evans, 1977.

Mason, Theodore K. *Across the Cactus Curtain: The Story of Guantánamo Bay*. New York: Dodd, Mead, 1984.

Maurer, Maurer. *Aviation in the U.S. Army, 1919–1939*. Washington, DC: Office of Air Force History, 1987.

Morris, Joe Alex, ed. *The Private Papers of Senator Vandenberg*. Westport, CT: Greenwood Press, 1952.

Murphy, Marion E. *The History of Guantánamo Bay*. Guantánamo Bay, Cuba: U.S. Navy, 1953.

Murray, Williamson, and Allan R. Millett. *A War to Be Won: Fighting the Second World War*. Cambridge, MA: Belknap Press of Harvard University Press, 2000.

Nalty, Bernard C. *Tigers over Asia*. New York: Elsevier-Dutton, 1978.

Nixon, Richard M. *Six Crises*. Garden City, NY: Doubleday, 1962.

Ornes, Germán E. *Trujillo: Little Caesar of the Caribbean*. New York: Thomas Nelson & Sons, 1958.

Paterson, Thomas G. *Contesting Castro: The United States and the Triumph of the Cuban Revolution*. New York: Oxford University Press, 1994.

Pawley, William D. *Americans Valiant and Glorious*. New York: Caleb Printing, 1945.

———. *Wings over Asia: A Brief History of China National Aviation Corporation*. New York: China National Aviation Association Foundation, 1941.

Phillips, Ruby Hart. *Cuba: Island of Paradox*. New York: McDowell, Obolensky, 1959.

———. *The Cuban Dilemma*. New York: Ivan Obolensky, 1962.

Pistole, Larry M. *The Pictorial History of the Flying Tigers*. Orange, VA: Moss Publications, 1981.

Pogue, Forrest C. *George C. Marshall: Ordeal and Hope*. New York: Viking, 1966.

———. *George C. Marshall: Statesman*. New York: Viking, 1987.

Prados, John. *Presidents' Secret Wars: CIA and Pentagon Covert Operations Since World War II*. New York: Morrow, 1986.

Preston, Paul. *Franco: A Biography*. New York: Basic Books, 1994.

Prevost, Charlotte Kaminski, and Effie Leland Wilder. *Pawley's Island: A Living Legend*. Columbia, SC: The State Printing Company, 1972.

Quirk, Robert E. *Fidel Castro*. New York: W. W. Norton, 1993.

Rappleye, Charles, and Ed Becker. *All American Mafioso: The Johnny Rosselli Story*. New York: Doubleday, 1991.

Roberts, Randy, and James S. Olson. *John Wayne: American*. New York: Free Press, 1995.

Rogers, George C., Jr. *The History of Georgetown County, South Carolina*. Columbia: University of South Carolina Press, 1970.

Romanus, Charles F., and Riley Sunderland. *Stilwell's Mission to China*. Washington, DC: Office of the Chief of Military History, Department of the Army, 1953.

Rosholt, Malcolm. *Claire L. Chennault: A Tribute*. Rosholt, WI: Flying Tigers of the 14th Air Force Association, 1983.

———. *Days of the Ching Pao: A Photographic Record of the Flying Tigers–14th Air Force in China in World War II*. Amherst, WI: Palmer Publications, 1978.

———. *Flight in the China Air Space: 1910–1950*. Rosholt, WI: Rosholt House, 1984.

Samson, Jack. *Chennault*. New York: Doubleday, 1987.

Schaller, Michael. *Douglas MacArthur: The Far Eastern General*. New York: Oxford University Press, 1989.

———. *The United States and China in the Twentieth Century*. New York: Oxford University Press, 1990.

———. *The U.S. Crusade in China, 1938–1945*. New York: Columbia University Press, 1979.

Schlesinger, Stephen, and Stephen Kinzer. *Bitter Fruit: The Untold Story of the American Coup in Guatemala*. Garden City, NY: Doubleday, 1982.

Schneider, Ronald M. *Communism in Guatemala: 1944–1954*. New York: Frederick A. Praeger, 1959.

Schultz, Duane. *The Maverick War: Chennault and the Flying Tigers*. New York: St. Martin's, 1987.

Scott, Peter Dale. *The War Conspiracy: The Secret Road to the Second Indochina War*. Indianapolis: Bobbs-Merrill, 1972.

Scott, Robert Lee, Jr. *Flying Tiger: Chennault of China*. Garden City, NY: Doubleday, 1959.

Seagrave, Sterling. *Soldiers of Fortune*. Alexandria, VA: Time-Life Books, 1981.

———. *The Soong Dynasty*. New York: Harper & Row, 1985.

Shamburger, Page, and Joe Christy. *The Curtiss Hawks*. Kalamazoo, MI: Wolverine, 1972.

Sheppard, Dick. *Elizabeth: The Life and Career of Elizabeth Taylor*. Garden City, NY: Doubleday, 1974.

Sherwood, Robert E. *Roosevelt and Hopkins: An Intimate History*. New York: Harper & Brothers, 1948.

Shilling, Erik. *Destiny: A Flying Tiger's Rendezvous with Fate*. Private printing, 1993.

Smith, Earl E. T. *The Fourth Floor: An Account of the Castro Communist Revolution*. New York: Random House, 1962.

Smith, Robert Moody, and Philip D. Smith. *With Chennault in China: A Flying Tiger's Diary*. Blue Ridge Summit, PA: Tab Books, 1984.

Snow, Edgar. *The Battle for Asia*. New York: World Publishing, 1942.

Stettinius, Edward R., Jr. *Lend-Lease: Weapon for Victory*. New York: Macmillan, 1944.

Summers, Anthony. *The Arrogance of Power: The Secret World of Richard Nixon*. New York: Viking, 2000.

———. *Conspiracy*. New York: McGraw-Hill, 1980.

Taylor, Elizabeth. *Elizabeth Taylor: An Informal Memoir*. New York: Harper & Row, 1964.

Thomas, J. Helsdon. *Wings over Burma*. Braunton, Devon, England: Merlin Books, 1984.

Truman, Margaret. *Harry S. Truman*. New York: William Morrow, 1973.

Turner, William W. *Power on the Right*. Berkeley, CA: Ramparts Press, 1971.

Walters, Vernon A. *Silent Missions*. Garden City, NY: Doubleday, 1978.

Weintraub, Stanley. *Long Day's Journey into War: December 7, 1941*. New York: Truman Talley Books/Dutton, 1991.

Weyl, Nathaniel. *Red Star over Cuba: The Russian Assault on the Western Hemisphere*. New York: Devin-Adair, 1960.

Whelan, Russell. *The Flying Tigers: The Story of the American Volunteer Group*. New York: Viking, 1942.

Whitaker, Arthur P. *Spain and Defense of the West: Ally and Liability*. New York: Harper & Brothers, 1961.

Wyden, Peter. *Bay of Pigs: The Untold Story*. New York: Simon & Schuster, 1979.

Young, Arthur N. *China and the Helping Hand, 1937–1945*. Cambridge, MA: Harvard University Press, 1963.

Dissertations, Theses, and Unpublished Manuscripts

Bauer, Boyd Heber. "General Claire Lee Chennault and China, 1937–1958." PhD diss., American University, Washington, DC, 1973.

Bonachea, Rolando E. "United States Policy Toward Cuba: 1959–1961." PhD thesis, Georgetown University, Washington, DC, 1975.

Brown, Philip N. "Claire Lee Chennault: Military Genius." Research paper, Air War College, Maxwell Air Force Base, AL, 1995.

Ennels, Jerome A. "Those Daring Young Men: The Role of Aero Demonstration Teams in the Evolution of Pre–World War II Pursuit Tactics, 1932–1937." Research paper, Office of History, Air University, Maxwell Air Force Base, AL, 1994.

Malek, R. Michael. "Rafael Leonidas Trujillo Molina: The Rise of a Caribbean Dictator." PhD diss., University of California, Santa Barbara, 1971.

McCoy, Mary Ellene Chenevey. "Guantánamo Bay: The United States Naval Base and Its Relationship with Cuba." PhD diss., University of Akron, OH, 1995.

Niznik, Monica Lynne. "Thomas G. Corcoran: The Public Service of Franklin Roosevelt's 'Tommy the Cork.'" PhD diss., University of Notre Dame, IN, 1981.

Pawley, William D. "Russia Is Winning." Manuscript, George Marshall Library, Lexington, VA.

———. "Why the Communists Are Winning." Edited by Richard R. Tryon. Manuscript, printed/photocopied for Pawley family by Dudley A. Whitman.

———. "The Bogotá Uprising." Monograph, George Marshall Library, Lexington, VA.

Pawley, William D., Jr. "Elizabeth Taylor's First White Diamond." Manuscript (1997).

Pickler, Gordon K. "United States Aid to the Chinese Nationalist Air Force: 1931–1949." PhD diss., Florida State University, Tallahassee, 1971.

Rys, John Frank. "Tensions and Conflicts in Cuba, Haiti, and the Dominican Republic between 1945 and 1959." PhD diss., American University, Washington, DC, 1966.

Smith, William M., Jr. "Claire Lee Chennault: The Early Years." Master's thesis, Northeast Louisiana University, Monroe, 1989.

———. "Mercenary Eagles: American Pilots Serving in Foreign Air Forces Prior to United States Entry into the Second World War, 1936–1941." PhD diss., University of Arkansas, Fayetteville, 1999.

Other

Air Corps News Letter. Washington, DC: Information Division, Air Corps, February 1, 1935.
19, no. 2, January 15, 1936.
19, no. 16, August 15, 1936.

Ayers, Eben A. Oral History Interviews, Harry S. Truman Library, Independence, MO.

Chapman, Oscar L. Oral History Interviews, Harry S. Truman Library, Independence, MO.

Clark, Tom C. Oral History Interviews, Harry S. Truman Library, Independence, MO.

Congressional Record, House
81st Cong., 1st sess., February 21, 1949, A993, "China—Statement of Hon. John F. Kennedy, of Massachusetts."
82nd Cong., 1st sess., June 26, 1951, A3898, "Ambassador Pawley and the India Grain Bill."

Congressional Record, Senate
87th Cong., 1st sess., April 18, 1961, A2581, "Ambassador Pawley's Grave Revelation."
89th Cong., 1st sess., March 9, 1965, 4472, "Agricultural Labor Shortage."
93rd Cong., 2nd sess., November 26, 1974, 37466, "Cuba."
93rd Cong., 2nd sess., December 19, 1974, 41083, "The Embargo Against Cuba."

Connelly, Matthew J. Oral History Interviews. Harry S. Truman Library, Independence, MO.

Cox, Oscar. Files. Franklin D. Roosevelt Library, Hyde Park, NY.

Department of State Bulletin
February 1, 1948, 18, no. 448, 149, "Ambassador Pawley to Assist in Preparatory Work for Inter-American Conference at Bogotá."
March 19, 1951, 24, no. 611, 477, "Appointment of Officers—William Pawley."

Fei Hu: The Story of the Flying Tigers. DVD. Transcript by Frank Boring. Directed by Frank Christopher. Santa Barbara, CA: Fei Hu Films, 1993, http://www.flyingtigers-video.com.

Flying Tigers. VHS. Written by Kenneth Gamet and Barry Trivers. Directed by David Miller. Hollywood, CA: Republic Pictures Corporation, 1942.

Frillmann, Paul. "Reminiscences of Paul W. Frillmann: Oral History, 1962." Columbia Center for Oral History, Columbia University, NY.

Leahy, William D. Diaries (Microfilm). University of Texas at Arlington.

Lyon, Cecil B. Papers, 1930–1971. Georgetown University, Washington, DC.

McHugh, James Marshall. Papers, #2770. Department of Manuscripts and University Archives, Cornell University Libraries, NY.

Medical Report, Office of the Medical Examiner, Dade County, Case# 77-62A.

Morgenthau, Henry, Jr. Papers and Diaries, 1866–1960. Franklin D. Roosevelt Library, Hyde Park, NY.

Morgenthau, Henry, Jr. The Morgenthau Diaries. Robert E. Lester, project coordinator. Microfilm. Bethesda, MD: University Publications of America, 1995–1997.

National Cyclopedia of American Biography. New York: James T. White, 1981, 60:215–16.

Pawley, William Douglas. Oral History Interview, April 4, 1967. Herbert Hoover Presidential Library, West Brank, IA.

Rankin, Karl L. Papers, 1916–1973. Seely G. Mudd Manuscript Library, Princeton University, NJ.

Rockefeller, Nelson. Papers. Rockefeller Archive Center, Sleepy Hollow, NY.

Smith, Sebie Biggs. "Reminiscences of Sebie Biggs Smith: Oral History, 1981." Columbia University Oral History Research Office Collection, Columbia University, NY.

U.S. Department of State, Office of the Historian. Foreign Relations of the United States (FRUS) series. Washington, DC: Government Printing Office.

    FRUS 1911 (1918).

    FRUS 1929, vol. 2 (1943).

    FRUS 1932, vol. 3, *The Far East* (1948).

    FRUS 1933, vol. 3, *The Far East* (1949).

    FRUS 1934, vol. 3, *The Far East* (1950).

    FRUS 1935, vol. 3, *The Far East* (1953).

    FRUS 1936, vol. 4, *The Far East* (1954).

    FRUS 1937, vol. 4, *The Far East* (1954).

    FRUS 1938, vol. 3, *The Far East* (1954).

    FRUS 1938, vol. 4, *The Far East* (1996).

    FRUS 1939, vol. 3, *The Far East* (1955).

    FRUS 1940, vol. 4, *The Far East* (1955).

    FRUS 1941, vol. 5, *The Far East* (1956).

    FRUS 1945–1950, *Emergence of the Intelligence Establishment* (1996).

    FRUS 1946, vol. 9, *The American Republics* (1969).

    FRUS 1947, vol. 1, *General; The United Nations* (1973).

    FRUS 1947, vol. 8, *The American Republics* (1972).

    FRUS 1951, vol. 2, *The United Nations: The Western Hemisphere* (1979).

    FRUS 1951, vol. 6, *Asia and the Pacific (Part 2)* (1977).

    FRUS 1952–1954, vol. 4, *The American Republics* (1983).

    FRUS 1961–1963, vol. 10, *Cuba 1961–1962* (1997).

U.S. House of Representatives, Select Committee on Assassinations. Investigation of the Assassination of President John F. Kennedy, vol. 10, *CIA Plots Against Castro.* 95th Cong., 2nd sess. Washington, DC, March 1979.

U.S. Senate, Subcommittee of the Judiciary to Investigate the Administration of the
    Internal Security Act and Other Internal Security Laws.
    State Department Security: The Case of William Wieland. 87th Cong. 2nd sess. Wash-
        ington, DC: Government Printing Office, October 4, 1962.
    Morgenthau Diary (China). vol. 1., 89th Cong., 1st sess., Washington, DC: Govern-
        ment Printing Office, February 5, 1965.
United States Relations with China with Special Reference to the Period 1944–1949.
    Washington, DC: Department of State, 1949.
Who Was Who in America. New Providence, NJ: Marquis Who's Who, 1977–1981, 7:440.

INDEX

ABOUT THE AUTHOR

Anthony Carrozza has spent ten years researching and writing the life of William Douglas Pawley. This is his first book. He lives in Elmira, New York, and is currently working on *Cactus Curtain: George Parr and Texas Politics,* a biography of George Berham Parr.